Advance Praise

All the priceless information that it took me years to collect, all in one easy-to-read book! Barbara Gilman pulls together the collective wisdom of decades of parents and professionals, from identification to accommodations to acceleration and beyond....This is the manual we all wish came with our gifted children.

~ Carolyn K., Hoagiesgifted.org

The wisdom in this book is so important to know when planning for success for your child or student. This is a must-read for every parent or educator of gifted children. If there were only one book to read on the gifted, this is the one!

~ Joyce R. Schilling, parent and advocate, Denver, CO

If you are the parent of a gifted child, you MUST READ this book! Author Barbara Gilman gently guides the reader through the maze that is educational advocacy...(to ensure) that gifted children receive an education appropriate for their special needs.

~ Nancy Golon, Highlands Ranch, CO

I am a mom of gifted children and have read much of the literature available on giftedness. Two reasons to buy this book are: one, there is a wealth of knowledge offered here that is extremely helpful in understanding giftedness, and two, much of this information isn't readily available elsewhere. If you suspect your child...may be gifted, then this is THE book to buy.

~ Sarah B., Maryland

Academic Advocacy for Gifted Children:

A Parent's Complete Guide

Formerly titled
Empowering Gifted Minds: Educational Advocacy that Works

Barbara Jackson Gilman, M.S.

With observations on the inner experience of giftedness by Quinn O'Leary

Great Potential Press™

Academic Advocacy for Gifted Children: A Parent's Complete Guide
(formerly titled *Empowering Gifted Minds: Educational Advocacy that Works*)

Edited by: Jennifer Ault
Interior Design: The Printed Page
Cover Design: Julee Hutchinson

Published by
Great Potential Press, Inc.
P.O. Box 5057
Scottsdale, AZ 85261
www.giftedbooks.com

Printed and Bound in the United States of America

12 11 10 09 08 5 4 3 2 1

Library of Congress Cataloging-in-Publication Data

Gilman, Barbara Jackson, 1950-
Academic advocacy for gifted children : a parent's complete guide / Barbara Jackson Gilman.
p. cm.
Originally published: Empowering gifted minds. Denver : DeLeon Pub., 2003.
ISBN-13: 978-0-910707-88-6
ISBN-10: 0-910707-88-X
1. Gifted children. 2. Gifted children—Education. 3. Parents of gifted children. 4. Teachers of gifted children. I. Title.
LC3993.G523 2008
371.95—dc22

2008020839

For Nick,
the experimental child,
who handled undeserved educational difficulties
with uncommon grace

Acknowledgements

Much of this book derives from the loving tutelage of Linda Silverman, Director of the Gifted Development Center in Denver. A one-woman *tour de force* in our field, she combines a generous spirit with the best diagnostic ability in the business. Over the years, I have seen clients begin a post-test conference in tears because they are at last with the person whose writings touched them most—and explained their child. I once watched a longtime director of a school for gifted children introduce Linda to a parent group, taking 10 minutes to describe how she met the qualifications for sainthood! This was unexpected, Linda quipped, as she is Jewish! Hearing her speak just once, I decided to bring my own children to her for testing, and I soon returned to the workforce myself as a tester in her employ. She has been my mentor, staunch supporter, and the dearest of friends, while teaching me much of what I know about gifted children.

Linda's insistence that we look at children "through the lens of giftedness," that we support strengths first and then accommodate any weaknesses, and that we see the internal characteristics of giftedness, not just external achievement is integral to the philosophy of this book. No one picks apart the strengths and weaknesses of a gifted/learning disabled child better or knows with more certainty that such a child *can* become a late bloomer when early indications are to the contrary. She also has a wealth of experience with the very highly gifted, including the personality characteristics and needs that so compellingly argue for educational modifications.

Linda views each gifted child from the background of her early training in special education tutoring learning disabled children. Gifted children, like special education children, are simply children with unusual enough needs to require modifications at school. Accommodations for such needs are never elitist. What could be more just than to insist that all children have educational programs that permit them to reach their full potential?

Linda's experience of more than 40 years in this field has allowed her to pursue many areas of interest. Her books and articles have been on the cutting edge of understanding gifted learning styles, especially the visual-spatial learner; the emotional and social aspects of giftedness; issues in counseling the gifted; gifted girls going underground with their abilities; underachievement; testing the highly gifted; and auditory, sensory, and visual processing problems. I came to adopt these as my own causes, as well, following in her footsteps.

I am further grateful to Linda for allowing me to take time away from my duties at the GDC to work on this book and, over the years, to advocate for my own children, serve on G/T committees, start a charter school, etc., all of which took considerable time. "I'll take you as much as I can get you," she said years ago, and she has kept her word. Thank you, Linda.

I thank Quinn Finnian O'Leary, the wild Irishman, for adding immeasurably to this book. His powerful writing described vividly the frustration many gifted students encounter in school. Young enough to remember multitudinous slights and a few truly traumatic events, Quinn writes with captivating maturity.

Originally tapped for an interview for the chapter on underachievement, Quinn graciously gave permission for considerable personal information to be disclosed. He began to share his own writing, which led to his collaboration on this book. He deserves special credit for providing a sounding board for my work and for encouraging me to finish the manuscript. His interest grew as he read and edited succeeding chapters (this was information he needed to have), and his interest helped me to complete the next chapter and the next. When he finally said, "I think this book would have helped my mother," I felt that we might have something to offer. The experience forced Quinn to redefine himself, to understand the real cause of his rebellion. There were reasons why he didn't fit in at school—beyond laziness, craziness, or undefined teenage angst. Thank you, Quinn, for illuminating this book with the richness of your thoughts.

Kathi Kearney was especially helpful to me, reviewing the original manuscript and offering suggestions for further reading and, most recently, helping me to update it. Inviting me to her cottage on the Maine coast after a flurry of writing would have been enough. I was exhausted and happy to support the local lobster industry. However, she also provided wonderful insights on the book. She is probably the best resource on home schooling gifted and highly gifted children in the country. A longtime teacher of the gifted, there is no better tester. So thank you, Kathi, for your much-appreciated help.

I am thrilled to be able to include ideas from the wonderful teachers profiled in Chapter 9: Lin Greene, Sharon Sikora, Rich Borinsky, and Betty Maxwell. All were sincerely interested and generously contributed their time for this book. While there is no cookie cutter "best teacher of the gifted," they demonstrate the essential passion for teaching that teachers of the gifted must have, along with genuine appreciation for gifted children—they expect wonderful things from them. I am also grateful to the school principals I have known—Bob Martin, Don Groves, and Bob Rea—who showed a willingness and flexibility to meet the individual needs of gifted students.

Betty Maxwell, one of the teachers profiled, now serves as Senior Staff Director of the Gifted Development Center. Her extensive teaching experience (augmented by later counseling and testing work) lends special weight to her concerns about educational practices that do not support the gifted (e.g., homework that doesn't teach and attendance rules that discourage attendance). Thank you, Betty, for supporting the Quinn O'Learys and Nick Gilmans, whose inherent personal worth begs to be acknowledged and whose educational needs must be accommodated. Thank you also for supporting the parents of such kids to view their rebellion as reasonable and honorable. You have both empowered gifted young people and worked hard to teach other educators best practices for teaching them. Your friendship is precious to me, while your philosophy has become integral to my thinking.

Karen Rogers has my sincere appreciation for reviewing this manuscript and contributing to the book's content. Karen's research on instructional grouping practices provides a basis for restructuring gifted education, in general. She has looked unflinchingly at what actually works to accommodate advanced learners. She also suggests superb individual learning plans to meet the needs of various children in her book *Re-Forming Gifted Education: How Parents and Teachers Can Match the Program to the Child*. Thank you, Karen, for your help with my book and your years of service in support of gifted students. Your research, curriculum development, and endeavors to teach future teachers of the gifted have a far-reaching, positive impact on our field.

Thanks also to the many young people featured in this book: Emma, Quinn, and others whose stories will, I hope, not only move us, but move us to action.

Two parents were kind enough to review the manuscript: Carolyn Kottmeyer and Kenneth Arenson. Carolyn, a highly active parent advocate and webmistress, created and busily maintains the popular online Hoagies' Gifted Education Page www.hoagiesgifted.org. The preeminent gifted information website for parents, students, and teachers, Hoagies provides invaluable information for advocates of gifted children.

Ken Arenson, a trial attorney and parent advocate, is an articulate contributor to the gifted advocacy community, always willing to share his experiences and thoughtful insights with others. Both Carolyn and Ken provided suggestions that improved every chapter of the final manuscript.

I owe warm thanks to the staff of the Gifted Development Center, especially Lee Ann Powell for trying to schedule me in ways to preserve my sanity when book, testing, supervision, and consultation duties collided. Lee Ann maintained a smile while patiently reminding me (as many times as necessary) of what I was doing! A big thank-you is also due my testing colleagues, especially Betty Maxwell, Helen McVickar, and Dawn Kinard, who are constant sounding boards for all we are observing and learning from gifted children.

My husband, Bob, has never failed to support my endeavors or keep his sense of humor when I needed it. I offer him loving thanks and a big hug. He bought me a laptop, solved every computer problem I encountered, and even typed when I was overwhelmed! My sons, Nick and Ben, graciously accepted fast food on many occasions when I was writing, and my stepson, John, showed me that gifted students can pull together their lives in their 20s. John's accomplishments gave me confidence that his brothers would eventually succeed as well. Thank you also to their many gifted friends, whose daily challenges, often discussed in our kitchen, enriched my understanding of the gifted.

Finally, I am grateful to Jim Webb, Janet Gore, and the staff of Great Potential Press for their commitment to supporting my vision of this book and their pleasure in the prospect of publishing it. They provided the crucial close reading that enables a book's message to come through clearly, offered excellent assistance with additional books and articles, and were always responsive and helpful. And thanks also to Julee Hutchinson for her thoughtful and distinctive cover design.

—Bobbie Gilman

Contents

Introduction

This book could only have been written by a parent. No amount of training in issues of the gifted or generalized desire to help gifted students could create the insistence that fuels this book. That can only come from the outrage that a parent feels when a child has been hurt. In this case, the hurt was not physical, but it was profound. Our oldest son, very highly gifted and with tremendous promise, dropped out of high school on the Monday following senior prom. By the time it happened, we actually supported his choice because no student that ambivalent about school for that long needed to be there. But he had joined the ranks of high school dropouts, about a quarter of whom (the G/T coordinator at our high school insists) are gifted.

Whatever happened from then on would certainly not be straightforward or particularly easy. At the very least, we would all be in for difficult times ahead, with the greatest burden borne by the most intense individual in our family—this son.

Even more frightening to me, because I work with gifted children at the Gifted Development Center in Denver, was the fact that the events leading up to our son's decision were so similar to those of many gifted children. Offered essentially traditional educational programs with little or no accommodation for their giftedness, gifted children *are* at risk. Moreover, parents may not realize the extent of damage being done to these children until it is too late to stop the downward progression—at least for a long time. At some point, a frustration sets in with school that is highly resistant to change.

Because I had a testing background before I started my family and understood the quality of reasoning that gifted children display on IQ tests, I was fairly aware of our first son's high intelligence. What I completely misjudged, however, was the likelihood that his educational needs would be reasonably met in public school. I had no reason to question his placement there. After all, we lived in the West, where people had trusted public schools for generations; the middle class did not send its children to private schools, as they did in some other parts of the country. Then, too, my husband and I had both done well enough in public schools.

My husband grew up in California during the space race, at a time when the nation highly valued gifted young science prospects. His mother recalled the principal of his neighborhood junior high school calling her into his office, saying, "You need to start planning *now* to send Bob to a good school. I don't just mean a good school, but a GOOD school." It was on his advice that my mother-in-law began a real estate career that would allow her to be at home with her son when she needed to be and save for what turned out to be Cal Tech.

Likewise, my own mother told me years later about being called to a meeting at my elementary school when I was in fifth grade. Parents at the meeting were told that their children were gifted, and the outcome of that meeting, as I look back, was probably that we were all tracked into higher level classes (at least in English, math, and science) throughout junior high and high school. I was unaware of such a division at the time, but I recall always being in classes with the same friends—Sally, who later became teacher of the year in Colorado; David, who won all of the math and science awards; Janet, who graduated first in her medical school class; and similar others. I remember most of us being challenged most of the time.

I didn't realize how different our son's experience in school would be. Moreover, I didn't anticipate the reactions of school personnel to his giftedness. Not only was he underchallenged, but the schools resisted even recognizing him as a gifted student. They certainly did not initiate the discussion, as school personnel had done for Bob and me.

Educational philosophy was changing, and the emphasis on tracking and advanced classes that had challenged my husband and me gave way to a new philosophy that was diametrically opposed. While gifted children had benefited from tracking, the mounting concern that other students had *not* resulted in new educational standards emphasizing the *heterogeneous grouping* of children for instruction. As our son was moving through elementary school, we didn't realize the revolution that was quietly occurring. We saw only the increased emphasis on *cooperative learning* groups in the lower grades—until we faced middle school! There, an entire three-year program had been designed to teach all students together, regardless of their individual needs, with few or no honors classes (ours had math) and the certainty that somehow the mix would produce "excellence."

It was into this unknown, redefined world of education that our son ventured. Although he was identified as a talented and gifted (TAG) student in second grade, little was done to accommodate his needs in the classroom that year or later. We had originally nominated him for TAG because he wanted to advance in math in first grade. However, we had to study first- and second-grade math books with him on our own, and then no modifications were made in his second-grade math instruction. We thought that a tutor was initially possible, but what finally materialized was a high school girl coming to his elementary school once a week in third grade during her lunch hour. When we asked why they were simply playing math games, the teacher said, "We don't want to interfere with classroom instruction."

Of course, interfering with classroom instruction was exactly what our son needed, but he didn't get it. It wasn't until fifth grade that his teacher moved him to a sixth-grade math book and he worked independently. Sadly, that teacher was forced to take a medical retirement mid-year, and the inexperienced substitute teacher who finished the year made our son do the regular fifth-grade work in addition to his advanced sixth-grade work. The teacher was afraid that there would be holes in our son's knowledge, and he also decided to grade only the fifth-grade work. The effect of these decisions, coupled with the fact that the teacher was extremely punitive (he punished the entire class whenever one student misbehaved and regularly made children cry each day), was dramatic in our son's life. He began having difficulty getting to sleep, he cried frequently, and didn't want to go to school. In short, he was clinically depressed. To his credit, he stood up one day for another student who was treated unfairly and told the teacher what he thought of him. The entire class applauded. Our son then voluntarily went to the principal and explained what he had done and why. Although the teacher finished the last few weeks of the year, he was not hired back the following year. Our son's depression thankfully ended, but his (and our) hopes that middle school would finally offer the challenge he needed went unfulfilled.

It was at this time that I attended a panel discussion by educators and counselors on the social and emotional needs of gifted children in Boulder, Colorado. On the panel was a psychologist, Linda Kreger Silverman, the Director of the Gifted Development Center in Denver, a non-profit organization dedicated to "supporting giftedness through the life span." Listening to her speak, I realized that she approached the gifted as she did any child with special education needs. She assessed their needs and designed programs to meet them. For her, gifted education was about accommodating children with discrepant educational needs and not about providing advantages for the elite. Dr. Silverman was equally knowledgeable about both the education and the psychology of the gifted. Intuition told me that this was a woman who truly did understand children like mine, and I made plans to pursue assessment and consultation at the Gifted Development Center.

Testing for our son at the GDC yielded information that we desperately needed, as well as support for the advocacy that we would have to provide for our children. It documented the reasons why our son's educational program was a poor fit for him and gave us, as parents, support for the concerns that we had had through the years of his education.

However, even after gaining a better feel for what our son needed and advocating more strongly, we still encountered many barriers. The most immutable were found in our beautiful new middle school that offered virtually no challenge. By eighth grade, our disgusted son's mostly A grades became widely variable, beginning a pattern of resistance to school and haphazardly done work that improved only occasionally with special teachers until he finally dropped out of school during his senior year at age 18.

Meanwhile, we had also learned at the GDC, as so many parents before us had, that where there is one gifted child in the family, there are likely more. Our younger son's testing at age six actually took place at a much more propitious time, which allowed us to advocate for him much earlier. The GDC not only became a support system for our family, but I accepted a testing position there and began to meet and work with other families similar to ours. My husband and I became more aggressive and careful consumers of education, joined local advocacy committees, and even helped create a new charter middle school (not for the faint of heart!).

Since I began my work with the gifted in 1991, I have seen some improvement in gifted programs. Middle school philosophy has moved away from strict, heterogeneous grouping, and supportive educators are finding ways to differentiate and offer challenge for advanced students. However, I continue to be amazed at the lack of truly successful educational programs for gifted children in various types of schools. For this reason, I believe that parents must be extremely knowledgeable advocates if they are going to prevent real damage to their children.

Testers and educational consultants who work with families of gifted children can offer an important service by evaluating children, determining initial needs, and helping parents understand how important their advocacy will be to their children's educational success. We can answer their questions and discuss at length those issues that are uppermost to them now. We can even offer occasional consultation, as needed, as gifted children mature. However, the broader questions about educating and parenting the gifted are vast, the decisions that arise will be difficult, and parents need excellent preparation for this most important job as advocates.

Our firstborn was forced to be the *experimental* child who taught his parents what we needed to know to advocate for his younger sibling, too late to benefit himself. Too many parents have an experimental gifted child. This book is meant to be a crash course in everything you need to know to advocate for your gifted child—immediately. It is meant to share with you the knowledge and experience of experts in this field about the relevant issues regarding giftedness.

Our family has been fortunate to see our older son rebound from the school experiences that cost him so dearly. However, some parents have not been so fortunate. It is my sincere hope that you will find these pages helpful, that you will find support for your own good judgment, and that your children will mature with their love of learning intact.

This entire program will soon be available on DVD. Look for it at www.icanreadyoucanread.com.

Chapter 1
The Experience of Giftedness

Six-year-old Zachary was brought to the Gifted Development Center (GDC) because he was extremely unhappy in kindergarten. His mother hoped that we could assess his needs and give her some guidance. Placed in a respected private school because he was unusually advanced, Zachary was supposed to be challenged and motivated by his first year in school. Instead, he was miserable and his confidence was shaken. The school he attended was teaching him little that he had not known before. In addition, his teacher found his personality characteristics, interests, and favorite activities so unusual for a kindergartener that she began to criticize Zach and blame his mother's child-rearing techniques. Behaviors that had at first appeared eccentric seemed increasingly pathological to her.

Although Zachary was an excellent reader when he entered school, interested in world events, he stopped watching the news and reading the newspaper after his teacher called him an "information junkie" who "already had too much information." He refused to do *inventive spelling* because he didn't want to misspell words he knew. He also refused to continue doing simple addition problems because "the answers will always be the same; they never will change, so why do we do them day after day?" Zach came to believe that nothing he did was right for his teacher. His teacher believed that he was overly sensitive and a "cry baby" due to separation anxiety. Zach said that he "was just a dolphin jumping through hoops." His teacher instructed him not to say "but what if..." or "that depends," and she limited him to "one curious question per day."

Zachary finally came home from school reporting that he had "emotional problems" and had been referred to the school psychologist. When contacted, the psychologist indicated that Zach did not have emotional problems but did need praise instead of criticism from his teacher. He experienced stomachaches, did not want to go to school, and finally developed chest pain and a rapid heart rate related to stress.

His high degree of sensitivity, mature reasoning ability, and advanced reading and math skills were highly unusual, but nothing about him was pathological.

Advanced Developmental History

Zachary's history was that of a very highly gifted child developing at a faster pace than normal children. Since birth, he had shown a long attention span and a high energy level. In fact, his mother did not recall him ever napping (a characteristic that we see occasionally), and he had continued to view sleep as "a waste of time." Zach reached developmental milestones early, especially in intellectual and verbal domains. He said his first word at five months and spoke in sentences at nine months. He sight-read an Easy Reader at 2 years, 3 months and sounded out new words at 2 years, 11 months. He wrote his first word at three years. Zachary developed within the normal range physically; he sat without support at six months of age and walked at 13 months. Initially ambidextrous, he had become right-handed.

Because Zachary was clearly not progressing as baby books described typical development, his mother kept careful records of his activities. He was an intensely curious child with a wide range of mature interests, and he would frequently wake his mother during the night to ask questions. He had studied fields as varied as American Indian tribes, dinosaurs, aircraft and flight, the solar system and space, the Gulf War, and anatomy. His mother wrote, "Zachary didn't go through the terrible twos...[he] was too busy learning." Zach's love of reading had resulted in a collection of 1,500 books, which were kept in a closet in which he loved to spend time. Also at age two, Zach told his grandmother that he had a "B-R-I-T-E" idea, and he spelled the word for her.

By age three, he was asking questions that were difficult to answer without research ("Does a shark have a tongue, and if so, does it have an epiglottis?"). In addition, he was so preoccupied with the concept of time that his family bought him six clocks to inform him of the time in major cities around the world. That same year, he was concerned with the lack of NASA funding, world crises, and natural disasters and ecological problems.

At age four, Zachary began to tell everyone he was six so that they wouldn't tell him he was too young to do things. This actually worked quite well and helped him cope. He routinely checked to see how the New York Stock Exchange was doing, studied adult literature and poetry, became a vegetarian to avoid "hurting wildlife," studied 25 separate tribes of American Indians (wearing a loin cloth and cloth leggings whenever possible), and concluded about the Aztecs that "just because they do things we do not approve of does not mean that we should not study who they were."

Zachary's sensitivity and compassion were evident at a very young age. At nine months, he was a participant in a university child development study. Asked to pick up a tiny pill and put it in a pillbox, he performed perfectly. However, when asked to turn a girl doll over and spank it three times, he was reluctant. Zach finally spanked the doll, then glared at the examiner and refused to return it. He hugged it repeatedly. This compassion was reflected in his regard for the well-being of friends and relatives, as well as global concerns.

Previously tested at the age of 4 years, 11 months on the Wechsler Preschool and Primary Scale of Intelligence, Revised (WPPSI-R), Zachary reportedly earned a Full Scale IQ score of 150+. It was this assessment that resulted in the recommendation to find a highly challenging school. Zach's score—in the highly gifted range—was probably a minimal estimate of his abilities, given his history. However, his teacher's contention that Zachary "had more of a 105 IQ than a 150" left his mother uncertain about both his educational needs and his actual abilities. And it left Zachary devastated. A full evaluation was scheduled at the GDC to address these issues.

Once Zachary and his mother arrived at the center, she revealed privately that her son was quite worried about the testing because he felt that it would determine whether the kindergarten teacher's low assessment of him was correct. We asked her to have Zach bring some of his favorite toys, and he brought along dinosaur books and plastic dinosaurs to share. Taking time to discuss the dinosaurs was both an icebreaker and an opportunity to observe Zach. He spoke precisely and in depth about various dinosaurs, passages in the books that he had brought, dinosaurs in movies, and museum experiences. He seemed calmer almost immediately and was smiling and talkative. He was concerned with details and was careful to place his books back in his backpack in a preferred order. During the testing, he generally appeared confident. Occasionally, with only the most difficult questions, he would bite his nails and was reluctant to guess. Sensitive to the conditions of the room and his clothing, he stopped several times to adjust his socks.

When the IQ scores were given to his mother from the WISC-III and Stanford-Binet L-M and it was clear that Zachary again had scored within the highly gifted range, Zach's mother chose to share this information with her son. Aware of his teacher's comments, he already knew that high scores provided some justification for his differences. When told what the scores were, he held his arms out from his sides, breathed a sigh of relief, and said, "I am finally free."

Unnecessary Damage

Such a story of absolutely unnecessary damage to a child is both heartrending and telling. In a nation with an excellent history of valuing education for all citizens, sadly, we lack understanding about the needs of our most able learners and permit considerable pressure for these children to simply fit in. The goal to educate *all*, at least to a moderate degree, falls short for gifted students. Worst of all, the failure to nurture our best minds can result in a failure to reach full potential, with both personal and national ramifications.

Zachary's story is typical of the situations that are most damaging to gifted children in school. Not only are such students inadequately challenged day after day, which could certainly undermine their motivation to learn, but also their self-esteem suffers as they sense subtle (or not so subtle) disapproval for their differences. Gifted children, as a group, do not fit the expectations of teachers or curriculum developers because of development that is proceeding at a much more rapid pace than is typical for the average child. It is their degree of difference from the norm that defines them as a special needs population requiring special accommodations in school. However, because these accommodations are rarely offered (few strong mandates exist in this country), we see these children suffering.

Teach to Their Level, Pace, and Learning Style

Gifted students need educational programs designed to meet their needs, just as the regular curriculum is designed for the majority of children it serves. Such programs must consider students' levels of content mastery, pace of learning, learning style, and the most effective instructional approaches. An impediment to the simple consideration of gifted students and their educational needs is the perception that they are advantaged. Must the second-grade teacher provide above-level material to the child who has mastered second-grade work, or can she simply feel that her job is done where that child is concerned? If a child is already advanced, do we really have an obligation to help him progress further? Couldn't this child merely help others to learn so that all students could end their year at more or less the same point of mastery? The experience of many gifted children attests to the fact that their needs must be met adequately enough to avoid destroying their motivation to learn or limiting the realization of their potential.

All gifted children, who typically fall into the 98th percentile and above, have difficulty with educational programs planned for the majority of children. Their learning rates outpace such programs, they need advanced material earlier, and they can and need to reason abstractly before most children are ready for it. Children who score at the 2nd percentile and below are considered discrepant enough from typical children that special education modifications in school are mandated to accommodate their slower learning rates and other specific needs. Children between these two extremes may also need modifications at times (teachers must be sensitive to the needs of all children), but we know that both gifted and developmentally delayed children need accommodations, and we must plan and provide for them.

The issue of making accommodations for gifted children has never been about high achievers whose parents demand special privileges—a sort of "tax credits for the rich" situation. On the contrary, it has always been about more basic, universal values that all parents share about the education of their children—maintaining a child's interest in school, developing healthy self-esteem, nurturing social development, teaching a strong work ethic, and preparing a child for a satisfying life. Such values are never elitist by themselves; gifted education only becomes elitist when it is denied to children without means. This can occur when a public school system denies appropriate education to gifted children and only those with the financial means to afford private schools are able to obtain the educational programs they need.

We have a responsibility to educate all children to reach their full potential. Inappropriate educational strategies can derail a child's learning altogether. The gifted high school dropout is as much a failure of our system as the less able dropout who struggles and receives insufficient help. The issues are the same for all children. Children have specific needs, and we are obligated to find ways to serve them.

An analogy to the plight of the gifted may be helpful. What if we were to mandate grouping all average children (IQ 100) with mildly retarded children of IQ 70 and somewhat below? Knowing that developmentally delayed children require significantly more drill and practice to master concepts, we would need to create a curriculum with sufficient practice and repetition to meet the needs of our slowest learner. Because we could no longer cover as many topics during the year, we would need to reorganize the scope and sequence of our multi-year curriculum and add years of education prior to high school graduation. We might believe that this plan would be a significant improvement because we would be supporting egalitarian ideals and because, eventually, more students would reach a level of high school graduate competency.

There is little doubt that there would be an outcry as average students became increasingly frustrated in the classroom. Kids would complain of boredom, and many would condemn the extra years required in school to earn the credits necessary for graduation. Many would insist that the extra drill and practice is counterproductive to those who don't need it and harmful to a positive attitude about learning. Of course, they would be right, but when exactly the same situation occurs for gifted students placed in average classrooms, there is resistance to the same expressed concerns. Sometimes gifted children are even admonished to be satisfied in order to get along with others in the world. What seems clearly inappropriate for one group is character-building for the other—unless the gifted child is close to us and we see the genuine suffering that can occur. Gifted children are too discrepant for the educational programs that generally serve them.

Personality Characteristics

In addition to their intellectual differences, the personality characteristics and interests of gifted children are out-of-sync with those of their age peers. Gifted children can, for example, become knowledgeable enough in a subject area that they appear quite eccentric when compared with average children their age. Some teachers find this disturbing. Often, the written observations that we receive from teachers contain a concern that Heather or Demetrius "just needs time to be a kid." Teachers assume that out-of-the-ordinary interests and abilities are the result of pushing by parents rather than natural tendencies of the child. Surely a child wouldn't choose such interests independently!

Our experience has shown exactly the opposite; gifted children do choose to pursue unusual interests (or perhaps their curiosities and interests reach a mature level quickly, and that appears abnormal). We find that parents do not tend to push but usually struggle themselves to keep up with these curious, high-energy children. It can be exhausting to answer children's incessant questions and support the interests that they express. It can be financially difficult to provide the enrichment opportunities that such children crave. These are not parents who instruct their children with flashcards in the highchair and push to give them a competitive edge in life. They are, more likely, barely hanging on and in need of both sleep and support for trying to meet needs that few adults around them understand and appreciate.

Gifted children exhibit other differences that come with the territory. Their high degree of sensitivity, intensity, and concern for injustice can raise psychological red flags for teachers. Their tendency to want to make their own decisions about life at an early age can frustrate adults working with them. Because teachers often have little background in gifted education, they may not understand that these differences are a normal part of the domain of giftedness. In fact, they are part of a larger group of characteristics—far beyond simply high achievement in school—that we recognize as typical of advanced development.

Even when teachers do support the differences that gifted children display, other students may not. The gifted child in elementary school may be isolated by her peers not only for her unusual interests, but also due to her adult speech. Young children are often quick to exercise prejudice against a gifted child who is different, just as they might a child with racial or ethnic differences or a disabled child. Teachers may feel less comfortable addressing prejudice against the gifted, as in the case of Jose.

Jose came to us as a fourth grader feeling very isolated in his public school classroom. His interest in history—particularly military history—was unusual; he enjoyed discussing military leaders, their campaigns, and their strategies. He spoke so articulately about these interests that one could visualize an adult Jose teaching university courses in history and spending considerable time researching and debating his passion.

His classmates, however, were not impressed, and Jose was the target of the class bully, who did everything possible to make his life miserable. The bully consistently rallied others against Jose, making the situation for him almost unbearable. He spoke of recurring nightmares about the bully and dreams in which the bully "flew off the earth." That, he admitted, was what he most wished could happen. His teacher did not intervene because she believed that children need to resolve such matters themselves. Jose's sensitivity and introversion made this highly unlikely, and he was miserable.

Social Development

Another concern in Jose's case was his social development. There is a common misconception that gifted children should be placed with age peers for social development to progress. But situations like Jose's halt social development. Children who must constantly defend themselves do not and cannot make strides socially. Rather, they need to find others with similar interests from which friendships develop. It is within the context of friendship that social development occurs.

This is undoubtedly why, with all of the pressure to place children with age peers in school, we have seen the best social development in gifted children who attend schools for the gifted. Because they are accepted by others and are confident that they fit in, they learn how to be good friends. Interestingly, they seem to be more tolerant and open to others with diverse backgrounds, interests, and abilities than gifted children placed in heterogeneous groups. Most of the latter experience persecution to some degree and lose some of their tolerance. Because Jose earned gifted-level IQ scores, placement in a school for the gifted was important. He desperately needed a program that would support not only his interests and learning needs, but also his personality characteristics.

Out-of-Sync with Middle School

As gifted children mature and leave elementary school, new problems arise. Older gifted students, particularly in middle school, may be persecuted for caring too much about their studies. Possibly arising out of the emphasis on heterogeneous grouping and "excellence for all," many writers have commented on the "anti-intellectualism" prevalent in middle schools. We have seen gifted students struggle for acceptance, enduring slights ranging from name calling ("geek," "brain") to bumper stickers proclaiming "MY KID BEAT UP YOUR HONOR STUDENT." Gifted middle-level students often perceive themselves as so different from what is considered popular that they wonder if something is wrong with them. They may see no point to the activities that their classmates value so highly and may find virtually nothing relevant in the classroom. Kathryn was one such young lady.

Kathryn came for evaluation at age 12 because the pace of academic work in seventh grade was "stultifying," and she felt very different and isolated from her peers. Although she still maintained a 4.0 average, Kathryn hated school and complained that it was painfully boring. Many gifted students reach this point after the accumulation of years in elementary school, moving at too slow a pace. They hold out hope that middle school, with its greater choice of courses, will afford them opportunities to finally have more challenging coursework. Regrettably, many find sixth grade a disappointment due to the continuing emphasis on basic skills.

Although school personnel had been cooperative, a series of meetings with Kathryn's mother every few weeks had not been effective. This mother felt that her daughter was bright, delightful, sensitive, and aware. Moreover, she wrote that Kathryn "has a fine character and more understanding and concern for the world than many adults." Yet Kathryn had difficulty finding others with similar interests and concerns, forcing her to "choose between being herself and fitting in." Middle school coursework had been particularly disappointing. Kathryn liked math best; it was the only class that was ability grouped and therefore came closest to offering the advanced material and fast instructional pace that she needed.

Kathryn arrived for the testing feeling both anxious and relieved that she would finally be evaluated. She explained that there had been plans to test her at age nine, but the evaluation was never done. It seemed very important to her to at last have information about her abilities, and she was visibly nervous about performing well. Nevertheless, she was friendly and poised, displaying a warm smile and a subtle sense of humor. When asked how she liked middle school, Kathryn replied that she spent most of her time coloring. She added that the work was very concrete because "we don't have abstract reasoning ability until we're 13 to 15."

Kathryn's test scores soon explained her sense of isolation. She missed only two items on the Stanford-Binet L-M, the IQ test with the highest ceiling available at the time. Her IQ score of 170+ was in the exceptionally gifted range, with an equivalent mental age of 22 years, 4 months. The "+" signified that she never reached a level in testing at which she could no longer answer questions; therefore, her score might have been higher, given harder items. In the conference, she tearfully described how poorly she fit in at her school. She said, "I will never be pretty or popular. All I have is my grades." A lovely, sensitive person, Kathryn was suffering from considerable loss of self-esteem for no justifiable reason. It was simply the result of being too discrepant from her age peers in a program designed to fit the majority of students.

Mental Age

The mental age computed on the test that Kathryn took is actually an excellent estimate of a child's level of functioning. Because a child may be mentally one age and chronologically another, mental age is useful in describing both advanced and delayed development. This is the conceptual basis of the Intelligence Quotient, or IQ. Originally, one's mental age divided by the chronological age times 100 equaled the IQ score. Although normative scaling is employed on modern tests, in which the child is compared statistically with age peers in a normal curve, perceived mental age is helpful in estimating a child's ability. For example, a child who has a mental age close to his chronological age is likely to be comfortable with age peers in a typical school. If his mental age and chronological age are the same, his ratio is equal to 1. Multiplied by 100, this yields an IQ score of 100, which is considered average and at the 50th percentile for children of that chronological age. On the other hand, a six-year-old child who is generally uncomfortable with age peers and has concepts and interests similar to 12-year-olds may well have an IQ score approaching 200.

Kathryn's mental age of 22 years, 4 months placed her totally outside the realm of typical middle school students and rendered her unable to fit in. Thinking at so different a level, Kathryn could only hope to accelerate to a higher grade level, where her mental age would not be so discrepant, or to a school with more advanced students. It would be ludicrous to assume that she could happily exist as a middle schooler, valuing the same things that her classmates found important. Moreover, it would be cruel to insist that she continue in this environment based on conventional wisdom. Parents frequently receive advice that acceleration will harm their children socially or are told that their child "can't have everything her way" and must learn to fit in. Such a moralistic approach has no place when a child suffers to this degree.

Because Kathryn was a straight-A student who was highly advanced academically, we suggested that she skip eighth grade and enter a high school program with a large number of Advanced Placement courses or an International Baccalaureate program. Research on acceleration has been largely positive, and Kathryn was likely to be considerably happier in high school. There, she would be a better fit, although still more advanced than most and a significantly faster learner. These differences would persist, even after acceleration or movement to a different school, and Kathryn's academic program would need to be frequently reevaluated. Even placed in a school for the gifted, Kathryn would advance through the curriculum so quickly that an individualized education plan would be needed to adjust her academic program. Such a school best meets the needs of children with IQs just into the gifted range—130 and up. The curriculum is not designed for someone like Kathryn, but it would come closer to meeting her needs and offer more emotional support. There would also be the chance of finding a friend there—a true peer who might share Kathryn's interests, understand her views, and appreciate her humor.

Underachieving Older Boys

Most testers of the gifted see their share of middle and high school-age boys. Brought in by worried parents, they are usually underachieving in school, perhaps failing some courses, refusing to go to school, about to be kicked out of school, or in danger of not graduating. Many high school students have attendance trouble; their ambivalence about school causes them to skip classes or arrive late. Sadly, current high school policies (designed for good students not suffering from this type of angst) are quick to remove course credit for such problems, thus pushing these students out of school.

Most of these boys share a pattern of highly gifted reasoning ability, increasing boredom with the regular curriculum, and a drop from mostly A grades to poor ones in middle school. Some suffer from inadequate challenge in coursework; gifted students may be bored even in advanced classes. Poor work habits and study skills, never a problem before, may also be a factor as students face multiple teachers and classrooms. Sometimes mild learning disabilities or other deficits make the increased workload difficult. If poor performance is not fully explained by inadequate challenge or weak organizational skills, a thorough evaluation is needed.

Gifted boys without deficits need a faster paced, higher-level educational program that allows them to move ahead when they have mastered concepts. This program needs to be available before they assert their independence too strongly and before too much cumulative damage has been done in programs that are underchallenging for them.

Poor Study and Organizational Skills

More challenging programs not only engage gifted boys more effectively, they teach work habits and organizational skills. Gifted children often fail to learn study and organizational skills until their work is difficult enough to require them. Why learn to take notes when one can still remember everything the teacher says in class that will be needed for the test? Why schedule work for a large assignment when it can be pulled together impressively at the last minute?

Failure to learn such skills can prevent some boys—as well as some gifted girls—who are bored with middle school from succeeding in International Baccalaureate or other challenging high school programs that would seemingly rekindle their interest. Such programs usually carry with them an impressive homework load, as well as more challenging, enjoyable work. Students who are poorly prepared may be so upset when they initially struggle that their confidence is shaken. Teachers may be less than understanding when students are obviously talented and underachieving, and these highly sensitive children take their criticism to heart. They may not be able to continue in the challenging program, creating a negative cycle that may take years to resolve.

Boys do tend to react more overtly in defiance of a system that is hurting them. Although parents instinctively counsel them to do their best and keep as many options open as possible, we must acknowledge their just cause. They rebel against educational programs that ignore their needs and undermine their natural love of learning. Unfortunately, the ramifications of their rebellion may include years of struggle to regain options that are appropriate and essential for their happiness as adults.

Girls: Suffering Silently or Going Underground

Whereas many boys underachieve to protest an educational program that they perceive to be harmful, many girls suffer silently at great cost to themselves. They may maintain the highest grades, as Kathryn did, or they may go underground with their giftedness, appearing to be only as intelligent as any group in which they are placed. Girls are particularly adept at sensing the social expectations of others and too frequently choose simply to please. Such was the case for 13-year-old Chantrelle, who had been previously tested and found to have gifted-level abilities.

Chantrelle's parents brought her for additional evaluation and advice regarding high school. She was an eighth grader taking honors algebra and a gifted language arts class. Her middle school offered these advanced choices. Although proud to be an A student, she was not working particularly hard and preferred to focus more on her social life. Somewhat concerned, her parents wanted her to consider an International Baccalaureate or other highly challenging high school program, but Chantrelle resisted. She liked being the top student in her less challenging classes and enjoyed some degree of leadership in her social group. She frankly did not want to work any harder but still planned to become a pediatrician. Pursuing a school program at the academic level popular with her friends was not going to support her career goals adequately.

As Chantrelle participated in the post-test conference, Dr. Silverman discussed these concerns with her and remarked that, in our experience, most 13-year-old girls express similar socially based goals. "But," she said to Chantrelle, "you have to understand that the world wants you to become a secretary." Gifted girls may lose their determination to challenge themselves and find it extremely difficult to diverge from the pathways that others envision for them. The failure of academic programs to push such students more is a failure to nurture giftedness.

The tendency for women to hide or deny their gifts and pursue more socially acceptable or traditional activities has persisted for generations. Testers of gifted children sometimes see mothers of their clients begin to accept their own giftedness following their children's evaluations. While some initially claim that their children inherited their intelligence from their fathers, mothers must have had a hand in it, too. The underestimation of self that these mothers have accepted and lived with has often led to less-than-challenging early careers. It is always a pleasure to see such mothers move ahead with additional education or a new career pathway as they accept their own capabilities. Many have proven to be enormously talented individuals, highly concerned about the plight of the gifted.

Girls, and even adult women, require substantial encouragement to realize their full potential. Efforts must be made to support their interests, develop their talents, and find true peers who will appreciate their abilities. Gifted females can support each other, and friendship can minimize social pressures.

Teachers Vary in Their Knowledge of the Gifted

Teachers are the most important variable in the success of gifted students in the classroom. Because most states lack strong mandates for gifted education, the required education for teachers of the gifted may be limited. Some states require teacher endorsements in gifted education, consisting of 18 or more credit hours of instruction, while in others, required training may amount to only a small portion of an Exceptional Child course, in which the subject of *gifted* is covered in one short chapter on special education needs. As a result, teachers vary tremendously in their ability to create appropriate learning experiences for gifted students. Although most teachers have their students' best interests at heart, they may lack the expertise and experience to consistently challenge gifted students and thus ensure their continuous progress. Without training and experience, teachers are likely to underestimate the degree of accommodation needed and are vulnerable to misconceptions about gifted children.

Such misconceptions tend to proliferate and be compounded by affirmation from other teachers. For example, the belief that gifted children will be fine, regardless of their situation, justifies that nothing be done for them. Reflecting the confusion between *gifted* students and *high achievers*, many teachers believe that the gifted, when given lemons, will make lemonade. In actuality, gifted students often fare poorly in the wrong learning environment and do not necessarily earn high grades. They are more likely to be high achievers in challenging classroom environments, but they may be lackluster students when more basic, grade-level material is stressed. Teachers should not withhold more challenging work solely because a child fails to impress them with basic performance.

Parents have also been warned by teachers, "If you put your child in a school for the gifted, he will just shut down socially." This statement reveals the common misconception that children must be placed with *normal children*, particularly chronological age peers, for proper social development. This belief keeps schools from considering grade skips or other acceleration accommodations, even though research on acceleration has generally been positive. Gifted children typically relate better to mental age peers and develop social skills when they feel confident that they fit in. Children who have chosen to accelerate fare very well. In fact, it is surprising what a non-issue grade skipping has been for many of my clients after only a short time in the new classroom.

The prevalent but misinformed notion that "gifted children just need a little enrichment" seems to have guided the development of some fairly ineffective gifted programs. Enrichment in the classroom that truly increases the depth and breadth of the material studied is an improvement for the gifted student, but the term *enrichment* can be used in almost any context. Programs that maintain traditional whole-class instruction in classrooms for all children but add a few extracurricular enrichment outings for the gifted group both fail to make a significant contribution to meeting their needs and incur the wrath of the parents of children who are below the gifted range. Why gifted children—and not others—would receive special advantages not directly related to their educational needs is indeed a reason for concern, and such concerns can lead to resentment and eventual discontinuance of a gifted program before a more appropriate program can be developed.

Likewise, a monthly brown-bag lunch or occasional after-school activities for gifted students do little to meet their intellectual needs and generally only provide opportunities to commiserate with each other about their inflexible programs. Most programs limited to activities outside of the classroom arise because there is resistance by classroom teachers to modifying regular schoolwork. Although such programs represent a commitment to do *something* for gifted students, they do little to save children from the frustration that they feel. An inappropriate educational program that must be endured six hours a day, five days a week, week after week, year after year causes considerable damage to gifted children. Significant accommodations must be made in the *daily* classwork that the gifted child completes, the pace at which he or she is allowed to progress, and the instructional approaches taken.

There is a pressing need for teachers to gain experience in gifted education and for gifted students to be placed in the classrooms of teachers with expertise. Incredible teachers of the gifted exist and have positive, life-changing influences on students. However, we need many more than we currently have; the quality of the teacher is critical for any student with special needs. The natural good fit of the curriculum is not sufficient for such children if chemistry with the teacher is poor. Unlike special education children who have federally mandated programming and often smaller classes, gifted children are more dependent on the regular classroom teacher's willingness to voluntarily provide appropriate learning experiences, as well as the teacher's knowing what that is—quite a tall order with some of these children.

Of course, there is the question of whether it is fair to expect teachers to do a good job with each and every student when students in large heterogeneous classrooms vary in ability from developmentally delayed to profoundly gifted. Given the range of student needs, it is a wonder that even a master teacher can provide something appropriate for all on any sort of consistent basis. Yet there is currently a very strong preference in public school districts to meet the needs of the gifted within the regular classroom, and self-contained gifted programs continue to be rare.

Gifted Introverts Are Vulnerable

Gifted children are at risk in classrooms with teachers who insist on grade-level curriculum. Teachers may be honestly unaware of students' higher levels of mastery before they teach them. Because gifted students are largely introverts, they are not likely to complain or to reveal to teachers that the work is too easy. Identifying gifted children in schools through testing helps teachers know when such a child will be in their class, and frequent classroom assessment (through pre- and post-testing, using both casual assessment and standardized tests) ensures teaching at the right level. Ignoring children's abilities and requiring them to complete assignments based on concepts that they have already mastered has the effect of confusing and devaluing them. If their advanced skills are worthwhile, surely they should be noticed and applauded by the teacher. Why wouldn't gifted children react negatively when forced to complete all regular assignments if they have already mastered the material in question?

Two kindergarten-age girls, both with IQ scores in the 130s (moderately gifted range), typify this problem. Both girls had learned to read before entering school, both felt horribly out of place in the kindergarten classroom, and neither was offered any accommodations. Savannah, age 6 years, 2 months, had already advanced through the developmental milestones related to reading so quickly that she needed very accelerated reading in kindergarten. She had recognized letters at 17 months of age and read her first sight word at age three. At 3 years, 10 months, she could sound out words, and she could read Easy Reader books at age four. When we saw her, her mother noted on our Developmental Questionnaire that in the summer, Savannah liked to read from 8:00 to 12:00 P.M. and sleep until 11:00 AM. On a sentence completion test, Savannah completed the sentence stem "When I wake up at night..." with, "I read some books and go back to sleep." She particularly enjoyed reading the American Girl, Bobbsey Twins, and Berenstain Bears series.

Savannah was of course frustrated learning the ABCs and numbers in kindergarten, having no opportunities whatsoever to work at her actual level in reading. She liked only "Choice Time," during which she taught other children how to use the computer. She needed immediate acceleration in reading, and her needs would have been better served in a school for the gifted, where she could avoid becoming a teacher's helper and could progress academically. Savannah was also very sensitive and sometimes prone to regressing to baby talk when stressed. If not placed in a more suitable environment, she could not be expected to handle her situation well for long.

Sierra, also a kindergartener, felt so out of place that she told her parents that the other children were "babies," and she began to make up excuses that would keep her from going to school. She had difficulty finding appropriate clothes in her closet—nothing was right for each day—and her parents were, frankly, frightened by her behavior. She simply could not be the student that her teacher expected, and she was reluctant to try.

Children like these would be better placed in first grade with, perhaps, even higher level reading instruction. Skipping kindergarten is usually the least problematic grade acceleration because all of the children start school together not knowing if any are younger. Unfortunately, the school district serving these girls had ended its program to allow early entrance to first grade. All children had to begin as kindergarteners, with acceleration to first grade possible only after a short period in kindergarten and with the agreement of school personnel that the acceleration was appropriate. Though not optimal for gifted children, such a change would be better than remaining in kindergarten.

A National Discomfort with Giftedness

American society has always exhibited conflict between egalitarian ideals and respect for high intellectual ability. We both honor our most brilliant thinkers (Thomas Jefferson, Albert Einstein, Margaret Mead, Eleanor Roosevelt) and assert that all men (and women) are created equal. We have difficulty deciding whether equality in education means that all students reach an equal level of performance or whether it means that we offer equal support to each and every student to reach his or her full potential.

Whereas many adults remember when high ability and achievement were celebrated in school, there is considerable reluctance now to acknowledge it. Some schools stubbornly assert that "all of our students are gifted," effectively undermining efforts to accommodate advanced learners. In addition, there is a marked contrast between acceptance of intellectual differences and acknowledgement of differences in a variety of talent areas. We readily celebrate and nurture outstanding talent in sports, music, or drama. We not only ask our children to accept that they may be less talented than others in these areas, but to "toughen up" and show good sportsmanship when they sit on the bench, fail to make the team, or miss winning the role in an audition. However, our keenest minds are rarely sought out for special training or accolades, and our discomfort with the concept of giftedness limits our ability to handle different educational needs effectively.

Egalitarian ideals, such as those stressed in middle schools in the 1990s, superseded rational consideration of special needs. For example, the "Middle School Essentials," the written policy of one local school district, stressed "inclusion of all students regardless of abilities, needs, backgrounds and interests, in common learning environments" (in other words, heterogeneous grouping) as a means to ensure that "all children will achieve excellence." Ideology is behind this educational philosophy, not empirical data about how well children with different needs and abilities learn. If the desire to meet the needs of all children is sincere, then the effectiveness of our educational policies must stand up to scrutiny. Whole-class instruction without differentiation strategies for children with special needs virtually guarantees problems for them. Special education mandates currently do provide further support for students with limited abilities. However, without a similar federal mandate or federal funding, gifted children face a considerably more uncertain future in such schools.

The Need for Vigilant Advocacy

Parents of gifted children, usually gifted themselves, share the same sensitivity, compassion, and likely introversion that their children display. They may find it very difficult to advocate strongly for their children and can be as uncomfortable with the term *gifted* as critical opponents of special services. Usually sensitive to the plight of all special needs students, parents of the gifted are reluctant to push their own students' agendas too strongly in fear of implying that they are insensitive to the needs of others. The fact that advocacy for gifted children is unpopular in our increasingly egalitarian society makes it even more difficult. For these reasons, parents of gifted children may be too trusting of the education that their children are receiving for too long, placing their children at considerably greater risk than they would ever deliberately allow. Parents need to educate themselves as fully as possible about their children's needs and accept the role of advocate early in their children's educational careers.

Parent advocates need to be more than casual observers of the fit between each gifted child and his or her educational program. A child's academic achievement must be constantly monitored to determine if the work that she is doing is appropriate and whether she is progressing. When a concept is mastered, is the child allowed to move on to new material? Gifted children reach mastery ahead of other children, creating the problem of what to do with them while the others finish. Is the gifted student learning something new every day, or is the bulk of instruction related to already-learned material? Is learning restricted to grade-level work? Can a first grader learn multiplication or a fifth grader begin algebra?

Most parent advocates discover that they need considerably more information than they have to do this job well. They must first understand giftedness and have some idea of the educational needs that gifted students have. Some estimation of the child's general level of ability, as well as strengths, weaknesses, and learning style, is critical. Advocates need familiarity with the forms that gifted education can take so that they can determine what is reasonable to request. They must have an idea of the options available for a child at his or her school and the people who can provide them. To whom does one go for help—the teacher, the G/T coordinator, the principal, the guidance counselor? If parent requests for help at school are denied, what other options are there? Is help available at the district or state level? Are there laws pertaining to gifted education? Where can supportive teachers obtain guidance? Is another school more appropriate, and how does one find other schools? Are there tutors, mentors, or other resources outside of school for instruction in various subject areas? To what degree can one circumvent school limitations to meet needs?

To educate themselves more fully, many advocates become avid readers and gifted conference attendees. They frequent computer websites and bulletin boards, learning what they can to negotiate a labyrinth of educational complications. What they have is determination and love for their children; what they don't have is considerable time.

Meanwhile, the learning discrepancy between young gifted children and their age peers increases, making accommodations increasingly necessary. For the children, the accumulation of frustrating experiences grows, threatening their inborn curiosity and love of learning that so characterizes them from their first years of life. This book is intended as a guide for advocates to better understand what giftedness is and to nurture it in their children—in time.

Observations on the Inner Experience of Giftedness, by Quinn O'Leary

> *"Today," grated the pedantic nasal caw that served the white-haired, wizened, tired-bodied teacher for a voice, "We will be writing about..." Her drone paused as she peeled the previous day's date from the department-store calendar full of ostensibly inventive ways to "inspire young writers." Mrs. "K" siphoned these ideas verbatim from the pastel-colored paper with the blaze-orange $4.99 sticker still clinging to the plastic backing. This admittedly ingenious plan saved her both the effort of actual invention and the risk of facing self-spawned creativity from her students.*
>
> *The fishlike movement of her lips as she silently read the calendar's suggestion lent her the aspect of an idiot. After a moment's consideration, she smiled and addressed the class. "Complete the following poem, 'I hope to have a horse one day, a beautiful pony to run and play...' " The last words were spoken slowly so that the, by and large, at least mildly attentive class could copy them.*
>
> *Throughout this, I had not raised my eyes or my pen from the page of my lovingly ragged notebook. Mrs. K had apparently noted this lack of attention and, as soon as she finished proclaiming the four-line assignment's due date as the following day, she approached and read over my shoulder. The obscure instinct of insecure writers dictated that I shift my free hand to cover the unfinished piece, a childish shard of a story concerning a tragic love between a toaster and a mouse.*
>
> *"That doesn't look like the assignment, Quinn," rasped the venomous voice of authority. "Perhaps you would be more successful*

in my class if you spent as much time on the material I assign as you do daydreaming."

The remark raised an equally venomous titter from the class. I felt the subtle flush of shame heat and stain my cheeks, and hurriedly turned the page, breaking off my tale to turn out a partly plagiarized poem.

"I suppose you expect me to read the assignment that you weren't paying attention to again," grumbled Mrs. K, turning away to retrieve the calendar cum lesson plan.

Without looking up, in the quiet voice that later teachers would learn meant I was being defiant, I recited, "I hope to have a horse one day...a beautiful pony to run and play," in a mockingly unsubtle singsong. Mrs. K clapped slowly, dramatically sarcastic. "I'm sure all your classmates are impressed, Quinn. Now stop showing off and get to work. Your poem is due today instead of tomorrow." Her acidic tone and pinched, strained demeanor brought a surreptitious smile to my lips. I had touched a nerve, bested someone my senior more than four times over. Five minutes later, I handed her this poem:

> *Shod hooves stamping, steady beat*
> *Cool wind banishing summer's heat*
> *Travel lands both fey and fair*
> *My horsey takes me anywhere.*

Satisfied in my ability, I returned to my seat and finished my toaster tragedy. Two minutes before the end-of-class bell, Mrs. K called me to her desk. When I approached she said nothing, but handed me my poem, slashed in the angry red angles of an "F." Her textbook perfect handwriting arched below it. "Perhaps I should have reread the assignment after all. You won't go far with the attitude you're showing."

I regained my seat, staring dumbfounded at the first failing grade of my life, though certainly not the last. The sharp sting of tears compelled me to hide my face in my folded arms as I quietly wept.

For Further Reading

Kearney, K. (1993). Discrimination against excellence. *Understanding Our Gifted, 6*(2), 16.

Kerr, B. A. (1997). *Smart girls: A new psychology of girls, women, and giftedness.* Scottsdale, AZ: Great Potential Press.

Kerr, B. A., & Cohn, S. J. (2001). *Smart boys: Talent, manhood, and the search for meaning.* Scottsdale, AZ: Great Potential Press.

Morelock, M. (1992). Giftedness: The view from within. *Understanding Our Gifted, 4*(3), 1, 11-15. Also available at www.gt-cybersource.org/Record.aspx?NavID=2_0&rid=11392

Silverman, L. K. (1986). What happens to the gifted girl? In C. J. Maker (Ed.), *Critical issues in gifted education, Vol. 1: Defensible programs for the gifted* (pp. 43-89). Austin, TX: Pro-Ed.

Silverman, L. K. (1993). Social development, leadership and gender. In L. K. Silverman (Ed.), *Counseling the gifted and talented* (pp. 291-327). Denver, CO: Love.

Silverman, L. K. (1995). To be gifted or feminine: The forced choice of adolescence. *The Journal of Secondary Gifted Education, 6*, 141-156.

Sykes, Charles J. (1995). *Dumbing down our kids: Why America's children feel good about themselves, but can't read, write or add.* New York: St. Martin's Press.

Tomlinson, C. A. (1992). Gifted education and the middle school movement: Two voices on teaching the academically talented. *Journal for the Education of the Gifted, 15*(3), 206-238.

Tomlinson, C. A. (1994). Gifted learners: The boomerang kids of middle school? *Roeper Review, 16*(3), 177-182.

Webb, J. T., Gore, J. L., Amend, E. R., & DeVries, A. R. (2007). *A parent's guide to gifted children.* Scottsdale, AZ: Great Potential Press.

Webb, J. T., Meckstroth, E. A., & Tolan, S. S. (1982). *Guiding the gifted child.* Scottsdale, AZ: Great Potential Press.

Chapter 2
What Do We Mean by *Gifted*?

> *Giftedness is asynchronous development in which advanced cognitive abilities and heightened intensity combine to create inner experiences and awareness that are qualitatively different from the norm. This asynchrony increases with higher intellectual capacity. The uniqueness of the gifted renders them particularly vulnerable and requires modifications in parenting, teaching, and counseling in order for them to develop optimally.*
>
> ~ The Columbus Group, 1991

Parents advocating for a precocious child must first understand how their local schools define giftedness. Today, we see a surprising range of definitions, many of which reflect our national discomfort with the notion of giftedness. Do we respect gifted intellectual ability in children enough to define it fairly specifically and try to ensure that it is nurtured appropriately? Or, to maintain egalitarian ideals, do we back away from concern about our nation's most able learners and identify as *gifted* a far larger percentage of students—or even *all* students?

How a child's school views this issue will affect not only the child's admission to a program, but also the level of service provided. For example, one public elementary school in a local district requires IQ scores of at least 140 (130 is typically considered *gifted*) because the school has a particularly able student body and feels that its program can provide for the needs of many gifted students without special accommodations. Yet we have also encountered programs for which only *above-average* ability, creativity, and task commitment are sufficient for entrance.

Thus, the top 1% or the top 30% of children in a school may be eligible for services, depending on the criteria. Some schools have taken the approach of creating an individualized education plan for every student, thus asserting that each child's needs will be met automatically.

Such a program could be successful, but it might also effectively eliminate accommodations for the highly able student. Even schools within a district may differ if each has chosen its own method of identification, so parents need to research this issue carefully. Schools should be able to supply literature to parents describing gifted and talented services and outlining admission requirements. Such documents usually provide insight into the school's perception of giftedness and commitment to supporting it. The following pages provide an overview of the current thinking on giftedness, as well as its recent history.

Definitions

The G Word

The term *gifted* is an unfortunate one in a society highly sensitive to the meanings of words and their political ramifications. Originally used simply to describe a high level of intellectual functioning (adjectives can be difficult to find for this purpose), it has unfortunate connotations for some. Perhaps labeling only some children as *gifted* comes too close to suggesting that all children are not the special gifts to their families that they are, or it offends by the fact that some children have gifts that are neither earned nor deserved. Furthermore, though we speak of nurturing giftedness, we don't usually speak of developing it from scratch. We acknowledge it as largely inborn—running in families, just as learning disabilities and other deficits do—a fact that rankles many. Whatever the reason, it invites criticism.

Susan Winebrenner, a nationally known expert in classroom accommodations for the gifted, suggested an alternative.[1] Because we are really trying to describe children who are "Discrepant In Learning From Age Peers," she proposed that "DILFAPS" might be a better choice. The term would refer to all students for whom the regular curriculum and instruction are not appropriate. "All children who are DILFAPS need different pacing or complexity and have learning styles that require atypical teaching methods," she wrote. But whereas DILFAPS would remove some of the unfortunate emotional loading that *gifted* has, the term is not exactly mellifluous and might be slow to catch on.

So many attempts have been made to rename and reframe the "problem" that the new terms tend to confuse the critical issues. For example, if we replace the term *gifted* with *talented*, there is a problem, because *talented* already has accepted meanings to some who do not want its usage changed. Comedian George Carlin[2] once observed that when Americans can't *solve* a problem, they *rename* it, usually with a longer, more complex name. He offers as examples the different terms applied to the traumatic effects that soldiers experience from combat: *shellshock* in World War I, *battle fatigue* in World War II, *operational exhaustion* in the Korean war, and *post-traumatic stress disorder* in Vietnam. He noted that each new name increasingly conceals the pain and "has the humanity squeezed out of the phrase." If Carlin is correct, we may simply prefer to keep *gifted* to avoid something far more cumbersome, impersonal, and likely devoid of any suggestion that being gifted is a good thing. Either way, the advocacy issues surrounding gifted children are too urgent to justify time spent debating new terminology.

The 130 IQ

The term *gifted* is a long-standing descriptor of advanced cognitive functioning. When I was an undergraduate psychology major, it meant one thing—individuals with IQ scores of 130 or higher on standardized tests of intelligence, generally the Wechsler or Stanford-Binet. The *average* level included scores from 90 to 109 (on a Wechsler test), *high average* encompassed scores from 110 to 119, and *superior* ranged from 120 to 129. The *gifted* level reflected scores two standard deviations above the mean of 100, at the 98th percentile when compared with other individuals of the same age (see Figure 1).[3] The 2% of the population labeled gifted corresponded with the 2% of the population considered retarded, with both groups exhibiting needs so discrepant from those of average individuals that special provisions were assumed to be necessary.

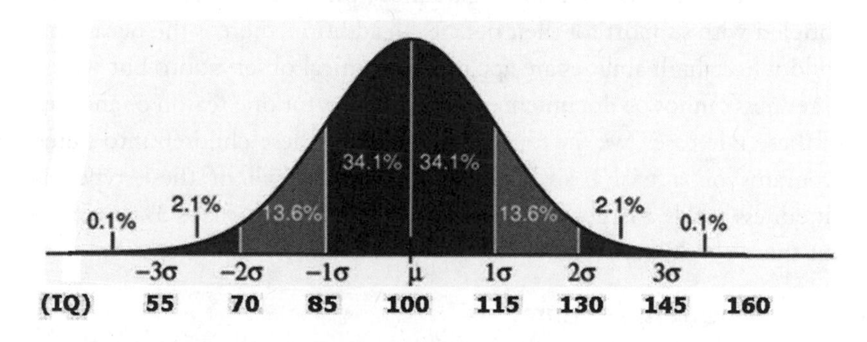

Figure 1. Distribution of Intelligence Quotients. Adapted from a chart by Wikipedia.

Many clinicians further defined a *highly gifted* level as well, beginning at three standard deviations above the mean (145 on a Wechsler test or 148 on the Stanford-Binet tests). Wechsler tests had ceilings of 160, effectively limiting the identification of higher levels of ability beyond *highly gifted*. Stanford-Binet scales through the Form L-M extended the range to 200 or more, allowing for the identification of even higher levels of giftedness: *exceptionally* and *profoundly gifted* (measurable only when the child was young enough to avoid reaching the test's ceiling). However, finding such children became more difficult when the Stanford-Binet, Fourth Edition was introduced in 1986. This version had a ceiling of 164 because it was felt that too few children scored in the extreme ranges to warrant the necessary extra test items. Riverside Publishing again raised the ceiling of the Stanford-Binet, Fifth Edition in 2003 by offering extended norms and other scoring choices. Wechsler tests boasted extended norms for the first time in 2008 for its WISC-IV for school-age children. Clearly, psychologists working with the highest levels of giftedness are quite dependent upon the scoring ceilings of available tests to find these children (see Chapter 3 for further discussion of this issue).

Children whose IQ scores identify them as being within the gifted range represent only about the top 2% of the population. However, more children are identified on comprehensive intelligence tests as gifted than just 2%, due mostly to *twice-exceptional* children, who demonsrate highly advanced reasoning abilities but who also have learning disabilities or other deficits that lower their overall IQ scores. These children are both learning disabled and gifted. They absolutely require educational accommodations—not only for their giftedness, but also adaptations that are coupled with support for their deficits. In addition, there is the occasional child whose high abilities are apparent in clinical observations but whose giftedness cannot be documented with our tests for one reason or another. In these rare cases, we try to gain entrance for these children into gifted programs on a trial basis. The combination of all of these types of giftedness yields a larger percentage than just 2%—perhaps 3% to 5%—but these children still remain a very small minority in our society.

What Do IQ Tests Measure?

Most scholars who study intelligence agree that it consists predominantly of abstract reasoning ability, which manifests itself in various domains such as verbal reasoning, spatial reasoning, or mathematical reasoning.[4] Abstract reasoning is the hallmark of giftedness. Intelligence tests assess reasoning ability by presenting the test taker with such tasks as finding similarities between concepts, discerning a mathematical pattern in a series, asking why certain things are done, or copying designs with blocks. Most have vocabulary measures as well, because the acquisition of words in a language and the ability to define them is a strong indicator of general intelligence, even for children from deprived backgrounds. IQ tests also assess other abilities, in addition to reasoning, that are felt to be clinically significant. Most have measures of visual and auditory memory (either short- or long-term), visual-motor coordination, visual perception, attention to visual detail, and processing speed.

The actual items on an intelligence test reflect the test maker's conception of intelligence. For example, the WISC-III (Wechsler Intelligence Scale for Children, Third Edition) manual describes the late David Wechsler's original view that intelligence is not a particular ability, but an aggregate and global entity—the "capacity of the individual to act purposefully, to think rationally, and to deal effectively with his or her environment."[5] Consistent with Wechsler's concept of intelligence, the manual states:

> *...[T]he subtests are chosen...to tap many different mental abilities, which all together reflect a child's general intellectual ability. Some subtests require the child to reason abstractly, some call on the child's memory, some call for certain perceptual skills, and so forth. All of these abilities are valued to varying degrees by our culture, and all relate to behavior that is generally accepted as intelligent behavior in one way or another* (1991, p. 1).

Test items are usually designed to assess a combination of *fluid* and *crystallized* abilities.[6] Fluid reasoning is general reasoning ability—"thinking on one's feet" in novel situations, especially perceiving relations in figural and spatial material. Crystallized abilities are the result of education and learning acquired from one's culture, accessed by tapping a child's general store of knowledge, verbal and quantitative reasoning, sequential memory, vocabulary, and reading comprehension.

Because they compare the child's abilities to those of other children the same age, modern intelligence tests are excellent measures of how discrepant a child is from others in terms of typical developmental expectations. The greater the variance from the mean of 100, the more discrepant or asynchronous the child is. Determining giftedness based on high IQ test scores is a reasonable approach to the identification of gifted children, provided that there is flexibility in the choice of tests to document the particular strengths of the child (see Chapter 3: Testing Considerations). IQ testing is preferable to basing identification solely on performance in school, teacher recommendation, or individual interview.

High Achievement

Although most children earning IQ scores of 130 and above on individual intelligence tests are labeled gifted by their schools and accepted for a gifted program, some schools insist upon performance-related definitions that require accomplishment in one or more academic areas. A child has to earn top grades in one or more subjects and show advanced mastery of the school's curriculum. Such requirements reveal a fundamental confusion between giftedness and high achievement.

Gifted students can process more conceptually complex material, need to be taught at a higher level, and learn at a considerably faster pace because they master concepts more easily. High achievers, by definition, perform well in a given subject area. Certainly some, but not all, high achievers are gifted. Many gifted students are high achievers; others are not. Gifted students who have been underchallenged for a considerable length of time or for whom the school's curriculum is otherwise a poor fit may not produce impressive work. One reason that testing is avoided by schools is due to concern that certain children, especially minority children and those without means, will be underidentified. Yet an identification process for giftedness that focuses on high achievement in school is at least as likely to miss these and other underachieving gifted students who are considerably at risk. The result is that schools fail to provide accommodations to those who need them most.

Whereas performance-related definitions of giftedness may *feel* more ethical to schools (one must earn one's giftedness) and may even tend to identify more children, they have other disconcerting ramifications. A school may consider a child gifted in some subjects but not others, and it may even identify a child as gifted at some times, but not consistently, based on performance. Certainly, schools want to offer services to gifted children most in need at a given time, but giftedness is advanced cognitive ability or intelligence that is relatively stable over time. It does not come and go and should not be measured simply by performance in the classroom at one moment in time.

Intelligence tests do a better job of finding gifted children, especially those at-risk students who are not performing well in school. IQ test scores tend to be remain stable enough that the child who was once documented as gifted remains so, unless there has been serious illness or injury to the brain or notable emotional problems. Scores may occasionally rise as interventions are undertaken for disabilities. The best rule to follow is that a gifted child who has been identified should stay identified and be continuously monitored to meet special needs as they arise.

Teacher Recommendations and Student Interviews

Some schools place considerable weight on teacher recommendations to find gifted children. However, we often see cases in which teachers have difficulty "seeing the giftedness" in introverted students, who may simply meet expectations and prefer not to stand out in the classroom. Likewise, teachers may not recognize giftedness in children who have become behavior problems when the classroom program is a poor fit. Most teachers believe that their teaching is sufficiently engaging for all children in their classrooms, so a child's abilities should be evident in his or her classwork. Unfortunately, this is not always the case.

Interviews with the child can also result in inappropriate conclusions if the interviewer is not familiar with giftedness. One first-grade boy who was turned down for his school's gifted and talented program (for which entrance considered only teacher recommendations, a parent questionnaire, and an interview with the child) wryly commented that he should have said that his favorite TV program was *Mr. Wizard* instead of *You Can't Do That on Television*. Those who still remember the latter program might realize that this first grader liked a comedy program for middle school-aged children—certainly a *gifted* choice. The next year, the same boy actually said that his favorite program was *Mr. Wizard*, made unexpectedly fast progress in reading (primary teachers usually expect that a gifted child will be an advanced reader), and was accepted into the program.

Educational Definitions of Giftedness

If a high score on an intelligence test is not the standard used to judge giftedness in children, what other definitions of giftedness/high intelligence should parents be familiar with in order to obtain services for their children? The operational definitions of giftedness that schools are using are becoming more inclusive, including more children who demonstrate giftedness in more diverse ways. This can be good or bad, depending on the individual child's needs, as the more inclusive definition can lead to over-identification of gifted children and make it less likely that the school can meet their needs. For example, a definition used by my children's school district around 1991 defined giftedness as follows:

> *Gifted students are those who possess exceptional intellectual and/or academic capabilities. Their demonstrated or potential ability is so outstanding that it becomes essential to provide them with qualitatively different educational programming which is individually prescribed.*

Note that the above definition includes both children acknowledged for high intelligence (probably those able to supply high IQ test scores would be accepted) and those who are high achievers in school. But compare that to the following definition promoted by the Colorado Department of Education in 2008:

> *"Gifted and talented children" means those persons between the ages of five and twenty-one whose abilities, talents, and potential for accomplishment are so exceptional or developmentally advanced that they require special provisions to meet their educational programming needs. Children under five who are gifted may also be provided with early childhood special educational services. Gifted students include gifted students with disabilities (i.e., twice exceptional) and students with exceptional abilities or potential from all socio-economic and ethnic, cultural populations. Gifted students are capable of high performance, exceptional production, or exceptional learning behavior by virtue of any or a combination of these areas of giftedness:*
>
> - *General or specific intellectual ability*
> - *Specific academic aptitude*
> - *Creative or productive thinking*
> - *Leadership abilities*
> - *Visual arts, performing arts, musical or psychomotor abilities.*

This definition very appropriately includes twice-exceptional students and students with exceptional ability or potential (possible underachievers) from all socio-economic and ethnic, cultural populations. Note, however, the expansion of types of exceptionality to include "leadership" and "psychomotor" abilities (football, perhaps?). "Psychomotor" has since been removed from the federal definition of giftedness because it was thought that there were plenty of sports programs for students with those talents.

Multiple Intelligences

Clearly the second definition from the two presented above responds to high ability in more diverse areas and requires the school to extend its services for the gifted. Howard Gardner's theory of Multiple Intelligences (MI), as described in his 1983 book *Frames of Mind*, recognizes even more ways to be gifted. Gardner initially proposed a group of somewhat discrete intelligences including the following: verbal/linguistic, logical/mathematical, spatial, bodily/kinesthetic, musical, interpersonal, and intrapersonal, with an eighth added later—naturalist. Gardner continued his MI tradition in his 1999 *Intelligence Reframed* with a discussion of whether spiritual, existential, and moral intelligences should be added to the list.

Although *intelligence* seems another poor word choice when discussing such things as bodily/kinesthetic abilities, Gardner's theory does acknowledge the different ways in which ability manifests itself in different individuals. Some schools have chosen to support these intelligences in their students, as evidenced by student performance in and out of the classroom. Schools are to be commended for efforts to support all advanced abilities in their students; however, some abilities extend beyond what schools can practically develop. Typically in the business of providing instruction in traditional curricular areas (e.g., in mathematics, science, and written composition), schools may be unable to support the serious ballet student or the child whose piano accomplishments have already eclipsed the knowledge of the school's music teacher. When class sizes are large, teachers are hard-pressed to accommodate the needs of all students.

Disappointingly, we have seen some schools extend Gardner's views to suggest that every individual must be gifted in at least one intelligence—a conclusion not intended by Gardner himself. In some schools, this misinterpretation has led to individualized learning plans for all students to support the "giftedness" of all. Supporting the learning strengths of every student is important, but the assumption that all are gifted tends to dilute accommodations for students who need significant changes made to their educational programs. And as one teacher noted, the faculty in her school had to concede very quickly that some students did not excel in *any* of Gardner's areas, an uncomfortable realization that the school might have avoided with a plan more carefully designed to meet previously unmet needs.

One positive result of Gardner's theory, however, has been an increased interest in teaching to the appropriate learning style of each student, as the seven intelligences suggest certain teaching strategies. Students often display a preference for learning through a particular sense modality: auditory, visual, or kinesthetic. They may prefer either verbal or visual-spatial tasks (or be adept at both) and learn more successfully through either a sequential or gestalt (big picture) approach. Because these elements of learning style lend themselves well to Gardner's intelligences, his theory has been extended to teachers' manuals to support instructional approaches for a range of learners.

Teaching has traditionally been highly verbal and sequential (emphasizing a lecture style and provision of some new information each day to build upon what was presented the day before). Any help for teachers to expand such approaches to include visual aids (e.g., maps, models, charts, pictures); hands-on experiences and creative projects; music, rhythm, and movement; and gestalt approaches (providing a conceptual framework or "big picture" before teaching) will benefit many students who have visual-spatial or kinesthetic learning styles.

Parents of children who need significant modification in their academic programs will need to find their way through the labyrinth of gifted identification in each school. Accomplishing this is a first step to being granted the privilege of accommodations—to the degree that they are possible. Every effort should be made to fully understand the school's view of giftedness and how it can be demonstrated by the child so that identification progresses smoothly. In some cases, it may soon become apparent that the school's perception of giftedness is inadequate to meet the child's needs. For example, parents of a highly gifted child in a program where 30% of children are identified and accommodations are minimal may want to consider a different school. Only if the child can be identified and receive meaningful accommodations is the gifted program worth pursuing (some do little more than identify).

While educational definitions of giftedness speak to the need for modifications in school, they do little to help parents understand the inner experience of giftedness in their children. There is one definition, however, that goes further.

Dealing with Asynchrony

Giftedness as Asynchronous Development

In 1991, a group including Dr. Linda Silverman met in Columbus, Ohio, to consider the question of what giftedness actually is. Still referred to as the "Columbus Group," this assembly of clinicians, theorists, and parents was concerned about definitions of giftedness that were based solely on external performance; they believed that giftedness was not only advanced abstract reasoning ability, but also a quality of experience that involved higher levels of sensitivity, intensity, and moral development. The possibility that giftedness could be reduced by educators to simply *high achievement in a subject area* placed many gifted students at considerable risk. Gifted children who were not also high achievers would fall through the cracks of our educational system and fail to reach their full potential. Thus, striving to agree on a more comprehensive definition that also reflected the totality and inner experience of giftedness, the Columbus Group wrote:

> *Giftedness is asynchronous development in which advanced cognitive abilities and heightened intensity combine to create inner experiences and awareness that are qualitatively different from the norm. This asynchrony increases with higher intellectual capacity. The uniqueness of the gifted renders them particularly vulnerable and requires modifications in parenting, teaching, and counseling in order for them to develop optimally* (1991, unpublished transcript).

This definition respects the unique experience of being gifted, with all of its academic, social, and emotional ramifications. *Asynchrony* reflects the special difficulties that the gifted child experiences because his or her abilities are not developing typically or in concert with each other. For example, reasoning ability may outpace physical development and fail to support emotional needs. The highly asynchronous gifted child develops in a minefield of potential problems and should not spark the envy of those who are concerned about the gifted being advantaged or elite.

The Asynchrony of Advanced Mental Age

The most notable asynchrony is that of the child's advanced mental age when compared with chronological age.

> *Mental age predicts the amount of knowledge [a child] has mastered, the rate at which the child learns, sophistication of play, age of true peers, maturity of the child's sense of humor, ethical judgment, and awareness of the world. In contrast, chronological age predicts the child's height, physical coordination, handwriting speed, emotional needs, and social skills* (Silverman, 1995).

One gifted child may have higher standards for the creation of a drawing than his or her physical fine-motor coordination can yet support; another may dictate wonderful stories to a parent but quit in frustration when asked to write them out by hand. The asynchrony of the child's higher aspirations and more limited physical coordination can cause considerable inner conflict and dismay.

Teachers usually gear instructional approaches to what is likely to work best with children of a particular *age*, and in many cases, these approaches are at odds with the needs of the gifted. For example, many gifted young students, like Zachary in Chapter 1, are reluctant to use the inventive spelling that their kindergarten and first-grade teachers encourage (to enable students to begin writing sooner) because gifted children immediately grasp the importance of correct spelling. This can paralyze their developing composition skills until they learn to spell enough words correctly that they are willing to take the risk.

In one case, a boy was horrified to learn that his teacher had been saying that his spelling was "fine" when it was, in fact, incorrect. "She lied to me," he wailed, and he insisted that his teacher had actually taught him to misspell. Considering that some of these children learn with only one presentation of material, he might have been correct.

As is true for the retarded child with an eight-year-old body and a five-year-old mind, asynchronous development is full of pitfalls. The retarded child must struggle daily with age expectations that cannot be met. The gifted child has the same problem, but with the eight-year-old mind trapped in the body of a five-year-old. This gifted child functions intellectually as an eight-year-old with eight-year-old aspirations, perfectionism, and reasoning abilities but is treated in school like a five-year-old.

The Further Complication of Emotional Age

The fact that emotional needs are tied to their chronological age renders gifted children more vulnerable. Whenever advanced cognition makes them aware of information for which there is insufficient emotional maturity for understanding, their suffering can be heart-rending.

For example, young children strongly need the stability that their parents' love and support provides, but when a preschool-age gifted child becomes aware that his parents may die, this is very difficult information to accept. "Nothing's going to happen to Mommy or Daddy" is an unacceptable statement on logical grounds (we can never be certain that disaster will not strike), even when the child has an age-appropriate need to believe it. Likewise, during the Gulf War, war in Afghanistan, and war in Iraq, we saw children devastated by the incongruity of adults killing other adults for a cause when children are taught to "fight with your words" because physical aggression is not right. Such highly conflicting realizations are encountered on a regular basis by gifted children.

The chronological age aspects of gifted children remain more age-appropriate (although some reach physical developmental milestones, such as walking, early), while the mental age qualities are usually very advanced (with notable lapses, parents insist), and emotional maturity varies with the situation. Gifted children can appear extremely mature in some situations and highly immature in others. Parents are forced to deal with a child of many "ages" at the same time—no simple matter.

Achievement vs. Developmental Advancement

In her 1995 keynote address at the Eleventh World Conference on Gifted and Talented Children in Hong Kong, Linda Silverman spoke on "The Universal Experience of Being Out-of-Sync." She emphasized that just as some want to move away from giftedness being determined by intelligence tests, a performance- or achievement-oriented definition invites other criticisms. Silverman noted that as early as 1926, Leta Hollingworth pointed out that achievement is very much a function of opportunity, and those who have greater financial resources have more opportunity to succeed. Moreover, Silverman reported that some experts[7] have even claimed that the notion of giftedness is culturally biased (even racist), related to socio-economic opportunity and a social construction that maintains hierarchical power relations. Silverman concluded that this is difficult to refute when children are identified by high achievement. Furthermore, giftedness as achievement is culturally determined so that the same performance may be judged differentially by members of different groups.

Conversely, if giftedness is viewed as developmental advancement, Silverman observed that there are children in every culture who:

> *...develop at a faster pace from early childhood on, are inquisitive to a greater degree than their agemates, generalize concepts earlier than their peers, demonstrate advanced verbal or spatial capacities at an early age, have superb memories, grasp abstract concepts, love to learn, have a sophisticated sense of humor, prefer complexity, are extraordinarily insightful, have a passion for justice, are profoundly aware, and experience life with great intensity* (1995, p. 2).

Of course, the gifted are developmentally advanced and may also be high achievers. But the developmental advancement is likely to be the more valid identifier, especially since achievement is tied to opportunity.

Personality and Other Traits of the Gifted

Extensive experience testing and counseling gifted children reveals typical personality characteristics common to the group. Not only do these children reason well, but they also exhibit many of the same personality traits. These traits apply regardless of the way in which their intelligence is manifested—in advanced mathematical/spatial reasoning or in remarkable verbal reasoning abilities.

Over the years, Silverman developed a scale of characteristics most predictive of high IQ scores. The following list is used at the GDC as a screener for giftedness and is available on our website (www.gifteddevelopment.com). When parents endorse at least 18 of the 25 characteristics as typical of their child's personality, our in-house research indicates that there is an 84% chance that the child will earn an IQ score of 120 or above. Profoundly gifted children can be predicted when parents endorse virtually every trait with multiple Xs (for emphasis) in the "very true" column. This happens often with this particular group.

Characteristics of Giftedness in Children[8]

- Reasons well (good thinker)
- Learns rapidly
- Has extensive vocabulary
- Has an excellent memory
- Has a long attention span*
- Sensitive (feelings hurt easily)
- Shows compassion
- Perfectionistic
- Intense

- Morally sensitive
- Has strong curiosity
- Perseverant when interested*
- Has high degree of energy
- Prefers older companions/adults
- Has a wide range of interests
- Has a great sense of humor
- Early or avid reader**
- Concerned with justice, fairness
- Judgment mature for age at times
- Is a keen observer
- Has a vivid imagination
- Is highly creative
- Tends to question authority
- Shows ability with numbers
- Good at jigsaw puzzles

*(Long attention span or perseverant *if interested.* Does the child stay with tasks for long periods of time?)

** (If too young to read, is the child intensely interested in books?)

Gifted children are complex and interesting. They love to reason, consider ideas, and debate. They are rapid learners in the sense that they do not require as much instruction as other children. Although the average child may need eight or nine repetitions to learn material, these children need far fewer repetitions, with drill and practice considerably reduced. Some are also fast processors (others are more reflective), but concepts are more easily grasped by all gifted children. Few need the review each fall that schools provide to ensure that students have not forgotten last year's work. Their memories are usually excellent, and parents often note that they remember verbal material discussed only once months or years before, or they seem to have a perfect visual memory of a place that they have been. Vocabulary is generally always strong, regardless of socio-economic background. Their speech usually resembles that of older children, adding to the social distance that they experience with age peers from the earliest grades in school.

Almost without exception, gifted children have long attention spans for material of interest. Even those with attentional deficits usually have the capacity to *hyperfocus* for long periods of time in areas of interest. Sensitivity (getting feelings hurt easily) abounds and tends to magnify the disparity between these children and others. Their differences are often not appreciated by other children, and they are made even more vulnerable to signs of rejection because of their heightened sensitivity. They may also be quite compassionate and empathetic about the plights of others. This is accompanied by moral sensitivity that allows them to consider deeply the events around them. Perfectionism is almost always seen in these children as well. It is evidence that they perceive a higher possible level of achievement than is expected and that they aspire to something better. It is the rare gifted child who is less than intense. Parents clearly view these children as challenging, exhausting, high-strung, or high maintenance; these are not children characterized by being easy-going or happy to just go along with the decisions of a group. Many show intense curiosity about the world, often leading to a wide range of interests.

Highly motivated to learn and accomplish, gifted children can persevere to unusual degrees. Their energy level is usually described as high, and most require less sleep than others (most also stopped napping earlier as small children). They commonly prefer to interact with older children, adults, and sometimes younger children (often feeling protective and caring for little ones) rather than with same-age peers. This is due to developmental advancement that makes them more similar to older children in both cognitive abilities and interests. Most sincerely enjoy humor and appreciate it during test sessions. Gifted children are clever and generally appreciate puns or funny situations.[9] They particularly enjoy the Verbal Absurdities items on the Stanford-Binet L-M that require them to find what is foolish or silly about a verbal statement.

Most gifted children are also early or avid readers. Many have taught themselves to read; those who learn later may learn very quickly. Reading provides, to a very large degree, the information that they crave and that is important to virtually all of them. Even gifted children with ADHD, who resist reading long novels, usually enjoy periodicals and browsing non-fiction books.

Concern for justice and fairness is enormously important to this population. Fueled by strong reasoning ability and high moral development, these children will go to great lengths to try to ensure that life is fair. Some have nightmares during wars and natural disasters; others begin "Save the Elephants" campaigns. Their advanced moral development is oftentimes even more impressive than their problem-solving abilities. The judgment of gifted children can be very mature, and they will question authority if it seems appropriate.

Creativity and a vivid imagination may abound, and these children may also show unusual ability with numbers or puzzles. Some gifted children even insist on assembling puzzles with the pieces upside down to increase the difficulty!

Other Gifted Characteristics

Beyond what is included on the Characteristics of Giftedness in Children scale, other tendencies are observed as well. Young gifted children typically progress through the developmental milestones more quickly than usual, at least in some areas. They may talk quite early or walk or ride a bicycle before others their age. However, there are some who will wait until they can walk, talk, or ride the bike almost perfectly before they show us, going through an extended period of mental rehearsal. Gifted children also tend to exhibit physical, as well as emotional, sensitivities and frequently have allergies, asthma, food sensitivities, or a history of colic in infancy. Tactile sensitivities to clothing are very common, most often with rough fabrics (some can wear only soft cotton knits), tags in the necks of garments, and seams in socks. Hypersensitivities to bright lights and loud noises are also seen frequently within the gifted population.

Introversion

Although some gifted children are extraverts (often with wonderful social skills), most are introverts. This is a concern, because the general population is predominantly extraverted, and as such, society provides considerable support for extraversion but little for introversion. Mothers do not admonish their children to stay in and read but rather to go out and play with other children. When a child shows introverted characteristics, there is usually pressure to "help" her change her "maladaptive style." Yet gifted introverts replenish their energy through time alone or with close friends or family members, so respect for and accommodation of their more introverted personality traits is very important. They need more time to observe and reflect before entering into discussions or answering a teacher's questions. Because introversion makes it more difficult for a child to be the "squeaky wheel" whose behavior forces some accommodation from teachers, parents may need to intervene and advocate more strongly for introverted gifted children, even when they are older.

Early Self-Efficacy

Elizabeth Maxwell (1998) has proposed that many gifted children show early self-efficacy. Not content to simply model their actions after adults until well through childhood, these children often insist while quite young that they should make many decisions pertinent to their lives by themselves. For example, one three-year-old profoundly gifted boy I tested had insisted upon making even the simplest decision himself since he could talk. His mother explained that he had been quite a challenge to handle, because most children do not question virtually every decision made for them by their parents as he routinely did. When tested in the spring, he had just informed his preschool teacher, "Now, I will write," after refusing to do written work all year.

Such children do not seem to come from parents who are overly indulgent; rather, they show these tendencies regardless of the response they get from adults. They view themselves as more in charge than others their age, although they may refuse to do some things until they can perform them well enough to meet their own high standards. More typical children would not think to make such decisions and could not be taught to try.

Familial Histories of Giftedness

Gifted children have familial histories of giftedness. A question on the GDC Confidential Developmental Questionnaire asks if parents or grandparents had indications of giftedness. Whereas most relatives have no test data to reference (a few note that they were given an IQ test but were never told the results), their answers frequently include academic honors and high SAT scores. Sometimes, parents mention skipped grades or relatives beginning college at a young age, or they describe unusual accomplishments. They may also include references to underachievement—struggles in public school and elsewhere due to the discrepancy between high ability levels and program offerings. The following response from one parent was notable for the number of highly accomplished relatives mentioned (specific details have been omitted to protect privacy):

> *Mom—in gifted pull-out program in middle school. PSAT-National Merit Scholar. GRE—790 math, 800 analytical, 710 English. Music very important—played flute/ piccolo throughout grad. school and professionally. Ph.D. in Molecular Ecology. Dad—not interested in school, but got good grades, finished a Ph.D. in*

> *Plant Physiological Ecology and is now a college professor. Paternal Grandfather—Ph.D. Recognized as the leading* [expert/job title] *in U.S. and probably worldwide. Harvard professor 30 yrs. Currently at Princeton. Paternal Grandmother—artist—deceased. Maternal Grandfather—Master's in Business, obvious intelligent underachiever! Maternal Grandmother—author of children's rhyming books—but unpublished. Also—Great Grandfather founder of* [major corporation]. *Great-Great Grandfather invented* [high tech gasket]. *Great- Great-Great Uncle was the* [European] *painter* [name]. *Grand Uncle important inventor.*

Although few children have family histories like the one above, it is especially helpful in evaluating a child to have information about relatives. For example, a child who earns lower scores on an IQ test but has a highly gifted sibling and parents who are successful professionals in their respective fields is likely to be far brighter than testing can document at that time. In such cases, the likelihood of learning disabilities or other deficits lowering scores is very strong.

Gifted adults show similar personality characteristics to those of gifted children. We use an adult scale, developed by Silverman, which expands the characteristics listed on the child scale. It includes the following:

Giftedness in Adults[10]

- Are you a good problem solver?
- Do you understand new ideas quickly?
- Do you have an extensive vocabulary?
- Do you have good long-term memory?
- Can you concentrate for long periods of time?
- Are you highly sensitive?
- Are you unusually compassionate?
- Are you perfectionistic?
- Do you have passionate, intense feelings?
- Do you have strong moral convictions?
- Are you very curious?
- Do you persevere with your interests?
- Do you have a great deal of energy?
- Do you often feel out-of-sync with others?
- Do you feel overwhelmed by many interests or abilities?
- Do you have an extraordinary sense of humor?

- Are you an avid reader?
- Do you often take a stand against injustice?
- As a child, were you considered mature for your age?
- Are you a keen observer?
- Do you have a vivid imagination?
- Do you feel driven by your creativity?
- Do you often question authority?
- Do you have facility with numbers?
- Do you spend time doing puzzles?
- Do you love ardent discussions?
- Are you perceptive or insightful?
- Do you have organized collections?
- Do you need periods of contemplation?
- Do you often connect seemingly unrelated ideas?
- Do you thrive on challenge?
- Do you often search for meaning in your life?
- Are you fascinated with paradoxes?
- Do you have extraordinary abilities and deficits?
- Are you often aware of things that others are not?
- Do you set high standards or goals for yourself?
- Do you have unusual ideas or perceptions?
- Are you a complex person?

Such characteristics run in gifted families, allowing parents some innate ability to cope with the issues of their gifted children. The highly sensitive child usually has a highly sensitive parent who is nurturing to the degree necessary. The highly curious child usually has a parent who is equally eager to find answers and will make that trip to the library, museum, or Internet site. Only in rare cases do we see parents who are baffled by children with unexpected or unappreciated gifted personality characteristics. When this does occur, it is essential that the parents understand all that goes with the territory of giftedness. No gifted child can "stop being so sensitive" or "stop asking questions" or "stop thinking life should be fair." Understanding the psychological territory of giftedness is essential to supporting, planning for, and appreciating the gifted child.

Levels of Giftedness

Schools usually acknowledge only a single level of giftedness, identifying students as either *gifted* or *not gifted*, since a score of two standard deviations above the mean is usually what is required to qualify for a gifted program. However, the range of ability above 130 is far-reaching and the differences among gifted children profound.

Some of the most advanced children have earned IQ scores above 250 on the Stanford-Binet L-M, more than seven standard deviations above children scoring 130 (which is two standard deviations above the mean, for a grand total of *nine* standard deviations above the mean!). Although all gifted children require accommodations in their educational programs, the accommodations for the higher levels of giftedness may be quite different based on the unique needs of the child.

The Moderately Gifted

The *moderately gifted* range, from IQ 130 to 144 (or 132-148 on a Stanford-Binet L-M), comprises about 1.5% of the total population and is the largest group within the gifted population. Most children we test earn IQ scores within this range, and most of the literature about giftedness pertains to these children. They have not only gifted abstract reasoning abilities, but also the accompanying personality characteristics discussed above. This is the group that public schools try to accommodate most, although even those programs are limited. Likewise, most self-contained schools for the gifted, whether public or private, plan curricula and instructional approaches based on the needs and learning pace of this group. Gifted children who are more highly gifted usually require an individualized education plan in such programs to ensure accommodations to meet individual needs.

All gifted children can be assumed to need considerably less drill and practice and to progress more quickly through new material. In fact, a rule of thumb is that these children can learn in about half the time it takes others. They do not require the usual review of material in the fall, and they have typically mastered some of the material that will be taught ahead of time; the rest they will learn much more quickly. They tend to be better at reading comprehension (understanding a passage) than decoding (identifying and pronouncing a word correctly). Their special gift of abstract reasoning allows them to discern a word's meaning from the context in which the word is found. Likewise, most gifted children are stronger at math reasoning than calculation. They hate the drill and practice required to learn math facts, and many fall somewhat behind when learning their multiplication tables. Most need strategies to make this learning more fun and considerably quicker. Moderately gifted students will generally need modifications in their educational programs in more than one academic area.

The needs of children in this range are rarely met in heterogeneous classrooms in which teachers use whole-class instruction. Likewise, it is a rare moderately gifted child whose special needs are served by simply assigning an extra project or providing services outside of the classroom in addition to regular work. These children all need consistent modification of their daily instruction to provide advanced material and accommodate their faster learning pace. This is best accomplished by developing a brief Individual Education Plan (IEP) each year that sets performance goals in each academic subject area based on current achievement levels.

Moderately gifted children should be assessed frequently to monitor their progress and to modify the yearly IEP if necessary. These children must be allowed to move ahead when they have mastered new material. Ensuring their continuous progress supports their motivation to learn. If they become too advanced for the general work of the class, they may need to advance a full grade or attend a higher-grade-level classroom for one or more subjects. Failure to acknowledge their need to progress further and/or any attempt to restrict their progress can place these students seriously at risk. Enrichment programs offered by colleges, museums, etc. are particularly helpful for gifted children and may provide a means to accelerate in a subject area. Likewise, correspondence or online courses, as well as tutors, can increase the options of moderately gifted students in public schools.

All gifted children need true peers, and it is essential that a child find friends of about the same intellectual level with whom he or she shares interests to promote social development. This generally requires access to other gifted children or those who are older. Of all gifted children, those at the moderately gifted level are most likely to value high achievement in school and be excellent students. But they absolutely need the highest level classes that schools can provide (honors classes may not be challenging enough), along with additional relevant enrichment and possible acceleration to reach their full potential. Self-contained schools or classrooms for the gifted can generally best meet the academic, social, and emotional needs of these children.

What are the concerns that parents have about these children? Consider Katelyn, who was brought for an evaluation because her mother felt that she was not adequately challenged in school and recognized in

Katelyn some of her own "gifted-girl-in-hiding" traits. A seven-year-old girl in second grade, Katelyn was starting to underachieve. Her mother wrote that she learns with "blazing speed when she's interested; otherwise, she just cruises." Katelyn's mother feared that her daughter already knew "the system" and would finish her work first to gain time to read or for other rewards while remaining unchallenged.

Because parents largely share their children's giftedness, they may also have shared a lack of support for it in school. Many hope to prevent problems in their children that they experienced themselves. Katelyn's mother knew the pressures on girls to deny their giftedness and hoped that her daughter would avoid this trap. The signs were already there, at age seven, of difficulties ahead. We documented Katelyn's giftedness and made a strong recommendation for a full-time school for the gifted to address her academic, social, and emotional needs. We noted that if such a placement proved impossible, Katelyn would need advancement in reading and possible grade acceleration to the next grade level. We also suggested that her love of drama, music, and singing be strongly supported to develop her talents. Supporting the strengths of the gifted is always of uppermost importance in supporting the self. Katelyn would also benefit from contact with other gifted girls with whom she could be herself and share her gifts. Where there is appropriate educational programming and similarly gifted peers, children such as Katelyn have a much better chance of reaching their full potential.

The Highly Gifted

Highly gifted children differ from those who are moderately gifted in their pace of learning and the intensity of their personality characteristics, and they are even more asynchronous. Usually highly articulate, these children may learn simply upon one presentation of material (if they are paying attention), without drill and practice. Comprising the group earning IQ scores from 145 to 159 on Wechsler tests, or 148 to 159 on older Stanford-Binet tests, these children often need more extensive acceleration (perhaps two or more years). This group will often show high school graduate grade-equivalency scores in reading and pre-algebra math before they complete elementary school. They also tend to make dramatic leaps in basic skills (e.g., reading), which necessitate very frequent evaluation to avoid teaching them material that they have already mastered. A highly gifted kindergartener who was tested last year for school admission who merely knew her letters then may be reading at the third-grade level when retested at the same time this year. Math skills may also be learned very quickly, and it is important for the child to move on to something new.

Frequent review of already-mastered material is mind-numbing for the highly gifted child and deadly for the child's love of learning and appreciation of school. These children may become valedictorians, or they may find few reasons to earn A's. They will often perform best in advanced classes with favorite teachers and far less well in easier classes or classes taught by teachers whom they don't respect. Alienation can be a considerable problem, as few others share their abilities or interests. Moreover, they may perceive school to be antithetical to their needs. They need true peers and opportunities to find them. In addition to taking all of the highest-level courses available, they should take advantage of Talent Search or other courses offered by colleges for younger students, distance-learning opportunities, computer-based coursework, opportunities to attend high school and college concurrently, tutors, etc.

Nine-year-old Kirk demonstrates the issues that highly gifted children face. A boy who was "born intense," according to his mother, he had enormous energy and a determination to focus himself and figure things out. Consistently somewhat reserved around other people and cautious regarding new situations (a strong introvert), he was also reticent about expressing his emotions. Kirk's feelings about school had changed dramatically; what he once loved, he had come to resent because there was too much homework and too much wasted time during the school day.

Third grade with a teacher who was unable to individualize work for him was a traumatic year for Kirk. He responded with crying, sleeplessness, and a refusal to go to school. He didn't understand why other students were happy with school and he was not. Finally, his mother arranged to have the Woodcock-Johnson achievement tests administered. He placed at the high school and college level in most subjects. His mother then home schooled him for the last two months of third grade, covering most of the fourth-grade curriculum as well. At this point, Kirk was willing to enter the district's magnet school for academically advanced students as a fifth grader. These accommodations helped tremendously, but Kirk continued to express many complaints about school. It was still difficult to find the right fit for him.

The Exceptionally and Profoundly Gifted

Beyond the highly gifted category, there is less agreement about what to call children who earn even higher IQ scores. The *exceptionally gifted* form a group that we define as having IQ scores of 160 to 174, whereas the *profoundly gifted* comprise the IQ range from 175 on. Because these populations are statistically very small (an IQ score of 160 represents approximately the 99.99th percentile), few professionals have worked with individuals at these levels. The needs of these children are so unique that documentation of their abilities is essential, and recommendations for them differ greatly from those for other gifted children. Parents are wise to read the works of Miraca Gross (see the For Further Reading section at the end of this chapter).

A special support system is POGO (Parents of Gifted Offspring), a support group for parents of children with IQ scores of 160 and above.[11] This group has chapters in the Denver metropolitan and Boulder areas of Colorado, as well as members who communicate by email from much more distant locales. POGO provides families with support and information to deal with the daunting needs of children at this level.

Groups such as POGO assist parents in learning how to provide extremely fast-paced, advanced instruction to allow an exceptionally or profoundly gifted child to make relatively continuous progress in school. Progress this rapid is virtually impossible to ensure all of the time, but parents must try. Reevaluation of each child's situation must be ongoing, with revisions to educational plans when the child makes unexpected progress and needs to move on. Resource information is critical, and in some cases, parents have to create the resources. They provide home schooling for their own children, start small educational groups in their homes, and even help to create charter schools. They find colleges willing to accept their much younger children for one or more courses, or college programs for high school-age students. Frequently, they have to move their children from program to program to create a reasonable educational sequence where none exists in a single school building or district.

These children may make incredible learning strides and graduate from college as pre-adolescents, or they may choose to accelerate only as much as is absolutely necessary. We have seen a surprising range of solutions be ultimately successful. Exceptionally and profoundly gifted children are considerably more vulnerable than gifted children at lower IQ levels, however, to damage from an ill-fitting program. Extremely sensitive and aware of every nuance of their predicament, they are unlikely to be a good fit with classmates until graduate school. However, placing them with older, more advanced students does help considerably and is necessary even in schools for the gifted.

Exceptionally and profoundly gifted students are often not our best students in terms of grades or academic performance. Because they are even more philosophical about the importance (or lack thereof) of grades, these students may either excel or become dropouts. One who excelled won a recent national science competition and at age 15 began attending a top college utilizing her $50,000 scholarship prize. She moved directly from sixth grade to high school and completed math coursework from Algebra I to Calculus in one year via computer-based instruction from a university. Unfortunately, many other exceptionally and profoundly gifted students tread a winding and uncertain educational path.

In the late 1990s, a group of POGO children and teenagers assembled at the GDC to assist a television production company researching high levels of giftedness. The company was not planning to make public any personal information from this meeting but hoped to gain some background perspective to help create a program on the subject. Virtually every student who attended had a story to tell about being terribly alienated in the classroom, of a teacher becoming defensive, and of being publicly criticized or humiliated.

One girl described an incident in elementary school when she was being taught subtraction. When asked by the teacher if a larger number could be subtracted from a smaller number, the girl replied, "Yes," knowing that the answer would be a negative number. Her teacher insisted this was not true and became so upset when she couldn't exact agreement from the little girl that the girl's mother had to remove her from the class and home school her. In fact, quite a few of these teenagers had been removed from school by their parents and educated at home. A highly articulate teenage boy in a biker-type black leather jacket described how an International Baccalaureate program at his high school had decided that he was "not appropriate" for their program because he looked and acted rebellious and was divergent thinker—clearly not a "teacher pleaser."

Some school programs have homework demands that exceptionally gifted students neither need nor see as important. The POGO students agreed that in some situations, it was not worth the personal cost to try to fit in; one had to give up too much of oneself for acceptance. A high school counselor working with a National Merit Scholarship contender failing his high school classes advised him to leave school immediately and take his G.E.D. She felt that he despised high school so much that remaining could only injure him further.

Children with the Highest IQ Scores

We have defined levels of giftedness upward through the profoundly gifted. However, there are children whose abilities are significantly greater and whose needs usually cannot be met even by creative acceleration in schools. Children with IQ scores above 200 are generally home schooled because their differences from age peers are simply too extreme, and they are unable to meet typical expectations.

As IQ scores rise from the moderately gifted level (130) to higher levels, we see increasing dissatisfaction with schools (even schools for the gifted), angst, and unwillingness to "play the game" expected of typical students. The more highly gifted children tend to value grades less and struggle more to meet average expectations (another good reason to avoid performance-based identification—these students may never *appear* gifted). At the moderately gifted level, we see many high-achieving students, whereas at the highly gifted level, we find some valedictorians and many underachievers. From the exceptionally gifted level on, students are increasingly at risk, with dropping out of school and even suicide as potential dangers. The most highly gifted children above 200 IQ usually cannot continue in school for long. Many are at least partially home schooled and take college courses quite early.

Such children push the envelope of asynchronous development and face its profound implications every moment of their lives. They experience the sensitive aspects of their existence to the most joyful and most painful degrees. Few would consider their challenges enviable or their needs elitist. Their needs simply are what they are. By acknowledging and labeling their giftedness, we merely recognize them as individuals who need our help.

What Is Giftedness?, by Quinn O'Leary

It was 5:37 in the morning by my watch when I stepped off my skateboard and mounted the slatted steps to my porch. The fog, thick and reminiscent of televised thrillers set in London, was melting swiftly as the world's colors shifted and climbed from greyness. The clouds lowering over the distant mountains were showing the first touches of blushing dawn, just as the grass-swarded pond bordering the street in front of my home was showing the nascent green of the amorous touches of uncertain mountain Spring.

Instead of entering my house, I laid my skateboard across my knees and sat on my porch, heels gently thumping over the edge. The awefully hushed quality of a foggy night was breaking up as birds woken by the traintrack clatter of my wheels against the sidewalk's sections trilled and warbled morning noise. The sighing breathing of the nearby highway was rousing itself from its nighttime lassitude as early-morning drivers bustled. I played careful fingertips over the wax-smooth skin of the apple that had ridden the night in my coat pocket, savoring the poignance of hunger and stilling the quiet concussion of my boot heels against the deck, willing for a moment the peaceful silence to remain.

The slight depression of the pond held the fog longer against the morn's incursion but its edges were consistently nibbled up like water swallowing a tidal island. In the still-predawn dark, a black shape dropped almost vertically into the fog. Startled, I peered hard for it until the familiar tri-note warble of a red-winged blackbird clarified.

As the fog grew increasingly less dense, the reflections in the glass-still, gem-smooth lake became more apparent, the fan of a skeletal tree becoming a drab pinwheel of intricate pattern. Close beside, the oddly oriental ornament of a stilt-legged heron doubled itself with the sedate stillness of its species.

The chill of the air, ignored in my nightlong exertions, made itself startlingly apparent, the chafing weight of my clothes notwithstanding. The part-rain scent of the fog's departure wafted from the tiny wildness, misting my mind with nostalgia befitting someone far older.

Breathing deep of the new day, I felt myself somehow renewed with its newness, made purer by its potential, made peaceful by its birth. When I bit into the apple, it tasted of spring.

For Further Reading

Feldman, D. H. (with Goldsmith, L. T.). (1986). *Nature's gambit: Child prodigies and the development of human potential.* New York: Basic Books.

Gilman, B. J. (2008). *Challenging highly gifted learners.* Waco, TX: Prufrock Press.

Gross, M. U. M. (2004a). *Exceptionally gifted children* (2nd ed.). London: Routledge Falmer.

Gross, M. U. M. (2004b). Radical acceleration. In N. Colangelo, S. G. Assouline, & M. U. M. Gross (Eds.), *A nation deceived: How schools hold back America's brightest students* (Vol. II, pp. 87-96). Iowa City, IA: The University of Iowa.

Morelock, M. (1992). Giftedness: The view from within. *Understanding Our Gifted, 4*(3), 1, 11-15. Also available at www.gt-cybersource.org/Record.aspx?NavID=2_0&rid=11392

Silverman, L. K. (1988). On introversion. *Understanding Our Gifted, 1*(2), 11.

Silverman, L. K. (1993a). A developmental model for counseling the gifted. In L. K. Silverman (Ed.), *Counseling the gifted and talented* (pp. 51-78). Denver, CO: Love.

Silverman, L. K. (1993b). The gifted individual. In L. K. Silverman (Ed.), *Counseling the gifted and talented* (pp. 3-28). Denver, CO: Love.

Silverman, L. K. (1997). The construct of asynchronous development. *Peabody Journal of Education, 72*(3&4), 36-58.

Silverman, L. K. (2002). *Upside-down brilliance: The visual-spatial learner.* Denver, CO: DeLeon.

Silverman, L., & Kearney, K. (1989). Parents of the extraordinarily gifted. *Advanced Development, 1*, 41-56. Also available at www.hoagiesgifted.org/parents_of_eg.htm

Skinner, W. (2007). *Infinity and zebra stripes: Life with gifted children.* Scottsdale, AZ: Great Potential Press.

Tolan, S. S. (1996). *Is it a cheetah?* Available at www.stephanietolan.com/is_it_a_cheetah.htm

Webb, J. T., Gore, J. L., Amend, E. R., & DeVries, A. R. (2007). *A parent's guide to gifted children.* Scottsdale, AZ: Great Potential Press.

For Further Reading

Chapter 3
Testing Considerations

Few experiences are more fascinating than testing a gifted child. From the first moments of meeting the child, that child's pattern of abilities and, perhaps, relative weaknesses begin to emerge. Once we begin the IQ test, I am observing verbal abstract reasoning, spatial reasoning, general knowledge, vision, audition, memory, motor skills, processing speed, attention, and a host of subtle cues that help to further explain the scores that the child earns. The sessions are usually very engaging for these children; the inherent challenge of the tests often eclipses what they experience at school. They are usually happy, frequently quite humorous, and virtually always well-motivated to do their best. For me, amidst the enjoyment of getting to know them, the pieces of a puzzle are being put into place, and the final picture seems always to be unique from all of the others that I have seen.

The IQ test was developed as a tool to observe the behavior of individuals under controlled conditions, and it is, indeed, a very useful tool, especially when used in conjunction with other observations. Those of us experienced in testing the gifted can usually make close estimates of the scores that children will earn based on our initial conversations with the child. Those qualities that we have learned to recognize as gifted—or highly or profoundly gifted—become recognizable. Likewise, the developmental history of a child is vital information in judging apparent or potential ability levels. However, the tests offer us standardized tools to further explore a child's intellectual functioning and to document it. They shortcut the process of observing the child's response to myriad situations over the course of days or months into two to three hours. Because the tests provide normative comparisons with age peers, we are able to tell exactly how advanced, typical, or delayed a child's abilities are.

It is always surprising to read a scathing condemnation of IQ testing. For example, the opinion that IQ scores offer an elitist way to rank individuals in our society according to some misguided scale of personal worth seems shocking to me. I view IQ tests as a means to clarify the educational needs of children who are discrepant from the average and to provide information needed to create an appropriate educational program for them. (Sometimes adults take these tests as well to answer long-held questions about their own strengths, weaknesses, and preferred learning styles.) Although the performance of average children is important in norming these tests, the tests are rarely used for average children experiencing no problems in school. They are used most with students who are developmentally delayed, those with learning disabilities or other deficits, and sometimes with children who are gifted because typical educational programs are not working well for these children.

Even when the scores are impressively high, parents usually keep the information private except when working with educators; the scores don't impress other children or parents and will never make a child more popular. But they do help parents make child-rearing decisions, and they offer excellent information about educational needs. They also provide documentation that what the parent thinks about the child's abilities is now confirmed by a professional. Parents are often put in the difficult position of justifying why they believe that their children are gifted, and testing becomes essential to provide a factual basis for discussion.

The information in this chapter draws heavily from my experience predominantly testing gifted children at the Gifted Development Center (GDC) in Denver since 1991. I share it here to familiarize parents and teachers with the relevant issues surrounding the assessment of gifted children. Because a wide range of testing and related services are offered by testers, those available in another location may or may not closely resemble the services described here. However, this information can provide a starting point for any family considering testing and will suggest questions that parents can ask potential testers.

Choosing a Tester

The decision of where to have the testing done is important (helpful resources are provided at the end of this chapter). Although private testing is costly, free testing at school has some limitations. Generally, school psychologists are hired with special education funding and are not available to test gifted children. When their services are made available, these professionals often lack experience with the gifted. This can seriously influence the interpretation of test score profiles. For example, relative disabilities that would concern us at the GDC because they represent a significant weakness when compared with often remarkable strengths might not appear to a school psychologist to be an issue when viewed on an absolute scale. I have seen reports that failed to view a discrepancy of 30 points between verbal and nonverbal composite scores on a Wechsler IQ test as indicative of anything when the lowest score is still within the average range (the test manual confirms that such a discrepancy is highly significant).

For example, if the child scores within the gifted range in verbal reasoning and language yet in the average range in visual reasoning, this suggests vision problems and the need for further evaluation of both acuity and visual processing. The verbal items on the test are presented auditorially, and the nonverbal items are presented visually. We have become aware in our practice that vision intervention (often with vision exercises) may well increase nonverbal scores upon retesting at least a year later. It is a travesty, therefore, to simply interpret the higher verbal score as a *strength*, ignoring the diagnostic implications of the lower score, when parents could easily address vision.

Moreover, testers with little experience testing the gifted may rush these children, being used to the testing taking a shorter amount of time. It generally takes longer to test gifted children because their thinking is more complex and they answer more items correctly before the discontinue criteria are reached. Many gifted children continue to hone their answers until a point at which they are finally satisfied. However, if the tester rushes to the next item, the child is quickly "trained" to offer the quick, concise answer that may not score as high. Allowing the reflective, gifted child the proper time to contemplate is as important as learning how to offer a speedy administration to the gifted child who is an especially fast processor and may lose focus if administration is too slow. Testers familiar with this population learn the skills needed to support optimum performance from gifted children. Therefore, it is generally advisable to have a gifted child tested by a psychologist or center with experience with many gifted children over the range of giftedness, not just the occasional gifted child.

Although extensive testing by school psychologists using individual IQ and achievement tests is not usually available for assessment of the gifted, most schools do offer some form of brief individual or group testing to qualify children for gifted programs. The tests are usually *unprotected tests*—brief screeners that can be administered by teachers, counselors, or paraprofessionals—as opposed to *protected tests* (e.g.,

Wechsler, Stanford-Binet, etc.), which must be administered by or under the supervision of a licensed psychologist trained to administer the particular test. The items on protected tests are kept strictly confidential, so the test remains a valid measure of abilities. Items on group tests should be kept confidential as well. Schools should store tests in a locked file cabinet.

The brief tests that schools often administer include the Cognitive Abilities Test (CogAT), the Naglieri Nonverbal Abilities Tests (NNAT), the Raven's Progressive Matrices Test (a nonverbal reasoning test), the Otis-Lennon School Abilities Test (OLSAT), the SAGES-2, the Slosson Full Range Intelligence Test (Slosson FRIT), Reynolds Intellectual Assessment Scales (RIAS), and Reynolds Intellectual Screening Test (RIST). Group IQ screeners have fewer items at the upper levels and are subject to ceiling effects. Some combine knowledge measures (what children have learned at school) with reasoning. A few represent only one type of ability (e.g., nonverbal), and because they are brief, they don't offer the detailed assessment of strengths and weaknesses found in comprehensive intelligence tests. For these reasons, we rarely obtain scores on major individual IQ tests that are lower than scores from these brief instruments, but we often obtain higher scores.

Brief tests appear particularly inadequate for documenting the giftedness of twice-exceptional (both gifted and learning disabled) children, and they frequently fail to document high levels of giftedness. For example, we have seen profoundly gifted children (175+) score in the 130s on the CogAT. Research as early as 1959 by Pegnato and Birch showed that highly capable children often expand the meaning of the multiple-choice questions on brief tests beyond what the test writer had in mind, and as such, they may answer incorrectly (comprehensive IQ tests favor questions which require the child to generate his or her own answer). My personal favorite of the brief tests is probably the Slosson FRIT because it is a reasonable test of abstract verbal and visual-spatial reasoning and seems to have a higher ceiling that allows for more scores above the 130-140 range. But individual IQ testing on the major tests is always preferable where the accuracy of the results is important.

Sadly, some schools will only allow children to be assessed on the brief test(s) that they use, believing that they must test all students on the same test to be fair. Tests and their limitations differ, so this is a poor policy if the school sincerely wants to identify all of its gifted students. It is fairest to all children to allow outside testing by a licensed psychologist and the opportunity for the child to be tested on a test that best documents his or her ability. Most schools will accept outside testing, but it is important to find out the school's policies to be certain.

Private testing has advantages in addition to providing access to the major individual IQ tests. If private testing is chosen, parents have the opportunity to assess the results before deciding what to do with them. Reports are given only to the parents unless the tester is instructed by the parents to send the report elsewhere (with a specific signed release). This can be advantageous for a variety of reasons. For example, parents may want to have a child assessed before choosing a school that is a good fit. Based on the child's results, a tester who has experience with gifted students can suggest a variety of programs or schools for further consideration by a family. A private tester works for the benefit of the child, not as a gatekeeper determining whether or not the child may enter a specific program.

Furthermore, if the child is tested by a particular school or program, it can be difficult to obtain a full report of the scores, and interpretation of the results may be minimal. Recommendations are rarely made—beyond whether the child qualifies or not— because such testing is done to satisfy the needs of the specific program, not the needs of the family for information. Additionally, parents may not select the tester; in fact, within private schools, many parents may be uncertain who did the testing.

Other problems arise as well. If the test(s) given must be re-administered, a waiting period must be observed. Major protected individual IQ tests cannot be given again for one year. In addition, cases have occurred in which the school would not relinquish scores because they were considered a part of the admissions process (parents should research the legality of this policy in their home state). One mother requested testing of her young daughter on the Wechsler preschool test. Because the little girl had been tested several months previously for admission into a private school on the same test, it could not be re-administered yet. The school was only willing to provide scores in a few more months, after its final admission decisions had been made for the coming year, and viewed releasing scores early as a threat to its highly selective, confidential process. Having a child tested privately ensures that scores are available as needed.

Testers experienced with gifted children are particularly concerned about documenting strengths, not just weaknesses, as it is the developmental advancement of these children that most often requires educational options. This is far different from the school psychologist who must primarily document weaknesses to gain educational accommodations for children with learning problems. Both testers are responsible for gaining admission for children to programs that will help them. And both want to make strong cases for these children to be included in programs that they need. However, the documentation of strength as a prime emphasis is not the way most psychologists are trained. Parents need to know that gifted programs can be swayed in their willingness to accept a gifted child if it appears that the child has too many weaknesses or if the report focuses most on the weaknesses. Experienced testers of gifted children are more likely to emphasize the level of strengths and the need for appropriate accommodations for those strengths. Where there are also weaknesses, a case is made for appropriate support for the child in those areas as well. Twice-exceptional children require a two-pronged approach; the child should be taught to his strengths first with appropriate gifted accommodations, then given support for his weaknesses.

The final choice of whom to choose as a tester involves consideration of all of these issues. How does a parent find the appropriate person? Parents are wise to attend local gifted conferences and presentations and to seek recommendations from professionals or parents of other gifted children via local organizations (gifted support groups, state and local associations for the gifted) or the Internet. The Hoagies' Gifted Education Page website listed at the end of this chapter offers a list of testers that is updated as circumstances change. This helps to ensure professional competency and boosts parents' ability to find a professional who can advocate appropriately for the gifted.

A psychologist or center that tests gifted children should be able to suggest specific services to support each child's individual needs. Talking with the tester or a representative of the center about such needs at length can not only be a good way to obtain advice about what tests are needed, but also lets the parents gauge their comfort level with the professional(s) involved. Do the suggestions seem reasonable? Does the professional quickly grasp and appreciate the issues of the child and fully recognize the different educational needs of gifted children? Does he or she understand the child's frustrations? As a tester and parent, I would want to know not only that the tester or center was professionally competent and experienced with gifted children, but also that we agreed on basic issues of gifted advocacy (gifted children won't necessarily be "just fine" in a typical public school program but will need significant accommodations). Furthermore, I would want to have a gut-level feeling of trust for that person by the end of the conversation.

I would also want to know that the person testing my child genuinely likes working with gifted children and is a person with whom my child would enjoy spending time. A psychologist who spends significant time testing and working with gifted children is more likely to have good rapport with them. Likewise, a center or group practice specializing in assessment of gifted children is more likely to draw professionals who will delight in the special qualities that these children possess: their interests, humor, and characteristic reasoning. They will understand when the little girl who misses an item begins to cry because she's used to getting everything right at school. They will be willing to spend considerable time supporting these children and answering any questions that they are allowed to answer during test administration. I am always pleased when our office manager, Lee Ann Powell, says, "You guys have been having entirely too much fun in there," because she has heard laughter emanating from a testing room. The tester's enjoyment of these children and comfort with high levels of sensitivity, reflectivity, perfectionism, and curiosity makes for a more comfortable session for the child. It also contributes to reports that appreciate and help the whole child in whatever ways seem appropriate, as opposed to being provided for a single purpose (such as program admission) utilizing only the options available at a child's school.

The Cost of Testing

The cost of private testing is based on the time spent by a professional actually administering tests to the child individually, scoring the instruments, interpreting the scores, noting observations of the child, having a conference with the parents, and writing the report for that child. Our experience at the GDC may be illustrative. We generally spend at least four to five hours in actual testing and 15 to 20 hours total when we do an IQ test, self-perception test, and achievement test (a combination of tests frequently requested), with their consequent report-writing times and post-test consultation. Additional tests and services require additional time and, usually, additional days, as testers are reluctant to push children too hard for too long. Fees are charged for each test administered and service provided, or they may be based on hourly rates. These are generally about the same, with contract prices reflecting an hourly rate appropriate for professionals in the field.

In rare circumstances, a tester assessing a child who takes considerably longer to test may need to ask for additional compensation. We have had several children who, because of significant learning disabilities or other disorders, have proven very time-consuming to test. One took three days to complete an achievement test that usually requires no more than 1½ hours. Testers are generally reluctant to ask for additional compensation, and it happens rarely, but additional trips to the office and possible rescheduling of other appointments make it necessary. If a parent is planning to have such a child tested, it would be wise to discuss the probable difficulties that the tester might anticipate and to ask how the costs will be calculated to avoid surprises. Likewise, a child with documented disabilities, a complex background, and a history of testing will require more report-writing time. Testers are professionally obligated to review past testing to understand the child and to report relevant previous results. Some children have had multiple batteries of tests through their lifetimes, which require summation in the report.

The professional may also provide other services, depending on specific needs. For example, extra time may need to be scheduled to get to know a child who is particularly anxious about the upcoming evaluation (some parents request this), or a clinical interview with the parents before testing may be advisable to understand a complicated situation better. Parents should also allow some flexibility for the tester to follow up on any observations of diagnostic significance (e.g., the tester might want to add one or more reading subtests to clarify a reading problem). Alternatively, he or she may suggest that adding an additional test or subtest will further document a child's strength in a particular area. In such cases, the tester should discuss supplementary tests (and their costs) with parents as the need arises. Minor additions to the planned battery of tests usually add little to the total cost; however, they can contribute significantly to the case made for accommodations at school. Other services might include creating an Individual Education Plan (IEP) for implementation at school. This is helpful when a school is willing to make accommodations but is uncertain about what is needed.

After the measures are administered, they are then scored and interpreted by the tester as part of the contracted price. Most parents choose to include a post-test conference to understand the test results more fully and discuss how they relate to the child's academic, social, and emotional needs. Billed according to length of time and the professionals involved, costs can vary. The GDC, for example, utilizes two-hour conferences that include the tester, another senior staff member, and the parents. Other people (including teachers, grandparents, etc.) may attend the conference at the request of the parents. Testers share test results and observations, and the parents offer their input. The second professional ensures maximum expertise in interpreting results and providing helpful recommendations. Parents should inquire about the type of documentation of test results and recommendations that will be available at the conference, pending receipt of the formal report. If results are needed immediately at school, how can information be transferred quickly? At the GDC, we provide an Evaluation Summary at the end of the conference that lists all of the test scores, as well as recommendations stated briefly. This signed summary can document the results until the formal report is received, or parents can request that scores be faxed or have the tester call the school (with a signed release from the parents).

Particularly time-consuming and requiring additional weeks for writing and review, formal reports are highly individualized and lengthy. Most GDC testers estimate that they spend about an hour per page writing these (this accounts for a significant portion of the testing cost); however, these reports are extremely important as the major documentation of the need for gifted services. The entire process is very different from the machine-scored ability or achievement tests administered at school that yield a short, computer-generated report. In the formal reports, the reason for the evaluation is explained, the child's developmental history is explored, and a current description of the child is created, with the help of information submitted by the parents. Then, each test is described, along with resulting scores and their interpretation. Test behavior is noted, and all results are combined and summarized, with a lengthy list of recommendations geared to the specific needs of each child.

A child's report will probably be used on several occasions throughout his or her school career to help determine educational needs, so it must be of sufficient quality for this purpose. Just as an example, our youngest son's report from GDC (completed at age six, modified at age seven to reflect an IQ test with a higher ceiling, and augmented several more times to add later individual achievement testing) was used many times. Submitted first to his elementary school, it was used to identify him as a gifted student in first grade, was consulted when planning his second-grade program, and was pivotal in the consideration to skip him from second to fourth grade. It was also considered when he entered a private school in sixth grade, was used for admission (in lieu of SAT scores) to a Talent Search math class following sixth grade, and along with samples of writing and descriptions of classes taken in seventh and eighth grade, it facilitated his skipping most freshman and sophomore courses in high school. It might be prudent to ask for a sample of the type of report that parents can expect from a tester to determine if it will meet such standards.

Costs are usually limited to one major individual intelligence test, as IQ scores remain relatively stable. Children need not be tested again and again on an intelligence test to obtain current assessments of ability unless there has been a brain injury or serious illness or there are disabilities that are likely to improve with interventions. One child I worked with had been originally diagnosed with pervasive developmental delay, autism, and sensory-motor integration problems based on initial testing as a young child, which yielded low scores. By age 12, he had completed years of therapy with several types of interventions and finally tested within the exceptionally gifted range. Such a child might be tested several times to assess progress. However, few children show such a pattern, and most who have only minor weaknesses earn scores that are fairly consistent if testing is repeated.

Sometimes the child's test scores are believed to be an underestimate due to immaturity when the child refuses to do parts of the tests or is reluctant to guess unless absolutely certain of an answer. When this occurs, the child might benefit from being retested when somewhat older. Parents may also be advised to have a child tested on an intelligence test with a higher ceiling if the child's abilities appear to be beyond the limits of the test taken. However, this is a matter of documenting the full range of abilities, not of expecting abilities to change over time (see "Ceiling Problems: Scoring beyond the Limits of IQ Tests" later in this chapter).

In most cases, the only testing that parents may want to consider doing several times is individual achievement testing in order to evaluate the child's academic progress and determine whether current grade placement is reasonable. Individual achievement tests provide a way to document achievement levels higher than those typically assessed on grade-level tests at school. Achievement tests can be given by themselves when there is no need to repeat the other tests, and they are usually available from good testers close to home.

As I have thought about the cost of testing my children, I have felt that it was probably the best money we spent to support their giftedness. Whereas tutoring, enrichment classes, summer foreign language camp, and private school for a brief time were all helpful, the testing was the most essential, as it documented our children's abilities and provided us with a game plan for advocacy. When families lack the means to afford individual testing, it is worth inquiring about low-cost options. Some private funding is becoming available for this purpose, and many testing centers offer a limited amount of low-cost testing done by supervised interns in training.

Which Tests Should Be Given?

Most testers of gifted children suggest several tests to provide different kinds of necessary information. To answer questions about general ability level, relative strengths and weaknesses (including learning disabilities), and whether a child meets requirements for entrance into a particular school or program for the gifted, an individual intelligence test will be needed. In addition, an achievement test is important to answer questions about current achievement levels. Achievement testing is helpful for various reasons: to evaluate the effectiveness of the child's current educational program, help with planning a home schooling curriculum, determine grade placement, or provide support for acceleration. At GDC, we currently also add a brief self-perception test for all of our children to rule out areas of concern for the child. Some have had their confidence and self-esteem affected by negative circumstances. Personality tests (we routinely evaluate children for introversion/extraversion) can provide more information about the child's personality style and how he or she may fit into the family or classroom environment, whereas emotional inventories and projective tests can further elucidate children's concerns. A number of diagnostic tests may also be used to evaluate apparent problems (e.g., visual-motor integration, ADHD, reading disability, etc.).

Such tests all provide important data to consider when evaluating a gifted child's needs, but not all are needed for every child. Ideally, testers of the gifted should carefully assess the testing needs and suggest tests that will be most helpful for an individual child. Then, parents can make an informed decision about what they want, can afford, and will be most relevant in their efforts to obtain educational accommodations. Here is what parents most need to know about the various types of tests used to assess gifted children.

IQ Tests

Different IQ tests reflect the individual test developer's philosophy of intelligence, but these tests ordinarily have many elements in common. Abstract reasoning ability is considered by most psychologists to be the most essential element of intelligence;[1] however, other abilities are assessed as well. There are measures of memory—visual and auditory, meaningful and non-meaningful, short-term and long-term, and working (in which the test taker is asked to manipulate remembered material in some way). There are assessments of visual/motor/perceptual abilities and processing speed. There are tests of attentional focus. Most IQ tests ask questions that assess both *fluid* and *crystallized* abilities, in terms of Cattell's (1963) two-factor theory of intelligence. Fluid abilities can be tested by questions that require the child to solve novel problems, especially those involving spatial relationships. Crystallized abilities are those that are constantly augmented through experience—for example, vocabulary and general store of knowledge. These reflect the child's curiosity, exposure to information, and long-term memory. Because the major IQ tests are *protected*, the actual questions must be kept confidential. A child cannot prepare for an IQ test, but parents can always support learning and encourage thinking and reasoning at home.

As previously noted, the major IQ tests all have some diagnostic capacity beyond providing an estimate of intellectual level. Because they have been given for many years to large numbers of children, recognizable scoring patterns have emerged that suggest various deficits and disabilities. Sometimes, for example, auditory memory seems poor in a child with a history of ear infections, even though an audiologist has previously found no permanent hearing damage. The child may miss mental math questions because he has difficulty keeping the question or his mental calculation in memory. Or the child can't repeat strings of digits; her memory for non-meaningful material is quickly lost. This could be Central Auditory Processing Disorder, a rather common problem for which new therapies are being developed. Or these symptoms could be caused by attentional deficits, which should be further evaluated. Likewise, visual processing problems (e.g., visual perception, visual tracking, focus, etc.) may be apparent in testing, suggesting the need for a vision evaluation. The child may appear to have good spatial reasoning ability but experiences visual confusion when copying designs with blocks or assembling puzzles. Problems with tasks of visual-motor speed can indicate inadequate functioning of the visual system, fine-motor coordination problems, or attentional deficits (because the child loses interest in the clerical task and cannot maintain focus).

When suspicious scoring patterns occur, supported by the observations of an experienced tester, it is reported to the parents and recommended that further evaluation take place with specialists. Testers often receive reports back from these specialists after the child has had further evaluation, so the testers obtain feedback about what was an apparent concern in testing. Over time, experienced testers improve in their ability to find subtle issues, and parents are wise to follow through on further evaluation where indicated. In most cases, weaknesses in the gifted are relative to their unusual strengths and are not serious by absolute standards. However, because many children respond to interventions, it is important to find them. In some cases, the weakness is seriously hampering the functioning of the child yet has been masked by the gifted child's ability to compensate. If further evaluation with a specialist is undertaken, it is important to share the testing information with the specialist. Gifted children have been known to compensate in other evaluations as well.

It is wise to begin assessment with an IQ test that is acceptable to most schools, followed by additional IQ measures if the child scores beyond the ceiling of the test or shows a need for a different type of test (e.g., a nonverbal measure). Tests acceptable to schools are usually the newest versions of nationally recognized instruments. Most IQ tests are revised and renormed every decade or so. Testers are ethically bound to use current tests or to justify the use of an older test; however, monetary limitations may determine how fast school districts and individual clinicians replace their tests. Schools may vary in their requirements for private testing, so it is always wise to ask not only which *test* is acceptable, but which *version* of a test is required when a child is going to be tested outside of the school.

Wechsler Tests

Wechsler tests have long been favored by schools as strong measures of reasoning and diagnostic information for children needing individual, comprehensive intelligence tests. Wechsler tests have real strengths for gifted children if they are interpreted properly and if alternative scoring approaches are used where applicable. However, parents will need to make sure that testers are aware of these developments and apply them properly.

Traditionally, Wechsler tests have successfully documented giftedness for children earning IQ scores as high as the 140s, and occasionally the low 150s. They feature normative scaling, in which scores are determined by comparing the child's performance with that of age peers. It is helpful to know a little about the various Wechsler tests. Released in 2002, the Wechsler Preschool and Primary Scale of Intelligence, Third Edition (WPPSI-III) replaced the WPPSI-R (Revised). The WPPSI-III features a shorter version for children ages two and three (only four subtests are required) and a child-friendly, streamlined version requiring seven subtests for ages four and five. Both offer supplementary subtests. The WPPSI-III subtests used to calculate the IQ score emphasize abstract reasoning well. The Verbal, Performance, and Full Scale IQ scores are important for gifted identification; the additional Processing Speed Quotient is not. Slower speed on paper-and-pencil tests is not cause for denying gifted services. The WPPSI-III can be given to six-year-olds, but the WISC-IV (described next) is usually a better choice when the child is likely gifted.

The Wechsler Intelligence Scale for Children, Fourth Edition (WISC-IV), for ages 6-16, replaced the WISC-III in 2003. This newer version adds more advanced questions at the upper ends of a number of subtests, which is helpful when testing the gifted. Five of six subtests are untimed in the two Composite areas that emphasize reasoning—Verbal Comprehension and Perceptual Reasoning—an advantage for reflective, gifted children. The increased emphasis on processing skills (Working Memory and Processing Speed) can lower Full Scale IQ scores, but the General Ability Index is an excellent alternative global estimate of intellectual potential (see discussion below). The WISC-IV can be used for gifted 16-year-olds, but the WAIS-III (described next) is typically more helpful.

The Wechsler Adult Intelligence Scale, Third Edition (WAIS-III), for ages 16 and up, revised in 1997, provides older teens and adults with Verbal, Performance, and Full Scale IQ scores (Working Memory and Processing Speed scores are optional). A new WAIS-IV is slated for release in the fall of 2008.

These newest Wechsler editions reflect structural changes important to gifted identification—primarily, an increased emphasis on processing skills, with a consequent reduction in abstract reasoning measures. Previous Wechsler IQ tests were divided into Verbal subtests (presented verbally) and Performance subtests (presented with visual prompts) and yielded Verbal IQ, Performance IQ, and Full Scale IQ scores. The subtests assessed abstract reasoning, (verbal, visual-spatial, and mathematical), acquired knowledge and language, and processing skills (short-term memory, processing speed). However, some processing skill subtests were supplementary and were not included in IQ scores. On the newest tests, the emphasis on processing skills has increased. For example, the WPPSI-III has added a Processing Speed Quotient, which can be harmful to gifted children with handwriting delays. Many young gifted boys (and some girls) show handwriting delays and should still receive gifted learning accommodations, despite the fact that their hands cannot keep up with their minds.

The WISC-IV has dispensed with Verbal and Performance IQ scores in favor of a Full Scale IQ and four Composite scores: Verbal Comprehension, Perceptual Reasoning, Working Memory, and Processing Speed. The weight of Working Memory and Processing Speed in the Full Scale IQ score doubled on the WISC-IV, with a consequent reduction in emphasis of Verbal Comprehension and Perceptual Reasoning. This was done despite the fact that the gifted group in the normative sample[2] scored lower in Working Memory and Processing Speed, potentially confounding results. Verbal Comprehension and Perceptual Reasoning better identify giftedness. When Composite scores differ greatly, a Full Scale IQ score should not be used. It may be better to calculate a General Ability Index (GAI), utilizing the scores from Verbal Comprehension and Perceptual Reasoning (six subtests) as the best global estimate of ability.[3]

The National Association for Gifted Children (NAGC) addressed this problem in January 2008 with a position statement titled "Use of the WISC-IV for Gifted Identification." The statement cited these concerns:

> *The WISC-IV introduces important structural changes that compromise the relevance of the Full Scale IQ score (FSIQ) for gifted children.... The weight of processing skills in the Full Scale IQ calculation has doubled, with a consequent reduction in the weight assigned to reasoning tasks (verbal, visual-spatial and mathematical).... In light of these circumstances, where comprehensive testing is available, NAGC recommends that WISC-IV Full Scale IQ*

> *scores* ***not*** *be required for admission to gifted programs. Instead, the following guidelines are suggested:*
>
> *When the WISC-IV is used for the identification of gifted students, either the General Ability Index (GAI), which emphasizes reasoning ability, or the Full Scale IQ Score (FSIQ) should be acceptable for selection to gifted programs. The GAI should be derived using the table provided in the Harcourt Assessments website (Technical Report 4) http://harcourtassessments.com/hai/Images/pdf/wisciv/WISCIVTechReport4.pdf.*
>
> *The Verbal Comprehension Index (VCI) and the Perceptual Reasoning Index (PRI) are also independently appropriate for selection to programs for the gifted, especially for culturally diverse, bilingual, twice-exceptional students or visual-spatial learners* (NAGC, 2008).

Parents need to know that the WISC-IV is an excellent, comprehensive intelligence test for gifted children, with a good balance between verbal and visual reasoning, as long as the Full Scale IQ score is used *only* when indicated. It is important when choosing a tester to ensure that the tester is aware of this issue and computes appropriate global scores for the gifted child.

NAGC's Task Force on IQ Test Interpretation, which suggested the position statement, also facilitated a change in the scoring ceiling of the WISC-IV by its publisher, The Psychological Corporation (PsychCorp). Data on 334 gifted children were provided to PsychCorp to substantiate concerns about the validity of the Full Scale IQ score. Some of these children had earned higher raw scores on the subtests than PsychCorp had previously seen. These raw scores extended well beyond those required to yield the highest subtest scaled scores (previously capped at 19), as well as the global IQ scores (previously capped at 150-160) that are derived from these subtest scaled scores.

As a result, PsychCorp agreed to extend the scoring ceiling on the WISC-IV, allowing subtest scaled scores to extend as high as 28 in some subtests at some ages, and global scores to rise as high as 210. These scores were offered after the original test manuals were created, so it is important for any tester who encounters a child with ceiling-level scores on the WISC-IV to go to the publisher's website and access *WISC-IV Technical Report #7: WISC-IV Extended Norms* for the correct scoring tables to use with this group.[4]

Stanford-Binet Tests

Released in 2003, the Stanford-Binet Intelligence Scale, Fifth Edition (SB5), for ages 2-86+, replaced the Stanford-Binet Intelligence Scale, Fourth Edition (SB4). The SB5 is the second wholly reformulated edition since the Stanford-Binet Intelligence Scale, Form L-M (SBLM) (1972), which was the culmination of decades of similarly structured tests that were successful in assessing gifted students. Binets through the L-M were organized into age levels, each level containing a selection of different types of questions that a normal child of that age could answer. The tester worked through the age levels to determine a mental age; then a ratio-based IQ score, placed in a normal comparison, yielded the single IQ score.[5] The tests offered excellent reasoning items (especially verbal) and had much higher ceilings and lower floors, extending the range of testing beyond the limits of Wechsler tests.

The SB4 was a departure to a Wechsler-like test, with different subtests assessing different kinds of abilities and a more limited scoring range based on normative scaling—the child was compared with age peers. Testers of gifted children yearned for the higher scoring ceiling of the L-M.

The SB5 retains normative—not ratio-based—scaling, but it reflects a wider scoring range with structure akin to the L-M, and it uses toys, which were a favorite feature of earlier Binets for young children. Based on a five-part model of intelligence, the SB5 taps Fluid Reasoning, Knowledge, Quantitative Reasoning, Visual-Spatial, and Working Memory, with verbal and nonverbal items to assess each. The SB5 has extremely advanced visual-spatial and mathematical reasoning items. However, many of the verbal items are really verbally presented math or spatial reasoning problems, rather than classic verbal items that measure facility with language and the verbal abstract reasoning abilities that are emphasized in gifted classrooms through discussion and debate of complex concepts and in-depth writing. Because more verbal reasoning items would have been preferable, some testers combine the SB5 with the more verbal L-M. The SB5 does offer one helpful feature for reflective gifted children: timing is virtually eliminated in the administration of the test.[6]

Lovecky, Kearney, Falk, and Gilman (2005) note that, "for programs that rely on one IQ test for admission to a gifted program, scores of 120 or higher on any section of the SB5 [Full Scale IQ, Nonverbal IQ, Verbal IQ—the three global scores] should be used" (p. 27). The SB5 often produces lower scores than others using the regular scoring tables, and testers should be familiar with alternate scoring approaches (e.g., the Roid Gifted and Nonverbal Gifted Composites,[7] the Rasch Ratio[8]) discussed in the test's *Interpretive Manual* and on Riverside Publishing's website (see the For Further Reading section at the end of this chapter). Endorsed by the publisher, these approaches are appropriate for use with gifted children, provided that they are reported as a change in typical procedure.

The Stanford-Binet Intelligence Scale, Form L-M is still useful as a supplemental test to assess the full range of intelligence for children who demonstrate abilities beyond the limits of other current tests. It is best administered to young children (see the discussion of "Ceiling Problems" to follow). This heavily verbal, largely untimed instrument has stood the test of time identifying the gifted mind, sometimes at extraordinary levels. It is, perhaps, the test that emphasizes abstract reasoning most, with meaningful questions that gifted children find engaging.

Other Cognitive Tests

The Differential Ability Scales, Second Edition (DAS-II) is another comprehensive test of cognitive ability, for ages 2.5 through 17 years, 11 months (not all subtests are used for all ages). The second edition offers extended assessment of processing skills. Some school districts use this test, but others are unfamiliar with it. The Woodcock-Johnson III Tests of Cognitive Abilities (WJ-III COG, WJ-III COG NU) is most useful in exploring deficits and fine-tuning recommendations for a child needing accommodations. It is less helpful in identifying gifted potential, as it strongly emphasizes processing skills rather than abstract reasoning and may produce lower IQ scores in children who test in the gifted range on other tests. The Raven's Progressive Matrices Test and Naglieri Nonverbal Abilities Test (NNAT) are popular nonverbal intelligence measures to use with children who show visual-spatial strengths, are from culturally diverse backgrounds, are deaf or hard of hearing, or are limited English-speaking.

Test authors strive to create tests that meet the broadest range of needs possible, which may or may not serve the gifted well. Using some tests or portions of tests and avoiding others makes sense. Most testers agree that gifted individuals are best identified by tests that maximize abstract reasoning (verbal, mathematical, and spatial) and minimize diagnostic assessment (memory, processing speed, fine-motor coordination).

This best identifies the children who need the characteristic gifted classroom that emphasizes fast-paced, advanced instruction and the development of higher-level thinking skills. Whenever tests are revised, we must determine which tests, or portions of them, best serve different gifted children and advise parents accordingly.

Ceiling Problems: Scoring beyond the Limits of IQ Tests

Gifted children may experience ceiling effects on intelligence tests. Every test has a ceiling in terms of the highest scores possible and the most difficult items contained on it. Once a child can correctly answer the hardest questions on a test, he or she has reached the ceiling. If the child is young enough that the ceiling-level performance is remarkable, the score will be quite high. However, if the same child is tested several more times on the same test over the next few years and can answer no additional questions because there are no harder ones, that child's score will go down because his or her performance will become less and less remarkable. Is the child's intelligence declining? Of course not. There are simply ceiling problems restricting the scores. What is needed is a test with a higher ceiling and more difficult items. However, if no such test is available, it is important to test the child early enough on an available test to obtain the best score and avoid a score reflecting any decline. In this case, the first test score is usually the best estimate of the child's true abilities, assuming that the test session went well. Any gifted child who has been tested on a test with a sufficient ceiling (the child cannot yet answer the most difficult items) and earned high scores should use those scores throughout childhood for program admissions. It is not appropriate to ask a considerably older child who was tested previously for current scores to document giftedness, as it may be more difficult to obtain an accurate measurement.

The major IQ tests have important ceiling limitations for gifted children, unless the procedures noted above are used. First, most of the tests have maximum possible global scores (Full Scale IQ and composite scores) around 160, with the highest earned scores generally occurring in the 140s (with an occasional 150+). These highest-scoring children may get their global IQ scores by earning just enough raw score points on each subtest to qualify for them; other children may have scored considerably more raw score points on the component subscales but yet get the same global IQ score because of the ceiling effect. In either case, their global scores cannot go higher.

The Wechsler Preschool and Adult scales (WPPSI-III and WAIS-III) and Differential Ability Scales (DAS-II) all have scoring ceilings around 160. The popular Wechsler Intelligence Scale for Children, Fourth Edition (WISC-IV) had similar scoring limitations until PsychCorp added its extended norms for children earning the highest scores (scoring caps were lifted, but no harder questions were added).

Scores from 145 through the 150s document at least highly gifted abilities, but they may mask considerably higher abilities beyond the ceilings of the tests. To those who do not work with gifted children, this issue may seem trivial. What difference does it make if a child is actually more capable than the test can measure? Does it really matter if a 145 IQ is an underestimate? The answer is that it matters considerably, because we advise parents differently about child-rearing issues and educational choices based on the level of scores above this ceiling.

The preferred test to explore the full range of giftedness has been the older Stanford-Binet Intelligence Scale, Form L-M. Having last normed this test in 1972, Riverside Publishing still supports its use for testing the extreme limits of intelligence and for research, provided that it is used as a retest following a test with current norms.[9] The L-M is indicated for children whose scores on other tests cluster around the ceiling. It can produce normed ratio IQ scores as high as 200+ in children not old enough to have surpassed its ceiling. It is best to administer it through age nine. Sometimes higher ability can be documented with slightly older children, but occasionally, a child younger than nine can do the most difficult items.

There is confusion about the higher scores sometimes obtained on the Form L-M. Some believe that children always score higher on the L-M or that the higher scores are due simply to older norms. Neither is true. Children do not always score higher on the L-M; those who score near the top of other IQ tests earn a range of scores on the L-M from about the same to much higher. Because testers are reluctant to suggest a second IQ test unless higher ability is strongly suspected, they recommend retesting only for those children with scoring patterns on other tests that indicate high abstract reasoning ability in order to maximize the chances of finding those likely to benefit from the L-M. For example, children who earn 99th percentile scores or higher on two or more of the Verbal Comprehension subtests of the WISC-IV (Similarities, Vocabulary, and Comprehension) should be retested; our research at the GDC indicates that they are likely to score higher on the Binet. Scores at this level on subtests that particularly measure abstract reasoning suggest intellectual abilities beyond the limits of the test.

Higher scores on the L-M have also been attributed to the *Flynn effect.* Defined as the general tendency of the population to score higher on intelligence tests over time,[10] this gradual increase in intelligence reportedly amounts to about one-third of an IQ point per year and is cause for the renorming of tests. If it were a factor, the Flynn effect would account for a point difference equal to one-third the number of years since the 1972 norms were published (or less, due to several rather antiquated items that modern children miss). However, the Flynn effect may not apply to our most highly gifted children. John Wasserman, then Director of Psychological Assessments at Riverside Publishing and project director of the fifth edition of the Stanford-Binet Intelligence Scale, wrote:

> *Although we standardly recommend that the most contemporary norms be utilized for any test, it has not been effectively demonstrated that phenomena such as the Flynn effect (the notion that norms become obsolete over time due to improvements in population intelligence) apply to changes in abilities at the extreme ranges (i.e., for individuals at very high or very low levels of ability). Indeed, there are sound statistical reasons for assuming that there may be only very minimal changes at the extremes of ability and that most of the changes in question occur for children and adults near the population mean. Moreover, Form L-M is one of the few reasonable options, given the dearth of intelligence tests with sufficient ceiling to assess extremely gifted children. . .* (J. D. Wasserman, personal communication, December 23, 1997).

More recently, some scholars have proposed that the Flynn effect may have ended beginning in the 1990s.[11]

With some rare individuals, discrepancies between Wechsler and Stanford-Binet L-M scores of greater than 100 points have occurred, which can only be explained by extraordinary advancement for a child's age, evident on a test with a high ceiling and the Binet's normed ratio IQ scores, which allow for greater expansion of scores at the extremes instead of forcing the scores into a more limited bell curve. These rare scores are sensible to clinicians familiar with the highest levels of giftedness and do indeed describe these unique children. However, normed ratio IQ scores are not favored by modern test authors because they believe that child development does not advance smoothly and consistently and that ratio-based scaling does not represent an equal interval scale. It is, for example, more understandable to describe a five-year-old child with a mental age of 10 than a 15-year-old with a mental age of 30. However, the Stanford-Binet L-M is effective for documenting higher levels of giftedness *only for young children*. Used in this way, the concept of mental age and ratio-based IQ scores can be quite descriptive to parents and teachers attempting to understand a child's advancement and plan appropriately for it.

For children needing this type of higher-level assessment, the additional option of WISC-IV extended norms is important.[12] Reflecting a smooth extension of the test's normative scaling, these norms recognize performance beyond the test's original scoring ceiling that was previously ignored. However, the test itself was not changed, and we often see children who need more difficult items. Typically, each subtest is terminated when a child misses a designated number of successive items and thus reaches a ceiling in terms of difficulty. But some gifted children fail to meet discontinue criteria on seven of 10 subtests, suggesting that there is still a problem with insufficient ceilings on the WISC-IV. We are seeing many gifted children whose scores rise only minimally using the extended norms but who can answer many of the hardest questions on the test. A valid measurement of a gifted child's abilities is only possible when both the scoring limits are adequate *and* the child clearly reaches a level of difficulty that is too hard—a true ceiling. Otherwise, we have no idea how much further the child could go.

The Stanford-Binet, Fifth Edition (SB5) also offers an extended IQ scale (EXIQ), which was originally designed to allow children who score 150 or above to use an extended norms chart with scores up to 225.[13] Unfortunately, very few children scored 150 on the SB5, so this option was very rarely used. Subsequent reconsideration of the 150 IQ requirement for use of the extended norms tables resulted in the following change by the test's author, Gale Roid: "As I re-read the *Interpretive Manual*, I can see now how overly restrictive the 150 might have been. Anyone can use the tables of the manual by simply accessing the table values with the total raw score values. In other words, you can ignore the 'worksheets' on pp. 24-25 and p. 131...."[14]

Rasch-ratio IQ scores, also provided by the test's author and using the 1980 Rasch statistical model,[15] offer yet another option on the SB5 to document extraordinary reasoning levels with scores as high as 200+ ("Profoundly Advanced").[16]

While appropriate use of the Stanford-Binet L-M and new scoring approaches for the WISC-IV and SB5 may all prove helpful in finding and documenting the abilities of highly gifted children, many testers are unaware of these issues. Parents need to share such information to ensure that the best approaches are taken when testing. Otherwise, unable to identify our most gifted children using traditional tests with typical ceilings, we threaten our most able minds.

IQ Tests and Minorities

Concerns have been raised that IQ tests favor specific groups and that they fail to document strengths in minorities. These issues are largely based on the fact that older tests did not use normative data from a large range of population groups, and parts of the tests may have been less relevant measures of ability for minorities. Modern tests, however, have generally been scrutinized carefully, and testing to develop norms has included a more diverse population with many population groups, as well as test items that are chosen so that they are equally relevant to all groups. Most schools these days try to use tests that are more culturally fair to assess giftedness. However, their good intentions have produced both positive and negative results.

Because schools typically have more limited testing capacity than private psychologists, they cannot provide a battery of tests to each child. Most schools rely on one or two multiple-choice screeners of intelligence, designed to be administered quickly. Sometimes a single test is chosen because it appears more equitable to insist that all children score high on the same test. Severely limiting test options lessens the quality of identification procedures for the gifted, including gifted children from minority groups.

In individual testing at the GDC, we begin with a frequently administered individual IQ test and then use additional assessment measures to clarify any weaknesses apparent on the original test and to further document strengths that the child exhibits. If the child's particular strengths would be better documented by another test, we suggest administering it, since every test tends to emphasize certain types of abilities.

The benefits of this type of approach are obvious. The choice of tests depends on the needs of the child. Group testing in schools can't provide this level of diagnosis, and the limited test use may or may not document a child's high abilities. *Whether the test is fair to a gifted child needing accommodations depends on whether it can document the child's unusually high abilities.* Children who have strong visual-spatial abilities will not do as well on a highly verbal test; likewise, highly verbal children may not be identified as gifted on a nonverbal test. Most tests include different types of items but vary in the balance that they achieve. Some tests specifically test only one type of ability—e.g., the Raven's Progressive Matrices Test. A classic identifier of nonverbal reasoning ability through pattern recognition, the Raven's would not be a good single identifier because it would not document the high abilities of children with strong verbal reasoning abilities. Different populations tend to exhibit certain strengths (although individuals within a group may exhibit very different strengths), so it is important to offer different measures.

The concern of schools to provide culture-fair tests sometimes backfires. For example, one district in California decided that it was unfair to test less verbal children with a verbal test, so the decision was made to use only the Raven's Progressive Matrices. This nonverbal test would presumably provide a level playing field for all children taking the test. However, this approach might fail to identify children who show strong verbal skills but weaker nonverbal skills. The assessment would be, from the outset, deliberately unfair to certain groups with verbal strengths. A better approach is to provide tests of both verbal and nonverbal/visual-spatial reasoning and to allow outside testing in the hope that throwing out a number of different nets will result in a catch of gifted children identified by their strengths in more than one way. No child should be at the mercy of a single test.

Achievement Tests

Tests that assess the academic progress of a gifted child are important to determine specific educational needs, and they are essential when acceleration is being considered. Achievement tests document the level of a child's skills in various academic areas, such as reading decoding and comprehension, math calculation and reasoning, and spelling and written composition. Some tests also offer assessments of acquired knowledge in such areas as science, social studies, and humanities, but these measures can be less useful because school curricula vary considerably and scores can be limited by exposure to the information assessed.

Individual achievement tests are especially useful with gifted children because they sample skills over a large range of grade levels in order to place the child's achievement at a particular level in each subject. In contrast, standardized grade-level achievement tests, such as those administered at school, have an important limitation—they offer relatively few questions above grade level. As a result, it is impossible to determine the actual achievement of a child who scores at the highest level of the test (99th percentile). The same child might also score at the ceiling of the test for the next higher grade. Tests for higher and higher grade levels would need to be administered to finally determine the full range of the child's mastery.

Individual achievement tests, though less detailed at a particular grade level, sample knowledge at many grade levels. They do a better job of determining achievement levels for the child who is advanced, whether beyond grade expectations in all subjects or asynchronous (e.g., extremely advanced in math but at grade level in reading). The tests yield grade equivalents for the various academic subject areas, which can be eye-opening for parents and teachers. They also provide a means to observe the kind of work that the child has mastered and what he or she is now ready to learn, thus helping to determine what level of instruction best fits the child.

There are several frequently administered individual achievement tests. Most have brief forms, as well as comprehensive ones, to offer choices for retesting. The Woodcock-Johnson III Tests of Achievement (WJ-III ACH, WJ-III ACH NU) offer subtests in reading, writing, math, and spelling, with supplementary subtests to explore problems in any of these areas. The most useful subtests in the WJ-III standard battery to document a gifted child's achievement are the following: Letter-Word Identification, Passage Comprehension, Calculation, Applied Problems, Spelling, and Writing Samples (sentence composition). Experience with the WJ-III suggests that the timed Fluency measures—which assess how quickly a child can read simple sentences, demonstrate automatic knowledge of math facts, and write short sentences—may be less relevant measures for gifted children, assuming that the child has no significant processing speed difficulties needing documentation and accommodation. The WJ-III has a very high scoring ceiling with standard scores beyond 200 for certain subtests at younger ages. This range is helpful when assessing more highly gifted children.

The Wechsler Individual Achievement Test, Second Edition 2001 (WIAT-II) allows correlation with Wechsler IQ test scores. The WIAT Written Expression subtest offers a flexible written expression evaluation using a writing prompt and criteria to score the composition that the child writes. This can be a good choice for the child who is a gifted writer. Other individual achievement tests useful for this group include the Kaufman Test of Educational Achievement, Second Edition (KTEA-II) and the Peabody Individual Achievement Test, Revised/Normative Update (PIAT-R/NU).

The individual characteristics of these tests and ceiling levels are important considerations for specific children, and the following questions should be considered:

- Does the test provide a way to document specific strengths, such as writing or math? For example, the child with knowledge of algebra, geometry, or calculus will need a test that samples skills well beyond arithmetic.
- Is the highest possible score beyond or similar to the child's scores on IQ tests? A child whose IQ scores are considerably higher than the highest score possible on the achievement test may simply earn ceiling-level achievement scores, without demonstrating a true ceiling of knowledge learned.

Such considerations guide the choice of achievement tests used to document a gifted child's developing skills. Knowing the child's current achievement levels helps determine whether his or her academic program is reasonable. A child whose achievement is far beyond that of classmates is unlikely to enjoy that classroom and needs accommodations or an alternative grade or school placement.

Parents may wish to monitor a child's achievement every 1½ to 2½ years through elementary school and into middle school by using a continuous, individual achievement test as a way to supplement the grade-level achievement tests at school. Whereas the individual achievement test indicates the full range of ability, the grade-level test will find small holes in the detailed assessment of grade-level skills, and this is important information to include in an Individual Education Plan (IEP) for the next year. (It should be noted that small holes are quickly filled by gifted children and are not cause for holding them to a lower grade level.) Ideally, a child's achievement scores (calculated as standard scores with a mean of 100) should approach his or her IQ scores, unless learning deficits prevent it. When a child's achievement scores fall considerably below IQ scores and no discernible weakness is evident, the educational program may be inadequate. Conversely, when achievement scores are close to or about the same as IQ scores, gifted children usually feel challenged and happy.

Personality Tests

At the GDC, we routinely assess introversion/extraversion—one aspect of personality. Gifted children are largely introverted and living in an extraverted world, so they can experience problems. Whereas gifted extraverts often have unusually well-developed social skills, gifted introverts may need support for their less common personality style and accommodation, both at home and at school. We cannot make extraverts of them because they are simply wired differently. Furthermore, respecting their introversion goes a long way toward acknowledging and valuing them as unique individuals.

We have learned many things about gifted introverts. For example, an introvert should be disciplined privately, allowed the extra time needed to adjust to changes, given projects to explore in depth, and allowed time to consider a question before being expected to answer in public. They don't do as well in large groups but benefit from one-on-one interaction or small group placements. In addition, because introverted gifted students are usually reluctant to talk to their teachers about work that is too easy for them, parent advocacy is important, even for older gifted students.

The Myers-Briggs Type Inventory or Murphy-Meisgeier Type Indicator for Children may be useful to evaluate other personality characteristics. Understanding a child's personality style is relevant for approaches in parenting and instruction in the classroom. In addition, on many occasions, we have given the Myers-Briggs to families to help members understand how their own underlying personality styles affect their interaction with each other.

Emotional Inventories and Projective Tests

Emotional indicators are important because the experience of feeling different or out of place is common in the gifted. These children may have particular problems making and keeping friends or coping with the stress of being out-of-sync in the classroom. Perhaps the child has been tormented by a bully or has simply been isolated by other children and feels terribly alone. Or the child's efforts to move ahead and learn new material have been frustrated by a teacher who insists that all students must do identical work. Sometimes the twice-exceptional child is struggling to overcome a disability that is unrecognized and the damage that comes with being considered "lazy." It is important to assess the magnitude of these pressures and to know the details of the child's concerns in order to suggest strategies to mitigate them.

Parents often find this information helpful. They may not have realized that their young daughter felt so isolated from classmates or that their gifted teenage son with a learning disability seriously wondered if he were as smart as others. We often learn of needs that can be addressed with teachers and at home. The older, more verbal child may be asked to answer questions and complete sentences to gain more information about thoughts, concerns, and hopes for the future. The younger child may be asked to draw pictures or create stories to explain pictures. The patterns of recurring themes in a child's answers help us to understand the issues of greatest concern. Gifted children may give responses—reflecting such characteristics as their vivid imagination, intensity, and sensitivity—that appear pathological to some. Experience with the personality characteristics of gifted children is necessary for professionals who use emotional inventories and projective tests.[17]

Further Diagnostic Tests

Additional diagnostic measures may be warranted to further investigate a difficulty—explore a reading problem, understand why a child resists writing, rule out ADHD, etc. The Woodcock-Johnson III supplementary subtests are helpful for exploring problems with phonetic skills, written work, or basic math concepts. Newer comprehensive tests generally include more subtests to explore such weaknesses.

In other cases, the tester may ask to administer another ability measure or portion of an IQ test to substantiate a child's particular strengths. For example, when dealing with children with apparently strong nonverbal/spatial reasoning, it may be helpful to give one or more of the following: the Naglieri Nonverbal Abilities Test, the Raven's Progressive Matrices Test, or the Universal Nonverbal Intelligence Test (UNIT). Sometimes even a portion of an adult test is useful to document extremely advanced abilities in children. The Matrix Reasoning subtest of the Wechsler Adult Intelligence Scale, Third Edition (WAIS-III) is an excellent, untimed, nonverbal measure. Demonstrating that a much younger child can score high on this test, using norms for 16-year-olds, is convincing evidence to many that the child has a considerable strength.

A thorough knowledge of available testing instruments allows the experienced tester of the gifted to accommodate the strengths and weaknesses of any child. Parents are paying for a highly individualized evaluation and should gain as much helpful information as possible during the initial assessment, since it is not likely to be repeated.

Preparing Your Child for Testing

Parents should prepare their children for testing so that it will be a pleasant experience for all. Our rather introverted young clients need a little time to adjust to the idea. Rather than telling them that they will be "playing games," it is better to say that they will be involved in activities that help us to find out more about how they think and that this information will be used to help them in school. Especially with younger children, parents can provide support by remaining at the tester's waiting room during testing (bring a good book) so as to be there when the child comes out for short breaks. Parents are then available to cuddle with their children for a few minutes, watch them play, or provide healthy snacks to keep blood sugar levels stable. We always insist on a suitably lengthy lunch hour that allows the child to get away from the office and the testing for a while. Additional breaks are taken as needed for comfort.

If children are to be tested at school, make sure that they will be tested at an agreed-upon time when they are prepared for it. Under no circumstances should a child be unexpectedly pulled out of the classroom for testing or tested without being previously informed that it will occur. Most would be upset and could not be expected to perform well.

Preparing for the Follow-Up Conference

Most parents who bring their children to be tested opt for a follow-up conference, and planning for the conference can maximize its value. Think carefully about what is most important so that the most critical issues are addressed. Is it understanding the ramifications of a high level of giftedness, or creating a workable educational program where none exists? Is it helping a twice-exceptional child to understand her strengths and weaknesses, or helping a lonely gifted child find a friend? Making a list of questions is very reasonable. Parents may bring grandparents, teachers, or anyone they wish, and some ask that the session be audio recorded so that it may be reviewed at a later time (a great idea, as the amount of information can be a bit overwhelming and both parents are not always able to attend). We have even used a conference call to unite our staff and one parent at the Center with a parent in another location who cannot attend.

Providing two experienced clinicians at the conference—the child's tester and one additional senior member of the staff—works well. The combined contribution of all parties—parents and professionals—results in conclusions being drawn about the child's level of intellectual functioning, strengths and weaknesses, and learning style. Recommendations are then made to support the child's needs, both at school and at home.

Whereas most parents choose to attend the conference without their children, later deciding what to share with them, older children or teenagers can be included at the parents' discretion. Younger children are sometimes very helpful joining a conference toward the end and helping to determine what recommendations should be made to the school, including whether or not acceleration is an appropriate idea (since the child must concur with this decision for it to be considered). Parents who choose to have their child participate in some or all of the conference need to request it.

If children are to be involved, clinicians must fully understand what can be shared with them. Some parents would like test results to be limited to general levels, strengths, and areas in which the child will need to work a little harder. Parents of teenagers may prefer to be very frank and share specific scores. Parents will need to consider the specific characteristics of the child tested to determine this. Also, when siblings are tested, caution is warranted so that children don't become competitive. We do not recommend giving scores to children in such cases. Parents may also attend the conference alone, then set up a separate appointment just for the tester to explain results to the child according to guidelines discussed within the parent conference.

For children whose scores document gifted-level abilities, the first recommendation is generally placement in a school or full-time program for gifted children, even when one is unavailable where the family resides. Such programs usually meet the academic, social, and emotional needs of gifted children best. We have seen families decide to relocate to improve their children's educational options. It is important, whether or not the child eventually attends such a school, to document this need. Other recommendations follow to create a better fit for the child in school, cultivate interests, and nurture talents. Ways to support social and emotional needs are also a priority in the recommendations. Where apparent deficits exist, further evaluation is recommended with specialists.

Professionals who test gifted children usually offer additional follow-up services as well. Phone consultations may be available to inquire about issues that have come up since the evaluation, as children mature and move on to different schools. Advocacy services may also be available, whereby the tester consults with school administrators and teachers or helps create an Individual Education Plan (IEP) for the child at school. Testers can usually recommend schools locally or offer guidelines for choosing a school out of state. Counseling is often available, as well as resource materials such as informative articles, books, and audio recordings.

Understanding the Gifted through Testing

Testing provides us unusual access to understanding the highly complex cognitive abilities of gifted children, as well as insight into ways to support their rare gifts. Exploring the intricacies of intelligence, we gain information—and documentation—that augments and clarifies our own observations. Because assessment tempers our conjectures with a healthy dose of realistic analysis, it allows us to arrive at more meaningful conclusions about the needs of these remarkable children. More confident to make perfectly arguable requests of teachers and school administrators, we become empowered, effective advocates.

Testing, by Quinn O'Leary

The test center surprised me. Upon hearing of my multitudinous, albeit somewhat over-dramatized and self-pitying problems, a counselor friend had recommended this particular center, but despite her downplaying, I had subconsciously envisioned a stark building of unpainted concrete and mirrored windows, an amalgamation of the latex-and-fluorescent sterility of hospitals I unwillingly frequented as a child and the gently threatening impersonality of a government facility. I expected the population to be much the same, a swarm of cookie-cutter professionals in lab coats, toting clipboards and wearing the same empty expression of subtle disdain.

With this picture fermenting in the back of my mind, I nearly walked past the actual testing center. Its entry hunkered like a shy child between and slightly back from the larger street-butted fronts of two venerably encrusted townhouses. It was apparently a converted house, the busy, cramped verdancy of its infinitesimal front yard speaking of a time before the city and its cheek-by-jowl street plan had encroached quite so far.

I navigated the awkward angles of the foyer with a nascent sense of relief already manifesting itself as general good cheer. I greeted the woman working as secretary and was shortly introduced to my tester, a woman whose stature and open, guileless smile put me in mind of an elf from a child's book, kind but capable of a certain brand of gentle mischief. After a brief round of banter, we retired to a Spartan room to conduct the testing.

The test itself was a surprise, in that despite my half-panicked feelings, I enjoyed it. A half-day's worth of verbal and visual absurdities, vocabulary, patterns and puzzles of colored blocks. It put me in mind of my first day of school, the same hollow anticipatory fear in the pit of my bowels, similar relief at my apparent capability. The glaring difference was that the test challenged me and was therefore fun for more than the first fifteen minutes. By the end of the final subtest, I felt as though my attention had been sifted like flour through a series of increasingly fine screens and that every subsequent weave had required more attention, had demanded more powerfully that I be aware of the mesh.

"Now these scores are a bit less accurate because of your age. Had you been tested as a younger person, these would be more indicative of your actual IQ." With these words, my birdlike tester led me into a concise explanation of what my scores meant. The numbers, with the slithy mien that is their wont, slithered quickly from my consciousness, but a few admittedly flattering words filtered through. The phrase that most caught my attention, however, was offered as an explanation: Asynchronous Development. *I was different in more than attitude; I was singular in awareness.*

Those two words, their pairing making them almost incantatory, struck to the core of my worry, slightly soothed years of self-doubt and guilt, started to abolish the idea that my always-apparent if somewhat unsuccessful intellect was nothing more than pedantry paired with laziness and angst. Relief flooded my head like liquor and, on my way out the door, I grinned into the sun with the expression of a joyful madman, reveling in a sense of well-being that I hadn't felt for years.

For Further Reading

Books and Articles

Gilman, B. J. (2006, Spring). Testing your gifted child: A springboard for effective advocacy. *Duke Gifted Letter, 6*(3), 1-2, 11. Also available at www.dukegiftedletter.com/archives/author/gilman_barbara_jackson

Gilman, B. J., & Revel, A. (1999, Spring/Summer). Current use of the Stanford-Binet L-M. *Highly Gifted Children, 12*(4), 10-12. Also available at www.hoagiesgifted.org/current_use.htm

Osborn, J. B. (1998, Winter). Assessing gifted children. *Understanding Our Gifted, 10*(2), 9-12. Also available at www.hoagiesgifted.org/assessing_gifted.htm

Rimm, S., Gilman, B. J., & Silverman, L. K. (2008). Nontraditional applications of traditional testing. In J. L. VanTassel-Baska (Ed.), *Alternative assessments with gifted and talented students* (pp. 175-202). Waco, TX: Prufrock Press.

Rimm, S. B., & Lovance, K. J. (1992). How acceleration may prevent underachievement syndrome. *Gifted Child Quarterly, 36*(2), 100-105.

Ruf, D. L. (2003). *Use of the SB5 in the assessment of high abilities* (Assessment Service Bulletin No. 3). Itasca, IL: Riverside.

Silverman, L. K. (1997). Using test scores to support clinical judgment. *Gifted Education Press, 12*(1), 2-5.

Silverman, L. K., & Kearney, K. (1992a). Don't throw away the old Binet. *Understanding Our Gifted, 4*(4), 1, 8-10. Also available at www.hoagiesgifted.org/dont_throw.htm

Silverman, L. K., & Kearney, K. (1992b). The case for the Stanford-Binet L-M as a supplemental test. *Roeper Review, 15*, 34-37.

Websites

Gifted Development Center (information about a variety of testing issues)
http://gifteddevelopment.org

Hoagies' Gifted Education Page (offers a list of testers by location, as well as articles about testing issues)
See "Psychologists Familiar with Testing the Gifted and Exceptionally Gifted"
www.hoagiesgifted.org/psychologists.htm

The Psychological Corporation (webpage with all WISC-IV technical reports)
http://harcourtassessment.com/haiweb/Cultures/en-US/Harcourt/SupportAndResources/ResourceLibrary/Reports/TechnicalReports/reslist.htm

Riverside Publishing
www.riverpub.com/products/sb5/pdf/SB5_ASB_3.pdf

For Further Reading

Books and Articles

Chapter 4
Curriculum and Instruction

A Typical Curriculum

Those who have watched a child pass through the public school system have some idea of the curriculum or learning sequence that public schools typically provide. Kindergarten stresses pre-reading skills and basic math concepts that underpin the acquisition of reading and formal math skills. In first grade, children focus heavily on reading and begin to learn addition and subtraction. By third grade, basic reading (having a repertoire of recognized words and the ability to sound out words) should be mastered, and arithmetic is expanding to include multiplication and division. Teachers are more concerned now about proper spelling, moving away from the inventive spelling used to empower their students to write. Science and social studies topics are presented as well at basic levels in primary grades and more complex levels as children mature.[1]

Foreign language may be introduced minimally in elementary school, then taught in classes in middle school. The equivalent of one or two high school level years in foreign language is offered in middle school, the first usually split into two years. By seventh or eighth grade, most students are concluding arithmetic study, having integrated into their knowledge the four basic operations (addition, subtraction, multiplication, and division), concepts of money and time, decimals, fractions, positive and negative numbers, percentages, and square and cube roots. At this point, they generally begin to learn to solve simple algebraic expressions, first by a "guess and check" method, then by strategies that are taught to them. Algebra instruction in eighth or ninth grade introduces a whole new series of higher-level math concepts—logarithms, functions, and slope—as students advance to geometry, trigonometry, and finally calculus. In language arts, students have expanded their knowledge of literature, reading age-appropriate selections as they pass from grade to grade. Their writing has progressed from instruction in writing a sentence to learning to write effective paragraphs, and they've probably encountered the three- to five-paragraph essay format. With minor variations, students have learned the same things at about the same ages for a long time. The curriculum has stood the test of time and met the needs of the majority of students.

But does it work for all students? Curricula are developed by arriving at a consensus about what educated people should know and determining what content and skills must be taught year by year to achieve the desired end result after a certain number of years in school. Curriculum specialists must decide how a set of knowledge and skills should be taught, beginning with the youngest school-age child. They must make decisions about how children learn best and about the quantity of material that can be covered in a given period of time. How much review is necessary before concepts are mastered? Must periodic review take place following mastery so that concepts once mastered are not lost?

School districts seek to meet the needs of the most students possible, so for the most part, they match the level and pace of instruction to the needs of their average students. This ensures that the educational program will be a good fit for the majority. Yet some students will learn far faster or slower than the standard curriculum can accommodate. These students will find themselves either bored with material that they mastered some time ago or frustrated and unable to keep up with classmates who are ahead of them.

What should the school do about the first grader who is multiplying and dividing, the third grader who is reading at the seventh-grade level, or the fifth grader who is ready to start algebra? Gifted children often find the curriculum relevant but the pacing inappropriate. They may be ready for advanced material much earlier than most children. The typical curriculum can be modified individually for such a child, but not without later ramifications. With such an enormous, detailed structure, flexibility is problematic; changing a child's program in first grade threatens second grade and the entire sequence that follows, and most teachers are reluctant to do this. Moreover, it is the responsibility of each teacher to prepare a student well over the range of topics that must be covered in that grade level. Teachers take this responsibility seriously, and some feel that acceleration or a grade skip will increase the risk of holes or gaps in the child's content mastery.

Sequential Teaching

Most material is taught sequentially in schools because this is the way in which most children learn. Instruction begins with the most basic concepts and continues with a bit more each day. Yet not all students are sequential learners. Many (particularly highly gifted and visual-spatial learners) prefer to learn holistically, beginning with an overview of the whole and then proceeding to the details of the various parts. These students need to know where they're going first in order to integrate new learning into a conceptual framework. They are wonderful systems thinkers and appreciate complexity. Instead of being taught the steps to complete an arithmetic calculation, they may benefit more from being given the answer and asked how the problem must be done. Rather than showing continuous, step-like learning progress, they are more likely to learn in intuitive leaps, mastering large amounts of related material quickly.

Learning Style Needs

Students may also have a strong preference for material presented auditorially, visually, or kinesthetically. Whenever the primarily auditory-sequential approach that is typically used in America's classrooms is not a match with the learning style of the child, teaching is more problematic. Within the gifted population, we commonly see combinations of ability and learning style that don't fit well with traditional public school teaching methods and programs. Gifted children may be auditory-sequential learners who are prepared for traditional classrooms, but there are also many visual-spatial learners who require different approaches to learn.

Linda Silverman has studied these children extensively and finds that they benefit from gestalt learning, visual aides, and hands-on activities that provide visual input—anything that requires them to visualize. In her book *Upside-Down Brilliance: The Visual-Spatial Learner* (2002), she notes that these children usually have difficulty following any step-by-step approaches and are divergent thinkers. They hate sequential approaches to math calculation and are reluctant to "show their work" for credit because they usually arrive at answers in different ways from their teachers. They fail to excel because instruction is seldom geared to their preferred learning style.

Gifted children who have both auditory-sequential and visual-spatial strengths may be termed "abstract conceptual learners," as the strong abstract reasoning abilities of the gifted characterize their thinking in both domains. They learn readily through both visual and auditory modalities, with holistic or sequential approaches. They can learn with varying teaching styles, but they may flounder with instruction too concrete for their needs (e.g., in middle school programs in which hands-on instruction for concrete learners is stressed because middle school philosophy assumes that most students have not developed abstract reasoning capacities yet). All gifted children reason abstractly quite early, and this capacity needs to be tapped if they are to engage in their studies.

In addition, we see gifted children with other learning styles, such as gifted kinesthetic learners, who usually have both visual and auditory deficits. Our highly and profoundly gifted students usually have both auditory-sequential and visual-spatial strengths, along with a preference for holistic learning. Regardless of learning style, all gifted students are efficient learners in the sense of grasping concepts quickly with minimal drill and practice. They are likely to advance through material very quickly, if taught reasonably well.

How do these children, for whom the regular curriculum and instructional approaches are not geared, move through the system successfully? Experience tells us that ignoring their different needs simply does not work and is a dangerous risk to take. Some will suffer silently but endure the poor program fit and manage to succeed. Some will become underachievers who lose, at least temporarily, their motivation to learn. Some will become behavior problems as a means to express frustration with being a captive in a system that is hurting them. Some will drop out of school. Once gifted students experience such failures, the final realization of their dreams seems all too dependent on luck, assuming that they receive strong support from their families. Their frustrations must be taken very seriously, despite what should be "fine for all students," because the risks are simply too great to ignore.

How Different Are the Gifted as Students?

Learning Rate

Dr. Charlotte Mendosa of Colorado College recalled an anecdote with a teacher in the college's summer enrichment program for gifted children. The teacher wrote to thank Dr. Mendosa for the opportunity to teach in the program and, particularly, for the daily planning period scheduled into her day. The teacher admitted that initially, she had thought that the planning period would be a waste of time because she had already completed her lesson plans for the entire three-week course before arriving. However, when by Thursday of the first week of class her students had exhausted everything she had planned for them for the entire course, she was very grateful to have a planning period![2]

Professor Brian Start found a difference in learning rates in heterogeneous classrooms of eight to one—that is, the fastest learner learned eight times faster than the slowest.[3] This is an enormous difference with serious ramifications. How can a child who learns at the slowest rate be learning successfully in that classroom without special accommodations? Likewise, how can the fastest learner in that room be challenged adequately enough to learn good work habits and maintain an interest in learning? Unfortunately, needed accommodations are often not available. Although there are strong laws to support the needs of students with disabilities, the current tendency to mainstream these students sometimes results in less capacity to meet their needs in heterogeneous classrooms in which teachers have a wide range of students and class size is large. Gifted children suffer as well because teachers have similar limitations dealing with them and because a lack of pre-service training in gifted education restricts teachers' understanding of gifted students' learning needs.

The National Research Center on the Gifted and Talented (NRCG/T) published a report titled "Why Not Let High Ability Students Start School in January?"[4] alluding to the fact that gifted students usually do not need the extensive review of material undertaken every fall and could simply begin with new concepts usually taught at the beginning of the new year. A full 40% to 50% of the material that would typically be taught has already been mastered by these students. In fact, gifted students generally can progress at least at twice the normal pace, assuming no disabilities (requiring accommodation) that slow them down, and some progress even more quickly. Yet virtually no schools are prepared to allow students to progress this fast. Gifted students' pacing difficulties persist throughout their elementary through high school years. Even when a child skips a grade, he or she is likely to need faster pacing after only a few months in the new grade. The problem is never fully resolved without a program in place designed for gifted children at the level of the particular child. With regular public school programs (and even gifted programs when the child in question is more highly gifted), parents must frequently review their children's programs for appropriate fit and consideration of what to do next.

Typical Test Score Patterns for Younger Gifted Children

The individual achievement testing of gifted children best describes their unusual academic progress. The following is a sampling of actual scores from six- and seven-year olds in a school for the gifted in Boulder, Colorado. The test used was the Kaufman Test of Educational Achievement (K-TEA) Brief Form, which assesses pre-algebra mathematics (both calculation and reasoning), reading (both decoding and comprehension), and spelling. K-TEA standard scores have a mean of 100 and standard deviation of 15, and this test has a standard score ceiling of 160 (corresponding to the exceptionally gifted range). Note the grade equivalents, which include the grade and month of the school year (e.g., 5.2 means the second month of fifth grade; 13.4 means the fourth month of the first year of college). Grade equivalents are based on raw scores earned and equate those raw scores with the scores of average children at a particular grade level.

Child A, Age 6-6 (6 Years, 6 Months)

K-TEA Subtests	Standard Score	Percentile Rank	Grade Equivalent
Mathematics	112	79	2.0
Reading	160	>99.9	4.8
Spelling	152	>99.9	4.2

Although this school does not have age-based grade levels, it is clear that Child A, who would be a first grader in most public schools, is very advanced in reading (fourth-grade level) and would have difficulty in a classroom in which the basics of reading are stressed for the majority of the school day. This young child is also very advanced in spelling, which is not formally taught in typical first-grade classes. Inventive spelling might be frustrating for Child A, who would want to know when words were misspelled to avoid learning them incorrectly.

Child B, Age 6-8

K-TEA Subtests	Standard Score	Percentile Rank	Grade Equivalent
Mathematics	112	79	2.0
Reading	142	99.7	3.5
Spelling	100	50	1.7

Child B is of a similar age to Child A and is also very strong in reading, but he or she is at a typical level for a first grader in spelling and a high average level in mathematics.

Child C, Age 6-10

K-TEA Subtests	Standard Score	Percentile Rank	Grade Equivalent
Mathematics	120	93	2.5
Reading	160	>99.9	7.3
Spelling	155	>99.9	4.9

Child C is also a very strong reader (seventh-grade level) who would be difficult to challenge, even in a school for the gifted. This child will need appropriately challenging books without objectionable content and literature study that engages his or her abstract reasoning. This child's spelling is so strong that more advanced composition assignments are possible.

Child D, Age 6-10

K-TEA Subtests	Standard Score	Percentile Rank	Grade Equivalent
Mathematics	118	88	2.4
Reading	160	>99.9	10.8
Spelling	130	98	3.3

Child D has an even more remarkable reading level (nearing the end of tenth grade). Such children have often begun to read early. As parents read to them, they develop their own reading skills. Many parents don't teach formal math skills early unless the child has requested to learn certain concepts, so reading is often the more advanced subject at this age. In fact, we have encountered few parents who take the lead to teach any formal skills to their gifted children; most only respond to their curious children's questions.

Note that the children presented up to this point are all six-year-olds. Most would have been placed in the first grade in public schools based on age, even though reading levels range as high as the tenth-grade level. All of these children would find the typical beginning reading emphasis of first grade stultifying.

Let's look at some children who are a little older.

Child E, Age 7-2

K-TEA Subtests	Standard Score	Percentile Rank	Grade Equivalent
Mathematics	143	99.8	3.8
Reading	148	99.9	4.4
Spelling	116	86	2.8

Child E, who was seven at the time of testing, is advanced in both mathematics and reading, with spelling somewhat lower (a not uncommon pattern for gifted children). Scoring at this level in mathematics, Child E is probably doing simple multiplication and division, which would not normally be taught in a second-grade classroom.

Child F, Age 7-6

K-TEA Subtests	Standard Score	Percentile Rank	Grade Equivalent
Mathematics	114	82	3.0
Reading	140	99.6	5.2
Spelling	155	>99.9	6.7

Child F reads and spells at the fifth- and sixth-grade levels and would also have serious difficulty being challenged in a second-grade classroom.

Child G, Age 7-11

K-TEA Subtests	Standard Score	Percentile Rank	Grade Equivalent
Mathematics	160	>99.9	>12.9
Reading	150	>99.9	>12.9
Spelling	156	>99.9	9.2

Child G, another potential second grader, is remarkably advanced in all areas assessed, scoring at the level of the average high school graduate in reading and pre-algebra math. This demonstrates the rapid progression in achievement that we may see, with children exhibiting a widening range of skill levels as they mature. This particular child is profoundly gifted and scoring virtually at the 160 ceiling in all three areas of this achievement test. An achievement test with a higher scoring ceiling would provide a better measure of actual achievement levels.

The children above, a typical mixture of students in a school or program for the gifted, differ in age by only 17 months, yet their grade equivalents vary by 12 grade levels! Each would likely be placed in the first or second grade in most public schools. A fair assumption would be that children in the gifted range (IQ 130 to 144) will usually reach the high school graduate level in one or more academic areas at least during middle school. Highly gifted students (IQ 145 and up) will have reached this point by the end of elementary school. Not only is rapid learning pace to be expected, possibly resulting in extreme advancement, but this assortment of skill levels demonstrates the need for individualized programs for gifted children. Even within a school for the gifted, where instructional pace can be increased for all students, individual accommodations will also be needed.

Choose Achievement Tests Carefully

To consider the academic progress of gifted children as they mature, one must choose achievement tests with a sufficient ceiling to assess these children's developing skills. Make sure that the test offers scores at least as high as the child's highest IQ score, and that the knowledge sampled on the test is advanced enough so that a child learning algebra, for example, can demonstrate skills that extend beyond arithmetic. Individual achievement tests generally work better than the standardized group achievement tests given at school for the reasons noted earlier.

Regardless of school placement or level of achievement (even if well beyond that of the child's classmates), a child should be making reasonable progress each year in school. If we accept as a minimal expectation of annual progress a full grade level's advancement, then the third grader reading at a seventh-grade level this year should, at the least, be reading at the eighth-grade level by next year. Of course, the gifted child who has new, challenging programming should pace more quickly, but under no circumstances should this child's meeting of third-grade expectations this year or fourth-grade expectations next year be cause for doing nothing additional! We want the child to continue to progress.

Typical Test Score Patterns for Older Gifted Children

Grade equivalents of older gifted children reflect their accelerated learning, but they also show variances between gifted children of similar ages and between skill levels in the various domains within each child. Keep in mind that not all gifted children score high in achievement; some score lower when held to a rigid curriculum with no exposure to advanced topics. Others struggle due to weaknesses. The following scores on the Woodcock-Johnson III Tests of Achievement (WJ-III

ACH) from gifted students tested at the Gifted Development Center chart advanced achievement that will require accommodations in school. Standard WJ-III ACH subtests that are useful in gifted assessment include Letter-Word Identification (word reading) and Passage Comprehension (reading comprehension), Calculation (math calculation) and Applied Problems (math reasoning with word problems), and Spelling and Writing Samples (sentence composition).

Child H was tested twice on the WJ-III ACH, once at 6 years, 2 months (scores in parentheses) and again at 8 years, 1 month. A comparison of grade equivalents reveals the significant progress that Child H made in less than two years.

Child H, Age 8-1

WJ-III ACH Subtests	Standard Score	Percentile	Grade Equivalent
Letter-Word Identification	139 (163)	99.5	12.7 (8.5)
Passage Comprehension	155 (157)	>99.9	>18.0 (8.9)
Calculation	164 (146)	99.5	12.9 (3.2)
Applied Problems	151 (147)	>99.9	9.4 (4.1)
Spelling	149 (141)	>99.9	13.2 (3.1)
Writing Samples	138 (146)	99.5	>18.0 (5.1)

This child, who would generally be a third grader, made remarkable progress as a home schooler. Passage Comprehension jumped from the eighth-grade level at age 6-2 to the level of an average graduate student at age 8-1. Similarly, Applied Problems progressed from the fourth-grade level to the ninth, while Calculation rose from third grade to high school graduate equivalency. Spelling improved by 10 grade levels, and Writing Samples placed Child H at the 99.5th percentile compared with age peers (the grade equivalent for Writing Samples appears to inflate skills on this version of the test; this scoring considers only composition, with spelling generally ignored and punctuation scored only on some items).

Child H's grade equivalents do not mean that this child has mastered everything typically learned through high school or beyond, but if Child H's scores are compared with those of all ages taking the test, they equate with scores of average students at the reported grade levels. High math scores on such tests can be earned at this age by showing mastery of arithmetic skills, without knowing algebra or higher-level math skills. Child H's fast-paced learning would require significant program accommodations, even in a gifted classroom. Home schooling is an excellent solution to provide the individualized program that this child needs.

Child I, Age 8-9

WJ-III ACH Subtests	Standard Score	Percentile	Grade Equivalent
Letter-Word Identification	134	99	5.9
Passage Comprehension	127	97	5.8
Calculation	139	99.5	4.1
Applied Problems	146	99.9	7.2
Writing Samples	115	85	4.0

This eight-year-old (Child I) reads at the fifth-grade level and has math reasoning at the seventh-grade level, with math calculation skills and writing at the beginning fourth-grade level. Actually held back a year before starting school because of a November birthday, this profoundly gifted child, with an IQ score of 187+, was in the second grade, not third! Such a placement, no doubt, has been both a source of frustration and lower achievement scores due to lack of exposure to more advanced materials. Full-grade acceleration is needed.

Child J, Age 8-11

WJ-III ACH Subtests	Standard Score	Percentile	Grade Equivalent
Letter-Word Identification	131	98	10.6
Passage Comprehension	128	97	11.3
Calculation	160	>99.9	>18.0
Applied Problems	154	>99.9	13.5
Spelling	124	95	9.0
Writing Samples	126	96	11.9

Child J has remarkable math achievement for an eight-year-old. To be at the level of an average college freshman in math reasoning (Applied Problems), this child had to demonstrate some knowledge of higher-level mathematics, as well as general mastery of arithmetic. Calculation skills are at the level of an average graduate student. Reading comprehension is at the level of a junior in high school.

Child J's current achievement is six to 15 grade levels above third grade! If this child were actually placed in a third-grade classroom, full-grade acceleration would be strongly indicated, if the child agreed.

If so, moving him or her to the fifth grade in the fall (or the fourth grade, if this situation were encountered in the fall of third grade) would be wise. Because grade acceleration is usually attempted one year at a time, frequent review of the child's situation is needed thereafter. If Child J had reservations about acceleration, accommodations would be essential in the third-grade classroom. Acceleration to a higher grade level in only one subject might also be tried if the child found limited acceleration more comfortable. This solution would help to meet educational goals in that subject and would also acquaint Child J with the older group to ease a future full-grade skip.

It is difficult for teachers to accommodate students with such varying needs. As gifted children mature, the discrepancy between their actual achievement levels and grade-level expectations increases. Most gifted children can cope with typical kindergarten and perhaps first-grade curricula, unless they enter school with very advanced reading. However, it becomes harder for them to find comfort in the regular classroom as they acquire basic skills in reading, math, and writing more quickly than other students. They soon begin to surge ahead.

Moreover, each child's achievement in the different academic areas may vary; a child may need significant accommodations in one area but not others. As a result, the teacher responsible for a range of gifted children of about the same age may face huge variability in his or her students' readiness to learn new topics. Some children's achievement may place them in the stratosphere in all academic areas, whereas other students may need only moderate accommodation in one area. Imagine when these needs are encountered by a teacher in a regular classroom, in which the gifted students exist in addition to other children with special needs. Knowing that children learn best when taught approximately at their correct level, we see the inherent complication with the typical public school classroom.

Child K, Age 9-10

WJ-III ACH Subtests	Standard Score	Percentile	Grade Equivalent
Letter-Word Identification	132	98	12.7
Passage Comprehension	137	99	>18.0
Calculation	126	96	8.0
Applied Problems	127	96	8.7
Spelling	136	99	13.9
Writing Samples	130	98	17.7

Child K, who would likely be placed in the fourth grade in a typical school, demonstrated reading (Passage) comprehension at the level of a typical graduate student and spelling at the college level. Writing skills are very advanced, and skills in math reasoning (Applied Problems) and calculation are eighth-grade level. Note that as gifted children continue to mature, we see grade equivalents extending well beyond the high school graduate level (>12.9) at young ages.

Child L, Age 10-3

WJ-III ACH Subtests	Standard Score	Percentile	Grade Equivalent
Letter-Word Identification	133	99	14.1
Passage Comprehension	128	97	13.0
Calculation	129	97	9.7
Applied Problems	122	93	8.7
Spelling	135	99	13.9
Writing Samples	144	99.8	>18.0

Note that Child L, at age 10, has college-level grade equivalents in reading, spelling, and writing. Consider the ramifications of limiting literature study to typical fifth-grade fare. Though content that is both challenging and appropriate for such a child is more difficult to find, it is needed to engage this child. Only math is as low as the eighth- and ninth-grade levels, due to a lack of exposure to higher-level concepts. Child L breezed through addition, subtraction, multiplication, division, and some problems requiring the finding of a common denominator with fractions. This student is ready to extend arithmetic knowledge to multiplying decimals (correctly placing the decimal point), simplifying and dividing fractions, and multiplying positive and negative numbers. Child L is just beginning to solve simple algebraic equations by a guess-and-check method and will probably enjoy mathematics more at the more abstract level of algebra and geometry. Like several of the children presented here, Child L would be an excellent prospect for full-grade acceleration.

Child M, Age 10-11

WJ-III ACH Subtests	Standard Score	Percentile	Grade Equivalent
Letter-Word Identification	124	94	10.6
Passage Comprehension	129	97	>18.0
Calculation	148	>99.9	>18.0
Applied Problems	143	99.8	>18.0
Spelling	124	94	12.9
Writing Samples	122	93	12.9

Child M has very advanced math skills (Calculation and Applied Problems), resulting in scores at the level of a typical graduate student. To earn them, Child M showed mastery of addition, subtraction, multiplication, and division; operations with fractions and mixed numbers; multiplication of decimals; addition and multiplication of positive and negative numbers; finding a simple cube root; finding percentages; and solving for unknowns in algebraic equations. Again, such children require higher-level, abstract math. This typically means moving the child past arithmetic study sooner and into formal algebra. This 10-year-old is ready now—not only for acceleration in math, but also in language arts as well.

Child N, Age 11-10

WJ-III ACH Subtests	Standard Score	Percentile	Grade Equivalent
Letter-Word Identification	127	97	14.1
Passage Comprehension	128	97	>18.0
Calculation	141	99.7	>18.0
Applied Problems	135	99	>18.0
Spelling	124	94	12.9
Writing Samples	123	94	14.5

Child N also needs very advanced math instruction, including rapid pacing through arithmetic concepts and early formal algebra. In a typical sixth-grade placement in middle school, Child N might experience significant frustration in math, as curricula for the remaining years before students are allowed to take algebra usually provide few new math concepts and emphasize mastery of arithmetic. Substituting an outside math instructional program for math at school would be an option (e.g., the self-paced math programs for gifted students from Stanford University or Johns Hopkins University, or other such programs as ALEKS). Note that Child N's achievement is high school graduate level or higher in every subject.

Child O, Age 13-1

WJ-III ACH Subtests	Standard Score	Percentile	Grade Equivalent
Letter-Word Identification	134	99	>18.0
Passage Comprehension	131	98	>18.0
Calculation	109	72	9.7
Applied Problems	103	58	8.7
Spelling	142	99.8	>18.0
Writing Samples	152	>99.9	>18.0

At age 13-11, Child O is performing at the level of a graduate student in the language arts, while math is grade-appropriate. Literature study should be very advanced, offering considerable opportunity for abstract reasoning. Books with heightened complexity and existential dilemmas will provide food for thought. Child O, a young teenager, is a talented writer who would likely benefit from a writing mentor and writing opportunities of all types to develop writing talent. Note that despite ceiling-level grade equivalents of >18.0, the corresponding standard scores vary from 131 in reading comprehension to 152 in writing. Such discrepancies begin to appear as a child's achievement approaches the test's ceiling.

Child P, Age 14-5

WJ-III ACH Subtests	Standard Score	Percentile	Grade Equivalent
Letter-Word Identification	130	98	16.8
Passage Comprehension	143	99.8	16.9
Calculation	120	90	12.2
Applied Problems	134	99	16.9
Spelling	95	38	7.4
Writing Samples	142	99.7	16.9

Child P, a 14-year-old, also shows strengths in reading and writing. However, note that the standard scores for several of our older children are not as high as we find with some of the younger children. It becomes more difficult for young gifted teenagers to score high as their achievement nears the graduate school equivalent level, the highest assessed by this test (>18.0). Child P is scoring in several areas at the college graduate level (16.9), so he or she probably should not take this test again.

Several of these older children would be excellent candidates for early high school admission, skipping at least one grade in middle school. High school graduation requires a specific number of credits, but middle school has no such requirement, so acceleration *before* high school is often a good choice.

Instructional Approaches

Teachers who have successfully taught gifted children learn strategies to meet and match their students' advanced and varied learning needs, their faster learning pace, and their earlier abstract reasoning. They use a variety of tools, including curriculum compacting, enrichment, grouping strategies, grade acceleration, subject acceleration, and other approaches designed to accommodate these able learners. Adept at analyzing the learning options available within a school, successful teachers of the gifted learn to use them flexibly to meet a child's specific needs. Though they have to abandon many traditional assumptions about what and how a child should be learning at a particular grade level, they are successful at teaching and continuing to motivate these children.

Unless a gifted student is home schooled, it can be difficult to create a program for a child to be taught at his or her assessed level in every subject with pacing determined by the child. A home schooling parent can order materials exactly geared to the child and can order new ones as needed due to unusual progress. The grade-level teacher in a typical public or private school, however, is accustomed to teaching many children together at the same level, with similar materials designed for average children. Therefore, accommodations for a gifted child within a classroom usually involve careful consideration of the existing curriculum to discover which parts will work and which will not before determining what else will be needed. A gifted student requiring modifications of regular work is likely to have already mastered some of what will be taught—but not all—and can learn new material quickly.

Curriculum Compacting

Curriculum compacting is a powerful tool for teachers to use when a child needs faster pacing through new material than other children in the class and/or has already mastered a portion of the curriculum being taught. Susan Winebrenner and Pamela Espeland, in their book *Teaching*

Gifted Kids in the Regular Classroom (2001), instruct teachers in the technique of determining what children know before teaching, eliminating already-mastered material, teaching new concepts with less drill and practice, and providing additional enrichment with the time gained. For children who have not encountered the material before but can learn it more efficiently, they offer suggestions to increase the interest level of the topic being studied. For example, while other students complete a textbook-based unit, the gifted child who learns quickly might read the text independently and focus on a related project that can be shared with the class.

Curriculum compacting provides the gifted child with much-needed accommodations within the regular classroom, studying topics and materials related to what the rest of the class is learning. At the same time, it frees the gifted child from the lower-level, slower-paced learning that can undermine a child's motivation, and it can be very effective when used consistently. Teaching methods that rely on scope-and-sequence charts or regular and cumulative review are not generally compatible with how gifted students learn.

Advanced Independent Study

When the material that the child requires is clearly beyond what his or her classmates are studying, the classroom teacher might accommodate the child by creating an independent study program, sometimes referred to as a "learning contract." Although it somewhat isolates a child within the classroom, it allows him or her to remain in close proximity to friends. For the child reluctant to attend a class with older students, this can be a welcome solution. Independent study is possible in all subject areas. Students might read different literature than the rest of the class or undertake a research project in an area of interest. Teachers must teach any independent learning and research skills that the child may need, however. Although they are advanced, gifted children are not born with research skills.

The end result of an independent study program must be reasonable. If it involves accelerated work typical of a higher grade level, it should lead to activities in the next year that are an appropriate next step. It should not take the child through a portion of the next year's curriculum with the expectation that he or she will simply repeat learning those concepts next year. What makes gifted children most at risk is their inability to maintain progress in their studies, so acceleration offered at one point without planning for future options is as unwise as ignoring needs now.

Subject Acceleration

Significant advancement can often be more easily achieved by having the child go to a higher grade-level classroom for the subject(s) needed. This is sometimes called single-subject acceleration. The teacher of this class has already prepared to teach this material, and the child can learn with others. Arrangements have to be made to accommodate a student's attendance at the given time, as teachers usually do not teach the same subjects at the same times of day. However, this can usually be accomplished when flexible teachers agree that there is a need. In cases in which a child has reservations about whole-grade acceleration, attending a more advanced class for one subject can be an introduction. Once the child makes friends among the older group, the prospect of moving to that grade for all subjects is less daunting.

It is important to note that pacing difficulties are likely to reemerge at some point at the higher grade level. After the child settles in with the older children and any holes in mastery of previous material have been filled, he or she will likely grasp new concepts more quickly than the other students. The acceleration will not eliminate this need, but it will improve the fit for the child within the curriculum for the time being.

Mentors and Other Opportunities Outside of School

Instructional strategies for gifted children may also include the use of outside mentors, projects, and other opportunities to broaden a child's study and build on activities within the classroom. A mentor in the community or at a local college might be willing to meet periodically with a child to nurture his interest in math or writing, and those experiences might become part of his program at school. In this way, the teacher supports the child's passions and advancement in specific areas beyond the boundaries of the classroom. Scientific investigations, shadowing experiences with the mentor, and literary accomplishments with a local writer are all potential ways to substitute more meaningful outside work for typical grade-level classwork.

Acceleration vs. Enrichment

Acceleration and enrichment warrant discussion here as they relate to instructional approaches. Because many educators are reluctant to make a change in a gifted child's regular curriculum because it may significantly affect the entire curriculum sequence, there is a bias in favor of offering *enrichment* opportunities instead of *accelerative* options. The belief is that it is always beneficial to enrich a child's study, and if that can be done without presenting concepts from the next year's curriculum, the child will benefit. However, enrichment unrelated to the child's regular work or interests may not motivate the child. Only *relevant enrichment*, which increases the depth and breadth of the child's study, significantly improves the child's situation in the classroom.

If a truly enriched curriculum is offered, it will lead to *acceleration* at some point. This is because curricula are designed to cycle through the same concepts a number of times at different grade levels, adding more depth and breadth as the child matures. So the curriculum of one grade, now significantly *enriched*, resembles the curriculum of a higher grade, especially in less sequential subjects such as science, social studies, and language arts. Southern and Jones note:

> *In truth, advanced study in any discipline may entail the kinds of activities normally associated with enrichment. Some of these include original investigations, productive and critical thinking in the content area, moral and ethical implications of procedures, and advanced levels of analysis, synthesis, and evaluation* (1991, p. 22).

There is nothing wrong with offering interesting enrichment opportunities, provided that the teacher is always assessing the child's grade-level placement and whether it continues to be appropriate. The concepts of *enrichment* and *acceleration* overlap considerably; however, *acceleration* confers credit for material that is mastered and affirms the right of the child to move on. These issues are discussed in *A Nation Deceived: How Schools Hold Back America's Brightest Students,*[5] an excellent national report available via the Internet for parents to share with schools.

The Individual Education Plan

All of the above instructional approaches imply that planning has taken place for the gifted child's educational year. Since planning is vital to successfully working with any special needs child, it is important to complete an Individual Education Plan (IEP) or Personal Learning Plan (PLP) each year. Each school will have its own terminology, and some will resist the "IEP" because it is the term used in special education planning, which is mandated by law; gifted programming usually operates under a softer mandate, depending on state education law, policy, and rules. Parents can request a copy of their current state law and rules by contacting their local state department of education or their local parent advocacy organization for gifted children. Most states will post this information online as well.

The education plan should detail the child's specific needs in each subject area, listing ways to meet those needs. The IEP requires the input of parents, the teacher, and the child to be relevant, since each brings important information to the planning process. It should be reviewed during the year and revised, if necessary. Goals that were set should also be evaluated at the end of the year to provide information for the next year's teacher to use in further planning. Although IEPs for the gifted are rarely mandated by state law, it is still very important to create them. Even a brief IEP contributes to better accommodations for gifted students offered consistently throughout the year. Highly, exceptionally, and profoundly gifted children placed in full-time schools or programs for the gifted will need IEPs as well to plan for needs beyond those of the moderately gifted.

Successful Instructional Assumptions

Good teachers of gifted children bring to their classrooms valuable assumptions about teaching. First, they know to always engage their students through abstract reasoning. They instinctively "bump up" the level of classroom conversations to challenge these excellent minds. Teachers familiar with Bloom's Taxonomy (1956) know to encourage the higher-level thinking skills of analysis (e.g., categorize, compare, contrast), synthesis (e.g., create, construct, compose), and evaluation instead of the simple acquisition and parroting back of facts learned. The model that one middle school teacher of the gifted used for literature study specifically directed students to begin with the concrete details of each piece and then move to an understanding of its universal truths. With such an approach, study is always expansive and supportive of the gifted mind, which simultaneously sees many sides of an issue and recognizes different levels of meaning.

Second, these teachers understand that some students will find different, less traditional ways of reaching an answer. Especially in math, some gifted students struggle to follow typical problem-solving sequences. Successful teachers are more flexible reviewing their students' work and following alternate lines of reasoning. Of course, it is important to teach students logical ways of thinking and to prepare them for future teachers; however, teachers must also respect divergent approaches, as long as they are correct. In subjects other than math, it is important to see alternate answers as well. Essay questions on tests should be chosen to generate more than one answer from students. An acceptable answer will be one that is well-supported.

Another basic tenet in teaching gifted children is to have naturally high expectations, ignoring what others think that "children this age can't do." For example, one new science teacher for an accelerated charter middle school noted that her biology lesson plans, previously used in teaching college freshmen, were "just about right" for the bright group of middle schoolers that she was expecting to have. Indeed, she went on to sponsor many state science fair winners by supporting unusually advanced research and by teaching what looked like high school- or college-level lab-based classes. An English teacher at the same school, who came from teaching high school seniors Honors English in a private school, had similarly high expectations for her middle school students. Although she initially noticed that her students were good thinkers but not yet good writers, she focused on how to help them accomplish the goals that she felt they could meet. Doing a masterful job of teaching what was most essential and promoting extremely high expectations in her evaluations of student writing, she proclaimed her finishing eighth graders "ready for college English courses." Most were.

A successful teacher of the gifted will observe no ceiling in the classroom in terms of questions that can be asked or topics discussed. Discussions are allowed to rise to any level, embracing higher-level observations and never restricting students to grade-level concepts. One teacher divided his class time into three parts: discussing planned topics with the entire class, helping students who were struggling, and exploring the most difficult material that he could find related to the day's topic with his gifted students. Such teachers tend to be advocates for gifted children even when other teachers create roadblocks. Strong, independent thinkers, they forge ahead with novel plans and create options that allow gifted students to progress.

A willingness to modify a gifted student's educational plan when the original plan isn't working is another common thread among these teachers. They recognize that there are no prescribed methods that always work for gifted students. In every case, the plans made are the best guess by the teacher, parent(s), and the student of what will meet the student's needs. If plans fail, they simply modify them or try something else.

Understanding the special relationship that a gifted student may have with a teacher is also important; the student may relate better intellectually to a teacher than to her classmates, so the quality of the relationship is important. Good teachers of the gifted can be life-changing role models.

Grouping Strategies

Anti-Tracking

Although grouping gifted children to provide accelerated instruction is a reasonable approach to save time and effort accommodating them, it is addressed separately here because the concept of grouping arouses considerable controversy.

The school reform movement of the 1980s and early 1990s brought an end to *tracking*, which previously had been a common instructional strategy in America's schools. Students were divided into low-, medium-, and high-ability groups by the end of elementary school, with these placements lasting throughout junior high and high school (classifications like "college prep" or "vocational track" were applied). Over time, problems emerged, and educators reacted sharply to the perceived abuses of tracking children. Valid concerns were raised about the reluctance of schools in a tracked system to move students to a different track and to meet the needs of children achieving at different levels in different subjects. While there was some comfort for the low groups in being grouped for remedial work, critics were apprehensive about schools assigning lower track classes to less qualified teachers, who placed greater emphasis on discipline than on course content. Tracking was an overly simple system, with serious flaws that led to its demise.

In reaction, educators turned to *heterogeneous grouping* as the new panacea, which demanded an equally extreme emphasis on grouping everyone together for instruction. In its most egregious form, this resistance eliminated even the ability grouping of children within classrooms (perhaps for reading or math) and tolerated no more special schools or pull-out or other grouped programs for the gifted. A few schools managed to keep gifted programs intact, but very few.

While tracking for gifted students was very successful when the coursework taught them at their actual level, heterogeneous grouping placed them in considerably less challenging classes. Rather than being seen as students who needed faster-paced, advanced instruction, gifted children were increasingly viewed as role models for the slower students in the heterogeneous classes and as teachers' helpers.

Reinforcing the emphasis on heterogeneous grouping, a new middle school philosophy emerged to support the social and emotional growth of pre-teens. An attempt to supplant traditional junior high schools with programs deemed more appropriate to bridge the gap between elementary and high schools, middle schools became some of the strongest proponents of heterogeneous grouping for instruction. Not only was the new teaching philosophy viewed as more ethical and democratic, but it was also the natural outcome of grouping children into *pods*, or smaller groupings within a grade for all of their courses, to provide the additional emotional support that adolescents were felt to need. Most middle schools established several groupings of students within each grade, each tied to a team of four or five teachers. A group of 100–150 students would, more or less, stay together with these teachers for all of their classes, creating a more intimate, nurturing school experience. However, for all to stay together, students had to take classes at the same level. Most middle schools eliminated or severely restricted optional advanced classes.

Although teachers are certainly using ability-grouping strategies in classes today, opinions are mixed as to whether such grouping is ethical. Many schools of education are turning out graduates indoctrinated against ability grouping, or at least with strong views that *instructional grouping* should be short term and with the groups changing composition frequently. Especially within middle schools, where heterogeneous grouping has been a hallmark of middle school philosophy, there are teachers who feel that they would be acting unethically if they were to create a small cluster group of gifted students within a class and modify the group's curriculum to address advanced learner needs. These are generally not teachers with a background in gifted education; these are well-meaning teachers who are unaware of the tremendous damage that can be done to the gifted by holding them back.

Cooperative Learning

One very prevalent form of grouping deserves further explanation here. *Cooperative learning*, an instructional method in which children learn in small groups, was a strategy designed to teach students communication skills needed to work in a team. Pushed ardently by schools in the early 1990s, it is still respected and used today.

Cooperative learning groups were usually deliberately heterogeneous, composed of one high-ability child, one low, and several average children. In theory, all children could profit from this approach. Gifted children would ostensibly gain leadership skills from teaching the others. Exposure to high achievers helped the other students who were struggling. All benefited from learning to work together in an increasingly team-oriented world.

Yet many gifted students were frustrated when held to grade-level work through this approach, which certainly had a leveling influence, and they resisted pressure to serve as leaders or teachers for other students. Moreover, the fact that many teachers assigned group grades for cooperative learning projects (to mimic team rewards in the outside world) made this approach extremely upsetting for gifted students who felt that they had lost control over their grades.

Fortunately, there are solutions to the problems encountered. Cooperative learning does not have to be practiced with heterogeneous groups. Gifted children do much better when they choose their own groups, and actually, homogeneous groups mimic real-life work experiences more closely. Teachers can also allow different children in heterogeneous groups to contribute at different levels of complexity, extending the potential challenge of the gifted student's work and accommodating struggling students better. In addition, teachers can give individual rather than group grades.

We have seen encouraging philosophical change about grouping in the late 1990s and the early 21st century among thoughtful educators across the United States. Seeing that gifted students are often not excelling in heterogeneously grouped classes or cooperative learning groups, good teachers are relaxing rules and are once again beginning to embrace a variety of options for these students.

Research on Grouping

When gifted children are underchallenged in school, parents and supportive teachers often look to homogeneous grouping strategies as a potential solution. If advanced students can be grouped and taught together at the proper level and pace, this approach can often meet their needs. However, some educators still balk at this notion, sometimes citing "research" to support their views. This occurred in one local school district when a superintendent insisted that "the research" proved that grouping would produce dire consequences, armed with only a single study by Jeannie Oakes,[6] who criticized tracking. While Oakes' work pointed to important concerns about rigid tracking systems, it did not represent the bulk of research on instructional grouping, which generally documents positive gains when advanced students are grouped and instructed appropriately. Because more schools for the gifted, gifted classrooms, and other grouped gifted accommodations are so desperately needed, it is important that parents and educators become familiar with the research of Dr. Karen Rogers. Rogers reviewed all of the studies, not just one, and her work is indispensable to gifted advocates.

Rogers' 1991 work *The Relationship of Grouping Practices to the Education of the Gifted and Talented Learner: Research-Based Decision Making* was a meta-evaluative synthesis of the research on grouping, including all research up to that time, which included more than 700 studies on ability grouping, more than 300 studies on cooperative learning, and more than 300 studies on accelerative options involving forms of regrouping. The executive summary of Rogers' work (Rogers, 1991) was distributed through The National Research Center on the Gifted and Talented (NRCG/T), funded by the Javits Act Program, and administered by the Office of Educational Research and Improvement, U.S. Department of Education. This summary, a brief and readable document, is discussed below and can be helpful in dealing with grouping issues with school personnel.

Rogers' subsequent book, *Re-Forming Gifted Education: How Parents and Teachers Can Match the Program to the Child* (2002), updates all of the research on ability grouping, acceleration, and individualization through 1998. This essential information strongly supports the use of grouping strategies for the provision of accelerative and enrichment options for the gifted. Gifted students who are grouped with similar peers who are offered programming that is modified to meet their learning needs show marked academic achievement gains, as well as moderate positive changes in attitude. Rogers found no research support for mixed-ability cooperative learning.

The research results in interesting conclusions about ability grouping. Full-time ability grouping (tracking) for regular instruction makes no discernible difference in the academic achievement of average and low-ability students, but it does produce substantial academic gains for gifted students enrolled full-time in special programs for the gifted and talented. In addition, high-ability student groups have more extensive plans to attend college and are more likely to enroll in college. Ability grouping for enrichment, especially when enrichment is part of a within-class ability grouping practice or as a pull-out program, produces substantial academic gains in general achievement, critical thinking, and creativity for the gifted and talented learner. It also produces a moderate improvement in attitude toward the subjects in which students are grouped. (A moderate improvement in attitude toward subject has been found for *all* ability levels when children are grouped homogeneously on a full-time basis.)

It should be noted that ability grouping is not synonymous with tracking. Ability grouping may take many forms beneficial to gifted learners, including full-time enrollment in special programs or classrooms for the gifted, regrouping for special subject instruction, cross-grade grouping for specific subjects or for the entire school curriculum, pull-out groups for enrichment, and within-class ability grouping, as well as cluster grouping. The major benefit of each grouping strategy for gifted students is its provision of the format for enriching or accelerating the curriculum that these students are offered. It is unlikely that grouping itself causes academic gains; rather, what goes on in the group does.

Rogers reports that the research on cooperative learning for regular instruction of gifted students fails to support its use as a learning tool when employed in mixed-ability groups. Likewise, there is no research below the college level to support cooperative learning in like-ability groups for gifted students. Although there is some evidence to support sizable academic effects for those forms of cooperative learning that incorporate individual task accountability, there is little research that would support this being extrapolated to the gifted population. Likewise, although there is some evidence to support sizable affective outcomes for mixed-ability cooperative learning, particularly for increasing students' acceptance of culturally diverse and academically handicapped classmates, no research has been reported which would allow this to be extrapolated to the gifted population.

Research on the effects of *grouping for acceleration* yields important conclusions for the gifted advocate. Grouping for the acceleration of curriculum for gifted students produces substantial academic gains for the forms of non-graded (multi-age) classrooms, curriculum compacting (compression), grade telescoping (rapid progression at junior or senior high), subject acceleration, and early admission to college. Advanced Placement (AP) programs produce moderate, nearly significant academic gains as well. None of these forms of acceleration appear to have a direct impact on self-esteem, either positively or negatively. Because a primary emphasis of The National Research Center on the Gifted and Talented is the dissemination of research results to educators in the field, Rogers offers the following specific recommendations, drawn from the research syntheses for educators who are considering various grouping options.

Guideline One Students who are academically or intellectually gifted and talented should spend the majority of their school day with others of similar abilities and interests. Both general intellectual ability grouping programs (such as school within a school, gifted magnet schools, full-time gifted programs, or gifted classrooms) and full-time grouping for special academic ability (such as magnet schools) have produced marked academic achievement gains, as well as moderate increases in attitude toward the subjects in which these students are grouped.

Guideline Two The cluster grouping of a small number of students, either intellectually gifted or gifted in a similar academic domain, within an otherwise heterogeneously grouped classroom can help gifted students progress when schools cannot support a full-time gifted program (demographically, economically, or philosophically). The "cluster teacher" must, however, be sufficiently trained to work with gifted students, must be given adequate preparation time, and must be willing to devote a proportionate amount of classroom time to the direct provision of learning experiences for the cluster group.

Guideline Three In the absence of full-time gifted program enrollment, schools might offer gifted and talented students specific group instruction across grade levels according to their individual knowledge acquisition in school subjects, either in conjunction with cluster grouping or in its stead. This "cross-grade grouping" option has been found effective for the gifted and talented in both single-subject and full-time programming (i.e., non-graded classrooms).

Guideline Four Students who are gifted and talented should be able to choose from a variety of appropriate acceleration-based options, which may be designed for either a group or on an individual basis. It is, of course, important to consider the social and psychological adjustment of each student, as well as cognitive capabilities, in making the optimal match to the student's needs.

Guideline Five Students who are gifted and talented should have various forms of enrichment experiences to extend the regular school curriculum, leading to the more complete development of concepts, principles, and generalizations. This enrichment could occur within the classroom through numerous curriculum delivery models currently used in the field, or it could be in the form of enrichment pull-out programs.

Guideline Six Mixed-ability cooperative learning does not promote academic growth and progress for students who are gifted and talented, and it is probably useful only for social skills development. Until there is evidence that this form of cooperative learning provides academic outcomes similar or superior to the various forms of ability grouping, it is important to continue with grouping practices that are supported by research and to use mixed-ability cooperative learning sparingly.

A Curriculum and Instruction Challenge

This chapter has deliberately *not* focused on an ideal curriculum for gifted students; that is the domain of curriculum developers and the unlikely dream of most gifted students and their families. Rather, the parent advocate or supportive teacher must find ways to provide for a gifted child's needs to the degree possible each year that the child attends school. Concerns about scope and sequence and a seamless flow from one piece of coursework to the next must take a back seat to ensuring opportunities for gifted students to study at a higher level and to tackle a passionate interest. The more fortunate gifted child usually has a patchwork of educational experiences that, together, are just adequate to maintain interest and motivation and nurture self-esteem. Rarely do these children enjoy long-term educational planning, advisors within the schools who take responsibility for meeting their unusual needs, consistently advanced coursework, or opportunities to develop strong work ethics and organizational skills. We could provide so much more.

The good news is that gifted students do succeed—and some succeed beautifully—with proper advocacy and reasonable options. The fact that their programs are often odd conglomerations of offerings from diverse sources at various levels does not render them ineffectual. For example, the Intel Science Competition winner who went directly from elementary school to high school, skipping middle school and completing many years of math with the help of a computer-based program, is doing well at MIT. Another student skipped third grade, went to an accelerated charter middle school, began high school with essentially junior-level coursework, graduated (perhaps a year later than would have been best for motivation) at 15, and was still reasonably satisfied. For some gifted children, partial home schooling offers the opportunity to study very advanced subjects at home while maintaining contact with friends at school. For others, the opportunity to take just one advanced class is enough; the middle schooler who takes AP calculus with seniors at the nearby high school may have adequate challenge. All of these students were able to find options that were tolerable.

Flexibility from the school systems made these options possible. While the typical school curriculum supports the majority of learners, curricula that support gifted children may look very different. Ideally, options will address a child's achievement levels in each subject area, creating a *diagnostic-prescriptive curriculum* allowing for continuous progress in school. When material is mastered, the child moves on. If our students are spending the majority of their days learning new material, then we know that education plans for them have been relatively successful.

Happily, there seems to be no inherent loss when first graders are reading at a fourth-grade level or fifth graders are studying algebra. Students who choose whole-grade acceleration usually do very well socially, relieved that older classmates tend to laugh at their jokes a bit more readily. Advocacy that results in such opportunities is not fraught with danger at every turn. Gifted children who veer significantly from typical educational paths can succeed magnificently when the changes in their programs address their unique needs. Unusual placements, older friends, and unlikely course choices all play a possible role in ensuring that the gifted maintain the natural curiosity and love of learning that so characterized them as young children.

In situations in which the gifted student has only the regular grade-level options of public school, the risk is enormous that those offerings will be insufficient. When we restrict an individual's opportunity to stretch and grow, we threaten his or her innermost curiosity about the world and excitement of discovery. We risk damage to the gifted student far greater than any nontraditional education could pose.

Curriculum and Instruction, by Quinn O'Leary

I didn't notice my fatigue until, in the space between blinks, I passed out. It was more than simply falling asleep, it was sudden, an almost violent venture, the annoyed flick of Morpheus' casual hand. I woke two hours later with my mother shaking me. I was going to be late for school again.

The harried monotony of morning preparations, the ritual of brushes and water and carefully sniffed clothing, gave me time to groggily reflect over the evening previous. I had discovered new things, an excellent Internet site on Native American mysticism—really nothing more than the animal-based creationism myths. Coyote was quickly joining other benevolently roguish troublemakers as a personal hero. After devouring everything the site could offer, I deliberately sought out other similar myths; the religion of the Maya and the campfire tales of Hawaii's first settlers were taking root in my fertile imagination.

There was so much more to know, I reflected, as I brushed cursorily at my teeth and rushed out the door, backpack spine-telescopingly heavy with textbooks I had not yet needed to open, had done nothing with save carry, for several weeks. The conversations of other, older peers referenced such elusively magical names as Kazinzakis, Thoreau, Joyce, Nietzsche and Faulkner. They mentioned with the insouciance of familiarity worlds beyond my current scope, great orchards of beautiful and unknown wisdom. I envisioned these orchards to be littered with windfalls, small, delectable gems of knowledge that set my mind awhirl with their imagined sweetness.

The unfairness of that struck my reeling mind suddenly. Why did I never find the thrill of discovery in the dense collections of rote recitation currently curving my spine? There was no personal gain, no joy in pounding out hundreds of similar equations, in rereading and analyzing pieces of literature usually enjoyed by children years my junior, stifling in a classroom peopled by bored kids, antagonistic teachers and dry curriculum. Eight worthless hours stolen from my studies and squandered, adding up to a travesty. I spent sleep-hazed years wasting away in the comfortless plastic of a school desk, too angry to enjoy myself, too hopelessly bored to care. That day, like many days both before and after, I didn't make it to class—on time or at all. I spent my precious school time at the library in the best possible way, self-medicating with a real education.

For Further Reading

Books and Articles

Colangelo, N., Assouline, S. G., & Gross, M. U. M., (Eds.). (2004). *A nation deceived: How schools hold back America's brightest students* (Vols. 1-2). Iowa City, IA: The University of Iowa.

Gentry, M. L. (1999). *Promoting student achievement and exemplary classroom practices through cluster grouping: A research-based alternative to heterogeneous elementary classrooms* (RM99138). The National Research Center on the Gifted and Talented. Also available at www.gifted.uconn.edu/nrcgt/nrconlin.html #99138

Reis, S., Burns, D., & Renzulli, J. (1992). *Curriculum compacting*. Mansfield Center, CT: Creative Learning Press.

Robinson, A. (1990). Cooperation or exploitation? The argument against cooperative learning for talented students. *Journal for the Education of the Gifted, 14*, 9-27, 31-36.

Robinson, N. M., & Weimer, L. J. (1991). Selection of candidates for early admission to kindergarten and first grade. In W. T. Southern & E. D. Jones (Eds.), *The academic acceleration of gifted children* (pp. 29-50). New York: Teacher's College Press.

Rogers, K. B. (2002). *Re-forming gifted education: How parents and teachers can match the program to the child*. Scottsdale, AZ: Great Potential Press.

Southern, W. T., & Jones, E. D. (Eds.). (1991). *The academic acceleration of gifted children*. New York: Teacher's College Press.

Winebrenner, S. (2001). *Teaching gifted kids in the regular classroom*. Minneapolis, MN: Free Spirit.

Winebrenner, S., & Devlin, B. (2001). *Cluster grouping of gifted students: How to provide full-time services on a part-time budget* (ERIC Digest; E 607). Also available at http://eric.hoagiesgifted.org/e607.html

Websites

ALEKS
www.aleks.com

Benjamin Bloom (an Internet search will produce many websites with information about encouraging higher-level thinking skills in the classroom)

ERIC Clearinghouse on Disabilities and Gifted Education (digest articles on gifted education, including cluster grouping, curriculum compacting, etc.—archived online on the Hoagies Gifted Education Page)
http://eric.hoagiesgifted.org

A Nation Deceived: How Schools Hold Back America's Brightest Students
www.nationdeceived.org

National Research Center on the Gifted and Talented (NRCG/T) (articles on curriculum, program options, and grouping)
University of Connecticut, Storrs, CT
860-486-4676
www.gifted.uconn.edu/nrcgt.html

Why Gifted Children Fail to Achieve: Preface to Chapters 5 and 6

When a child who is exceptionally bright fails to achieve in school, it can be bewildering. Is something at school very wrong? Have we overestimated the abilities of a beloved child? Is the school program inappropriate for the child? Are there hidden learning disabilities or other deficits that need to be identified and addressed? Are there attentional issues beyond what is normal for the active boy or girl? Or, where disabilities have always been apparent, has a child's giftedness been ignored, causing a lack of motivation? Myriad possibilities exist that require further investigation.

Gifted children may be so unmotivated by average work that they perform at a mediocre level, effectively preventing teachers from recognizing their gifts. But other possibilities exist, too.

Just because a child is intellectually gifted doesn't mean that he or she will have any innate protection from deficits. Giftedness and disabilities may co-exist in the same child, and families may have one profoundly gifted child and another child with multiple learning disabilities. Since intellectual potential clearly runs in families, we can usually assume similar ability. Learning disabilities often appear in several members as well, but they may present themselves to greater or lesser degrees in the various individuals within a family.

The fact that teachers have little exposure to training in gifted education is certainly a problem when underachievement is involved. Teachers often have difficulty acknowledging a child's giftedness when the child does not excel at grade-level work. If the child is far more capable than average, wouldn't he or she find typical work easy and do well? Likewise, many teachers don't realize that children can be "twice exceptional," having both gifted intellectual potential and deficits. Because these teachers are more thoroughly trained in special education issues, learning disabilities, and disorders such as ADHD, they are more likely to see signs of deficits. However, those deficits can be obscured by the gifted child's ability to compensate, or the disabilities can be recognized and the giftedness overlooked. Chapters 5 and 6 explore reasons for underachievement and their interventions.

Chapter 5

Underachievement: When a Child Is Too Advanced for the Educational Program

When testing documents gifted abilities with no apparent weaknesses, the cause of underachievement is typically an educational program that doesn't fit the child. The child is in an "age-appropriate" grade level, being taught according to assumptions about average learners of that age. Yet he or she knows most or all of the material being taught and could easily pace more quickly though new concepts. This type of underachievement typically becomes apparent after the child has spent some time in school. The child probably entered school with enthusiasm and an enormous desire to learn, yet he or she encountered, on multiple occasions, pressure to conform to the learning patterns of the majority. If this situation continues year after year, the child begins to lose motivation to learn and perform.

Underachievement in Girls

Underachievement usually, but not always, takes different forms in boys and girls. In girls, their extreme sensitivity to the social expectations of others often causes them to "dumb down" and appear to be at the ability level of any group in which they are placed. They are patently aware (often from early elementary school age) that being smart is not *cool* and thus make the choice to do what is more acceptable. Their special educational needs then become invisible to the classroom teacher, and their high potential goes unnurtured.

How do we keep gifted girls from going underground? We frequently recommend that gifted girls (with the help of their parents) actively seek out other gifted girls because there seems to be safety in numbers. When these girls are able to socialize with each other, they gain strength to achieve at higher levels with less embarrassment. We suggest that they read books such as *Reviving Ophelia*[1] to become aware that they need not downplay their abilities, even though much of the world will be satisfied if they aspire to far less than they're capable of accomplishing. They need to have information about professional career options and insist on academic preparation that will support their most demanding career choices. Awareness and support help considerably, but parents need to be continually watchful that their daughters will not place too much emphasis on popularity at the expense of their education.

It is important to note that girls who choose *not* to dumb down and underachieve must often lead their own silent rebellion. They have to choose between being themselves and being acceptable to others, and if they choose to be themselves, they endure a quiet suffering in the hope of better times ahead. Girls often have a strong capacity to be patient and delay gratification. They may also have a highly developed sense of ethics that prevents them from ignoring academic responsibilities, even though they feel a strong sense of rebellion. Better times usually do occur for these girls, eventually, but perhaps not until they find true peers in high school AP classes or they enter college. Some are not comfortable in the classroom until they reach graduate school.

Underachievement in Boys

Boys, on the other hand, are more likely to openly rebel against school situations that they perceive to be hurting them. It is usually, but not always, the boys who act out in school; fail to turn in assignments; refuse to attend, despite danger of being expelled; threaten to drop out; and even consider suicide. Schools usually react poorly to such cases, with a show of authority and a plethora of attendance rules that further alienate the boys and may lead to their leaving school entirely (if they are not forced out).

Most male underachievers feel alienated for years, but their rebellion is usually strongest in middle and high school. As upper elementary students, they are usually eager to attend middle school, with its increased class options, having spent years with grade-level material and few, if any, gifted accommodations. Elementary school is clearly not the fun place that they originally thought it would be, and they are angry. They assume that middle school will provide the higher-level coursework that they crave. Unfortunately, middle school philosophy in many parts of the country means that there are limited advanced classes, and the emphasis is on students remaining with their age peers. As a result, many gifted boys find their middle school experience to be their most frustrating years in school. If their efforts to find meaningful instruction are ignored, they become increasingly resistant to school and school programs.

Building upon these difficulties, high school-age underachievers may express even more intense displeasure. If they were not high achievers in middle school, they may not be eligible for advanced high school classes that would be a better fit; high schools often require recommendations from middle school teachers to place students in these classes. Or gifted boys may have access to such classes but refuse to fully engage in work that they feel is still beneath them. When this occurs, such students may respond in more dangerous ways than just failing to attend class or turn in assignments. Efforts to cope may result in experimentation with substance abuse, skirmishes with the judicial system, serious depression, or even threats of suicide.

Gifted underachievers suffer not only from the intense pressure of being different, which by itself can bring about the need for counseling, but also from the lack of alternatives to the traditional high school experience. These students have no acceptable way to refuse to participate in the high school environment. Punishments for those who rebel are enormous and threaten to limit options in later life. Students' belief that there is no way out of an untenable situation places them at extreme risk. Individuals considering suicide have this perception, so it is of uppermost importance that we provide struggling gifted students with options.

No matter how much a parent may have depended upon a student graduating, making good grades, and going to a good college, such assumptions are unimportant when the life of a young person is in the balance. Gifted underachievers do drop out of school, do experience frightening times, and can, eventually, find their way with adequate support. We have sometimes marveled at the students who survived dropping out or those who remained within school when they were truly miserable. They should be commended for their resilience.

Quinn

One such student is Quinn O'Leary, who was later tapped to write his inner impressions of giftedness for this book. This young man, a senior in high school at the time of our initial interview, agreed to share his story for the sake of his "progeny." Declared a National Merit Semi-Finalist after taking the PSAT, he was unable to become a finalist because student grades are taken into account, and his rarely exceeded

B's and C's. As gifted as he is, he didn't decide to attend college until his senior year.

Quinn recalls his earliest experience in public school being one of alienation. He didn't like kindergarten, didn't relate to his age peers, and didn't get along with his teacher, who seemed boring and trite to him. Moving to a smaller school in first grade, he recalls the school being a "vicious place" with frequent schoolyard fights. Quinn was a sensitive boy who cried easily, lost his temper, and hit other children. He was also a poor fit with the other students, speaking at an adult level quite early and having different interests than his age peers.

Quinn's experience of school finally improved in grades four through six, when he fared better with teachers. Fourth grade brought participation in a weekly pull-out program for 12 gifted students for in-depth instruction in various topics. One unit studied was the popular Voyage of the Mimi, which utilizes a marine excursion to teach concepts in various subject areas. Quinn enjoyed these opportunities very much. He remembers with great appreciation and affection the teacher that he had for both the fifth and sixth grades. She arranged for him to study eighth-grade math (algebra), along with two other advanced students. He remembers that she would teach him individually at times, and she took a special interest in him.

It is important to note that most gifted underachievers, like Quinn, have fond memories of a few teachers who supported and challenged them. They are not oblivious to the efforts that such teachers make. However, most have pitifully few such experiences to report—and many more painful ones. Most are highly sensitive; few, despite occasional bravado, seem to be hardened individuals. They need both a curriculum that is a reasonable fit for their needs and some degree of sincere acceptance from their teachers. Sensitive to subtle nuances of communication, they are painfully aware when their teachers find their knowledge annoying, their intelligence threatening, or find them somehow lacking in the qualities that typical students are expected to display.

After elementary school, Quinn's educational experiences worsened, and his social problems increased. He recalls fellow students in the seventh grade being cruel, and he rated his teachers "terrible." His honors English class was unchallenging, and the school stressed only basic reading. He was already an avid reader of literature well above the level emphasized. All of his classes seemed substandard to him. Although he had two close friends his age, he tended to choose friends four to five years older, which his considerably higher mental age allowed. However, he now refers to the older friends as clearly "bad people" who engaged in minor acts of shoplifting and received curfew and drug violations.

He escaped serious trouble when his family moved to Colorado during the summer following his seventh grade. He attended eighth grade in a suburban middle school that was considerably safer and where the students were more accepting. He met another very bright underachiever, Everett, who got into more trouble than Quinn but was nevertheless a kindred spirit. He still found the school to be "academically mediocre" but liked history class for his teacher's interesting lectures. More "entertaining and engaging," the class provided an environment in which he was able to do well. He also thoroughly enjoyed woodshop. Yet he despised his English class, and the teacher wasn't fond of him either. He and Everett often made a point of wasting class time, only to quickly finish a project in the last 15 minutes that deserved an A grade. His teacher resented that. Although Quinn had some positive experiences, he concludes that the whole experience was "pretty solid drudgery," and he responded with average grades (B's and C's), that were far less than average for him.

Quinn recalls his freshman year in high school being similar to middle school. He was disappointed that an honors version of the school's freshman "Core" (a combined class of English, geography, and U.S. government) would not be offered as promised, but the school allowed him to take sophomore "Literature and Composition." Writing was becoming a strength for Quinn. He was able to take geography and U.S. government at a nearby university instead of his high school. He was also placed in a higher-level math class, in which he didn't do as well, which was also becoming a pattern.

Quinn recalls that his social maturity level at this time was still "not great" and that he was a little overwhelmed by the high school atmosphere, with much older students and an "air of simmering hormones." He concluded that he didn't "enjoy the masses" because they avoided becoming individuals. "These are the years when people are supposed to be developing personalities," he insisted. At times, he felt that other students ostracized him for trying to develop one. Yet he reached a point at which he could say, "I got along decently well with everyone, as per always. Nobody hated me, and a few really liked me." He became involved with individual sports, participating in wrestling and swimming. He wouldn't have participated in a more team-oriented sport.

The beginning of Quinn's sophomore year marked a distinct departure. He attended classes for the first three days and decided that school was not *fun* anymore. He didn't want summer to be over. Of that time, he said, "I had a nascent rebelliousness I needed to express." He failed to go to school for the next three weeks, triggering attendance alarms at the high school. His mother was called in and told about his series of *excused* absences (Quinn had phoned in and excused himself while she was at work) and about the punishments that would befall him if his illnesses weren't real (he would, essentially, be kicked out of school). When asked if the absences were, indeed, excused, his mother answered, "Yes," to keep him in school. Quinn still feels terrible about putting his parents in that position.

Continuing to miss classes during his sophomore and junior years, he managed to stop just short of prompting serious disciplinary action, and he still maintained mediocre grades. He struggled socially with friends. "I was trying really hard to establish myself as a person. I was violent at times. I wasn't quite mature enough to associate with one particular group on their level at that time." There was "one-upmanship back and forth, cutting remarks, pointed insinuations." Quinn recalls painfully, "The group ostracized me. I felt horribly betrayed."

Quinn's senior year brought an improvement in his grades, thanks to two AP teachers whom he respected and enjoyed, and he subsequently decided to attend college. He noted that this was the first year that he chose to generally hang out with the "smart people," the most thoughtful students in the classes that he liked. He wrote articles for the school newspaper, which were always pensive, articulate, and a bit outrageous. He felt that he was growing up and finding "a happy medium between insane, wild nastiness and a mellow person." Quinn spoke with admiration and appreciation about his English teacher, who challenged his thinking, recognized his tremendous writing talents, and provided support. He talked of perhaps becoming a high school English teacher himself one day.

Discussing with Quinn the causes of his underachievement, it was clear that he was intellectually too advanced for his classes throughout his entire educational career. He was terribly out-of-sync before he was equipped emotionally to handle the mismatch—if anyone ever is. Though common for very gifted children, it can, at first, be confusing, then devastating. Quinn's highly sensitive nature made him even more vulnerable. He suffered deeply whenever his attempts to "develop a personality" didn't meet with approval from others whose experience of life was more limited than his. Quinn agreed that *will* also played a role. In some ways, he felt that he showed "a blazing lack of will power." Yet in other ways, he said, "Will power's the problem. You're too sure of yourself to say 'I'll do it your way.'" Quinn doesn't want to be a part of "mainstream society," and indeed, he should aspire to far more.

Quinn should find that life improves as he takes on greater intellectual challenges and continues to associate with more highly gifted peers. Such peers will be more likely to share his interests, his sensitivity, his strong will, his self-examination, and his ultimate hopefulness about the future. Although he feels that he has many acquaintances, there are "no soul mates, no brothers." Hopefully, Quinn's sense of alienation and isolation will fade as he finds lasting friends and a meaningful place for himself in the world.

When asked what type of educational program would have served him better, Quinn said, "Something like the Internet. The simple act of accessing information yields multitudinous results." He enjoys the speed at which information can be accessed online because curiosity can be satisfied far more quickly than in the slower-paced classroom. Likewise, the information available from the Internet is varied and representative of different points of view, and Quinn's mind will require no less. Yet he also admitted that he likes the personal, but guarded, contact of email and chat rooms. The latter, he added, "provide words on a screen. They can't hurt you. It's a more cerebral way to interact."

Scars of Alienation

Quinn's story is similar to that of other gifted underachievers. They all bear scars of alienation that may include a distrust of others, a tendency to be critical of teachers, a strong will, usually less-than-stellar study habits (they will not learn them unless their academic work is difficult enough), a greater willingness to miss classes, the tendency to perform much better for respected teachers, and inconsistent perfectionism (they may apply the highest standards to a particular piece of work that they feel is important, then miss another assignment that they feel is not). Being both critics of the systems within which they find themselves and individuals with the most abiding love of learning, they commit themselves to the educational process only as much as they are able.

The Effect of High School Attendance Policies

Most underachieving gifted boys also have some resistance to authority, particularly to those administrators who enforce attendance policies in high school. Our local high school gives a student who is five minutes late to class an unexcused absence. The student is not allowed to turn in homework or take tests when unexcused. Four unexcused absences in the same class bring an automatic grade of F on the student's permanent record, unless authorities choose to give the student a second chance. In our case, our son Nick was incensed that such rules were created for the expressed purpose of "keeping kids in school" when it was clear that they would be encouraging students to leave. In fact, our high school pursued these policies because other schools had found that attendance rose a few percentage points with such rules, and our school was eager to improve attendance, too.

Yet policies such as these are counter-productive with gifted students. Students struggling to find a reason to stay in school are frequently late and, under such circumstances, are easily convinced to simply not go at all. They see no point to a punishment that garners them a second chance to avoid a permanent failing grade, when it seems obvious to them that grades should depend on the student's work, not picayune attendance policies. Our son was told that he would be given a second chance if he spent 10 hours studying in the vice-principal's office. Under duress, he agreed yet later concluded, "You know I can't do that." The ambivalence about school, which dogged him every day, would not be lessened by studying for 10 hours in the vice-principal's office. In fact, the punishment made school considerably less attractive to him.

Gifted students who are at risk of dropping out would be better served by exempting them from such rules (letting their grades reflect their work) and by providing them with additional support to attend school. Assigning them mentors, for example, who would encourage them and take an interest in how they're doing would be a more positive approach and would support their high level of sensitivity better. Our son knew teachers who would have been appropriate, including several who had struggled themselves in high school even though they were very bright. What was inappropriate was that our school, like too many others, would respond to this type of dilemma with a show of force. Ken Seeley, in his chapter "Gifted Students at Risk" in *Counseling the Gifted and Talented* (1993), describes a study of gifted underachievers in which the number-one reason for dropping out of high school was attendance policies that tended to push students out of school (p. 267).

Closeness to Family

One heartening observation is that many gifted underachievers remain close to their parents during their most difficult times, at least in families in which authoritarian parenting is not used. Gifted children, in general, appear to thrive in homes where issues are discussed together and reasons are given for decisions. Loving, patient support is critical for most and is best provided by sensitive parents. Quinn notes that he has always remained close to his parents, despite his most intense rebellion against school, and that has given him strength. Our son, likewise, benefited from a close, supportive family that felt, ultimately, that it was more important to support him than the school.

Most parents of underachieving gifted students do not seem overly indulgent; rather, they look to the deeper issues of whether the student's school program is actually meeting needs or causing harm. Of course, parents struggle with these issues because they know that their child's rebellion will limit future options. However, the young person's well-being is ultimately far more important, and his or her experiences, with support, can become part of a stronger individual in the making.

Viewing Spirit as Strength

Mary Kurcinka, in her book *Raising Your Spirited Child* (1992), points out that many of the qualities that parents find difficult to deal with in their growing children are the same qualities that can empower them as adults. Speaking at a conference on the gifted sponsored by the GDC in the summer of 1999, she asked parents to jot down the most representative traits of their "spirited" children. A long list of characteristics was generated among the audience to describe our most challenging offspring, including "intense," "bossy," "high maintenance," "overly sensitive," and "rebellious." Kurcinka discussed each trait with an eye toward the future.

The "intense" child may become the passionate adult. The "bossy" child may become the able leader. The child viewed as "high maintenance" might turn out to be the adult with high standards and expectations. The "overly sensitive" child has the capacity to become enormously receptive to others. The "rebellious" child may ultimately become the adult with a vision. Although the idea of a happy and obedient child is pleasant to all parents, few of us would choose to create so uninteresting an adult. The gifted underachiever often has many of these traits of spirited children and challenges us to help him create something positive from his potential strengths and his negative experiences in school.

Despite apparent lost options, gifted students who survive their underachievement do have futures filled with promise. Even though they are more likely to be late bloomers, they usually do not depart completely from the values learned from their parents. As one of our son's teachers noted, "The apple doesn't usually fall too far from the tree." These students typically find a way at some point to pursue their education in earnest or find an acceptable substitute. For example, although Quinn initially lost opportunities to attend the "top" colleges with greater prestige and was even turned down by the state school from which his mother, father, and sister graduated (a hurtful blow), he did find an acceptable way to distinguish himself. Graduate school would certainly be a likely option for this English major, and he might eventually have considerably more schools to choose from depending upon his performance as an undergraduate.

Our elder son, Nick, who dropped out of high school in his senior year, had some work to do to place himself in a position for quality further education. He easily obtained his G.E.D. and took some community college courses to fill in holes in his high school education, particularly in math and science. Though frustrated by the slow pace of instruction in these classes, he worked responsibly and grew more concerned about earning A's and making himself a good prospect for colleges. Several subsequent jobs rekindled his belief that he was indeed competent and that he needed to get a good education to have access to work that he would truly find meaningful. At several points, it was instructive for him to hear co-workers ask, "What are you doing here? You need to be in college." At age 25, he began his undergraduate work in mechanical engineering and became a highly successful student. His conquest of his past clearly added to the strength of his personality.

Some gifted students conclude that traditional classes are *never* going to work for them, but they have high aspirations nevertheless. One such young man we know has taken an individual approach to his education, teaching himself computer programming and polishing his strong writing skills. Programming is now part of his livelihood, but he has also enjoyed success as a writer and playwright.

The Risk of Dropping Out

Every gifted child who is a poor fit in an educational program is at risk of losing his or her motivation to learn. Some parents realize this, even when their children are fairly young. One woman brought her elementary school-age son to be tested in order to gain advice early. He was becoming bored in the classroom, and she said, "I'm afraid he'll do exactly what I did—drop out of high school." It is important that all parents of the gifted realize this risk and know that creating an adequate program for a gifted student requires more than trivial changes. Providing just "a little enrichment" is not likely to satisfy the child's needs, nor is the parent's determination to make a traditional school work for a child necessarily going to be enough.

Few of us are prepared for the dire possibility of a child dropping out of school because we know that our children have such promise. We don't consider dropping out of school an option. Yet when this threat arises, our students are letting us know that they are miserable and having serious problems with school, and we must listen. Once we accept the fact that a young person will be unable to complete school in the typical manner (and this takes considerable soul-searching), we can consider reasonable options. Moreover, the sooner we reach this point, the better we can support our children as individuals needing to make a healthy change in their lives. Students in this situation find themselves on very shaky ground. It is not their fault if they are a poor fit in school because of their abilities, yet they feel terribly guilty about disappointing us. Listening to them, then supporting and assisting their decisions shows that we respect them enough to take their concerns seriously.

Be Willing to Accept Options

Parents facing serious underachievement by their gifted children or threats of dropping out of school need to know that there are always options for a student, and they need to work actively to find and offer these alternatives. A "time-out" from school is always a possibility, as is home schooling or a year abroad living in another country. A student may consider enrolling in a different school, especially one that offers a more challenging program. For gifted and talented students, the more *difficult* programs will generally be *easier* because they are more engaging, provided that the child's study skills are adequate. Avoid choosing easy class options in hope of raising poor grades; such students will usually perform worse.

Some gifted students choose to simply leave high school early, obtain a G.E.D., and move on to college. In fact, our son's principal noted that his failure to graduate from high school probably wouldn't significantly affect his future options, except to rule out the more prestigious colleges initially. Our son had high SAT scores and could always attend community college. These problems do not have to ruin lives permanently. However, it is essential that changes be addressed when a child is suffering. Failure to do so increases the possibility of serious depression or even suicide. If a child has made even a vague threat of suicide, parents must seek professional help. Adults should always take such threats seriously.

Supporting a Student's Motivation to Learn

Underachievement in gifted students, although not irreparable, is easily prevented. The best insurance against underachievement is an educational program that offers sufficient conceptual complexity and options to pace more quickly through the curriculum. Once concepts are mastered, gifted students need to move on to new material. The specific course offerings and progression need not be perfect, but they must be at least reasonable. Otherwise, the educational program can seriously undermine a gifted student's motivation to learn.

Parents need to monitor and take seriously children's comments about school. Is the child excited about learning in class? Is there satisfaction with work well done or high test grades? Is the child impressed with what the teacher is teaching about a particular topic? These are all healthy signs of children who are well-placed in their school programs. On the other hand, does the child complain of boredom? Does he or she want to move on to harder material and is prevented from doing so? Does the teacher complain, "I wish your son wouldn't talk to the other kids so much when he finishes his own work early"? These are red flags that the child is not thriving. Children can withstand less-than-perfect circumstances for a short time, but they should never be asked to endure a truly inappropriate program over a long period of time.

Underachievement, by Quinn O'Leary

I first ditched school in third grade. It was a spring morning and by seven, as I trudged to the bus stop, it was already shaping into one of the fine feathery days that seems crafted for outdoor romping, perfectly tailored to any of the gut-twistingly nostalgic notions usually drooped over the memory of that age. It was a morning full of nascent lilacs, sweet apple blossoms, and the crisp scent of dew-wet grass, smells that have always been the most conducive to caprice and carefreeness. Back then, school was hated only because it caused me to miss any number of momentous occasions, from staying up for a sunrise to finishing books as fast as I would have liked. It was disliked, assuredly, but certainly not to the level of extremity it eventually gained. It did not, in short, hurt me overmuch.

I was reading J.R.R. Tolkien's books at the time and I think the memory of the magical world he spread across the pages, the total immersion in a realm of sprites and goblins, of heroic fur-footed hobbits in whom I could see myself turned me around. I returned to the house and, latchkey kid that I was, had it all to myself until my parents returned home.

Recollection is fuzzy with the rampant ravages of day-to-day fadings, but I remember that day as one of the finest few weekdays I have spent, scholastic obligation and eventual punishment notwithstanding. A hand cramped with the ancient punishment of scribing my sin a thousand times could not compare to the simple release of a single day's layaway.

My true dalliance with failure came much later, however. Four years after that first fateful absence I discovered the truth about middle school and began hating it in earnest. I expected a collegiate atmosphere, a school full of kids like me working towards their own edification, in diversified, individualized plans of education, different routes for different people.

The first disappointment came in the form of the worthless selection of classes, the self-assured certainty of an administration touting drivel as enrichment. The classes I wanted, that I needed, did not exist. The ones I felt I could perhaps settle for were bureaucratically placed out of reach, guarded by hateful administrators.

My memories of the teachers are far from flattering, relics of archaic academia who meted out similar sentences to those who interrupted to ask a question and those who punched a peer. In an advanced language arts class, I was barred from reading my books in favor of the selected tome, an idiot novel of no consequence save as a warning against illiteracy. Still, I finished the book in a fraction the allotted time, hoping that I would be allowed, once my work was finished, to pursue more personally attractive modes of learning.

Such a dream, of course, was a juvenile fancy. I languished in class, routinely having my own books irrevocably confiscated (to be picked up at the end of the day in the office) because I was "inappropriately using class time."

Seven classes a day, roughly eight hours of similar torture one hundred eighty days of the year. An insistence on my own morals, values, voice and ideas earned me the distaste of the faculty as well as my peers. Shunned, hated and with a growing sense of anger, I stalked into high school with a tear in my frustrated eye and a dutifully bowed head.

High school was no turning point, no respite from the unfitting angles of my education, the burgeoning angst that was starting to spill over into my attitude. If I wasn't happy, surely there was something wrong. If I wasn't the only one unhappy, surely it was not my fault. I began to place blame where I saw it necessary, overwhelmingly upon the school.

That blame, however, did not change the low mediocrity of my achievement, nor did it help assuage the stomach-wound pain that came when I saw my parents' reaction to my poor grades or my apparent behavioral problems. Swayed by their arguments, I oscillated between accepting responsibility for my failures and hating my environment, a blend that led to an unparalleled number of unexcused absences from my school. With a school-wide policy of credit loss after the fourth unexempted absence, it was my glib lies, my handiness at forgery and my brilliance at circumventing a system of rules designed by idiots to corral idiots that kept me from ever receiving a NC-Fail grade on a report card.

Such a thing was not necessarily a victory, however. I avoided triggering all but the most sensitive radars to my ditching habit, but my grades suffered tremendously. My rebellion was transmuting mindlessly repetitive homework assignments into a string of zeros spiced with 100% test scores. Usually, my average was somewhere in the upper sixties until a week from semester's end, when I would churn out a hundred pages of retroactive regurgitant and raise it ten percent or so. Only so many teachers would accept this huge dump of long overdue work, however, and I found myself scraping the bottom levels of passing grades.

Meanwhile, I learned to separate the seeds and stems from pot. I learned a half-dozen ways to sneak silently out of and into my house at night, and a dozen ways to hide a hangover.

I also learned that colleges don't care whether I am brilliant, that being locked out in the dead of winter is painful, that not only can I not pay for college, but that I cannot even get accepted. I learned, as an unremembered writer once poignantly remarked, a hundred different names for tears.

For Further Reading

Books and Articles

Kearney, K. (1996, Summer/Fall). Highly gifted children in full inclusion classrooms. *Highly Gifted Children, 12*(4). Also available at www.hollingworth.org/ fullincl.html

Kerr, B. A. (1997). *Smart girls: A new psychology of girls, women, and giftedness.* Scottsdale, AZ: Great Potential Press.

Kerr, B. A., & Cohn, S. J. (2001). *Smart boys: Talent, manhood, and the search for meaning.* Scottsdale, AZ: Great Potential Press.

Kurcinka, M. S. (1992). *Raising your spirited child: A guide for parents whose child is more intense, sensitive, perceptive, persistent, energetic.* New York: HarperCollins.

Silverman, L. K. (1986). What happens to the gifted girl? In C. J. Maker (Ed.), *Critical issues in gifted education: Vol. 1. Defensible programs for the gifted* (pp. 43-89). Austin, TX: Pro-Ed.

Silverman, L. K. (1993). Social development, leadership, and gender issues. In L. K. Silverman (Ed.), *Counseling the gifted and talented* (pp. 295-307). Denver, CO: Love.

Silverman, L. K. (1995). To be gifted or feminine: The forced choice of adolescence. *Journal of Secondary Gifted Education, 6*, 141-156.

Supplee, P. L. (1990). *Reaching the gifted underachiever: Program strategy and design.* New York: Teachers College Press.

Whitmore, J. (1980). *Giftedness, conflict, and underachievement.* Needham Heights, MA: Allyn & Bacon.

Whitney, C. S., & Hirsch, G. (2007). *A love for learning: Motivation and the gifted child.* Scottsdale, AZ: Great Potential Press.

Website

AEGUS (Association for the Education of Gifted Underachieving Students) www.aegus.org.futuresite.register.com

Chapter 6
Underachievement: Gifted Children with Learning Disabilities or Other Deficits

The lack of a good fit between the gifted child's advanced learning capacity and the typical school curriculum is sufficient to produce underachievement in students such as Quinn, but there are many other bright students whose underachievement is more difficult to understand. Linda Silverman, in her 1989 article "Invisible Gifts, Invisible Handicaps," wrote that the "most fertile ground for unearthing learning-disabled gifted children is among underachievers" (p. 37).

Comparing the descriptions of gifted underachievers and learning-disabled gifted children, now commonly called "twice exceptional," she found intriguing similarities. First, Silverman noted Joanne Whitmore's traits of underachievers from Whitmore's classic 1980 text *Giftedness, Conflict and Underachievement*:[1]

- Perfectionistic
- Supersensitive
- Lacks social skills
- Socially isolated
- Has unrealistic self-expectations
- Low in self-esteem
- Hyperactive
- Distractible
- Has psychomotor inefficiency
- Chronically inattentive
- Frustrated by the demands of the classroom
- Fails to complete assignments
- Excessively critical of self and others
- Rebellious against drill and excessive repetition
- Disparaging of the work they are required to do
- Becomes "an expert" in one area and dominates discussions with own expertise

Then, Silverman compared these traits with those emerging from studies of twice-exceptional children and noted an identical set of characteristics! She pointed out that the coincidence between the characteristics of gifted underachievers and those of the twice exceptional is not surprising when we realize that both populations have been identified through discrepancies between performance on measures of aptitude and achievement, and thus the two groups overlap. However, the significant question is: "When we are looking at a student who *won't* do the work, how do we know we aren't actually seeing a child who *can't* do the work?"[2]

Adults are often quick to misjudge such students as "lazy," damaging their already fragile self-esteem. Gifted students with learning disabilities may do an excellent job of compensating, thereby keeping their deficits hidden from parents and teachers and receiving no help for them. The resulting loss of performance is sometimes mistaken for more average overall ability. Instead of the child being viewed as twice exceptional, with obvious gifts and handicaps, only the blend of averaged strengths and weaknesses may be apparent. The gifted traits hide the disability, and the disability hides the giftedness.

Twice-exceptional children tend to have a characteristic pattern of abilities on Wechsler tests. They generally score high on those subtests most highly correlated with abstract verbal and spatial reasoning ability (Vocabulary, Information, Similarities, Arithmetic, Word Reasoning, Comprehension, Matrix Reasoning, and Block Design), provided that a visual deficit doesn't compromise visual reasoning tests or that an auditory weakness doesn't undermine information taken in auditorially or affect verbal reasoning. Most twice-exceptional children show the largest discrepancies between reasoning strengths and processing skills weaknesses: memory, and especially processing speed on paper-and-pencil tests.

What Exactly Is a Learning Disability?

For parents who suspect that their child's underachievement in school may be related to a subtle disability, it is important to know how the term *learning disability* is defined. This term connotes some problem that interferes with learning, but it has more specific definitions at the national, state, and school district level. The 1995 Individuals with Disabilities Education Act (IDEA) viewed a learning-disabled child as one who achieves at a significantly lower level than his or her ability would predict. In assessment terms, a specific learning disability could be diagnosed if the child scores significantly lower in some area of academic achievement than he or she scores on an IQ test. The numerical discrepancy documents the degree to which the child is affected by the disability. This discrepancy model was, and continues to be, one of the best ways to detect a learning disability (LD) in a gifted child, who may achieve at the average level due to strong compensatory strategies but also have a significant disability that requires services.

Available special education services for children with a specific learning disability, including gifted children, are designed to help remediate the problem and/or teach the child compensatory strategies to deal with it. They might include special tutoring or help in a resource room. In addition, classroom accommodations are offered when the child requires modifications to his or her program. Such services can benefit the gifted child with LD; however, qualification for services is becoming more difficult.

A significant change in the *Individuals with Disabilities Education Improvement Act of 2004* (IDEA 2004), which took effect on July 1, 2005, eliminates the discrepancy requirement, stating that the criteria adopted by each state:[3]

- Must not require the use of a severe discrepancy between intellectual ability and achievement for determining whether a child has a specific learning disability,...
- Must permit the use of a process based on the child's response to scientific, research-based intervention; and
- May permit the use of other alternative research-based procedures for determining whether a child has a specific learning disability....

Some schools continue to use discrepancy formulas when they are helpful in documenting a disability; however, others believe that they should not. Response to intervention (the second point above) has become the major thrust of schools, based on the notion that if a child responds well to a learning intervention, he or she needs it. Such an approach is more useful when a child's disability is obvious (it may be subtle in a gifted child) and all who see him or her believe that the child needs intervention. The use of alternative research-based procedures for determining a specific learning disability (the third point) may signal the need for additional diagnostic testing for gifted children with LD—for example, a comprehensive reading test or evaluation with a reading specialist, in addition to IQ and achievement tests, for the gifted child with mild dyslexia.

Types of Learning Disabilities

IDEA 2004 includes requirements for states to determine the existence of specific learning disabilities in children. According to IDEA 2004 regulations, a child has a specific learning disability if:[4]

1. The child does not achieve adequately for the child's age or to meet state-approved grade-level standards in one or more of the following areas, when provided with learning experiences and instruction appropriate for the child's age or state-approved grade-level standards:

    i. Oral expression.
    ii. Listening comprehension.
    iii. Written expression.
    iv. Basic reading skills.
    v. Reading fluency skills.
    vi. Reading comprehension.
    vii. Mathematics calculation.
    viii. Mathematics problem solving.

2. The child does not make sufficient progress to meet age or state-approved grade-level standards in one or more of the areas identified in 34 CFR 300.309(a)(1) when using a process based on the child's response to scientific, research-based intervention; or the child exhibits a pattern of strengths and weaknesses in performance, achievement, or both, relative to age, state-approved grade-level standards, or intellectual development, that is determined by the group to be relevant to the identification of a specific learning disability, using appropriate assessments, consistent with 34 CFR 300.304 and 300.305; and the group determines that its findings under 34 CFR 300.309(a)(1) and (2) are not primarily the result of:

    i. A visual, hearing, or motor disability;
    ii. Mental retardation;
    iii. Emotional disturbance;

iv. Cultural factors;
v. Environmental or economic disadvantage; or
vi. Limited English proficiency.

Testers of the twice exceptional may find the following statement helpful as support for the discrepancy model, although the group making the determination of eligibility at the school must agree:

> *the child exhibits a pattern of strengths and weaknesses in performance, achievement, or both, relative to age, State-approved grade-level standards, or intellectual development, that is determined by the group to be relevant to the identification of a specific learning disability* (U.S. Department of Education, 2006, p. 46786, emphasis added).

Twice-Exceptional Children Refused IDEA Services

Changes in IDEA 2004 have robbed many twice-exceptional children of needed services in the public schools, most turned down because their performance is "average" and they are viewed as having no problems. Parents seeking services now need even stronger diagnostic confirmation of disabilities—with specialists, if possible. It is also wise to cite the difficult aspects of the child's educational experience—for example, the extra time that a twice-exceptional student requires to finish homework (often double or triple the time that the average child needs) or the amount of help that parents must provide for the child to maintain good grades (e.g., the parent should not have to be at the child's locker every day to make sure books and materials are brought home, or be needed to guide the child through every aspect of homework). Even if the child's performance is average, such problems are not.

Sadly, confusion about details of the federal law has resulted in varying regulations by states, and even school districts within states, which must individually craft regulations based on federal law—and regulations are still changing. Such confusion, coupled with tightened regulations governing services, makes obtaining services for a twice-exceptional child a formidable challenge. A sizeable percentage of gifted children who have subtle learning problems that affect their success in school will never receive services unless their parents pay for them privately or pursue legal action against the schools.

In some cases, parents prefer to avoid involvement with special education services because of the emphasis on weaknesses and the increased difficulty obtaining accommodations for giftedness. However, a letter dated December 26, 2007, from Assistant Secretary for Civil Rights Stephanie J. Monroe affirms that children receiving IDEA or Section 504[5] accommodations for disabilities have a right to participate in challenging academic programs (AP or IB classes and other accelerated coursework) if they would otherwise qualify. Conversely, it states that children participating in such advanced programs may not be refused accommodations for disabilities or required to give up services designed to meet their individual needs as a condition of participation in challenging coursework.[6]

When a child needs services for disabilities and schools refuse, parents are wise to pursue outside interventions, if possible. When testers encounter disabilities assessing these children, they can make formal recommendations that classroom teachers support the twice-exceptional learner, even if compliance is only voluntary and limited to classroom accommodations, not additional interventions with special education personnel.

Other Deficits

Gifted children sometimes exhibit other relative weaknesses/deficits that may not qualify as *learning disabilities* but require support nevertheless. Any physical handicap, for example, deserves accommodations in the classroom, and many handicapped students respond well to assistive technology. Attention Deficit Hyperactivity Disorder may also warrant modifications for the student to be successful (serious ADHD qualifies under IDEA 2004). These particular difficulties qualify for accommodations in the classroom or workplace through Section 504 of the Rehabilitation Act of 1973. This federal legislation guarantees the provision of modifications that a student or employee needs to be successful over the individual's life span (e.g., assignments to be provided in writing for students with hearing difficulties, or the use of a keyboard for writing tasks for students with motor weaknesses). It does not provide remediation or instructional services as IDEA provides for children in the public schools. Section 504 accommodations require a lower standard of proof of disability than is required for services under IDEA.

Whether or not the gifted child is offered services for disabilities within his or her school, it is important that parents follow up on any concerns that they may have about their child. Subtle disabilities in gifted children are so frequently overlooked that these children often suffer for years, criticized unfairly for their lack of effort. It is far healthier to identify problems, treat them to the degree possible, and teach compensatory strategies early. Doing so supports healthy self-esteem and the dream of a future with excellent potential.

Exploring the Disabilities of the Gifted

Because comprehensive, individual IQ tests have diagnostic capabilities, they reveal a considerable amount about each child's strengths and weaknesses. When we detect apparent deficits, we recommend specialists for further evaluation. Although many types of weaknesses are possible, here are the ones that we most frequently diagnose in gifted children.

Spatial Strengths and Sequential Weaknesses

One common pattern in the gifted is having spatial strengths yet sequential weaknesses. Linda Silverman noted this pattern early at the GDC because we saw many such children. They were visual-spatial learners with deficits not common to all of the visual-spatial population. These children were able to copy complex designs with colored blocks, count blocks in pictured stacks in which the existence of some must be inferred, and visualize how paper that is folded and cut would look if it were opened. They were usually wonderful abstract reasoners and divergent thinkers, and they understood complex systems. However, they sometimes had difficulty repeating digits in sequence, repeating a sentence, or recalling the days of the week or months of the year in order. They were poor spellers, poor with phonics, resistant to rote memorization, and performed badly on timed tests. They scored relatively low on the Arithmetic, Digit Span, and Coding subtests of the WISC-IV, which assesses sequencing, as well as other abilities.

Because these children make intuitive leaps, often understanding more difficult concepts before simple ones, sequential instruction doesn't work well for them. Yet most teachers are taught to begin with a simple concept first, then slowly build upon it day by day. Helping the learner who grasps the whole or *gestalt* before the individual parts to mesh with a sequential instructional approach can be tricky. Such students need to have a conceptual framework first, into which they can place new individual facts learned. They need flexibility from teachers who want them to "show their work" because they may devise their own problem-solving strategies and not see the sequential steps that the teacher sees.

The learning of these students is paradoxical in that they can often accomplish complex tasks, but they cannot master simple ones. In fact, many parents have said, "For my child, *what is difficult is easy,* and *what is easy is difficult.*" When teachers insist that such a child master easier concepts before proceeding to more difficult ones (e.g., mastering math facts before tackling more complex math reasoning), it causes extreme frustration for the child. Teachers should teach to these students' strengths while providing support for their weaknesses to the degree possible as they move ahead. Holding children back until they can learn in a typical sequence usually doesn't work.

Central Auditory Processing Disorder

Many gifted children who have a history of chronic ear infections as young children, and some who have parents with auditory weaknesses, exhibit auditory processing deficits. Virtually all have histories of ear infections beginning in their first year, which are treated with antibiotics and which persist through the period when they are learning to talk. Those who have pressure equalization tubes implanted in their ears to forestall further infection generally fare better, but many parents avoid tubes, relieved when their doctors don't press for them. Unfortunately, the damage seems most apparent where antibiotics are the sole treatment. Audiological exams, conducted on many of the children once the infections clear, confirm normal auditory acuity. However, these same children tend to have difficulty with short-term, auditory-sequential memory items, background noise, hypersensitivity to sound, and seem to have reduced listening capacity. (Many show the pattern of visual-spatial strengths and sequential weaknesses discussed above.) The fact that they learn to speak and process auditory information while their ears are infected and fluid-filled seems to affect their ability to process auditory information.

The physician mother of one of our clients noted a number of cases in her practice in which tubes were implanted in a child's ears, and the parents called the next day to say that the child had suddenly begun to talk or "was a different child." This pediatrician expressed the concern that middle ear infections (otitis media) should be monitored more carefully. Research by Lynn Feagans (1986) found auditory processing deficits in children who had nine or more bouts of otitis media before the age of three. Children who have fewer infections but several long-standing ones are also at risk, as are children with high pain thresholds, whose infections are only discovered in well-child check-ups.

In *The Mislabeled Child*, Brock and Fernette Eide (2006) further explore auditory processing as the combination of auditory *information input* and auditory *pattern processing.* Once auditory information is taken in through the peripheral auditory system (ear, middle ear, inner ear, brain), which may be impaired by collections of fluid, or *effusions,* in the middle ears, then the brain's pattern-processing functions commence to determine where the sound originated, what kind of sound it is, whether it carries linguistic information, whether it's worth paying attention to, and what meaning is contained in any parts that have become garbled.[7] In children with difficulties, a variety of central auditory processing deficits (CAPDs) can occur:

- Impaired hearing in the presence of background noise—The child's understanding of the teacher's words may decline in the normal buzz of the classroom.
- Impaired sound discrimination and mishearing—Children may mishear whole words or struggle to hear sounds in spoken words (phonemes), contributing to spelling and reading problems. (Because letter sounds are heard at different frequencies, even a mild hearing impairment can change sound thresholds affecting a child's ability to distinguish similar sounds.)
- Impaired hearing of the music or "prosody" of speech—The child doesn't hear the rhythm, pitch, and tone of speech, misunderstands the emotional implications (sarcastic, silly, kind), and may exhibit droning or robotic speech.
- Impaired sound localization—The child can't discern where the sound comes from and may misunderstand the source.
- Delayed sound processing—The child is always a step behind comprehending what has been heard and may hesitate to answer.
- Impaired auditory memory—Non-meaningful auditory memory is especially difficult because the child cannot rely on recognizable patterns to fill in what is not easily recalled.

- Auditory hypersensitivity (hyperacusis)—Overly acute hearing may cause distress during movies, fire alarms, or even a full school day in a noisy classroom.[8]

Sadly, CAPD is rarely recognized in a gifted child who compensates well, and if noticed, it is frequently diagnosed as Attention Deficit Hyperactivity Disorder (ADHD): Inattentive Type (without hyperactivity) because the child displays inconsistent attention. However, the apparent distractibility likely occurs when the classroom environment requires considerable close listening, such as story time for a young student or lecture classes for a teenager; when the child misses auditory instructions but not written or visual ones; or when background noise increases. Extended listening can exhaust such children, just as a noisy environment can lead to meltdowns or other behavioral problems. Eide and Eide also point out that children with impaired speech prosody who miss vocal inflection and other auditory social cues may be diagnosed with autistic spectrum disorders. Even the child with milder CAPDs can have trouble grasping what nearby children are saying, may respond inappropriately, and have difficulty making friends.

Auditory processing problems often invite unfair criticism from a child's teacher ("If she'd only listen, she'd get it the first time") or family members. One mother commented about her son, "As bright as he is, you almost need to tackle him and tattoo instructions on his arm in order to get him to listen and follow instructions. I can't tell if it is willful disobedience or he doesn't hear or doesn't process. I don't see him as willfully disobedient." This boy's history included both chronic ear infections and a past diagnosis of ADHD. His mother was right to view him sympathetically, as children generally do not choose to be "willfully disobedient." However, after being supported in her concern for him, she admitted that she really needed help to make his grandparents understand. "They think he's horrible," she said as she recounted years of their criticisms.

It is important to seek a Central Auditory Processing evaluation from a qualified audiologist for any child who frequently asks, "What?," mishears, or struggles in noisy environments—and especially for children who have been diagnosed as Inattentive or as having an autistic spectrum disorder and auditory issues may be involved. The cost of not diagnosing such disabilities in our children is measured in their loss of confidence and self-esteem. Fortunately, note Eide and Eide, "The auditory system has a tremendous capacity for change in response to targeted interventions," and they suggest a wealth of excellent options to help, including classroom interventions, assistive technology (e.g., FM speakers that amplify the teacher's voice), and a variety of auditory training exercises for each type of CAPD that can be done at home.[9]

Vision and Visual Processing Deficits

Young gifted children may struggle to see visual detail due to farsightedness. Many are early readers and may be reading more difficult books with small print when their eyes are still somewhat farsighted and would appreciate large-print Easy Readers. The problem can be temporarily addressed with bifocals to ease the stress of reading. The avid reader need not stop reading!

Visual processing problems can also cause difficulties, which may show up on IQ tests. In some cases, children show apparent visual perception problems (they experience visual confusion when trying to copy a design with blocks and may be unable to tell if their copy is correct) or may display visual tracking problems (their eyes can't follow a printed line in a book, can't track efficiently up and down between parts of a page, or they inadvertently skip items in a sequence). Children with such visual issues often do not visualize well, either, so their visual memory for abstract patterns or sequences is poor.

When we see evidence of visual processing weakness in testing, we frequently refer parents to a behavioral optometrist who is trained to assess how well the child's visual system is working (see www.covd.org for a referral). This approach is somewhat different from that taken by ophthalmologists who are concerned with the health of the eyes and distance vision. The behavioral optometrist additionally looks at the way the eyes function or team together, adjust their focus from far point to near point and back, track moving objects or lines of print, etc., and he or she can suggest short-term vision therapy to improve weaker abilities. Athletes often take advantage of such therapy to improve sports vision, but it also can make a significant difference for children with certain visual processing difficulties.

Consider the case of Maia, a bright, verbal nine-year-old who still struggled to read. Her parents provided a reading therapist who worked with Maia on pre-reading basics and helped her understand the building blocks of language and the rules of phonics. However, it was only after nine months of vision therapy for serious visual tracking problems that

Maia read her first billboard while riding in her parents' car! After her vision therapy, I tested her, and she earned a Full Scale IQ score in the 140s. What was amazing was that she was gifted enough to fool many who believed that she was reading. Her father realized while trying to do her vision exercises with her that some were "impossible" for him. A person who also struggled to read, he shared many of her same visual processing difficulties.

Although she improved immensely, Maia's mother reported a problem several years later. Maia became quite capable in mathematics but still struggled on tests. She admitted that she couldn't always see written math problems accurately because the numbers jumped around and the vertical columns blurred, causing her to miscalculate. She could do the same problems accurately if someone read them to her and she computed mentally. This is a case in which additional vision therapy would likely be warranted, as well as the use of lined paper turned sideways for calculations so that the columns stay put. In addition, such a child needs accommodations for tests so that her visual processing problem doesn't undermine her success in math.

Fine-Motor Deficits

Some gifted children struggle with fine-motor difficulties that challenge their ability to manipulate small objects (puzzle pieces, Legos, craft supplies, etc.) or successfully complete paper-and-pencil tasks. The struggling writers (often young boys) can't begin to write as fast as they think, and quite a large number are frustrated when they try to express themselves through their own handwriting. Children with significant weaknesses may be helped considerably by a pediatric occupational therapist (OT), who can often provide more effective teaching strategies. However, all gifted children with handwriting delays are encouraged to learn keyboarding skills as early as possible because computer word processors will undoubtedly best support their developing composition skills. Some will benefit from the use of a keyboard for all writing in the classroom, or even a computer with a voice-activated word processor.

Fine-motor problems cause gifted children the most difficulty in the early grades, when considerable emphasis is placed on learning to print and write in cursive (by middle school, most students are encouraged to keyboard compositions). Repetitive worksheets used to develop early writing skills make life difficult, and timed tests are a nightmare. Children who regularly struggle to finish work on time may develop an avoidance of composition altogether because the physical act of handwriting is so unpleasant. We have suggested keyboard accommodations for even our youngest school-aged clients, who learn to type using computer typing tutorials at home. Though parents may want to support developing handwriting skills through enjoyable activities (e.g., calligraphy), insisting that children with fine-motor difficulties write extensively by hand is usually counterproductive. These children are fortunate to live in the age of word processors. As they mature, their advanced learning of word processing skills soon becomes an advantage.

All children benefit from opportunities to express themselves and show what they know in ways that don't involve handwriting, but such options are essential for children with handwriting weakness. They might do a PowerPoint presentation or a creative project about a topic. Dictating a composition to a parent (teachers must trust their work) is another solution that invariably guarantees a more descriptive and detailed product than the student would create writing by hand.

In cases in which students have significant fine-motor problems that persist as they mature, they may need to take state achievement, College Board, or other standardized exams with the accommodation of extra time, a scribe, or a keyboard. Parents need to research the exact requirements needed to make such exceptions. Typically, a child needs a recent evaluation by a licensed or certified psychologist to document such needs, as well as a history of accommodation in school for the particular problem.

Sensory Processing Disorder/Sensory Integration Dysfunction

According to the Sensory Processing Disorder Foundation, "Sensory Processing Disorder (SPD) is a complex disorder of the brain that affects some developing children. Children with SPD misinterpret everyday sensory information, such as touch, sound, and movement. Depending on which type of SPD a child has, he may feel as if he is overwhelmed with information, he may seek out intense sensory experiences, or he might show other symptoms. This can lead to behavioral problems, difficulties with coordination, and other issues" (see http://spdnetwork.org).

Carol Kranowitz writes in *The Out-of-Sync Child* (1998) that the most likely causal factors for Sensory Integration Dysfunction (the newer general term is Sensory Processing Disorder) are a genetic or hereditary predisposition, prenatal circumstances, prematurity, birth trauma, or postnatal circumstances (e.g., environmental pollutants, excessive or insufficient stimulation after birth, a lengthy hospitalization or institutionalization, or the lack of normal sensory experiences) (p. 23). The GDC is also currently investigating the relationship between children with sensory integration issues and Pitocin administered to their mothers for extended periods of time to induce or accelerate labor. Pitocin was designed to be used for brief periods, perhaps three or four hours, but doctors medicated some mothers for 24, 36, or even 40 hours, and the incidence of sensory processing problems appears striking. We have some concern that the very hard labor that results from Pitocin, when maintained for long periods of time, may be especially damaging to gifted children with highly developed central nervous systems and, often, large heads.

SPD is often the culprit when gifted children are less coordinated and athletic than their peers (e.g., they learn to ride a bike late); are easily overstimulated by crowds or noise; are unduly fearful of peers who might be rough or aggressive (prefer to play with girls or younger children); struggle with visual processing issues or handwriting (SPD may be the underlying cause of the fine-motor problems described in the previous section); are especially clingy and dependent upon parents to negotiate the world for them; or have hypersensitivities to light, sounds, and tactile stimuli. Most gifted children have some of these sensitivities (e.g., they are picky eaters, have hypersensitive hearing, or are bothered by tags in the necks of their clothes), but not to a degree that causes them problems. Gifted children with Sensory Processing Disorder exhibit a variety of more significant symptoms which interfere with life and learning. SPD may also underlie other disorders such as attentional deficits, and it is usually apparent with children who have autistic spectrum disorders.

Occupational therapists can provide interventions that bring about vast improvements for children with SPD, and also usually lessen the secondary anxiety that they experience. We have seen some cases in which occupational therapy was especially effective for autistic spectrum disorders.

Parents who note in their children the symptoms listed above are wise to read Jean Ayres' original book on the subject, *Sensory Integration and the Child* (1979), as well as newer books like *The Mislabeled Child* (Eide & Eide, 2006) and *Sensational Kids: Hope and Help for Children with Sensory Processing Disorder* (Miller, 2006), which are listed in the For Further

Reading section at the end of this chapter. If the symptoms seem a good fit for what parents are observing, a sensory processing evaluation can be done by a pediatric occupational therapist (OT), and a directory of pediatric occupational therapists is available online (see http://spdnetwork.org/directory/search.html). Therapeutic intervention is most effective through age seven, so early assessment is warranted. OTs can suggest exercises specifically tailored to an individual child's symptoms. Many of these children also benefit from vision therapy.

Gifted Children with Severe Learning Disabilities

Whereas subtle learning disabilities in an obviously bright child may not be detected because the child compensates well, severe learning disabilities that are easily diagnosed may make giftedness difficult to document in any way. Families may see the advanced reasoning abilities of these children, but only their deficiencies are obvious to teachers, and their early lives may reflect a singular emphasis on remediating their deficits.

Emma

Consider the case of Emma, who came to us at age 13. Her parents hoped that her intellectual strengths might finally be documented so that she could find an educational program that would adequately challenge her. Emma's deficits were no secret to her family and teachers who had taught her. Her dyslexia made elementary school extremely difficult. She had to learn strategies to discriminate b's from d's, and she could not hear short vowel sounds. When asked to alphabetize, she had to run through the entire alphabet each time. Her spelling was so poor that even after she learned keyboarding, spell checkers were inadequate for her needs; her spelling did not approximate correct spelling closely enough to cue the software to the appropriate words. Math calculation was also very difficult for her. She had not been able to learn all of her multiplication facts and calculated using the few that she knew. She developed laborious, circuitous strategies to extend what multiplication facts she had internalized, often accompanied by counting on her fingers. Emma was also diagnosed with an auditory memory/sequencing disorder, which made it hard to get teacher instructions straight. With all of these issues, her early education was clearly directed toward her weaknesses. She attended a private school with a strand for students with learning disabilities and attentional deficits.

Tested at age seven on the WISC-III, Emma earned a Full Scale IQ score of 107—in the average range. The profile of her subtest scores showed significant peaks and valleys, common with learning disabled children, but her highest scores (Vocabulary and Symbol Search) were in the superior range (IQ 120+). There were no gifted-level scores, and it was highly unlikely that anyone outside of Emma's family would have considered her twice exceptional—both gifted and learning disabled. Yet Emma's brother had earned a 144 on the WISC-III, and their parents were highly intelligent individuals in professional positions. In fact, Emma's parents had always viewed her as "at least as intelligent as her brother," but the tests did not provide documentation of that.

There were a few others who saw Emma's gifted potential. Her verbal ability and social insights always made her ideas worth considering, and she stood out for this reason. Some of her teachers and several other adults who got to know her, especially as she grew older, discovered extraordinary capacities that appeared in various guises. Her fifth-grade teacher, for example, excitedly told her parents that Emma was a "genius" based on work that she did on the science projects that year. The task was to build a simple machine out of bits and pieces found around the home or at school. After completing her own project, Emma helped the five other children to build the machines that they desired. But it was the speed of her design and the deftness of her construction work, along with her ability to forage through the school collecting the needed pieces almost on the run, that was so striking to the teacher. Emma recalls, ruefully, that her take-charge attitude did not endear her to classmates, even as they benefited from her help. Other children almost never saw past the dyslexia, the Central Auditory Processing Disorder, and the way in which she dominated the classroom with her need to comment or ask orienting questions in compensation. Winning the elementary school (both LD and regular stream) speech contest two years running in grades five and six was the first official recognition of the excellence of her slowly blooming academic skills.

In seventh grade, Emma was moved to a regular classroom and made amazing progress. She learned to read, although she frequently misread words within passages and replaced them with synonyms. Her parents thought that this was odd but came to accept it as just what Emma does. Although her decoding skills were not sophisticated, her understanding of words from context was impressive (reflecting her gifted verbal abstract reasoning ability). She was able to reach a point at which her reading was quite good, although she often needed more time to finish her work. She learned to write compositions and to find a way to turn in high-quality work with the help of a word processor. She had good math intuition and could perform quite well within reasonable time limits when given a calculator. Math became an easy subject for her. She learned to write all of her assignments down carefully and to ask questions of her teachers whenever she wasn't certain of a detail. In addition, she developed excellent social skills, but she had no intimate friends or soul mates.

Emma made good grades, thanks to her compensatory skills and strong motivation to do her best. Her teachers allowed her extra time for exams and did not penalize her for spelling. That year, she won the seventh-grade English Prize. She was voted the school's community service representative in eighth grade, and she was also awarded the school's gold honor pin—only the second time it was awarded in the school's history. At graduation from the school that year, she won the Science Prize and the Mathematics Prize. She was co-chair of the graduation exercises, played violin in the senior band, and sang in the choir. Yet she was complaining of boredom. Her parents wondered if retesting might document her higher abilities to the extent that a school for the gifted or other challenging program would accept her. They brought her to the GDC for testing.

Emma was retested on the WISC-III (current at that time) at age 13. Although we saw some of the same highs and lows in her subtest score profile as before, all of her scores rose dramatically. She earned a Verbal IQ score of 132—in the gifted range, well above her Verbal IQ of 112 at age seven. Likewise, her Performance IQ score of 131 was in the gifted range, compared with a Performance IQ score in the average range of 102 at age seven. Her Full Scale IQ score rose from 107 to 134! Moreover, her Verbal Comprehension Index score, based on the verbal subtests most heavily weighted for abstract reasoning ability, was 140, at the 99.6th percentile. This score, we have found, is the best indicator of students who will perform well in a school for the gifted.

Though Emma's scores were very high, she still showed tremendous difficulty with subtests emphasizing short-term auditory-sequential memory. She earned a low average score repeating digit sequences (low-interest material) and an average score remembering mental math problems presented verbally. She also struggled with the mental math calculations on the Arithmetic subtest. Such difficulties brought down her IQ scores, as did the visual confusion that she experienced copying one design with blocks. Her difficulty copying angles, at times switching them to face in opposite directions than they were meant to face, mimicked her problem distinguishing b's and d's. Yet she still scored in the gifted range. It was reasonable to assume that this assessment still did not document the full extent of her abilities and that she was likely a very highly gifted individual.

Watching Emma work was impressive. An extravert, she had no qualms about talking herself through both difficult and easy tasks. The act of discussing the problem with herself (called *verbal mediation*) seemed to help. This was a young woman who had learned how to compensate to an incredible degree. For example, as she read several math problems, she would begin to read a multiple-digit number starting with the last digit, then correct herself and restart with the first digit. Taking the Woodcock-Johnson-Revised Tests of Achievement, she struggled to decode words yet would sound them out deliberately. She read passages haltingly but well, achieving a college graduate grade equivalent. Her only limitation was the amount of time such reading required, but this subtest was untimed. Clearly, she would perform better with books on tape if she had considerable reading to do. Her math calculation placed her at the college graduate level as well, although the math portions of the test took hours to administer because she could not use a calculator. Math reasoning (Applied Problems) was at the level of a college junior. Writing Samples required Emma to compose sentences according to increasingly specific and descriptive criteria. As spelling was not considered, she scored in the highly gifted range, again at the college graduate level. Her only low score was in Dictation, a test of spelling, punctuation, and word usage, in which she scored in the low average range (fourth-grade level). Her score of 84 in Dictation contrasts with a score of 154 in Passage (reading) Comprehension!

Emma's parents were delighted that, at last, gifted-level abilities had been documented because they hoped to enroll her in one of the more challenging local private schools where they lived. Unfortunately, none of the schools to which Emma applied felt that they could make accommodations for her, even after they met her and liked her immensely. One school apologetically noted that its teachers simply could not ignore spelling when grading Emma's papers. Fortunately, a public high school with a full-time gifted program was happy to accept her, and the latest test scores would be of some benefit after all. Emma was kind enough to share some of her experiences with us for this book. She sent both this early copy of a letter and a corrected copy; however, I asked that her first version be used so that Emma's challenge with her dyslexia could be better understood.

> *When I was little (about four, when I started J.K.) I was told I was slower in class then most kids, but I would ketch up when I was older. My parents weren't to worried because they know I was smart because of my huge vocabulary and my capability to talk to adults like I was an adult. But when it came to grade one I was no learning my A.B.C's and 123's. The teacher reassured my parents once agen that I would learn, but my parents were getting a little hesitant and worried. My mother especially was this why since she was the one who would have to drag me from underneath the living room table with me kicking and screaming when I, should say we, did Phonics or any homework. My mother got so distressed that she decided to send me to a specialist to test me for a learning difficulty. I was tested on the Wisk III and other tests and learned that I was very dyslexic. This was in some ways a relief but I wasn't sure what this meant at the time. At the same time it didn't seem to make me fell any more secure, I still was academically last in every thing.*
>
> *I didn't real know that I was last at the time; all that I know was that I never got the candy for minute math (60 multiplication, adding, subtracting, or/and dividing questions that you needed to do in 60 seconds). Grade one and grade two were not my best years they were mostly filled with frustation, isolation, and discernment. My parents thought that the [school] I was at was not the right school for me, and deiced to move me to another. The first day I visited I was only meant to stay a half day but I stayed the hole day. This school was ultimately better for me. I learned how to read and spell well enough that spell check gets my spelling about 1/3 of the time (trust me that is good considering when I when into grade three I couldn't spell 'the"), and I succeed academically too. I was in a small class of 6-7 kids from grade 3-6 with specialized teachers who were highly qualified to teach children with dyslexia.*
>
> *I loved it at my new school. I would have an activity every day at lunch, was on the honor role every year that I could, won the*

citizenship award, the speech contest twice, and got the gold and silver honor pins. I have many time consuming little strategies that help me with multiplication, spelling and about any thing else you can think of. When I was in grade 7 English, and won the English award that year. I have to say that my grade 7 English teacher was one of my greatest confidence busters and truly understood me and had the perseverance to look at my work with the 1000 mistakes. In grade 8, I was assessed highly gifted on the same test that I was tested dyslexic, Wisk-III and highly gifted on subtests of the WJ-R. This was an interesting revelation because know I had a new problem: how am I going to get the challenging work that I love that was getting increasingly harder to get? We figured that by dropping French (the augment we used was, "If our daughter took 10 years + to learn English her first language, and still can't spell, how do you expect her to be able to read and spell French?"), and challenge my self by taking accelerated Math, Science, and English courses.

Even though have I have been very successful, not every academic institutes understands my learning style. I live in [a large Canadian city] and all the high-end privet high schools didn't accept me. I can guarantee you that I got the politest rejection letters there are in this world, but for the first time in my life I felt almost ashamed of my dyslexia even though it was only for a day or so. I thought that know with spell check and extra time I was not that hard to handle. I thought for days why I didn't get in with an 80+ average in every thing I have done since grade five it would be dead certain entry. Instead I will go to a very good public high school that has a gifted program.

Through out it all I have had a very optimistic look at life. I guess it's was in my genes to be happy and to make every thing look as good as possible. All through my life I have been challenge, with out that challenge I would have nothing to work for, so life would be boring. My advice for any one dyslexia is that no matter what don't give up because there is always the computer, calulator, and the good old agenda to solve all the problems. With these tools we are equals or supers to those with out dyslexia, and with time like red wine we only get better.

Although Emma still struggles to express herself in writing, her speech is highly articulate and completely without obvious errors in word choice. Word processors with voice recognition software would seem a logical solution to her dilemma, yet they still do not record her speech especially well. Her father believes that she introduces subtle extra consonant sounds in many words, which human listeners ignore but the program "hears." However, frequent changes in technology make this her best hope for the future. As it is, Emma makes use of a text reader that audibly reads her more difficult documents for her. This spares her the time investment required to decipher the material herself. In fact, although she was able to score at the college graduate level on the untimed reading comprehension test administered to her at the GDC, she asked for the report of her evaluation to be emailed to her, as well as hard copies sent, so that she could hear it with her computer text reader.

Working with gifted children, I find that most testers want to see some evidence of giftedness (subtest scores in the gifted range) within a child's test profile before considering the possibility of gifted intellectual potential. A few want to know that, even with deficits, a child can still earn scores in the superior range (120+) if he or she is to be considered twice exceptional. Emma is the perfect exception to this rule. Tests can miss a child's potential when complex and overlapping deficits are at work. In Emma's case, she earned only an average Full Scale IQ score at age seven, with no subtest scores in the gifted range.

When considering such a child, it is essential to carefully view all of the background information and the child's test behavior, as well as the test scores. Emma's parents and brother documented a familial history of giftedness, and her parents had always felt that their daughter had similar intellectual ability. Their assessment of her was clearly the closest approximation of her ability for many years, until testing of the teenage Emma revealed a more realistic (if still minimal) estimate.

Her father reported that Emma asked her parents if they ever gave up on her being smart while she was struggling with the early remediation. "No way," her father had reassured her. Later, he told us, "but we had evidence of her deep wisdom from her spoken output." It is clear that Emma has not yet tapped her full potential. With her tireless motivation and irrepressible personality, I know that she will amaze us all.

Underachievement Due to Attentional Deficits

Many parents today worry about the misdiagnosis of Attention Deficit Hyperactivity Disorder (ADHD) and the consequent overuse of stimulant medications in children.[10] However, the parents of some underachieving gifted students shouldn't rule out ADHD too quickly. We have seen many parents rate their children as having a sufficient number of characteristics of ADHD to be significant for the diagnosis. Yet most are quick to note that their children *can* attend to high-interest material without difficulty. This is typical for the gifted child with diagnosed ADHD. Rather than showing consistent attentional inadequacy, the gifted child with ADHD has difficulty attending to low-interest material on demand but often has the capacity to *hyperfocus* on high-interest material. Virtually every one can attend to a video game for hours. Focus problems occur with repetitive, low-level material and are also evident in the child's struggle to activate attention (focus is fine when engaged in an activity, but starting is difficult). We cannot ignore the growing numbers of ADHD children, nor the complexity of making an accurate diagnosis when giftedness is a factor.[11]

The *Diagnostic and Statistical Manual of Mental Disorders* (4th ed.) of the American Psychiatric Association (DSM-IV) lists the typical characteristics of inattention, hyperactivity, and impulsivity used to make the diagnosis of Attention Deficit Hyperactivity Disorder (a child may exhibit behaviors in one or more of these areas). However, it also offers the caveat that "*Inattention in the classroom may also occur when children with high intelligence are placed in understimulating environments.*"[12] Sorting out the relevant issues to make a diagnosis is often difficult. Some children's symptoms disappear without medication or other intervention when they are placed in a full-time, highly challenging program for the gifted. Consider the case of Serafina.

Serafina

Eight-year-old Serafina came in for testing with her parents during the summer following second grade. Over the previous academic year, she had become increasingly unwilling to attend her public school, had developed chronic stomach pain of unknown origin, and generally appeared to be underachieving. Previous testing at age five indicated that she had an IQ of 142 (well into the gifted range) and would need modifications in her school program to offer more challenge. Unfortunately, Serafina's neighborhood school had provided little.

Serafina was initially placed in kindergarten based on her birthdate and size, even though she had previously attended school in another English-speaking country and was a third-grade reader at the beginning of the kindergarten year. Her skills appeared to regress as she tried to fit in with the other students and meet teacher expectations. Likewise, each succeeding year brought a similar lack of challenge, and Serafina no longer displayed her intelligence and eagerness to learn at school. She simply hated school and didn't want to go. Her mother concluded that the school did not believe that gifted children had special needs and gave Serafina few, if any, options. Allowed to attend only a brief, occasional gifted pull-out program, Serafina's teacher required her to make up all regular classwork missed. (Sadly, we have seen many other children whose teachers were similarly punitive about their participation in gifted pull-out programs.) Serafina was soon seeing a psychologist for her physical symptoms, low self-esteem, and underachievement. She told her mother, "I feel like a little possum that's been run over by a truck, and unfortunately, I haven't died yet."

Serafina's parents hoped that further assessment would clarify her needs and suggest a more appropriate educational experience. Her father noted that his two older sons had suffered similar difficulties in school, and both had dropped out of high school. He was concerned that his daughter might follow in their footsteps if things at school didn't change for the better.

Serafina earned a Full Scale IQ score of 132 (gifted range) on the WISC-III, with a Verbal IQ score of 135 (gifted) and a Performance IQ score of 123 (superior). These scores seemed somewhat low in light of her previous testing. Her profile of subtest scores was markedly inconsistent, with dramatic highs and lows ranging from the ceiling level of the test (highly gifted, 99.9th percentile) to the average range, more than three standard deviations lower. This is typical of children with learning disabilities, ADHD, or other problems, all of which can bring down scores and yield an underestimate of intellectual potential. In Serafina's case, her verbal reasoning was at or near the ceiling level of the test, and her spatial reasoning was high average, suggesting possible visual processing problems because visual confusion was evident when she attempted some of the items. When we discussed this, her mother told us that Serafina was getting headaches reading, and Serafina herself noted a problem when swimming—she couldn't tell how far she was from the end of the pool, so she couldn't judge when to turn. Visual processing problems were likely one reason for the lower scores.

In addition, Serafina's mother confirmed the girl's long attention span as a young child, but increasing distractibility as she got older. In the test session, Serafina needed to move through the material quickly to stay interested and was very active in her chair. Assembling puzzles, she became a bit boisterous with the pieces, although she was generally enthusiastic. This was unusual, since gifted children with ADHD often show minimal distractibility in the one-on-one test session because it is the ideal situation for them. They have the full attention of a supportive adult and are easily engaged with the high-interest, novel material. When children such as Serafina are distractible, requiring a fast-paced administration and frequent redirection to answer the questions, we take note. Serafina had some apparent difficulties, further supported by reports of her disorganization at home, but not enough to conclusively diagnose ADHD.

Also of interest were Serafina's achievement scores. Having just completed her second-grade year, her reading comprehension score placed her at the equivalent of the tenth-grade level, a fact that shockingly brought home the frustration she must have felt with Easy Readers and beginning chapter books. In addition, all of her academic skills were at the fourth-grade level or higher, suggesting a very large discrepancy between what she faced in the school curriculum as contrasted with what she had already mastered and was ready to learn.

We recommended that Serafina change schools to attend either a school or a full-day program for the gifted to meet her academic, social, and emotional needs better. If that was not available, whole-grade acceleration would help her maintain her motivation to learn. She would certainly need more challenging material in order to improve her attentional focus. We also provided information and references to educate her parents about ADHD and allow them to monitor her symptoms to see if that might be a component as well. We suggested an evaluation with a behavioral optometrist to assess many aspects of her visual system (not just distance vision) and provide vision therapy, if needed. In the meantime, Serafina would need large-print books and preferential seating. Assistance with study and organizational skills (a typical ADHD challenge) would also help her gain better control of her responsibilities.

In Serafina's case, an incorrect school placement was affecting her both physically and emotionally. She had developed stomachaches and anxiety related to school. An appropriate instructional level, along with supports for her deficits, was necessary for her physical and emotional health. Unfortunately, the family's requests and our report failed to adequately change Serafina's academic program at her school. She was not allowed to skip a grade and completed third grade with a defensive teacher who felt that she was *not* gifted, generally gave her C's, and noted on report cards that Serafina "does her best." At the same time, her teacher withheld some materials, ensuring that Serafina could never advance. For example, as each student learned the multiplication tables, for example the "5's," the teacher would then furnish materials for the "6's" and chart each student's progress on the chalkboard. However, Serafina was given no materials beyond the "5's" and appeared, on the board, to have the *least* developed multiplication skills in the class. Although Serafina's stomachaches disappeared after second grade, they were replaced with dizzy spells in third grade.

Serafina's mother, who by this point was not appreciated by some employees at the school, located a full-day, highly gifted program, housed within another regular public school in the district. It was a self-contained class for fourth through sixth graders. Children are generally referred to this school by teachers in their home schools, but Serafina's mother described the problems to program administrators and instead submitted our report. Serafina was accepted to the program because her need was so great, even though it was felt that she might not be *highly* gifted.

We had suggested that Serafina be retested in a year, following her likely vision therapy, to gain a better estimate of her abilities. We would retest her on several subtests of the WISC-III to assess visual processing issues and administer the Stanford-Binet L-M to see if her ceiling-level verbal reasoning abilities on the WISC-III were actually beyond the limits of that test.

When she returned after 14 months, several months into her new gifted program placement, the results were remarkable. First, Serafina described being thrilled with her new school, the teacher who was so nice to all of the students, and the friends she had made. She said, "We are like a family at that school," and she described how pleased her new friends were when she came back to school after being sick for a few days. Even the boy who always had to be first in line got out of line to tell her that he was glad she was back!

Second, Serafina was totally focused during the test session, with no apparent need to rush and a happy, poised demeanor. Her mother was pleased that her change in focus was apparent to us as well, because there had been no intervention for ADHD. The mother noticed huge differences at home following enrollment in the gifted program. Recounting that Serafina had always been horribly disorganized, losing materials and even forgetting to get dressed in the mornings once they awakened her, she was now the picture of organization. She couldn't wait to attend school, and she placed a high value on her work.

Third, Serafina earned a 148 IQ score on the Stanford-Binet upon retesting, placing her in the highly gifted range and documenting a mental age of 14 years, 8 months. She displayed vocabulary, verbal reasoning, and spatial reasoning at the Average Adult level. Serafina was, indeed, well placed in her program for the highly gifted.

Retesting on three of the WISC-III subtests, Serafina scored slightly higher (but not significantly so) on all three, having completed only three months of vision therapy by that time. We suggested that she return to the behavioral optometrist for a consideration of additional vision exercises. Ongoing research at the GDC suggests that six months of daily exercises is often very effective. In addition, optometrists are more successful with gifted children when they pursue higher levels of visual functioning than what would be expected for typical children of a certain age and grade. Although Serafina's scores were only slightly higher, we were pleased to note that she experienced significantly less visual confusion when presented with visually complex material.

Serafina's mother had struggled to arrange for her placement in the gifted class, but the truly frightening problems that her daughter experienced have all but evaporated. Serafina is a different child now, reminiscent of the little girl who was always exuberant about life and caring of others. She now has the opportunity to write frequently, whereas few writing assignments were given in previous years. She has to work hard to learn, and a strong work ethic is developing. She truly needs study and organizational skills to handle the level of her work, and she is displaying a newly discovered control of herself and her assignments. Most of all, Serafina fits in to a degree that she has never experienced before. Her mother said that she recently heard her daughter humming—something she hadn't heard in years. Serafina is so very happy!

The Difficulty of Diagnosing and Treating ADHD in the Gifted

Sadly, few children we see have the option of a relatively perfect educational placement, so we can only rarely observe the effects of greater challenge on apparent attentional issues. We have seen *some* children with serious inattention helped enormously by medication, so we are not prepared to conclude that there is no real ADHD within the gifted population.[13] In fact, one gifted father, who also struggled from dyslexia as a child, noted that his reading disability significantly improved only after he was treated with Ritalin in high school. Treating his attentional difficulties finally enabled him to deal with his reading problems. He still self-medicates with caffeine, as most adults with ADHD symptoms do, to maintain focus.

At the same time, we have seen others experience minimal benefits or be unable to tolerate medication. Because virtually all parents are resistant to the idea, medication is rarely our first suggestion. However, we do counsel parents to see an attentional specialist and consider that specialist's recommendation for a medication trial (to determine response and effectiveness) when the symptoms have been significantly problematic. When the child is beginning to run out of options—he or she has alienated teachers or been kicked out of schools—then that is usually a time to consider medication. We have also seen some cases in which the child felt desperately out of control and unlikable, and the medication offered a solution to help regain control of attention and impulsive behavior.

Some of our staff members have noted that within the gifted population, medication is not the "magic bullet" that it usually is within the average population. The school psychologists that we have working at the GDC, who also work with more average children in schools, have commented that medication alone usually makes a tremendous improvement in the ADHD symptoms of more average children, but they feel that the gifted don't respond as predictably.

John Ratey, co-author of *Driven to Distraction* (1994) with Ned Hallowell,[14] offered thoughts about the most common ADHD-*like* child that we see at the Gifted Development Center. This child is typically male; gifted or highly gifted; his organizational skills clearly hurt his schoolwork (he lacks control here); he fits Inattentive-type symptoms, without apparent hyperactivity or impulsivity; he did not show signs of ADHD by age seven (when the DSM-IV indicates that they should be apparent), but they appeared over time; and if medication has been tried, it likely has not been especially effective for a variety of reasons.

Ratey observed that the ADHD symptoms of children "often appear over time," as opposed to being in place by age six or seven, "as the environment changes and as the demands (external and internal) grow." He added:

> *I am always suspicious of [medication] trials—usually too much or too little—and not trying the variety of offerings today. It is not always easy to get the right key, and sometimes it is not possible to find it—one must be an explorer as a treater, and there are not many. I just think that we back off with children, as we see them as being too delicate. I think the consequence of ADHD and failures and frustration are much more a horror for the brain, mind, body than any possible effects of medication* (J. J. Ratey, personal communication, October 9, 2002).

Few of the children that we have seen who are taking stimulant medication for ADHD have worked with an attentional specialist. Generally, the child's pediatrician prescribed a dosage that was never altered or tried for long. A specialist in attentional deficits will follow the child carefully for a more extended period, varying dosages, medications, and times at which the medication is taken to support the child when focus is most critical. We have heard some very positive comments from patients who changed to newer stimulant medications and noted a distinct improvement.

The effect of challenge on the gifted-ADHD child cannot be overestimated. When the challenge increases, the symptoms are reduced; when the challenge decreases, the symptoms become more obvious. School personnel generally should *not* make a gifted child's program easier because he or she suffers from attentional deficits. Classroom accommodations for gifted children with ADHD must first support giftedness with advanced instruction and fast pace. However, other accommodations may be necessary as well. Help with study and organizational skills is usually essential, providing a quiet place to work without distractions can keep a child on task, allowing the child to move around in the classroom may assist the child in maintaining good control and focus, and offering ways for students and their parents to easily communicate with the teacher to keep track of assignments (detailed instructions and due dates) can be a lifesaver. Study and organizational skills will not develop unless the child cannot function without them, so a challenging curriculum helps. We have noticed that it is easier to train gifted-ADHD children to focus when the work is really difficult because they are more likely to engage.

Teaching gifted children to focus may be particularly critical because they are taking in so much more information than the average individual and must learn to prioritize their thoughts and sensory input in order to accomplish anything of value. One 11-year-old boy with hyperacuity was aware of every sound within the office and in the adjacent neighborhood during his testing. "You have no idea how much information comes in for me all the time. It's like information overload," he explained. He never lost his focus with the inherently challenging items on the IQ tests administered; however, his mother noted some attentional issues. His attentional capacity would be severely tested with material of low interest that he did not find challenging.

In general, gifted individuals are far more aware of the details of their environment. When they consider issues, they see more sides—multiple points of view. At any given moment, they must choose from myriad options for thought or action. It is far easier to focus when only one or two choices present themselves. Teaching gifted children at a level and pace that requires sustained focus will provide essential practice for them in culling out the most important aspects of their experience and using them in a deliberate, thoughtful exercise of intellectual power. Because we expect relatively little of gifted students in programs developed for average children, many leave high school with poor work habits, inadequate organizational skills, and fluctuating attention and motivation. For these, whether or not we diagnose them as having attentional deficits, ADHD-like problems will still have to be addressed at some point.

Enabling the Twice Exceptional to Bloom

Learning disabilities and other deficits are no less common in the gifted population than the general population, but they can be more difficult to diagnose. Linda Silverman stresses to all testers at the GDC careful examination of discrepancies of all kinds: between scores on different tests, between performance on various subtests or types of items within a test, between behavior at home and at school, between strong and weak subjects, even between IQ scores of siblings. For example, discrepancies of more than one standard deviation (15-16 points) between the IQ scores of siblings should be investigated. Research with 148 sets of siblings has shown that 36% have IQ scores within five points of each other; and 61% are within 10 points (Silverman, 1988). The child perceived to be non-gifted in a gifted family usually is a gifted child with learning disabilities.

Finding and treating gifted children with learning difficulties can make an enormous difference to the child challenged in this way. The fact that these children can often do advanced work while still struggling with simple concepts is confusing to them, as are the mixed messages that they receive about being "bright, but lazy" or simply *disabled*, when their parents view them as so much more capable. Every effort should be made to diagnose apparent weaknesses through careful assessment. Where they exist, they should be explained clearly to the child and interventions undertaken.

Twice-exceptional children need to be taught first to their strengths and consistently reminded that they are capable. However, in addition to supporting their giftedness, their deficits should be accommodated so that they can thrive and progress. The good news is that the twice exceptional *are* late bloomers. Linda Silverman recalls many examples of students feeling more capable as they matured, noticing the phenomenon at some time between puberty and young adulthood (few did well as young children in elementary school). Many had the sense that they were becoming more intelligent, that their brains were growing, or that they could do things that they had not been able to do before. Twice-exceptional children will struggle, but they will also improve, appear smarter, and compensate more effectively. With help, their gifts will become increasingly apparent as their deficits prove to be smaller obstacles.

For Further Reading

Books and Articles

Baum, S. (1984). Meeting the needs of learning disabled gifted students. *Roeper Review,* 7(1), 16-19.

Baum, S. (1991a, Spring). Gifted but learning disabled: A puzzling paradox. *Highly Gifted Children,* 4-6.

Baum, S. (1991b). *To be gifted and learning disabled: From identification to practical intervention strategies.* Mansfield Center, CT: Creative Learning Press.

Davis, R. D. (1994). *The gift of dyslexia.* New York: The Berkley Publishing Group.

Eide, B., & Eide, F. (2006). *The mislabeled child.* New York: Hyperion.

Hallowell, E., & Ratey, J. (1994). *Driven to distraction.* New York: Touchstone.

Hallowell, E., & Ratey, J. (1996). *Answers to distraction.* New York: Bantam Books.

Hollingworth, L. S. (1923). *Special talents and defects: Their significance for education.* New York: Macmillan.

Kay, K. (Ed.). (2000). *Uniquely gifted: Identifying and meeting the needs of the twice exceptional student.* Gilsum, NH: Avocus.

Kutner, D. R. (1999). Blurred brilliance: What ADHD looks like in gifted adults. *Advanced Development, 8,* 87-96.

Lovecky, D. V. (1991a). Highly gifted children with attention deficit disorder. *Highly Gifted Children,* 7(2), 1-2.

Lovecky, D. V. (1991b). The hidden gifted learner: Nonverbal learning disabilities. *Understanding Our Gifted, 4*(1), 3.

Lovecky, D. V. (1994). Gifted children with attention deficit disorder. *Understanding Our Gifted, 6*(5), 1, 7-10.

Lovecky, D. V. (2004). *Different minds: Gifted children with ADHD, Asperger Syndrome, and other learning deficits.* London: Jessica Kingsley.

Miller, L. J. (2006). *Sensational kids: Hope and help for children with sensory processing disorder.* New York: Putnam Adult.

Moon, S. M., Zentall, S. S., Grskovic, J. A., Hall, A., & Stormont, M. (2001). Emotional and social characteristics of boys with ADHD and giftedness: A comparative case study. *Journal for the Education of the Gifted, 24,* 207-247.

Ratey, J., & Johnson, C. (1998). *Shadow syndromes.* New York: Bantam Books.

Silverman, L. K. (2000). The two-edged sword of compensation: How the gifted cope with learning disabilities. In K. Kay (Ed.), *Uniquely gifted: Identifying and meeting the needs of the twice exceptional student* (Reference ed., pp. 153-165). Gilsum, NH: Avocus.

Silverman, L. K. (2001). Diagnosing and treating visual perceptual issues in gifted children. *Journal of Optometric Vision Development, 32*(3), 153-176.

Silverman, L. K. (2003). Gifted children with learning disabilities. In N. Colangelo & G. A. Davis (Eds.), *Handbook of gifted education* (3rd ed., pp. 533-543). Boston: Allyn & Bacon.

Webb, J. T., Amend, E. R., Webb, N. E., Goerss, J., Beljan, P., & Olenchak, F. R. (2005). *Misdiagnosis and dual diagnoses of gifted children and adults: ADHD, bipolar, Asperger's, depression, and other disorders.* Scottsdale, AZ: Great Potential Press.

West, T. G. (1991). *In the mind's eye: Visual thinkers, gifted people with learning disabilities, computer images, and the ironies of creativity.* Buffalo, NY: Prometheus.

Whitmore, J. (1980). *Giftedness, conflict and underachievement.* Needham Heights, MA: Allyn & Bacon.

Websites

College of Optometrists in Vision Development
http://covd.org

Eric Clearinghouse on Disabilities and Gifted Education (articles on dual exceptionalities—archived on the Hoagies Gifted Education Page)
www.hoagiesgifted.org/eric/fact/dualexep.html

GT-Special (an electronic mailing list for families, educators, and professionals who support gifted and talented children with learning disabilities)
http://gtworld.org/gtspeclist.html

Individuals with Disabilities Education Act – IDEA 2004
U.S. Department of Education
Office of Special Education Programs
http://idea.ed.gov/explore/home

Learning Disabilities Association of America – LDA (information and links to government agencies and support organizations)
www.ldanatl.org

Sensory Processing Disorder Network (SPD Network)
http://spdnetwork.org

Uniquely Gifted (Internet resources for gifted/special needs children edited by Meredith Warshaw)
www.uniquelygifted.org

Wrightslaw (special education law and advocacy website by attorney Peter W. D. Wright and Pamela Darr Wright)
www.wrightslaw.com

Chapter 7
Successful Programs for Gifted Students

Seek the Best Options Available

Self-Contained Classrooms or Schools for the Gifted

By far, the most successful option for gifted children is the full-time, self-contained classroom or school for the gifted. We have seen the best academic, social, and emotional development in gifted children who are placed in these programs. These schools are designed to accommodate the considerably faster learning pace of gifted children, and the teachers who teach in them typically have some experience and training in gifted education. At the least, these teachers have an interest in gifted children and usually have a background in modifying curriculum to accommodate special education needs, or they are accomplished at teaching older, more advanced children and can apply that knowledge similarly to younger, highly capable children. Ideally, they will use a variety of instructional approaches that best suit gifted students, and they are accustomed to more advanced materials and performance expectations.

Schools for the gifted have the luxury of creating curricula specifically for this population. Taking into account learning rate, learning styles, and other characteristics of gifted students, these schools can increase rigor, add depth and breadth of typical study, add topics that would not generally be addressed until children are older, and actually match the program to the students' needs. However, because so few schools for gifted children exist, either in the public or private domain, few families have the opportunity to choose the full-time option. For most families, providing an appropriate curriculum for a gifted student becomes an issue of working with the school to piece together the best options available, rather than choosing a ready-made school or curriculum.

Interestingly, self-contained schools for the gifted are the most cost-effective way to educate gifted children in public school. The common notion that schools simply cannot afford gifted programs only applies to models in which the child attends a regular program and gifted accommodations are added on, such as with a daily or weekly pull-out in which the child goes to a specialist teacher. Funds for the regular instruction of students, teacher salaries, and buildings can be spent as easily to place a child in a public school for the gifted (a self-contained school) as in a regular public school. Self-contained schools for gifted children eliminate the need to hire extra teachers for pull-out programs that extend the regular program. Moreover, with self-contained classes, gifted programming is not lost in difficult financial times when school funding is limited and special programs for non-majority populations are subject to elimination. Schools for gifted children (some are *schools within schools*) simply utilize regular funding and are not nearly as vulnerable.

While some school districts have created schools for the gifted, many others resist this approach. They assume that a gifted school would not be politically acceptable and fear criticism for catering to the elite. Many also believe that heterogeneous grouping of all students is essential for social development or think that gifted students should stay in regular classrooms to provide role models for other students. Virtually all are still sensitive to that ethical mandate of the 1980s and 90s that we should avoid any semblance of *tracking*.

However, the benefits for gifted students in a full-time program are obvious to those who work with them. When they are challenged sufficiently, gifted children maintain their love for learning and develop a solid work ethic. They progress as scholars, acquiring the study and organizational skills that they would not learn if the work were too easy. Socially, they reap the benefits that we take for granted for average children; they are able to find friends with similar interests who understand their jokes. They are more comfortable with mental age peers than chronological peers, but this placement allows them both. They are not allowed the comfort of always being the best student in the class, who is best with or without much effort. Although it would seem that gifted students in such a setting would become elitist, they generally learn more humility because others are similarly competent.

Self-contained programs for gifted children also help social development. Gifted children in regular classrooms are often isolated, teased, and ridiculed by other students for being different. Taunted with a phrase like "read-a-book, read-a-book," the gifted child develops a defensive posture that reduces openness to others and slows social development. Gifted children in a school for the gifted fit in, and it becomes a psychologically healthy placement for them. When they are no longer the "odd one" in the class, they are free to learn to appreciate the differences among all of their friends and the diversity that makes each friend unique and interesting.

Charter and Magnet Schools

But what if such a school is not available? Fortunately, there is still a range of other options that can work. Charter schools—publicly funded schools created by groups in the community who want to meet particular needs—are one alternative. In states in which charter schools have been adopted, they have generally done well. They meet a wide variety of needs and, in some cases, are good choices for gifted students. But because they vary tremendously in philosophy and quality, they must be evaluated carefully with the particular gifted child's needs in mind. A charter school that I helped organize in Boulder, Colorado, was created for "students who feel they want or need more challenge" and provided a considerably accelerated curriculum for middle school students anticipating challenging high school programs (i.e., the International Baccalaureate program or Advanced Placement courses and possible concurrent enrollment in a local college). Although this school was not specifically for *gifted* students, it proved to be a good option for most.

Some magnet schools have a particular academic focus (e.g., science, math, computer science, or the arts) and draw top-notch students; these may also be a good match for gifted students. Parents and other advocates should examine these schools carefully to determine if the level and pace of instruction will be adequate and if placement of students in classes is flexible enough to accommodate a student who has already mastered advanced work.

Home Schooling

Home schooling is another option. Although it places enormous demands on parents as teachers, it does provide an immediate solution to the problem of how to create a program that's substantially and qualitatively different. Parents are more willing to home school children in the lower grades than the higher, as gifted children quickly become more challenging to instruct as their content knowledge level rises. However, some home schooling parents teach their children through high school and note that their students increasingly become autonomous learners.

Home schooling is the best way to achieve a truly unique program or accommodate an unusually rapid learning rate. There is help available for parents wishing to try home schooling, including secular and religious support groups and online forums in all 50 states. Social development is not a problem for home schooling parents, who often combine efforts by getting children together for projects, field trips, and other social gatherings. Some parents arrange partial home schooling situations that allow the child to study some subjects at home (usually the subjects in which the child is most advanced) and attend school for other subjects and electives. This is a way to provide physical education, art, and music experiences beyond what is done at home and allow the child frequent access to friends at school. (See Chapter 8: Models of Advocacy for Parents, for an extensive discussion of home schooling.)

Typical Schools with Grade and Subject Acceleration

Whole-grade and single-subject acceleration at school provide other effective alternatives to the regular program. Movement to a higher grade level ensures that accelerated work will be provided on a consistent basis, whereas efforts to modify curriculum for an individual child within a lower-level classroom may be inconsistent. A child who accelerates is treated as one of the group and not singled out, and accelerated students usually relate better to students who are more likely to be at their same mental age and share interests.

Research on acceleration, despite the warnings that one occasionally hears, is quite positive when the child supports the placement. Because gifted children tend to be introverts, they may need opportunities to visit the older class and take time to decide. An escape clause can be built into the agreement to accelerate, allowing the child to return to the lower-level placement within a month if he or she is not happy. For children who are reluctant to skip a grade, acceleration in one subject area first can familiarize them with the older students and make the prospect of later full-grade acceleration less daunting. It is important that the receiving teacher in either case be willing to facilitate the child's adjustment. Acceleration is easiest when the child starts the new placement at the beginning of the school year.

For situations in which school personnel resist acceleration or are unsure about a child's readiness for a full-grade skip, parents or school personnel may wish to make use of the *Iowa Acceleration Scale, 2nd Edition.*[1] This tool contains a questionnaire designed to guide a child study team through a series of items, which include data about the child's ability and achievement (testing information); school history; and also academic, developmental, and interpersonal factors. A numeric score indicates whether the child is an excellent, good, or marginal candidate for a whole-grade skip, or whether another option such as mentoring should be recommended. Items in the IAS questionnaire have been tested for validity, and research on the instrument continues at The University of Iowa, so it may help even a school that has never accelerated a student consider this option.

Keep in mind, however, that the IAS also has strict rules about when to automatically refuse an acceleration request, which may not address the range of issues that occur with real students in real life. For example, one critical requirement automatically disallows whole grade acceleration for any student advancing into the grade level of an older sibling, even if they attend different schools, because it "will introduce the accelerated child into the social and academic territory of the older sibling" (p. 20). While this seems reasonable, what about the struggle of two siblings close in age, the older with Asperger Syndrome and the younger who is exceptionally gifted? If we know that exceptionally gifted students usually fare best with several years' acceleration over a K-12 school career, can we in good conscience refuse acceleration each year to the younger child? What are the ramifications of such an action long term? The IAS suggests other offerings in such cases, such as a mentorship, but such an option might be inadequate.

The IAS should not be the ultimate arbiter of full-grade acceleration in some situations, but it can facilitate reasonable decision-making. When difficult decisions arise, it makes sense to defer to families, who can often settle such issues supportively. In truth, some children attend gifted schools with accelerated curricula, while their siblings (usually with learning disabilities but high potential) attend more typical schools or even therapeutic programs. Good parents find options to support the gifts of each child, sometimes in very different ways.

Private Tutors and Mentors

Private tutoring or mentoring in one or more subject areas is always an option, regardless of the child's school placement. Although the terms overlap, *tutoring* is private instruction, sometimes with the goal of helping a child catch up or gain a more thorough or more advanced knowledge of a subject, while *mentoring* connotes an adult role model, adviser, or guide (adult professional, college professor, local writer, or scientist) who helps move a child ahead or exposes the child to a wide range of new ideas. Local mentors can usually be found to help a child extend writing skills, learn a foreign language, explore a career, or begin a subject such as algebra early.

It is important, however, that the child's school program be modified to reflect the advanced work if the result is a higher level of mastery in a subject. Children should never be expected to continue to do lower-level work in school while they are advancing rapidly in the same subject outside of school. Parents engage mentors to support the interests of children who are eager to explore a field, and the school should support the child's efforts as well. If the school fails to acknowledge this work, it can seriously affect the child's motivation to learn in the classroom.

Distance-Learning Courses

Increasingly, another option is emerging for gifted children: computer-based instruction, online coursework, and correspondence courses from distant sources. Stanford's EPGY (Education Program for Gifted Youth) has long offered computer-based math instruction from elementary school through high school that is self-paced (Johns Hopkins University has a similar program). EPGY has expanded to offer a variety of courses in English, the sciences, and computer programming, as well as a complete high school program. The coursework is computer-based for use on a home computer, consisting of multi-media lectures on CD-ROM supplemented by real-time virtual classroom sessions in which students and instructors interact. Instructors are available for additional instructional support by phone, electronic mail, and virtual classroom. Tuition is paid, and the materials (including textbooks) are sent to the child's home, where the child can progress as quickly as he or she likes.

This is an option that parents may want to consider temporarily when a child requests accelerated instruction but the school refuses. Generally, credit from Stanford's Continuing Studies Program is viewed by schools as reasonable evidence of mastery, and the child is then allowed to take higher-level coursework at school. Or EPGY may become the longer-term math program that the child whizzes through at a faster pace than the school could provide. One sixth-grade girl we know completed instruction from Algebra I through Calculus in one year.

Such a program, if undertaken, should substitute for mathematics at school. The student can do homework at school while math is being taught and then get instruction at home when homework for school would normally be done. These programs are increasingly being offered by universities with Talent Search programs and others interested in supporting gifted students. For example, Duke University provides Advanced Placement courses for younger students ready to take them early.

Correspondence courses continue to be popular with families of gifted children. For example, the University of Nebraska Independent Study High School offers a full range of courses leading to a high school diploma, and it is appropriate for younger gifted students who are not yet of high school age. Likewise, many colleges will allow advanced students of high school age or younger to access college-level courses.

Private and Parochial Schools (Not Specifically for Gifted Children)

Private and parochial schools, although usually not designed specifically for gifted students, are an option that many parents of the gifted consider, since these schools are generally more challenging than regular public school programs. However, they need to offer flexible placement in order to fully support gifted students. Parents exploring this option will encounter a range of different programs and must thoughtfully decide if such a placement will benefit their gifted child. One excellent local school, for example, places gifted students in their various subjects according to mastery so that a student can be working at various grade levels in different areas. This type of placement works beautifully for gifted children; it allows them to learn new material once previous material is mastered.

Another private school we know has a strict grade-level placement because school personnel are concerned that parents will not approve if some children are acknowledged to be more advanced than others. Although teachers at this school spend considerable individual time with students in small classes, they insist that they do not individualize because it might appear to be offering advantages for some. In addition, the headmaster of this school has stated, "I don't believe in acceleration, and I never will." Such a school can stifle the advanced student. Furthermore, schools that emphasize high achievement may require considerable homework—more than a gifted child needs in order to learn the material. Parents need to proceed carefully, ask many questions, and have their children visit when seriously considering this option.

Advanced High School Programs

For gifted high school students, common options include schools with rich offerings of Advanced Placement (AP) courses, high schools with International Baccalaureate (IB) programs, and magnet schools (high schools for the performing arts, math/science magnets, etc.). Advanced Placement courses are typically the highest-level courses that most high schools offer. They represent work at the level of college freshmen courses and are generally taken by juniors and seniors preparing for AP exams that confer college credit with high scores. These courses can be taken earlier than usual if the student can place or test out of entry-level courses (options to discuss with the principal or guidance counselor). Omitting entry-level courses allows the student more time to take advanced courses.

International Baccalaureate (IB) programs technically encompass only the junior and senior years of high school, but the schools offering them provide some type of Pre-IB experience for freshmen and sophomores. These Pre-IB programs are advanced freshman and sophomore course offerings which are highly desirable, especially when compared with high schools that offer few honors courses for underclassmen. Earning the IB diploma documents completion of a comprehensive, challenging program with college-level courses similar to AP level. Since the program is international, an IB diploma is highly regarded around the world.

However, an accelerated American student may want to choose AP classes because he or she can take AP exams at any grade level, whereas IB exams may only be taken at the end of the eleventh and twelfth grades. A student ready to take an upper-level IB exam early in his or her high school career must wait until later to take it. In contrast, the flexibility of AP testing has allowed some seventh- and eighth-grade students at a high-challenge local middle school the opportunity to take two AP social science courses, taught by a former AP high school teacher, and then take the exit tests. Some of the students earned high enough scores to ensure college credit at most colleges (colleges vary in conferring credit) before they entered high school!

Concurrent Enrollment in High School and College

Many gifted high school students also choose to take college courses while still in high school (states sometimes pay partial tuition through Post-Secondary Options or Dual Enrollment acts). If chosen to reflect high school graduation requirements, the college courses then count toward *both* high school graduation and a bachelor's degree. Students may attend local colleges or take college courses online. Most gifted students appreciate such concurrent enrollment, as it allows them to compact their high school and college work, and many feel quite comfortable on college campuses. They may enter college with a significant amount of college credit (further augmented by credit earned through AP or IB coursework), usually in the more basic classes required of underclassmen. This allows them to pursue studies in their major area sooner and shortens the time required to earn an undergraduate degree.

Be aware that concurrent enrollment may also limit scholarship opportunities open only to college freshmen, if the student earns enough college credit while in high school to begin full-time college work as a sophomore or junior. Nevertheless, some gifted high school students really need the opportunity to advance, and they love their early college experiences.

Individualization within the Regular Classroom

Probably the most common program option for gifted children, particularly in elementary schools, is individualization within the regular classroom, sometimes called *differentiating the curriculum*. The child is placed normally with age peers, and his or her work is modified where needed to accommodate special learning needs. This allows teaching children in heterogeneous groups (which is very important to some), but it also recognizes the child's unusual needs. The choice of teacher, specific program options, and the consistency of modifications are critical, as is continuing administrative support for such individualized classroom instruction. Unfortunately, many gifted children have programs of this sort, with only minimal accommodations for their special needs. Successful individualization is difficult for teachers who have large classes, particularly if they have students with abilities ranging from the mildly delayed (mainstreamed into the regular classroom) to the most highly gifted.

To be successful, teachers must both understand the needs of gifted students and appreciate their strengths. They must have creative ideas for modifying a child's curriculum and the firm resolve to accommodate needs consistently. Such teachers are usually experienced professionals who plan lessons and handle classrooms with ease. Furthermore, they are confident individuals, willing to take some risks teaching a student, despite criticism from other educators.

Less Successful Options

Irrelevant Enrichment

Although gifted students in America desperately need educational options, some of the alternatives currently offered are poor. Gifted students need access to advanced material, a faster pace of instruction, accommodation to their learning style, and work that engages their abstract reasoning abilities, but many enrichment programs fall short. The late Julian Stanley, a great pioneer in work with mathematically precocious youth at Johns Hopkins University, writes that the desire to limit our accommodations to *enrichment* rather than *acceleration* (to avoid affecting the entire grade-level curriculum sequence) often has interesting ramifications. He notes four types of enrichment typically employed: (1) *busywork*—e.g., the math class is given the odd problems to do, but the gifted student must do *all* of the problems because she's smart and can do more work; (2) *irrelevant*—e.g., gifted students are given a leadership class, whether or not that is appropriate for all and despite the fact that some non-gifted students may have excellent leadership potential; (3) *cultural*—e.g., we offer gifted students an art appreciation class; it is also irrelevant but has some socially redeeming value; and (4) *relevant*—in which the enrichment actually increases the depth and breadth of the child's study and is relevant to what he or she is learning. In such cases, the enrichment will lead to grade acceleration in the future.[2]

Stanley's point is well taken; the difference between curriculum at different grade levels on the same subject is usually a difference of depth and breadth. However, it is common to hear people discuss enrichment *versus* acceleration: "I believe in enrichment, but not acceleration." The two really cannot be separated if the enrichment is the type that most of us envision—i.e., the regular work is broadened, and more detail is added. Moreover, the simplest instance of giving a child something additional in a classroom can be called *enrichment* yet not be helpful as a gifted accommodation. Unless relevant enrichment is provided on a consistent basis as part of a planned accommodation for a gifted child, it is likely to be inadequate.

Sadly, many gifted programs are quite irrelevant to the child's regular classroom learning. For example, one teacher in a gifted pull-out program for elementary and middle school students sought advice to improve her program. Every week, for a few hours, the program provided "thinking skills training" and also taught "leadership skills." When she asked what else she might do, I responded, "What contact do you have with the students' classroom teachers? Could you work more closely with them to modify instruction for the gifted students in the regular classroom?" She insisted that there could be no connection; the classroom teachers did not want interference! Yet what most undermines the motivation of gifted students to learn is the feeling of being trapped in a lock-step system that does not respond to their needs, their interests, or their accomplishments. What they need most is appropriate daily work, not to be "gifted" only once a week for a few hours.

Likewise, we have seen efforts to meet social and emotional needs of the gifted without any educational accommodations. One middle school, described in a recent newspaper article, was proud of its monthly brown bag lunches for gifted students that allowed them to commiserate with each other about their frustrations in the classroom. Programs that only minimally address the needs of gifted students are simply irresponsible.

Acceleration Opportunities Too Small in Scope

Some modifications for gifted students are too small in scope. For example, one "gifted math" group for fourth graders allowed students to skip very small amounts of regular classroom instruction when they demonstrated mastery of the relevant concepts on tests, and then they were exposed to limited enrichment. These programs are typically preplanned, without knowledge of the needs of the specific students, to provide a measured amount of enriched material acceptable to teachers. But the amount that one can skip doesn't begin to fit the degree of advancement that we see in gifted children when we administer achievement tests. A better gifted math group would result if the children were all assessed initially and efforts were made to provide appropriate instruction at each child's actual level, along with the opportunity to move ahead when concepts are mastered. Minimal, preplanned programs offer a false sense of security that the needs of gifted students are being accommodated, yet the programs actually fall far short of meeting the students' needs.

The notion that the child's accommodation cannot extend beyond grade level is never true. In fact, many gifted children benefit from substantial acceleration. For example, our most mathematically talented students are usually ready to begin algebra several years early while still in elementary school. Any small holes in their arithmetic mastery can be filled easily in the context of algebra instruction, and algebra appeals greatly to their love of abstraction. Teachers are very reluctant to allow this because of the sequential reasoning that all arithmetic must be in place before beginning algebra. Yet our brightest students in math are hard-pressed to endure arithmetic until eighth grade, especially since the number of new math concepts presented in the years just preceding algebra diminishes. Early algebra is a motivator for these students to continue loving math.

The Teacher's Helper

Some teachers believe that using a child as a teacher's helper is of great benefit, particularly for a well-behaved girl. Regrettably, this approach often ensures that the gifted student will be limited to helping with regular grade-level work and will not have the opportunity to move ahead appropriately. Likewise, pairing the gifted student with a child who needs extra help ignores the educational needs of the gifted child. Pairing advanced readers with non-readers for large amounts of time may relieve the teacher of an added instructional burden, but it eliminates any opportunity for the advanced reader to progress.

Trying to keep the gifted child simply busy or occupied while others catch up cannot be justified either; every child has a right to learn primarily new material every day. One Executive Director of Curriculum and Instruction of a local school district remembered having a particularly advanced boy in her classroom years before. He had mastered virtually everything she attempted to teach that year, so he spent most of his time reading quietly at his desk. She consoled herself about this situation by thinking that as long as he was reading, he was okay. Although reading books was better than forcing him to do low-level tasks, years of little or no challenging work in the classroom take their toll. They have a cumulative effect that, at the very least, undermines the development of good work habits, threatens motivation to learn in school, and may contribute to behaviors that resemble attentional deficits.

The Least Restrictive Environment

Parents of special education students have long advocated that their students be taught in the "least restrictive environment," and current legislation mandates it. If that same principle were applied to gifted children, it would mean that students would be taught at their appropriate level and allowed continuous progress; they would move ahead whenever they mastered material. They would not be held to a slower learning pace or forced to drill and practice concepts already learned; they would be respected as learners, not reproached for their failure to be typical. They would have opportunities to interact with true peers who share similar interests and nurture their social development.

Because gifted students differ so much from one another, there is not even a perfect gifted program that would accommodate them all and provide an ideal education. Schools for the gifted try very hard to create a good match, but such programs usually fit the moderately gifted (IQ 130-144) best because most gifted students are within that range. Educators must remember that highly gifted students need accommodations in gifted schools, as well as in regular schools, and that flexibility is a key component in any excellent program. Schools for gifted children vary considerably. Some are quite traditional, providing advanced instruction which is sequenced into somewhat rigid levels that most students progress through together. Other schools are more individualized, with students advancing at different rates. They may feature teachers lecturing in traditional classrooms, or rooms with sofas, armchairs, and small tables where each student pursues his or her week's work individually, meeting with small groups and occasionally the teacher for discussions or projects.

The best curriculum is a rich and varied one that challenges the gifted student's desire to reason and learn in depth. It thoroughly engages the learner and requires real effort without overwhelming him or her. The student gains self-esteem from meaningful accomplishment. Beyond that, there are many other successful possibilities that we have observed.

Some students attend private elementary and middle schools for the gifted and then earn an International Baccalaureate diploma in high school or attend a high school with a large number of AP classes. Other gifted students attend public school exclusively but are accelerated minimally, moderately, or even radically in their public school educations. A few highly gifted students that we have known skipped middle school altogether and moved from elementary school to high school. This is actually quite reasonable when the student's middle school offers few, if any, honors courses, and the child can progress from being a very advanced student at the end of elementary school to a high school freshman taking honors coursework. We have seen home schooled children take college courses quite early and love them. Some of these students graduate from high school at age nine, 10, or 11 and move on to college work.

There is no body of knowledge that suggests a single model for success with these children. A fortunate gifted child might attend a school for gifted children with a carefully developed curriculum that provides enriched, in-depth material at a faster pace. Likewise, a profoundly gifted child (most likely to suffer in a typical public school environment) might emerge relatively unscathed from high school with a pieced-together conglomeration of efforts to provide challenge. The value of choosing teachers carefully, of skipping a grade, of moving to a more challenging school for a couple of years, and of placing out of lower-level classes in high school, taking college courses concurrently, etc. cannot be underestimated. We *rarely* see gifted students achieving well and loving school without these kinds of interventions or accommodations.

Choosing a Program

Prior to School Entrance

Parents preparing a gifted child for school can rest assured that it is always appropriate to support the child's learning at home. It is important for parents to foster the child's curiosity by providing information when it is requested and letting the child take the lead and pursue knowledge of things that interest him or her. Nothing is gained by withholding information from a child in hopes of preventing boredom at school. Parents of gifted children usually try to support their children's interests to the degree possible; few push their children into unwanted activities. In fact, the pressure exerted by gifted children on their parents to provide a wide variety of stimulation usually taxes both parental energy and monetary reserves. Parents should feel comfortable offering enrichment activities, opportunities to pursue hobbies and develop talents, and even help to learn specific skills taught in school, if asked.

When we help a child to learn, or give any type of information that they request, we are rewarding the child for his curiosity and reinforcing his inborn love of learning. Many gifted children show remarkable stores of knowledge, attesting to the rich sources of information accessible to them. Some learn from watching the Discovery and History television channels, others from reading or being read to, and still others from trips to museums or vacations. These are children who pursue myriad interests and want to sample what the world has to offer.

Choosing an Elementary School

When it comes time to send a gifted child to school, parents should carefully and deliberately choose the school. These days, parents often have a variety of choices, even in public schools. The neighborhood school is not the only possibility. There may also be *schools of choice* in a school district (magnet or charter schools) that have a particular emphasis, or schools that parents simply feel more comfortable with when they meet the staff or find out about the programs. A school's principal can be the parents' best long-term ally if he or she is willing to help place a child with supportive teachers and/or in the most appropriate classes. In fact, contacting the school principal before a child begins school or before relocating can be helpful in finding the one who is most willing to meet a child's needs. A friend of mine, moving to the Northwest, contacted a number of schools as she looked for the best placement for her twice-exceptional son. Her calls to principals were surprisingly revealing; the administrators differed significantly in their willingness to help plan a program for her son, as well as in their knowledge of how to support both his giftedness and his dyslexia. Her search resulted in the choice of one particular school, and the family moved to the appropriate geographic area so that their son could attend that school.

Teachers should be considered in the initial choice of a school as well and are a factor every year that a child attends school. Teacher choice may precipitate the move to a different school at some point or be a factor in grade placement decisions. Even in a school of preference, whether or not the gifted child is a good fit in that school depends on the child's chemistry with each teacher each year. Parents should avoid teachers who are not supportive of giftedness, inflexible about modifying curriculum, or simply not appreciative of the child.

Parents must be careful to ensure that children, once they enter school, are learning primarily new material every day and not spending considerable amounts of time on previously mastered concepts. The child who is fully reading and sounding out words prior to entering first grade should probably skip first grade, as the main emphasis is reading instruction. Some schools will accelerate a child within a few weeks once the teacher has had an opportunity to appraise the child's skill levels. Beware of advice to retain a child in the age-appropriate grade simply because social skills do not appear advanced. If the child shows some reluctance to enter into new groups of children without some time to observe and become comfortable, this is typical of gifted children who are primarily introverted (and struggle to find age peers with similar interests). It is not an indication that the child's social skills are too immature for placement at a higher grade level.

As gifted children progress through school, monitor them carefully to ensure a continued good fit with the curriculum and instructional pace. Note the child's comments about being bored or having to do things repeatedly. Pay attention to concerns about the work always being too easy. Note teachers' comments, as well—for example, about a child resisting work, finishing the work too quickly, or talking when work is done (when this occurs, it means the child is not challenged enough). Don't ignore these concerns or assume that it will be character-building for a child to learn to be patient and wait for others.

Assessment Aids Planning

Have your child tested individually to gain a better idea of her intellectual potential, her achievement level, and her strengths and weaknesses (if not done previously for admission to a gifted program). Many children are accepted to gifted programs based on brief group intelligence screeners, which confirm giftedness but offer little additional specific information that would be helpful in planning programs. Children should also be individually tested if the scores from school tests do not seem to accurately describe the child. Some obviously gifted children do not score well on group tests and do not qualify for gifted accommodations at school as a result. One nine-year-old girl earned solidly gifted Verbal, Performance, and Full Scale IQ scores in the 130s on the WISC-III (all in the 98th and 99th percentiles) but was rejected for the gifted program at school based on her Cognitive Abilities Test (CogAT) group scores. On that test, she earned a Verbal score at the 93rd percentile, Quantitative score at the 71st percentile, and Nonverbal score at the 97th percentile. The school considered only the last score high enough for program admission but felt that an excellent Nonverbal score alone did not measure giftedness. The girl's mother brought her in for individual testing based largely on her personality characteristics. When the mother read about common personality traits of the gifted, she said,

"That's my child." The child's score on the WISC-III showed that the mother was correct.

Assessment of current achievement levels in academic subject areas is also invaluable when determining a child's proper placement. If achievement scores indicate poor placement (e.g., the child is bored in class, and the achievement grade equivalent is two or more years above the child's current grade), be sure to share the results with the child's teacher or principal, as they undoubtedly relate to the child's frustration. Try to work out solutions. Test results document the child's abilities and skill levels for parents so that they will not be speaking out of intuition or prejudice for their own child.

An Individual Education Plan (IEP)

Working out a written plan for modifying a child's curriculum, however simple, is an important goal (see Chapter 11 for sample plans). Whether we call it an Alternative Learning Plan (ALP), Individual Education Plan (IEP), Personal Learning Plan (PLP), or some other name, the plan lists modifications to the regular program. Accommodating a child's needs requires a meeting of the teacher, parent(s), and the child. Each can provide needed information. Focus on the particular problem, and suggest a fix for it. Remember, there are no prescribed solutions—only a general need for advanced materials, faster instructional pace, and support of the child's interests.

Solutions that require a minimum effort to manage are more likely to be successful. For example, it will be easier to send a child to a higher grade level for math instruction every day than to modify his or her math program within the regular classroom for the remainder of the year. The single-subject math acceleration will be fairly easy for the two teachers involved. However, the classroom teacher may be able to substitute fourth-grade spelling lists for second-grade lists for an advanced speller, and this would be a simple modification to the regular classroom curriculum. Likewise, schools that establish reading groups for different levels of readers within each grade may be able to accommodate an advanced reader. Substituting a more advanced book for an easier book is easy for a teacher to do as well. However, teachers should also advance the level of literature study to engage higher-level thinking skills, not just mastery of the concrete details of the book.

To be successful, Individual Education Plans must address the child's improper fit with the curriculum. The provision of enrichment experiences may be enjoyable and even offer the opportunity to be with other gifted children, but accelerated curriculum modifications are needed as well. Consider full-grade acceleration if a child is significantly advanced in all academic areas and is comfortable with the idea. Many times children are willing to accelerate because they are bored and have few close friends anyway.

Middle School Choices

As a child approaches middle school, it is important to check out the various schools and the middle school philosophy in the public school district. Junior highs usually included grades seven through nine, whereas most middle schools encompass grades six through eight. The practice of "heterogeneous grouping of all students for instruction" was accepted by many public middle schools, causing them to eliminate some or all of the honors classes that they formerly offered. Though many such schools are now making adjustments because gifted children were not being challenged, it is particularly important to carefully evaluate any middle schools under consideration for a gifted child. The option to take advanced (honors or accelerated) classes must be available at this critical time to support the child's motivation to learn and to help him or her develop good study habits. If there is the option of a public middle school for the gifted or an accelerated middle school, parents should seriously consider that option.

A gifted middle schooler needs preparation before entering an advanced high school program to ensure both prerequisite coursework and adequate study skills. Modifications can always be made at the middle school level, if the school is willing. The gifted student can substitute distance-learning courses or move to higher-grade-level courses, including one or more high school courses, if transportation is manageable.

High School Programs

At the high school level, the choice of school and course options remains critical, with honors courses, Advanced Placement courses, and International Baccalaureate courses as important considerations. Make sure that required entry-level courses are truly needed. Many high schools let advanced students skip the entry-level science and freshman English courses, and they may allow other accelerative options as well. For example, most students are allowed to take the next math class in the sequence offered if they are quite advanced coming from a previous school. Some schools may offer the option for the student to test out of the freshman-level course and into the next level. Counselors often handle these common placement changes; however, the principal may need to approve more radical advancement.

High school principals exert varying degrees of responsibility when it comes to placement and the accommodation of students with unusual needs. In some schools, head teachers in the various academic departments make the final decisions about a student's placement in courses. This can work well when the teacher has broad knowledge of the coursework at each level and the requisite student achievement needed (e.g., when the head of the English department teaches classes at several levels, including the freshman and AP English classes). Such a teacher can assess the work of an incoming student and make an excellent placement recommendation. However, when the teacher making the placement decision teaches only a class that students frequently wish to skip, very few students may be allowed to move ahead. Choosing a school with a principal who invites parents of gifted students with significant placement issues to discuss these with him or her is more likely to produce a positive experience for the student that lasts throughout high school. Not all principals have training or experience with gifted children, and some may not be as helpful, but principals who choose to be involved can make ultimate placement decisions. Such a principal can help plan a student's courses based on previous work (not age or grade level), exempt the student from certain course requirements, and offer advice about the best classes for the student to take.

Parents who have successfully guided gifted children through school usually come to prefer accelerative options over enrichment opportunities unrelated to general learning. As one of my friends says, "Kids get tired of dessert. They just want a real meal." Gifted students usually appreciate the opportunity to move ahead to more difficult work. Also, accelerative options are more dependable in the sense that they represent a step up to higher-level material that remains consistent throughout the duration of the class. They are not dependent upon the teacher having extra time to offer special options when he is she is busy with other students. Finally, when the child has successfully completed the accelerated class, acceptance of the child's academic progress is a foregone conclusion. Accomplishments in enrichment projects at a lower grade level may appear less impressive to later teachers and may not adequately document the need for advanced work in the next class.

Finding the Perfect Program

The perfect educational program for a gifted child teaches the child at the appropriate level and pace in each subject area, with instructional provisions made for learning style and support of the child's passions. It is designed to accommodate the abstract reasoning ability of gifted students, realizing that they are most engaged by activities that require higher-level thinking skills. In addition, the program must support the personality characteristics of gifted children, honoring their sensitivity, intensity, and likely introversion.

The program most likely to meet such needs is the self-contained classroom or school for the gifted. Even if the child has varying abilities in different subject areas and perhaps is more highly gifted than children for whom the program is designed, the full-time gifted program comes closest to meeting the academic, social, and emotional needs of gifted students. A well-run gifted school can be flexible where needed for individual children and is virtually always more likely to provide the challenging work and fast instructional pace that gifted children crave. Unfortunately, gifted children rarely have access to self-contained gifted programs, either public or private.

Therefore, parents must research alternative possible schools and programs, interview administrators and teachers, and locate a setting where the gifted child's needs can be met. For most gifted children, teachers build a program of sorts utilizing options available within the school where the child lives or through distance-learning offerings. Parents invariably become the managers of the gifted child's education in the absence of available long-term guidance from school personnel. Parents must ensure that the gifted child's needs are met year by year, helping teachers to locate resources when needed. In this way, a patchwork of educational options can work to support the gifted child's learning.

Help is available for parents through support groups for gifted families, local and state gifted associations, gifted education consultants, specialists in the assessment of the gifted, Internet resources, and selected school personnel. Because parents bear such a heavy responsibility for the learning outcomes of their gifted children, it is critical that they educate themselves about their children's needs to the greatest degree possible. Perhaps the most difficult adjustment for parents to make when they have gifted children is to accept that others won't bear the primary responsibility for educating them. Our gifted children's education will not be primarily the domain of the public or private schools. Likewise, it will not be directed by education professionals. Educated parents who know their gifted children best are the most likely individuals to understand those needs and ensure that they are addressed.

Program Options, by Quinn O'Leary

It took me months to realize how good I really had it. It was not a sudden realization that I liked my teacher or enjoyed my class. It was a slower, dawning awareness of pleasure, the subtle, simple glow of general good cheer at random times throughout the school day—aside, that is, from lunch and recess.

Eventually I wound up adoring both the teacher and the curriculum so much as to request stridently that I be placed in her split-grade class again, for sixth grade as well as fifth. I was the only student in the few years Mrs. Starry and I corresponded who managed to insist strongly enough to be granted my wish.

Mrs. Starry, who often supplanted her name with an "e" scrawled in after a careless five-point of the variety often replacing red inked smiles atop a careful student's paper, was a pale woman with curly dark hair and rather sharp features. She had been an active thespian throughout her college years and now, with a classroom of boisterous kids under her gentle control, she produced casually frequent classroom plays to the students' delight.

Perhaps my remembrances are slightly clouded with nostalgia, but it seems to me that those two final years of elementary school were the two finest for several years before or after.

Mrs. Starry had a knack for engaging students at their particular level, a penchant for drawing the best from everyone.

Spelling was dependent upon ability, reading materials chosen by the particular student. My language requirements were traded for public viewing of amateur claymation made at home with a camcorder capable, if clicked rapidly enough, of half-second frames. I participated in a self-initiated pull-out program in math with books borrowed from the junior high school up the street. We learned in units, no lecture save an occasional jest that the projects we submitted were too numerous.

Mrs. Starry was a catalyst of sorts, the type of dynamically irrepressible person that draws groups together and force-forges lasting friendships simply by introducing two people.

It was her gentle insistence and unconcealed exuberance that pulled the three disparate social landscapes of the other fifth and sixth grade classes into a united whole, studying and competing as a single heterogeneously huge group.

By the end of my fifth grade year, incidentally Mrs. Starry's first at the school, she held enough trust and clout with administrators and parents to have her odd ideas not only taken seriously but often accepted. Her unorthodox plan was to spend the last week of school, time usually reserved for finding out how many times a student will put up with cleaning his or her desk, in a cabined camp in the nearby mountains.

The Environmental Field Trip, as the trip was termed, rose as a huge success, an example of iconoclastic education at its best. The week was composed of multitudinous small quirks of intellectual stimulation, from conservation tactics to long, rambling walks.

There, amongst the subtly vanilla-scented Ponderosas of Idaho's hills, I came to understand new things about the nuisance of school. I had never before conceived of it as a place for personal growth, but I have never since forgotten its potential.

For Further Reading

Full-Time Schools and Full-Time Self-Contained Classrooms for the Gifted

Books and Articles

Rogers, K. B. (2002). *Re-forming gifted education: How parents and teachers can match the program to the child.* Scottsdale, AZ: Great Potential Press.

Silverman, L. K., & Leviton, L. (1991). In search of the perfect program. *Gifted Child Today, 14*(6), 31-34.

Websites

Governors' Schools (state residential high schools for the gifted)
www.ncogs.org

NAGC Resource Directory (general website with a variety of offerings, including gifted schools, enrichment programs, gifted support groups, and educational books)
www.nagc.org/resourcedirectory.aspx

NAGC Summer Opportunities for Gifted Kids (a listing of summer programs, summer camps, enrichment programs, academic programs, and special schools)
www.nagc.org/index.aspx?id=1103

Schools for the Gifted (lists and articles)
www.hoagiesgifted.org/schools.htm

Home Schooling

Books and Articles

Feldman, J. H. (1986). *Nature's gambit: Child prodigies and the development of human potential.* New York: Basic Books.

Kearney, K. (1984, May/June). At home in Maine: Gifted children and home schooling. *G/C/T*, 33, 16-19.

Kearney, K. (1992, September-October). Home schooling highly gifted children. *Understanding Our Gifted.* Also available at www.hoagiesgifted.org/the_highly_gifted_3.htm#homeschool

Rivero, L. (2000). *Gifted education comes home: A case for self-directed home schooling.* Manassas, VA: Gifted Education Press.

Rivero, L. (2002). *Creative home schooling: A resource guide for smart families.* Scottsdale, AZ: Great Potential Press.

Suzy (no last name given). (n.d.). *Home schooling—A family affair.* Available at www.hoagiesgifted.org/success_stories.htm

Wallace, N. (1983). *Better than school.* Burdett, NY: Larson Publications. (Out-of-print account of a year in the life of an unschooling family with two profoundly gifted kids; may be available through inter-library loan.)

Websites

Free Online High School Courses
www.homeschoolersofmaine.org/high_school_&_beyond.htm#Free%20 Online %20Courses

Home Education Magazine (resources on home schooling, state laws, etc.)
www.home-ed-magazine.com

HSLDA Home School Legal Defense Association
540-338-5600
www.hslda.org

John Holt and Growing without Schooling Website
www.holtgws.com

Westbridge Academy
www.westbridgeacademy.com

Grade/Subject Acceleration (Website)

Texas Tech University Outreach and Distance Education (offers distance-learning courses and the opportunity to test out of grades and courses using the "credit by examination" program, K-12, in an accredited public school; Texas public schools are supposed to honor passing test results and exempt students from the courses)
www.depts.ttu.edu/ode

Distance-Learning Courses (Websites)

Center for Talent Development
Northwestern University (including Gifted Learning Links, K-12)
847-491-3782
www.ctd.northwestern.edu

Distance Education – Center for Talented Youth (CTY)
Johns Hopkins University
410-735-6277 or 410-735-6278
http://cty.jhu.edu/cde/index.html

Distance Learning Programs, Hoagies Gifted Education Page
www.hoagiesgifted.org/distance_learning.htm

Duke University Talent Identification Program (TIP) e-Studies
919-668-9100
www.tip.duke.edu/e-studies/index.html

EPGY (Education Program for Gifted Youth)
Stanford University
800-372-EPGY
http://epgy.stanford.edu/courses/index.html

Independent Study High School
University of Nebraska
866-700-4747 or 402-472-2175
http://nebraskahs.unl.edu/index.shtml

Internet Academy (K-12)
253-945-2230
www.iacademy.org

Advanced High School Programs (Websites)

Advanced Placement (AP) Program Website (Includes AP course descriptions and syllabi. Note: all AP courses must go through an "AP Audit" by the College Board in order to be labeled an "AP course" on the transcript. However, students may take the AP exams without having been enrolled in an AP course.)
www.collegeboard.com/student/testing/ap/about.html

"Early College High Schools" (Allow many students to take college courses in their high school or on a nearby campus and earn both a high school diploma and an associate's degree upon high school graduation. Although not specifically developed for the gifted, gifted students would benefit. The Bill and Melinda Gates Foundation has funded many of these. This link to The Early College High School Initiative provides more information about these programs.)
www.earlycolleges.org

International Baccalaureate (IBO)
www.ibo.org

States with Post-Secondary Options or Dual Enrollment Acts – Many states have a state law that allows gifted and academically advanced high school students to take college courses at public expense, including Maine, Iowa, Colorado, Minnesota, and others. Check with your state Department of Education consultant in gifted education to find out if your state has such a law. Note: many high school students take college courses, regardless of whether the cost is covered by the school district.

Early Entrance College Programs (Websites)

EarlyEntrance.org (programs, comparisons, testimonials)
www.earlyentrance.org

Hoagies' Gifted Education Page (list of schools; perspectives of parents, students, and educators)
www.hoagiesgifted.org/early_college.htm

Standardized Testing (Website)

College Board Test Information (includes exam dates and fees and how to prepare for the SAT Reasoning Test, SAT Subject Tests, PSAT/NMSQT, AP, and CLEP)
www.collegeboard.com/testing

Chapter 8
Models of Advocacy for Parents

Once we realize that a gifted child needs our help to improve an inadequate educational program, we have to decide what form our advocacy will take. Do we contact the child's teacher and ask for modifications? Or, fearing that the teacher may not be willing (or allowed) to make the necessary changes, should we approach the principal first? Is this a matter for the school counselor because the child is unhappy in school, or the school psychologist because the child's abilities may suggest unusual needs? Is there a gifted and talented coordinator in the building (perhaps a teacher or paraprofessional hired for this purpose) who could help?

When parents have concerns with a public school, must we go beyond the level of the individual school to the district level? Does the school district have a gifted and talented coordinator who might be responsible for such cases? Are there other district-level administrators who could lead such an effort? Finally, what do district regulations and state laws say about gifted education that would support such a request? Are there legal ramifications for the school denying accommodations?

Would it be helpful to become a member of the school's gifted committee or the school improvement team or some type of site-based advisory/accountability committee within the child's school (given that most schools today give considerable power to committees consisting of teachers, parents, and school administrators)? What about membership in the school district's gifted advisory committee? Could changes be made that would benefit not only this student but others as well? If state laws are inadequate, would legislative efforts be in order?

When a child is suffering, where do we place our energy and direct our efforts for change?

Demonstrate a Documented Need

To have the best chance of success when asking for significant accommodations from school personnel at any level, we must first show a documented need. If the child has already been identified for the school's gifted program, then his or her giftedness is not in question, but we need to provide reasons for the accommodations that we are seeking. If the child has not been identified for the gifted program or there is no program, we have more work to do to justify need.

Most schools will require the child be identified as a gifted student before considering accommodations. As discussed in Chapter 3: Testing Considerations, an educational evaluation substantiates our request by documenting a need that other professionals would support. IQ tests usually provide the basis for entry into the gifted program—or gifted accommodations in general—by justifying the overall need for challenging programming and faster instructional pace. Achievement tests yield the necessary ammunition for requested changes in instructional level.

Parents should be sensitive to the fact that schools are proud of their programs, and most teachers work hard to meet the needs of their students. When parents ask for changes, they are, in effect, saying that the program or teacher is inadequate. Documentation allows the discussion with school personnel to focus on finding appropriate solutions for the child ("We've discovered that our child has these needs...") and helps teachers avoid feelings of personal failure or defensiveness. Without documentation, it is difficult to counter the arguments that school personnel often make that the standard program is adequate.

Follow the Chain of Command

Once the child's giftedness has been documented and there is no question that this child will need some accommodations, the next step can begin. Most longtime gifted advocates advise parents to follow the chain of command, beginning with the person closest to the child: the classroom teacher. When a child is already enrolled and attending a school, this is the best place to start.

Arrange a Conference with the Teacher

In such cases, it is usually best to arrange a conference with the teacher to discuss concerns. Many times, the teacher may be unaware of the extent of the child's abilities and may lack training in gifted education. It is essential that meetings be as upbeat, honest, respectful of the teacher, and oriented to finding *joint* solutions as possible. It is best not to go to the school in anger, not to demand specifics, and not to imply that this is entirely the teacher's problem or that the parents have no responsibility. Parents need to work in partnership with the teacher in the education of this child. Usually, the teacher cares about doing a good job with the child and, hopefully, will be willing to try some new approaches.

Test results give us a starting point. For example, high math scores, along with a recommendation from the tester that the child needs accelerated work, can initiate a discussion about how to provide more challenging math. Achievement test scores that show that a second grader is reading at the seventh-grade level can spark consideration of literature options and whether it would be better to have the child attend a higher-grade-level reading group.

Parents can also provide anecdotal data about what the child is doing at home. Does your first grader have a chemistry lab in the basement and an already-large store of knowledge in science? Has your third grader already published poetry? Some parents have created portfolios of their children's advanced work, which can be invaluable when trying to convince teachers of a need for higher-level instruction.

Bring an Expert

Where appropriate, it can be helpful to bring an expert along. Testers at the GDC have been asked many times to attend meetings at the school or to speak with a teacher or principal on the phone locally or long distance. Sometimes parents even bring a child's teacher to the post-test conference. The expert can usually discuss the child's needs with the teacher easily, whereas parents find this to be more difficult. (I personally can advocate more easily for children with whom I've worked than my own.) Parents of gifted children are painfully sensitive to the possibility that they might be perceived as elitist and are asking for accommodations for an advantaged child. Likewise, they are often perceived as "just parents" by school personnel, regardless of their expertise in gifted education issues; therefore, experts have some advantage presenting the necessary arguments on the child's behalf. (I have used my colleagues at the Center in school meetings about my own children for this reason.)

Create an IEP

Ideally, the mismatch between the child's needs and the instruction in the classroom can form the basis of an Individual Education Plan (IEP) devised for the child as a result of one or two meetings with the teacher. It need not be lengthy or complicated, but it should address modifications in every subject area in which something different is needed. If the child is advanced in just math and science, the IEP should include modifications in the teaching of math and science. English and social studies can be left alone and not included in the IEP. A child may need accommodations in only one subject area—or in all of them. This individualized plan corrects the inadequacies of the regular program.

The IEP may also include some "extras." Perhaps the child will work with a mentor in some area of interest or participate in other activities outside of the classroom. These extra accommodations can support passions, develop talents, and encourage interests not directly related to classroom instruction. If the teacher is willing to devise a plan, it is best to include the child in the planning process. However, this should be done only when it is clear that the teacher is amenable to modifications. The child should not be involved in a rancorous meeting with a teacher who is unwilling to consider any changes.

Obtaining an IEP that attempts to meet the child's needs for that year in a reasonable way is a very positive accomplishment. However, all parties need to view it as a best guess for what will benefit the child. If something is not working, the plan should be revisited and revised. Parents need to let the teacher have flexibility to try things and flexibility to fail. There are no certain ways of ensuring success with gifted children, but a positive plan developed by all parties is a wonderful start.

Meet with the Principal

If, on the other hand, parents approach a teacher and receive an absolute refusal to consider modifications, or if the teacher has been generally reluctant to make agreed-upon changes over several months, it is time to contact the principal. Principals vary in their willingness to support parents when there is parent-teacher friction. The best principals will try to make everyone happy, either working for a compromise or considering the child's placement with another teacher. Although principals today tend not to rule with an iron hand (site-based committees and teachers have some decision-making power these days), they are still the most powerful individuals within their schools and have the most influence. If a principal is willing to accommodate a child's needs, he or she often knows about many options that might be available within the school. For example, the principal might be able to choose a teacher whose strengths and interests are compatible with those of the child. Where a principal is willing to get involved, the child has an important ally.

Consult Counselors, School Psychologists, and G/T Coordinators

Counselors and school psychologists usually are less influential than teachers and principals. They can offer input but generally do not make binding decisions about what will happen in the classroom. Gifted program coordinators, likewise, can only offer enrichment opportunities, brief pull-out options, or ideas for teachers, but they cannot determine classroom modifications such as single-subject acceleration or a full-grade skip, though they may recommend such options to the principal.

Consider Involving District Personnel

If the teacher and principal have shown no support for accommodations for the child, it is time for parents to contact district personnel. We have seen cases of teachers stubbornly asserting that a child has no special needs and of principals supporting them. Some principals will blatantly admit that they are uncomfortable with giftedness, and an occasional principal will declare that all children are gifted, effectively blocking most accommodations.

The school districts that we have dealt with all acknowledge responsibility for gifted students, but they are usually reluctant to bring any considerable, immediate pressure to bear on a principal who is reluctant to comply. If parent complaints accumulate, however, they might make a difference in the results of the next periodic evaluation that the principal undergoes, but district involvement is not likely to be swift and decisive. Immediate help occurs only where there are strict laws and rules in place which outline specific services that are mandated for the gifted. School districts do not want lawsuits. Unfortunately, for most of us residing in states with softer mandates regarding the education of gifted students, district administrators will not always help us to solve our immediate problems.

District-level personnel can help in another way, however. Usually privy to what is going on in the various schools in the district, they can suggest school choices. They know which principals support gifted children, which ones have a background in gifted education, which ones are more flexible, and which are likely to accommodate parents in this situation. They can inform parents of special program options and provide test scores from various schools. They know where the math teacher works who has taught the district's best mathematicians. When parents have a serious need, district personnel often have some ideas, if parents approach them in a positive, problem-solving manner.

Pursue Committee Membership When You Have Extra Time

Some parents have sought membership in school committees, hoping to support relatively quick changes in their child's classroom via changes in school policy. Although there is an immense need for schools across the country to better accommodate gifted students, committee membership tends to produce only small improvements in policy, which are often abandoned once the individuals who propose the changes leave the committee. Furthermore, committee decisions are rarely binding; they usually address goals but have no real clout. Making a difference in this way is important, but it is better to address the pressing needs of a child in a current classroom more directly.

I spent a considerable amount of time on gifted committees, but my time within the school district was best spent helping to organize a charter school. Committee work was time-consuming, filled with the frustration of never having a real mandate for gifted education (some states have stronger laws), and seemed to produce so little. Once, I served on a middle school talented and gifted committee that met simply to exchange ideas. Asked to attend by the principal, I agreed because the school's gifted accommodations were so poor. At one meeting, I broached the subject of engaging gifted students through abstract reasoning. The principal responded that this was impossible because the majority of middle school students had not matured sufficiently for their abstract reasoning ability to be in place. When I asked, "But what about the children who *can* reason abstractly?" I was given a blank look. School personnel were committed to hands-on instruction, concrete learning, and an avoidance of abstraction!

One small committee success that I recall was being on an elementary school improvement team and proposing a school goal to modify curriculum in one subject area within the classroom for each identified gifted student. The goal was approved because it was combined with a similar goal for developmentally disabled students, and educators at the time liked the idea of heterogeneous classrooms in which students had unusual needs met through individualization. The committee also passed a third achievement goal that year for *all* students. An advantage of the goal for the gifted was that teachers had to make a plan to enrich or accelerate curriculum by October 1st of each year, effectively forcing some planning for each gifted child. The next year, the committee agreed to extend the goal to "all academic areas necessary," and the resulting procedure made a difference for a few years. Teachers filled out brief IEPs for each gifted child by October 1st. Interestingly, there was considerable resistance from the teachers the first year because there were three goals passed and the teachers expected only one general "achievement" goal. We were asking too much of them. Yet it was clear that just a single school goal relating only to gifted children would never have been passed. Unfortunately, the process was ended due to lack of support in the building less than a decade later.

Over two decades, I have seen our public school district begin three different district-level gifted committees in succession. Each was charged with the responsibility of defining *giftedness*, determining the needs of gifted students, and finding ways that schools could meet these needs. Each committee took considerable time to create a body of work, which was largely recreated by the next group. When I worked with the second of the three committees, our efforts resulted in large notebooks of good ideas sent to each school. Yet today, G/T services in our district remain largely voluntary, vary considerably with each school, and are subject mostly to mandates to identify and count the students.

What was most apparent from that committee work was the feeling of frustration that parents had. Some came to our meetings saying that they had chosen our school district after reading district literature about gifted programs. "But now that we're here, we see there is nothing!" many said. Like others in the gifted education field, I've tempered my optimism that things will change significantly, short of a massive change in laws at the state level.

Some states enjoy very strong legal mandates, including gifted children under laws covering all special needs children. However, in states less supportive of gifted students, parent advocates are sorely needed to strengthen state laws and teacher training requirements. The Hoagies Gifted Education Page (www.hoagiesgifted.org) offers basic information about state mandates, identification requirements, IEPs, etc. Links to state organizations in the United States and also gifted organizations in some foreign countries can clarify specific policies.

When Do We Give Up?

When the classroom situation remains inadequate, the teacher is defensive, the child is unhappy, the principal offers no reasonable alternatives, and the district will not help, it is best to find another placement for the child. At this point, we must set aside our personal need to fight injustice and to insist that the school meet its ethical (and possibly legal) responsibility to educate a gifted child adequately. Why? Because resistant teachers rarely respond appropriately when pressure is applied, and sensitive gifted children are easily damaged. Parents encountering such a situation must act first to protect the child. That was the case with Tyrell.

Tyrell's parents contacted us because their nine-year-old son refused to go to school and had been at home for the past month. The family had relocated to a neighboring state for the purpose of placing Tyrell in a public Extended Learning program that would, ostensibly, meet his needs as a gifted student. What he experienced, however, was a program with extensive drill and practice (which he did not need) and mind-numbing homework that took him three to four hours a night to complete. The program seemed to have both gifted and high-achieving students, as well as a teacher dedicated to making the students work *very hard*. Tyrell had been accelerated to the fourth grade from second grade and had earned virtually all A's in the first half of the year. However, in January, he had had enough and refused to attend.

A sensitive, sometimes anxious boy, Tyrell had gone from loving school to being school phobic. He had a history of chronic ear infections, as well as asthma, allergies, and hypersensitive hearing. A child who refused to go to movies without ear protection, he was a member of a large, noisy class with a teacher who yelled frequently when students misbehaved. She had difficulty controlling classroom behavior and seemed pushed to the limit. Sometimes she didn't appear to enjoy teaching children this young, saying that she had formerly taught a higher grade level. Tyrell struggled with handwriting and was slower than others completing paper-and-pencil tasks (no doubt adding to his homework time). He had difficulty working in the noisy classroom and, at times, missed recesses finishing written work.

When Tyrell arrived for the testing, which his parents requested to clarify his needs, he seemed anxious but was soon smiling and talkative. When topics were broached in conversation, he spoke in a happy, animated manner. However, when asked about school, his anxiety increased dramatically. He began to stutter as he spoke about his teacher yelling, his class becoming unruly, the noise in the classroom, and his difficulty working in that environment. Only as we became involved in other activities did he appear calmer.

Tyrell's parents had tried to talk with the school about modifying their son's program. He did not need all of the required drill and practice and would have benefited greatly from reduced writing assignments, emphasizing quality over quantity. He needed a quiet place to work, and his parents had asked if he could go to the library if he became overstimulated. All of these requests were initially denied before Tyrell was brought to the GDC. The teacher seemed defensive and resistant to conversation with his parents. Both the school and a private psychologist who had worked with Tyrell were waiting for our recommendations before deciding what to do next.

Based on his test results, we felt that Tyrell needed a full-time gifted program with a small class size and a plan to accommodate both his sensory processing deficits and his giftedness. Under no circumstances did we think that he should return to his previous classroom because it was overstimulating and extremely stressful for him. Because there was no classroom appropriate for his full-time placement, we suggested a home-based teacher for half of each day (school districts will sometimes provide these), with part-time placement in another, gentler teacher's classroom to enable Tyrell to interact with his friends (several important friendships had been made with other gifted boys, and he missed his friends terribly). By reducing drill and repetition, Tyrell would be able to complete most academic work in half of the day. Because he was very advanced in math, we suggested a computer-based math instruction program from a university that could be done with the help of the home-based teacher. If Tyrell became overstimulated and anxious at school (common in children with sensory processing issues), he could be allowed to go to the library. He was a responsible boy who would use his time wisely. We suggested that he do any writing on a word processor and wear headphones to reduce noise; we also advised that he learn some relaxation techniques.

When Tyrell's parents returned with our recommendations, school personnel refused to provide a home-based teacher and offered to put Tyrell back into the same classroom, but with an IEP. His parents were worried about this offer and called to ask our opinion. Given Tyrell's extreme anxiety about his school situation and the fact that the teacher was stressed herself and had been resistant to accommodations, this was not a situation that we could recommend. Instead, we suggested further negotiations with the school for other options, and we recommended connecting with an expert in the home schooling of gifted children until another placement could be found.

Tyrell's parents acted appropriately when they allowed him to stay at home while they sought outside help. They had noted his increasing calmness after time at home following a stressful climax of tension in the classroom. Their fears about his returning to his previous classroom were absolutely justified. Though we would like a simple solution in such situations, capitulating to the school's plan was not the best answer. We have seen children damaged so severely by their school experiences that counseling and considerable time were necessary to help them. When parents pull a child out of school suddenly, they are usually correct about the need to do so.

Interviewing Principals and Choosing a School

Living in a small Texas town with his wife and two gifted children, a father was concerned about having no schools for the gifted and no gifted program options as he saw them for his children. Realizing his dilemma, I explained ways that he might address his children's lack of challenge in school—how he might visit the schools in his area, meet with principals, and talk about how his children's needs might be met in each school in order to choose the best placement for them. He looked at me and said, "*You* might be able to do that, but I wouldn't know where to start." This is for all of the parents who feel that they wouldn't know where to start.

It is often difficult to modify poor school situations, but we can always take a proactive approach to the education of gifted children. Even though most communities lack full-time, self-contained schools for the gifted, many have excellent, flexible teachers and at least some programs that might be good placements for gifted students. Across the country, there is movement within public school districts to offer *schools of choice*: alternative schools, magnet schools, and charter schools. The neighborhood school is not the only choice any more, but even neighborhood schools are trying to develop unique programs to compete with the alternative schools.

Our school district publishes a guide to school choices with a brief summary about each school's focus and offerings. Parents can request several choices for the coming year by a deadline in February and be advised of admission possibilities. Though many schools impose a lottery system because requests outnumber openings, the opportunity for real choice should not be ignored. We have noted that it is generally easier to find a more appropriate teacher or school for a child than to effect substantial change in the child's current inadequate program.

If any school appears attractive, it is important to meet with school personnel and learn more about it. When principals are willing to meet or speak on the phone about accommodating an unusual child, it is a very good sign that they value the differential needs of the gifted. Principals vary enormously in their knowledge of giftedness, appreciation of learning differences, willingness to suggest teachers and appropriate options, and flexibility. Such conversations are very revealing. Does the principal automatically begin thinking of ways to meet the child's needs in his or her school? Is there willingness to set aside usual policy in placing a child? Will the principal allow placement at the level of the child's mastery?

In middle schools, can the student study at various grade levels, as needed, or must he or she stay with age peers in block-scheduled classes? In high schools, can the gifted student skip one or more entry-level courses for freshmen or start with Advanced Placement courses in an academic subject area in which he or she is particularly advanced? Can a child visit the program, either the classroom of the most appropriate elementary teacher (in the principal's view) or, in middle or high school, classes in favorite subject areas? The budding high school scientist may want to visit the school's best teachers of chemistry, biology, and physics, whereas the advanced writer may want to view AP English. Given such options, families can choose the most flexible, supportive program for a particular gifted child and have a better chance (nothing's perfect) of a successful placement.

Home Schooling

When the options are simply unacceptable within the local schools, families are increasingly turning to home schooling. A 1996 Florida Education Department survey found that 61% of parents ranked dissatisfaction with public school environment and instruction as the foremost reason for home schooling, beyond religion.[1] A *Mensa Research Journal* article, titled "What Are Four Myths about Home Schooling?" notes that one unique aspect of the home school community is its demographic diversity, which includes most races, religions, socio-economic groups, and political viewpoints.[2] Home schooled students are doing as well or better than publicly schooled peers, and they no longer surprise critics when they are accepted to Ivy League universities. Likewise, home schooling does not produce social misfits—children are involved in numerous activities outside of the home with peers, children of different ages, and adults. Nor does home schooling fail to prepare children to be good citizens.

A 2007 study by Jones and Gloeckner of first-year college performance of students who were home schooled concluded: "Although not statistically significant, the average first-year GPAs, credits earned in the first year, ACT Composite test scores, and ACT English, Mathematics, Reading, and Science and Reasoning subtests for home school graduates were all higher than traditional high school graduates."[3] Brian D. Ray, of the National Home Education Research Institute, examines the growth and success of home schooling as an educational option.[4] He notes that home schooling has grown dramatically—only about 13,000 students (grades K-12) were home schooled in the early 1970s, but an estimated 1.9 to 2.4 million K-12 students were home schooled during the 2005-2006 school year. Citing his 1997 study of standardized achievement test scores for home-educated students, Ray reports that average scores for all areas of the tests ranged from the 81st to the 87th percentile. He reports a similar nationwide U.S. study by Rudner (1999) that yielded achievement scores from the 62nd to the 91st percentile, with most scores clustering between the 75th and 85th percentiles. Key factors in the success of home schooled students appear to include customization or individualization of curriculum for each student, increased feedback to the student, holding high and reasonable expectations of students, emphasis on direct instruction by a teacher, and increased academic learning time.

Home schooling is especially suited to children with unusual needs. Not only can the topics of study be chosen and the appropriate level offered, but instructional pace can be adjusted for the accelerated learner, an almost impossible element to modify within typical schools.

Kathi Kearney, a longtime consultant to gifted home schooling families in New England, explains that home schooling is growing at a phenomenal rate for gifted students as public schools continue to offer less-than-optimal support for gifted learning needs. Although the prospect seems daunting to many parents, home schooling offers freedom available nowhere else. Kearney notes that there are generally at least two home schooling organizations in every state: a secular group and a

Christian group. State organizations are further affiliated with numerous support groups. Parents considering the prospect of home schooling are wise to contact these groups, which offer both support and information about resources available in the area. The groups are knowledgeable about state laws and are usually superior to local school district offices in interpreting them. Kearney compiled many of the resources for this book. Parents can find her articles, annotated bibliographies, and resource lists on various websites—the Hoagies Gifted Education Page, GT-CyberSource, and The Hollingworth Center for Highly Gifted Children (a support group that she started), all of which can be found in the For Further Reading section at the end of this chapter.

A tester, teacher of the gifted and curriculum developer, Kearney is experienced in developing programs for gifted students that are sensitive to their strengths and weaknesses, learning preferences, and level of giftedness. However, she also agrees that some gifted children may lay waste to the best planned curricula as they master concepts far more quickly than anticipated.

Kearney's experience with families shows that home schooling offers the ultimate educational choice. The parents of one large home schooled family (they had five children who were all teenagers at the same time) created a "grand plan" for each of their children.[5] Designed to meet the unique needs of each child, the plan contained specific goals to be met, but within a timeframe chosen by each child. The children met their goals at various times, ranging from a typical number of years in school to very few. The students in the family determined their own rate of acceleration.

Home schooling allows families to view education in very atypical ways and consider possibilities that do not occur to most. Kearney recalls an eight-year-old girl who quickly accelerated in elementary school yet was frustrated in her efforts to learn what she wanted. The little girl hoped to learn French, which was not offered at the elementary level in her school district. Her mother, a college student, suggested that she study the language on her own or take a high school correspondence course (through the University of Nebraska Independent Study High School). Though the girl was willing to do either of these things, she asked if it wouldn't be better to take the course with other people so that she could speak with them in French. Why couldn't she go with her mother to college and take a course there? This initiated a discussion about the difference between courses at different levels (i.e., the difference between an elementary-level course versus a college-level one), and the girl's mother explained that courses at higher levels progress more quickly. The little girl pondered this and concluded that if all of the beginning French courses started at the same level but progressed at different rates, then why couldn't she take one that progressed quickly? In the end, the college that her mother attended allowed this girl to take beginning French, and she did well. This launched a series of college courses that the little girl loved.

Because gifted students can become so disenchanted with learning in school before home schooling is even attempted, can they become too jaded to be home schooled successfully? Kearney notes that it is not uncommon for new home schooling families to need a period of "deschooling" before they can actually begin. As the term suggests, some children need an extended vacation from school and the situations that were oppressive for them. They need time to rekindle their inborn, natural curiosity and regain their love of learning. This is not surprising, as parents, too, need time to come to the realization that school is not likely to meet a child's needs, and home schooling may be the only reasonable alternative.

Jean, a mother of three, stands out as an advocate because she consistently relied on her own instincts, research, and home schooling efforts to meet the needs of her children. When her eldest child, a son, was experiencing boredom and stress at school, the school offered to evaluate him. Administration of the WISC-III yielded a Full Scale IQ score of 124; however, his mother questioned this score. She had received considerable information and support from other parents of gifted children on the Internet, and she used this to accurately diagnose higher ability. In fact, Jean correctly thought, from her reading, that her children were all highly gifted and suffered from ADHD. When she received no support from anyone locally, she packed the kids into the car and drove them to Colorado to have them all tested at the Gifted Development Center. We absolutely agreed with her diagnoses and were able to offer additional suggestions.

Jean and her husband removed their son from school after first grade, realizing that public school was not going to be a successful placement for him. Although she became a successful home schooling mom of her three children, she admits that a period of deschooling was necessary for her eldest. He was "too sensitive for that environment—overwhelmed, distracted, upset by other kids' actions and inabilities." His love of learning was disappearing, and he had developed nervous habits, tics, and stomachaches. Once removed from public school, these symptoms ceased, and he became curious again. Because he was positive for ADHD, exhibiting both symptoms of Inattention and Hyperactivity/Impulsivity, home schooling was ideal; his mother could make sure that he was spending most of his time with new, novel material and progressing quickly. He could move ahead as soon as he mastered concepts. This minimized attentional deficits by emphasizing high-interest material that was more engaging.

Because Jean's son at age nine earned a Stanford-Binet, Form L-M IQ score of 152, she planned significant acceleration. With achievement scores in the 150s as well, it was clear that this boy was being well-challenged in his home schooling program.

For many parents, home schooling offers the option of a more child-centered program, emphasizing the individual needs of the child over learning for the purpose of satisfying district or state standards. Lisa Rivero writes in "Progressive Digressions: Home Schooling for Self-Actualization" that home schooling need not be "school at home," which attempts to duplicate classroom education in the home through the use of packaged curricula, online coursework, and classroom-like time schedules and graded assignments.[6] Home schooled children can study what interests them most and, by doing so, learn valuable research skills.

Home schooling can take many forms, such as classical education, unit studies or theme studies, or unschooling. Although many families begin with a school-like model, parents such as Kathleen, a home schooling parent of two, find this model lacking.

> *The approach that we began using initially with home schooling (more of a formal curriculum) did not work with my gifted children. Their drive to learn about what interests them is so strong that to force a curriculum changes who they are as learners. We have had to adjust our thinking to a place where their sense of self is being served by how they are learning...* (Rivero, 2007, p. 50).

Rivero argues that home schooling can be creative learning, which is "primarily interest-based rather than curriculum-based and is beyond the scope and sequence of our traditional ideas of grade-level education" (2007, p. 49). She cites Deirdre Lovecky's notion that such learning is "highly individualistic and idiosyncratic, as the learner follows internal rather than external cues and pursues a topic not for extrinsic rewards but for intrinsic closure" (p. 50). Divergent thinking occurs, with the child often learning by immersion, "wallowing in a topic and all the resultant tangents until the learner reaches a 'point of vanishing interest'" (p. 50). Rivero writes, "While we need not, and perhaps should not, avoid all formal instruction for young children, we can work to provide more of a balance between true self-directed learning and teacher- or parent-directed learning" (p. 51).

Home schooling can reflect the philosophical views of the family and whatever structure fits best. Some home schoolers begin with only partial home schooling, sending the child to school for part of the day for certain subjects, perhaps art, music, physical education, and anything that parents think the school does well. Subjects saved for home school might include those in which the child is advanced and needs accelerated instruction, or topics that would benefit from outside experiences, programs, or mentors. Some families home school only temporarily for a variety of reasons: until a more supportive teacher is available, while therapeutic interventions are being done (occupational or vision therapy, for example, can require considerable daily practice), or when relocation initially restricts program availability. When working with gifted children, few families spend more than a few hours a day home schooling and weave much of their educational effort into typical daily activities. In fact, many parents are surprised at how their children have more free time when they begin home schooling. They cover subjects more quickly and have time for other pursuits like music, art, drama, or hobbies.

Home schooling is the default option—the option that most parents have when all other alternatives fail. But today, thanks in part to the college entrance and college achievement successes of so many home schooled students, it is now regarded with new respect as a desirable educational option.

Choices in Advocacy

Parents should trust themselves to assess the level and urgency of their child's needs, and they can wisely consider various alternatives. Sometimes the best choice is to work with the school and the current teacher to provide accommodations; sometimes it is to move to another classroom, grade, or an entirely different school; and sometimes it is best to remove a child from school altogether. There is no benefit to teaching a child to graciously accept being held back.

Most parents choose to keep their gifted children in school, and it is often possible to support a reasonable education there, as did one couple who were excellent advocates for their two daughters. Estella and Reynaldo first learned to advocate for their daughter with Asperger Syndrome, whom they realized would not have a reasonable education—regardless of the support of law—without their involvement. Having educated themselves as fully as possible about her needs and having learned to advocate successfully for her, they then began to advocate for their younger, highly gifted daughter. They have learned some interesting lessons.

First, they realized the need to become experts about their daughters' needs. They had both girls individually assessed and learned what they could from professionals. They participated in support groups and read the latest books available. They understood that teachers also needed help in learning about Asperger Syndrome and high levels of giftedness (which both girls likely possess). However, they felt that teacher in-services were not especially effective. Reynaldo noted that teachers need access to information and expert advice, but that they also need "buy in." The teachers appreciated help more when the expert met directly with them, and they could then formulate ideas for working with the child.

Reynaldo and Estella have asked for many things from their schools, but they have also been helpful members of school communities, willing to volunteer their time and energy when needed. They have made every effort to approach school personnel with courtesy and patience, knowing that some of their requests may require processing time. I attended a meeting of teachers, the principal, and a counselor with them to discuss the grade acceleration of one daughter. They asked me to explain testing results and provide more general information as needed. While the meeting produced the expected concerns from staff about the child's social development being hampered, Estella and Reynaldo's kind, reasonable approach allowed school personnel, who were also kind and reasonable people, to consider the issues without prejudice and to decide what would be best for the child. Although some teachers still had reservations, a plan was made to allow the girl to visit an accelerated classroom and have contact with the counselor about her experience.

Estella and Reynaldo's daughter did accelerate, found skipping a grade a relative non-issue (as it usually is for children who are bored and asking for more challenge), and is happier now in her new classroom.

Especially satisfying to her recently was an advanced rocks and minerals project that involved crystal structures that she grew and constructed with a Zometool kit. Her new teacher provided special support for this project. He even invited several younger gifted children who had an interest in crystals to his classroom to see her models.

For Further Reading

Books and Articles

Gilman, B. J. (2008). *Challenging highly gifted learners.* Waco, TX: Prufrock Press.

LaBonte, K., & Russell, C. (1999, Spring/Summer). Preparing for and holding an effective school meeting, *Highly Gifted Children, 12*(4).

Lloyd, M. P. (1999, Winter). The tea and terrorist society: Parent advocacy at the district level. *Highly Gifted Children, 12*(3). Also available at www.gt-cybersource.org/ =Record.aspx?NavID=&rid=11228

Neville-Garrison, C. M. (1997, Spring). Portfolio: An effective way to present your child to the school. *Highly Gifted Children, 11*(1). Also available at www.gt-cybersource.org/Record.aspx?NavID=&rid=11263

Rivero, L. (2002). *Creative home schooling: A resource guide for smart families.* Scottsdale, AZ: Great Potential Press

Rogers, K. B. (2002). *Re-forming gifted education: How parents and teachers can match the program to the child.* Scottsdale, AZ: Great Potential Press.

Ruf, D. L. (2005). *Losing our minds: Gifted children left behind.* Scottsdale, AZ: Great Potential Press.

Websites

Davidson Institute for Talent Development
www.ditd.org

GT-CyberSource (includes a large archive of articles)
www.gt-cybersource.org/ReadArticleNew.aspx

Hoagies' Gifted Education Page: Gifted Advocacy (includes a comprehensive selection of articles)
www.hoagiesgifted.com/advocacy.htm

Hoagies' Gifted Education Page: Home Schooling the Gifted Child (information on all aspects of home schooling)
www.hoagiesgifted.org/home_sc.htm

Hoagies' Gifted Education Page: Home Schooling Gifted Children (recommended books)
www.hoagiesgifted.org/home_school.htm

The Hollingworth Center for Highly Gifted Children
www.hollingworth.org

Chapter 9
Teachers of the Gifted

What are the qualities that define a wonderful teacher of gifted children? Parents seeking to ensure a good classroom placement for a gifted child naturally hope to find a teacher who will see the child's strengths and nurture them in a way that allows for true growth. Likewise, teachers who want to truly support a gifted student hope to find strategies that aid in planning and programming, dealing with social and emotional issues, and interacting with parents and fellow teachers to meet needs. Many of the children profiled in this book had negative experiences with teachers at some point, yet wonderful teachers of the gifted do inspire such children and change their lives in profound ways.

Elementary school teachers, who generally have the child for all academic subjects for a full school year, can be pivotal people in the child's life. But even in middle and high schools, where a student has multiple teachers, finding teachers who have high academic standards and who support advanced students is important to gifted students' continued motivation to learn.

Having a teacher who values teaching gifted students and knows how to teach them successfully is invaluable. Teachers have different personalities, backgrounds, and strengths; some are known to be kind and supportive, and some are especially effective with children who struggle. What kind of teacher best supports a gifted child? Below are profiles of some excellent teachers for gifted children who offer their experience and insights about how best to teach these students.

Lin Greene: Teaching Gifted Elementary Students

Youthful and spirited, Lin Greene's presence belies her 31 years of experience as an elementary school educator. In 1994, we co-authored an article in the journal *Understanding Our Gifted* titled "Challenging Ben," about individualizing a second-grade curriculum for a profoundly gifted child. Recently retired, Greene has an impressive record of meeting the needs of a variety of children in her classrooms, including gifted children within a heterogeneous classroom. She strongly believes in empowering children to set goals for themselves and become independent learners.

Make a Written Plan

Lin Greene's first step to accommodate a gifted child in her classroom was to make an overall written plan. The plan, however brief, requires careful consideration of the child's learning needs at the beginning of the year and throughout the time spent in her class. Better than simply making multiple, unrelated efforts to enrich, the plan acknowledges that a child will come into the classroom with certain knowledge in every subject and will need to make appropriate progress during the year in all academic areas. Greene believes that it is important to start early in making the plan. Ideally, she believes that the teacher should sit down with the parents even before school starts. Parents have unique knowledge of their child and can provide insight into the child's strengths (e.g., advanced reading or math skills, or high-level knowledge and interest in science), as well as discuss areas that need improvement (e.g., organizational skills such as "follow through," slowness or difficulty with handwriting, poor knowledge of math facts, or a significant learning disability).

Next, Greene suggests that the teacher and parents meet a month later to finalize the plan. By this time, the teacher has had time to assess the child's strengths and weaknesses and get better acquainted with the child. In addition, the teacher now knows the options to be offered during the year within the school that may not have been finalized prior to the start of school. For example, a local Toastmasters group may be willing to provide a weekly opportunity for students to learn the art of public speaking, or a retired math teacher may agree to serve as a mentor.

Once the needs and options are clear, the parents and teacher should agree to an overall plan for the year—but meet at least quarterly to review it. Things can change. An initial plan can prove insufficiently interesting to the child, or a program that the teacher thought would be available may not have materialized. Quarterly meetings allow the teacher to "stay on the same page with the parent." Greene found that some parents would come in and talk with her, but others felt that they were intruding or simply didn't have the time. "Please schedule it," she advises. Then everyone knows what the child is doing and how the child is progressing. She also agrees that it is important to include the child when possible, especially if the child is verbal. A gifted kindergartener might find this difficult, but most gifted second graders can add important information to the planning process that adults cannot provide.

Look for an Advanced Placement in a Subject of Strength

"One thing I like to do is see if another class besides the general classroom will fit the gifted child," Greene advises. Perhaps the child can be placed in a higher grade level for math or participate in a more advanced reading group. Is the child mature enough to handle leaving the classroom and coming back in? Since many plans are best implemented with the child going alone from the home classroom to another, teachers don't want to lose the child going or coming. At seven years of age, that's important! Yet most gifted second graders view such an opportunity as a welcome challenge and handle the responsibility beautifully, even remembering when it's time to leave without being reminded.

Next, make compromises with the other teacher. Greene always believed that it was especially helpful to let higher-grade-level teachers know that she was available to help if one of their students needed remediation. She could offer to take such a child into her classroom for extra help. This allowed her to help a teacher whom she might at another time need to ask to take a gifted child who needed acceleration. Likewise, Greene was always willing to take accelerated younger children into her own class. However, she admits this is not a normal occurrence for many teachers. Because the teacher is ultimately responsible for every child in the classroom—whether the child leaves or not—taking on one more can seem daunting. "You already have 30 children; now you have 31," Greene explains, and the receiving teacher must accept two additional parents and another teacher checking on how she or he is doing with the child. This may be more than the teacher wants to do. However, Greene concludes that such placements are worth pursuing. "You have to make the compromises if you're the teacher sending the child, but I think it's good for the child's morale. They will put up with a lot if they feel that their needs are being met."

Once placement in another classroom has been arranged, Greene, as the general homeroom teacher, considered what she needed to teach the child in preparation for the new classroom placement. Whether it's cursive writing, multiplication facts, long division, or regrouping, Greene wanted to ensure that the child knew all of the entry-level tasks that the other teacher's class already knew. "You can teach those tasks to a gifted child quickly. Of course," she admits, "there is no extra time to do this." It must be done during the lunch hour or recess, and the gifted student may be running up at inopportune moments asking for another long multiplication problem during social studies. However, Greene concludes, "Be flexible enough to do that because it's going to be so helpful to them."

She feels that it's important to help a gifted child to feel good about where he or she is going and the results that are happening—how the student is moving along—because so many of the problems occur when gifted students see themselves stagnating, unable to use any of the talents that they have. "Usually a gifted child has one area—math, reading, writing—that you can facilitate the extension of right away in September. It's not something you have to spend weeks on; they can go immediately."

What Level of Advanced Work Does the Child Need?

Greene admits that it was helpful to her in making placement decisions to have taught all of the elementary grades, one through six, during her career. She learned the academic levels of children beginning each grade and adds that those are quite different from the levels at which students finish the year. Greene believes that understanding where kids normally are at different grade levels also improves a teacher's willingness to let a child accelerate when appropriate. Such a decision is much more difficult for the teacher who has taught only one grade level for many years.

In general, Greene feels that a gifted second grader can fit into a third-grade class or, if he or she is quite advanced, a fourth-grade class at the beginning of the year. The first few months of each school year include considerable review; this can help the very advanced accelerating student ensure coverage of previous material. She adds that gifted students are usually more than willing to do any additional work needed. "They're even anxious to take home homework—if it's on their level."

Consider Additional Opportunities

After initial accelerated placements are made, Greene advises looking for any appropriate programs that may become available: Science Fair, dance classes, a mentor, etc. "Have your antennas up for anything said in a staff meeting that might be helpful to your child." Perhaps there is an elderly person who is willing to donate time mentoring a child in geography. "You have to be the first to sign the paper. If you don't, your child misses out." With such opportunities, a teacher has to be thinking about all of the children in the classroom.

Be Aware of Social and Emotional Issues

Unfortunately, Greene adds, many teachers feel that gifted children don't need any help. They are "already above where everybody else is at the start. They're already there." Yet she insists that if teachers merely give them more of the same classwork to do, "It's just death for a gifted child. They may start to act out, if they tend toward that anyway, or proclaim loudly how 'bored' they are. This can make the other children wonder about the classroom activity they had thought was fun."

Greene believes that teachers may also not realize how much gifted children want to be accepted by the other students in the room. These are the children that they went to kindergarten with. "This is their class." The gifted child sometimes wants to run around and do silly things on the playground, but then also likes to work on long division!

Greene adds, "The class itself wants to know that this child is working, too, because they feel they are always working. For them, everything is hard; to the gifted child, hardly anything is hard." Unless the teacher teaches at the appropriate level for that gifted child, nothing will be challenging. It is the teacher's responsibility to make the gifted child struggle, think, have meaningful homework, and be expected to really work in class. The class wants to know that this will happen, too. Greene feels that this is where the teacher's expertise in devising appropriate accommodations is particularly useful.

Providing direct instruction to the gifted child in what to say to others can be beneficial as well. For example, Greene taught gifted students that when classmates ask for help, the gifted children should ask questions instead of simply giving answers. "Don't assume these children know what to say because they talk to the teacher on an adult level," she cautions, "because their emotions and social skills are not at that level."

If the gifted students visit another classroom for advanced instruction in a subject, teachers should train them in what to do when they come back from the upper-level classroom. What do they do with that wonderful thing they've made? Classmates may be jealous if gifted children rush to share their experiences. Greene believes in teaching gifted children to come in appropriately, acting respectful. She tells teachers to advise them not to share their creations immediately as they come in the door, but to know that there will be a time to share later. Gifted kids are good at telling time and waiting. Right after lunch is a great time to share; they can count on it every day. In fact, Greene encouraged them to share on a regular basis; otherwise, the other children may think that the gifted kids just went to play! It is also a time to acknowledge what the gifted child has accomplished. "Second graders like to see a page of note taking or long division. Wow!" Everyone benefits from the sharing of praise.

Don't Rely on the Gifted Program

Greene cautions that some children have been told at home that everything in the regular classroom will just have to be endured; it will be "boring" and they're not supposed to like it, but things will be better once the "gifted program" starts. In truth, parents have little idea of what will happen in the gifted program or what a minimal role (in most schools) it is likely to play in their child's programming. The reality is that most gifted children spend the majority of their time in the regular classroom, with only minimal and part-time accommodations through the gifted program. Moreover, the gifted program is highly dependent on current funding and rarely provides any continuity of educational goals for the child from one year to another. The primary responsibility for gifted accommodations almost always falls to the regular classroom teacher. "That's where the conference at the beginning really helps," Greene says. "A positive attitude from the parents is vital to a successful year [in the regular classroom]."

Identify Gifted Children in the Classroom

Greene also warns that initial identification for the gifted program doesn't always happen quickly. "By the time they test them, it's nearly spring! If you've been there more than one year, you know you can't wait." Asking the assistance of a more experienced teacher can help find children who have not yet been identified, including some who have not been brought to the teacher's attention by parents. Greene liked to get a sample of the children's writing, see what comments they make, and discover what their thought processes are. "If they're thinking that many steps beyond the normal seven-year-old, let's see what they can really do!" she advises. Give them an assignment that will reveal their abilities; see if they'll pick up on it. An experienced teacher learns the most from informal, ongoing assessment within the classroom.

However, Greene cautions, "If the child is used to always having to fit in and you ask for them to write a couple of sentences, that may be all that they write." There's also the gifted child who won't write anything. Some gifted students may have difficulty determining the level at which to respond, perceiving that their best work is not what is being requested. "Assessment at the beginning of the year is tricky at best, but well worth the extra effort," Greene concludes.

Teach Research Skills and Independent Learning

When the needs of gifted children have been identified and some programming is in place, the teacher can begin to develop other skills that support their learning. For example, "Gifted children can really get their teeth into research," notes Greene. Gifted second graders can actually search out information, not just regurgitate it. Before the Internet, one had to know alphabetical order to look things up in encyclopedias. Gifted students already know alphabetical order; it's easy to teach them how to use the encyclopedia to research information. "Here's where you can really integrate the child's work with what's happening in the general classroom." Allow them to go to the library by themselves, look up something by themselves, and then come back with a written product. If given small amounts of instruction, they can do it. They love it.

"The class is learning about the Aurora Borealis. You weren't even going to expand on it except to say these are the Northern Lights; they look like ribbons of color in the sky." The gifted child takes notes on note cards and teaches the class about the Aurora Borealis with a passion! This not only teaches the research skills which gifted students enjoy learning, but also goal setting and independent learning. "I want everybody in my class to be independent to whatever level that is. For some, it's to use the tape dispenser or stapler because they're not allowed to use it at home." The gifted child can do so much more.

"When a child shares his or her cards, artwork, and sits in the chair where the teacher sits, it shows that he or she is respected by the teacher and has something to offer that they need to listen to—just like everybody else." The feelings and expectations that the teacher has for this child are an essential part of a successful student-teacher relationship. If the teacher feels that this is just another child in his or her harried workload, the child will not work up to potential.

Use Parent Volunteers

Helpful to both the gifted children and the children who struggle were the parent volunteers in Greene's classrooms. They were not counters of papers or folder stuffers or just party helpers; Greene trained them to actually work with the children. "I had some really wonderful volunteers, but not a huge plethora of them. A lot of them went on to be very good at, for instance, creative writing." Greene would train them to work with small creative writing groups, focusing on what to say and how to elicit good questions from the children rather than criticism. "How did you come up with that great idea?" the parent aides would ask, and they, in turn, would teach the children to ask those same types of questions of each other. This would free up the teacher.

Greene planned for the aides to be the ones who would go around, kneel down, and help the child who was stuck. She taught them how to "unstick" the child; then, just before the child was ready for the aide to do the work, the volunteer would move on to help someone else. "I trained them to be little clones of Lin. That was helpful to the gifted child, too."

Avoid Pairing Gifted and Struggling Students for Instruction

Asked about the frequent practice of pairing gifted students with struggling students, Greene recalls that this approach did not work very well in her classroom. First, it could cause a problem because gifted children were held to grade-level work. Second, when the two students were from the same classroom, she felt that the struggling student had to deal with the dilemma of "I live with you, and you're better than I am, and it's embarrassing." She therefore avoided such pairings within the classroom; however, she did find that occasionally having a child come from another classroom to help on the computer, for example, usually worked very well. "They weren't a part of your classroom, so they were like little teachers, and no one was uncomfortable. They could be helpful and didn't put anybody down." When the "Fifth-Grade Buddies" would come to the second-grade classroom for an activity, Greene made sure that gifted children from the fifth grade were paired with the younger gifted children, too. "That made for extra special bonding."

Accommodate Different Classroom Learning Rates

How does speed of learning affect instruction in the classroom? Greene recalls that only about one-third of the students needed significant repetition at her school. The gifted students mastered new concepts right away. "Then you had to risk them being bored because they already had it, while you worked with the average child, who almost knew the concept but was going to lose it right away if it was not reviewed. Some children would not ever learn the task, and you had to move on. That was hard." She further notes, "That's why grouping in math is so important."

When a teacher is not meeting each student's needs while teaching to the entire heterogeneous group, then instruction has to be done differently. Greene once trained her students to move in thirds in math to three centers in the classroom, each providing different elements of math instruction: (1) manipulative work, (2) time with the teacher, and (3) guided practice. As the students came to her center (the teacher center), she provided remediation, practice, or enrichment. It became much easier when the entire team of the four second-grade teachers in the school worked together providing *leveled instruction*. "One teacher took the top 18 of our 100 second graders. They stayed within the math strand being taught but expanded into areas way beyond the rest of the grade level. It was a tremendous help for all of the above-average and gifted students, as well as those needing extra help in just the basic skills."

Be a Strong-Willed Teacher

Asked if good teachers of the gifted need to be fairly strong-willed, confident people, Greene agreed. "That's true; you have to be a little out-of-sync yourself, I think. Most teachers are not like that." She went on to recount her frustration with teachers who refused to take a child for one subject if there were scheduling difficulties. "If I was trying to get them to take a child who was higher in reading and have them read with their class, it would just be incredible that they couldn't make any allowances. I like my schedule, too, but I've taken kids from first grade into my room." How much is scheduling and how much is resistance? "More is just resistance, not a scheduling problem. It happened more than you would like," Greene adds.

What does a teacher do when the higher-grade-level teacher refuses to take an advanced child? "Luckily, I was in a large enough school that if one teacher said no, I could go and ask another one at the same grade level," Greene notes. "They also knew if the child was coming from me, I was still going to be responsible for the child's behavior and make sure rules were obeyed. However, it was an honor to be going to another classroom, so of course my gifted child would want to behave!"

Greene believes that excellent teachers of the gifted, or of any special needs children, must be willing to buck the system. "You don't get help for children who are out-of-sync by following the normal path. When you want to get a child out of Special Ed and they've always been in Special Ed, you have to be willing to stake your reputation on that." Greene feels that teachers should be willing to say, "I think he could handle the Toastmasters group," or "She deserves to be in the Spelling Bee. She can't be the winner because that's the way the rules are, but she's a great speller and deserves to be there." Greene observes that most teachers are more passive than that, and she admits that the unusual request for a child's accommodation "sometimes doesn't make you very popular."

One place where teachers can be strong advocates is in team meetings to plan programs for gifted students. Known by various titles (child resource team, child study team, or some other name), such teams meet with a child's parents for the purpose of deciding future plans for the child at school. Depending on the purpose of the meeting, team members could include two or more teachers, the school nurse or counselor, the school psychologist, and the gifted coordinator or other administrator. Most of these meetings involve children with disabilities; team meetings are rarely called to consider a gifted child.

Greene notes, "I've seen many children's lives helped or hindered by those meetings. You never get together before those meetings to hear what everybody's viewpoint is." Having the child's teacher be a solid advocate is very important, especially since most teachers are not accustomed to offering unusual options to gifted students (e.g., grade acceleration) and may be resistant. The group leader can call an outside expert, if it would be helpful. The Gifted Development Center often sends personnel to such meetings in our area to assist parents and supportive teachers, when requested.

Besides being a staunch advocate for gifted students, what other characteristics contribute to being a good teacher for these children? Some teachers simply are better at working with gifted students than others, and personality styles should mesh. Principals or other administrators can help if they are willing to consider a choice based on the child's needs and personality (different gifted children might be optimally placed with different teachers). For example, Greene notes that while some teachers are better at coddling, she feels that she was not. "I wasn't the nursemaid or grandmotherly type. Both the gifted child and

Special Ed child were challenged in my room. They knew they would have to stretch. And that's a good thing!"

Advice to Parents

Asked what advice she could offer parents, Greene says enthusiastically, "Come in with the positive attitude that the teacher might have something to offer." She admits, "If they come in with no respect for what you've taught or what you might know, it's just human nature—you close your doors to them." Also, it is best *not* to have too specific a program in mind. "When the parents of my students came in with an open mind and a willingness to work with the teacher for the combined benefit of the child, that was the optimum situation. I knew it was going to be a great year."

Advice to Teachers

Greene advises teachers to keep an open mind as well, "because that gifted child has a parent who has been dealing with this challenge from the day he or she started public school. That parent is going to come with important information and a set of 'givens' also." She reminds teachers that just because parents may have had poor experiences in other classrooms, "That doesn't mean they couldn't have a good experience in yours. Start by being as understanding as you can. If the parent is also open, then it is just wonderful."

Asked how to improve gifted education within the public schools, Greene thinks that teachers should be paid for being terrific at what they do. Typically, the only benefit good teachers receive is "harder kids the next year." Greene sees virtually nothing in the system to reward outstanding teaching, especially when compared with private-sector jobs that offer substantial financial incentives for hard work, such as merit-based salary increases and bonuses. In addition, she believes that teachers need more training in gifted education and the experience of teaching at various grade levels to fully understand and guide these out-of-sync students through the educational sequence.

Lin Greene has enjoyed her work with gifted students through the years, watching them progress in their studies and conceptualize in new and interesting ways. She still recalls the little second-grade boy who asked, "You mean when you tell me to do something, I'm supposed to do it? Is that how it works?"

"I said, 'Yes'!" Greene laughs nostalgically.

Sharon Sikora: Teaching the Gifted Middle Schooler

Sharon Sikora is a former science teacher at Summit Middle School, a charter school for students who are seeking a more challenging educational environment (profiled in Chapter 10). The middle school discussion below is based on a personal interview that took place prior to Sikora leaving the school to pursue other aspects of science education.

Having a Ph.D. in Biochemistry, and as a parent of gifted children herself, Sikora was eager to apply her knowledge and teaching experience with college students to high-ability middle schoolers. Here, she describes the challenges that she faced while dealing with an influx of lower-ability students drawn to the school by high state test scores (unfortunately, this charter school must be "open to all," despite its mission), as well as her role in creating a curriculum rigorous enough to withstand the pressures of state assessments with ease. She also shares her views on working with gifted students.

How Does the Range of Student Ability Restrict Teaching?

Sikora's small school of 250 students, which will increase to 300 this year, has faced dramatic changes in the makeup of the student body during its six years of operation. Although the self-selecting school honestly advertises its accelerated curriculum (which overlaps with typical high school offerings) and the high expectations that it has of its students, many families seem to choose the school simply for its high test scores. This has created a difficult situation for students and teachers alike. Some students coming to the school find the work far too challenging and finally leave for placements in more traditional middle school programs. Others struggle but stay, requiring teachers to extend their program downward and increase their teaching skills to include a very different population of learners than the school initially wanted to serve.

Summit has maintained its commitment to the high-end learner by continuing to place children where they need to be and offering unusually advanced coursework where needed. For example, math classes extend through Geometry and Algebra II/Trigonometry, and two students last year took a university correspondence course in pre-calculus. There are two levels of English offered that are considered to be high school level, and science students often place into the tenth-grade Pre-IB (International Baccalaureate) science class at a neighboring high school after completing the program at Summit. Sikora notes that in the first two years of the school's operation, 60% of Summit students placed into that higher-level, tenth-grade Pre-IB class, with 40% placing into the ninth-grade Pre-IB class. Today, however, about one-third place into the tenth-grade Pre-IB class, one-third into the ninth-grade Pre-IB class, and one-third into regular ninth-grade physical science. She explains:

> *It is frightening to me because I work well with the high-end kids. Now I have students who can't read well, who can't sit still, who can't see beyond the surface of information, and aren't critical thinkers—they're not at that point yet—so I'm guiding them to reach that point instead of really fine-tuning and developing critical thinkers. From my perspective, it's made me a better teacher, but my preference is really taking kids who are neglected because they are so high-end and providing opportunities for them to grow and expand—for them to be nurtured—because I think the system so often teaches to the middle of the road. Or, if you have a lot of low-end kids, it teaches to those low-end kids because you can't lose them. It's often not fair to those upper-end kids.*

Sikora points out that the school has a huge waiting list of students who desperately need an accelerated program that they can't find elsewhere. The Summit program was designed to meet these unmet needs, but when students who would be better placed at other schools take the few slots available at Summit, the school is less effective fulfilling its mission. Stretching extensively to meet the needs of all Summit students, Sikora feels that she still can support the gifted student, "but I wouldn't want to see it go any further," she notes. At what point does the range of ability in the classroom preclude adequately teaching the high-end student?

Must Today's Teachers Teach to State Tests?

Sharon Sikora was recently involved, after helping to create a successful standards-based curriculum at Summit, in a curriculum project to aid other schools concerned about their performance on state tests. Unlike some educators, who believe that the pressure of the state tests forces teachers to abandon quality curricula in favor of "teaching to the test," Sikora believes that the process can lead to an excellent, rigorous curriculum that negates the need for excessive test preparation. "We created a process so we can go to a school and help them take the national and state standards, interpret them so that they're standards for their own school, and then create benchmarks so that that happens [students are successful]."

How do the benchmarks fit into a scope and sequence for a course? "We created templates and examples for every one of our disciplines in the core subjects: English, each of the individual languages, science, social studies, and math," Sikora explains. "We showed them examples set up in each subject of a scope and sequence that was standards-based and benchmark-based, and then this whole process of the template." Summit teachers went from school to school, did workshops with the teachers, and showed them how to turn what they were doing into a standards-based education.

Sikora is not adverse to the state tests, which often worry gifted advocates because they think that overadherence to grade-level material may rule out accelerative opportunities. "If you have a very rigorous curriculum, you're meeting those state standards," she says.

> *Even though there's a pull and a shove and you just want to say, "I'm going to take those standards and that's all I'm going to teach—that's how I'm going to get my kids though these tests," the bottom line is the standards are still so very vague that if your curriculum is rigorous and standards-based, your kids are going to be fine.*

Sikora understands that teachers may want to focus solely upon the standards (perhaps teaching each for three weeks) because their survival as teachers and the survival of their schools is at stake. Job security depends upon it. However, she insists that educators can learn to trust their programs. "The issue is that you're teaching well and following a rigorous standards-based curriculum. The cross-check is as much with the kids as with your curriculum. Is your curriculum hitting these standards, and when? And do you know that you're hitting all of them?" Sikora does not believe that such tests are an infringement that forces educators to teach to the test and "not be true to ourselves and our mission."

She feels that Summit was "incredibly lucky" because Amanda Avallone, an English teacher who had just finished her master's degree in curriculum, took a lead role in creating a standards-based curriculum for Summit before most schools in the rest of the state attempted it. "That's the bottom line," Sikora explains. "The reason we were successful was because we had done that."

Asked to give examples of the standards, Sikora noted that in science, the first standard is that students know the scientific process. The benchmarks in that standard might include how to write a proper conclusion, create a hypothesis, distinguish between a hypothesis and a conclusion in a problem statement, and know how to collect data (read a thermometer, or know that having more data is better than having less data). Sikora concludes, "So that's standard one. How do you hit that?" Considering the school's science projects, the curriculum "hits" all of that, but Sikora notes:

> *We've actually carefully taken apart the sixth-grade curriculum so there are different things students work on; they work on writing a hypothesis and collecting basic data (and get hints of this), and then we reinforce it in seventh grade and add on further data collection and data analysis. In eighth grade, I break the news to them that there really is a standard way you write a conclusion. You've taken that standard and broken it apart into three years and given them little doses of it along the way. The beauty of it is that students are writing a hypothesis and learning how to do that in sixth grade, which is one of the first things they do. They do that again in seventh grade; they probably cover it 20 times. The curriculum is rigorous.*

She cautions that teachers must be somewhat critical of the curriculum they're teaching. Some of the books and handouts, for example, only hint about actually writing a hypothesis. The teacher has to lay this foundation, then build upon it through the years spent with the student.

Sikora continues, "The question is how do you teach them that scientific process? Must it be covered just in biology or chemistry?" She insists it can be taught in many ways: with goldfish breeding in cold water, determining whether or not a substance is going to create bubbles when it's testing different minerals, through the use of a plate tectonics model, through chemistry experiments, or studying physics and the motion of a matchbox car on an inclined plane. "The bottom line is you're going to hit this concept in every single discipline." She adds that the other standards in science are very specific to earth science or biology or chemistry or physical science. They are very content driven, so it's essential to make sure that students are being taught the content.

Sikora emphasizes, however, that mandated curriculum content need not be taught at the typical pace, year by year, to meet state and federal standards. Since the inception of the Summit program, the typical science curriculum offered over three years in middle school has been taught in the first two years at Summit. "We hit all of those standards in sixth and seventh grades." This has remained the case, even as the student body has changed. She feels that the program still works well because third-year instruction at Summit can then either address the need for remediation or allow students to progress to high school work. "If we know kids got C's and D's along the way and didn't quite get [the master concepts], they go into our Advanced Topics class. If they got A's or B's, they can go on to Chem/Physics because they've mastered the middle school curriculum," she explains. She adds that teachers can make this determination by grades or by other assessments, which, up to now, haven't worked as well as grades. "We're still working on fine tuning that."

Summit's approach to varying the pace of instruction for different students has met both the varying needs of learners and produced high state test scores. Summit eighth graders scored at the 97th percentile in science, the 87th percentile in math, and the 92nd percentile in English utilizing this standards and benchmark approach. "The high schools have finally come to accept our kids," Sikora is pleased to report.

One way in which teachers can support advanced students is by advocating for their appropriate placement at their next school. Students will face considerable pressure to take the courses that most students in their same grade take. When their former teachers make a special effort to ensure that these students are placed appropriately in higher-level courses, it's tremendously helpful. If the receiving school agrees to a more advanced placement, the student avoids repeating work already mastered, maintains higher motivation to learn, and has time to schedule more of the most advanced courses. Many students also choose to take college courses concurrently because they enjoy the challenge and can earn both college credit and credit toward their high school diplomas.

Teachers initially encounter some resistance when they recommend more advanced placements at the receiving school. However, as that school gains experience that the recommendations that it is receiving are appropriate, the process begins to go more smoothly. "Boulder High decided they would really like to have our kids for their AP scholars program. Boulder High even sent us a cake thanking all the faculty," Sikora states. High schools realize at some point that recruiting advanced students helps them to offer their highest-level classes, for which there might otherwise be insufficient demand. Advanced students who have skipped entry-level courses have more time left during their high school careers to take such higher-level classes.

Preferable Teaching Approaches: Maintain High Standards

Asked to share her general views on teaching the gifted, Sharon Sikora first describes the necessity of having high standards for gifted students. "Make it very clear what you want them to do, and assist them in achieving that goal," she says. Sikora routinely expects her middle school students to handle college-like, lab-based classes, in which a high level of understanding by the students is expected. Even with this rigor, she cautions, "Don't put a ceiling on! Who knows how high they can go?" Allow students to explore high-end knowledge, and be surprised! She adds, "A little bit of mystery is a good thing" when the teacher has not taught higher-level material that the student can discover independently.

Learn to Trust

Second, Sikora advises, "If the area of their greatest interest is not your expertise, you must learn to trust." She explains that a teacher can find the right mentor for a student, seek out the community that the student needs, or find the books that will be required—that's easy. However, the teacher must then trust what the student shares as his or her resultant learning. "You trust that the information they've given you is correct." Of course, the teacher can still look at the student's analytical processing. "As a science teacher, you know when the critical thinking isn't quite right, and it's not flowing right, and they're jumping to conclusions—it doesn't matter whether it's biology or chemistry or geology or astronomy," Sikora notes. "I've recently had many students whose interests were not in my field, and I've had great success with them—if I treat them as if they are the experts and they're teaching me." She helps them fill in the holes or gaps in their knowledge by asking questions and recognizing where those gaps are. "Trust that they're the experts, that they've done good work, and that they're willing to work," she insists. She adds that it's important for the teacher to take on the role of a student and say, "You teach me because this is something that I don't know much about. It is a great opportunity for them to communicate what they know—and for the two of you to become colleagues instead of this teacher/student relationship."

Ensure that Teachers Have a Strong Content Background

Third, Sikora believes that a strong content background is critical to a teacher of the gifted. "I've met some amazing teachers, but none of those amazing teachers in science have only a bachelor's degree; they all have at least a master's," she says. Noting that this is a particular need when working with gifted students, she admits that it is also "tricky" because some teachers with higher degrees don't know how to communicate—how to teach. "You do need your teacher training; there are tricks, and there are things you have to know," adds Sikora. She also believes, "You don't personally develop your critical thinking until you've done some strong research on your own, and then you learn how to think."

Sikora's students have won an unusual number of awards at the highest levels in science competitions. She is particularly adept at supporting their research. "I think you have to write a thesis—do some research that takes at least a year—to grasp that," she insists. "In English and social studies, our most successful teachers have higher degrees as well. For that really high-end kid, you have to have spent some time in your discipline that is very integral to your being in order to be able to translate that to the students and teach them in the right way."

Allow Any Question

Fourth, Sharon Sikora believes, "It's critical in the classroom that you allow any question to happen." She advises teachers to admit when they don't know something. "There's a certain amount of respect that the gifted student understands when you say, 'I don't know the answer to that; we can find out.'" With gifted students, it is not so much the issue of a teacher admitting that he or she doesn't know something; it's the teacher letting the student know that it is okay to not know everything—perfectionism should not apply to knowledge. "Here, they respect you in the classroom and realize you're not perfect, which lightens up their load. The other thing that happens is that they see you as a colleague," Sikora explains. She strongly believes that gifted students seek out colleagues among their teachers. "They want someone who's on their level, who can be at their level, and who they see at their level. Even the age thing doesn't matter." She adds, "Intellectually, you're their colleague because you don't know everything, and therefore, they can learn from you." With such respect, she believes that the student and teacher can then "link arms and go forward." The understanding between them becomes, "I'm going to guide you sometimes, and you're going to guide me sometimes. I have more knowledge right now than you do, but I don't have all the knowledge. We can pursue intellectual endeavors together." With her most gifted and talented kids, Sikora feels that she is still viewed as their teacher and respected, but there is also a colleague relationship, and "that's what promotes their learning more than anything else."

Interestingly, she believes that her less capable students value such a relationship less. "There are some students you don't want to be colleagues with. They are not usually the high-end kids. They need a different relationship." She explains that these students are more comfortable having her apply a traditional teacher role dispensing information to them.

Sikora believes that, unfortunately, colleague relationships are not always an option for gifted students with other teachers. She suspects that teachers who are insecure with their knowledge may be the most resistant. Citing her own difficulties teaching meteorology, she admits, "I'm so insecure that I have to come across as, 'That's the way it is.'" Especially in middle schools, teachers are asked to teach things that they're not necessarily comfortable with. They don't have extra time for outside learning, and there's no professional development to ensure their competence. "That's where the discomfort comes in," Sikora notes. "When a teacher's uncomfortable, the kids pick up on it right away, and you get, 'I hate science. I hate....'" Yet, she adds, "When you have a teacher who truly loves what he or she is doing, that love is really contagious. When you're really passionate about what you're teaching, you can say, 'I don't know the answer to that. I've never thought about that before.'"

When a high-end question is asked in the classroom for which there is an answer, Sikora will virtually always take the time to answer that question in class. She believes that this is vital, even if the other students have totally lost the thought and don't understand why it was an important question. Sikora explains:

> *At that point in time, I've lost 90% of my class, but I will stop everything I'm doing and answer that good question. For the 10% of the kids who are following along, they feel really good about this; they're getting an answer, and they're thinking. It promotes their thinking at a very nice, high level. For the student who asked the question, it's validated his thought processes. He feels good that this was considered an important question. For the 90% of*

> *kids you've lost, they realize that there are questions out there that they can't imagine.*

Sikora recalls that her own son had an experience in which he asked one of those questions and the teacher replied, "That's too high-level for this class. You're going to have to hold on to that question and wait a couple years."

"That is the worst possible thing you can do to these kids!" she exclaims. "They're not going to hold onto it for those years, and suddenly, in that class, they're going to stop thinking at a high level. Their high-level thinking isn't even acknowledged."

Sometimes the questions are so complex that they need to be carefully considered before the teacher can offer an answer or facilitate a class discussion. In these situations, Sikora will say, "Let's talk about that after class, even if I have to write you a pass. I need to really process that." She makes sure to address the question with the student who asked it that day. Sometimes other questions seem too "off base" for classroom discussion. "You have to weigh whether or not it will be too disruptive to go off on that tangent." Even with questions deemed unsuitable for class discussion, Sikora feels that it is important to give the student a gentle explanation after class. Sensitive gifted students tend to be embarrassed easily in public.

Ask Open-Ended Questions

Sikora believes that teachers should ask their share of good questions as well. "Have a lot of open-ended questions on labs and tests—oh, tests are key," she advises. There is the tendency for all teachers to give exams with a lot of multiple-choice items because they are very easy to grade. "It cuts your time in half," Sikora admits. "The other tendency, especially in chemistry, is not to give partial credit for where their thoughts are—not to give problems where you actually have to see their thought processes." She notes that when only the final answer counts, a multiple-choice mentality prevails. Sikora believes that tests should generate a lot of discussion ("This is where you went wrong. Do you see where you went wrong?") and contain questions in which partial credit is given for correct thought processes. "I still give maybe eight points worth of multiple choice items because the whole world is set up for multiple choice. If I don't give multiple choice, it tends to hurt them later on," she explains.

Sikora also insists that about 10% of the test questions cover something that the students have never seen before. "They've seen it, but in another form," she clarifies. For example, questions of the form: "Scientists have observed ________; why might this happen?" are frequently used on college science exams, and Sikora believes that students should be introduced to them. Unfortunately, this sometimes draws the ire of both students and parents. "I've been called to the principal's office a few times!" Sikora admits, "and I stand on my ground." She explains:

> *Science is new. It's applying your way of thinking to totally new situations. And that's something that gifted students just love! They are able to see the connection. That goes to their hearts and souls. If you only make it 10% of the test and you give partial credit if they've sort of gotten there, they see where science is going and understand how the nature of science changes. A lot of teachers won't do that because it takes so much time.*

Finally, Sikora likes to flexibly meet the needs of her individual students as they arise. For example, "I had a great group of girls this year," she recalls with a smile. "Outstanding, brilliant. Four gifted young women worked together this year on a project." She explained that each was a past Science Fair winner or had some contact with high-level scientific work through their families. "I put these four together," she states. Sikora didn't encourage another Science Fair entry in middle school because the girls had placed at the state level before, had the basis of scientific inquiry down, and really needed to do Science Fair next in high school, when awards and scholarships would be at stake. Instead, Sikora wanted them to consider a team project, because despite the girls' gifted abilities, each needed to learn to work with a group. She suggested the Bayer NSF Competition, a team community innovation project, so that they could learn to work together.

Sikora provided support as the girls found their way to a highly scientific project. "Outstanding work," she proudly recalls, noting that the girls were regional finalists, won a subscription to *Discover Magazine* for a year, and were given a beautiful trophy. "The district has come to respect so much the work that we're doing," she admits proudly. "One girl on the team, now heading on to high school, was given the chance to do her senior science research project as a sophomore." In four out of the six years that Summit has competed in science competitions, its students have placed at the state, regional, or national levels. Sikora, along with other outstanding Summit teachers, had a hand in this.

Richard Borinsky: Challenging Gifted High School Students

Rich Borinsky, an experienced, highly talented teacher (now retired), is renowned in our school district for his many years of successful teaching of Advanced Placement Biology (usually taught to high school seniors), regular Biology (usually a tenth-grade course), and assorted other related courses of interest. His interview for this book took place just before he retired.

As a teacher who always managed to prepare a higher percentage of students to earn 5's on the Advanced Placement (AP) exams (the top grade available), Rich Borinsky achieved a level to which any teacher could aspire. He notes that most of the students in his high school AP classes were not gifted; he would classify most as high achievers who really cared about their grades and worked very hard. However, he always drew some gifted students (they "get it the first time") to his classes and was perceived by the gifted students as a teacher who could challenge even the brightest among them. "I don't put limits on their learning," he explains, "I allow them to get there in a lot of different ways."

Noting that all teachers seem to have students with whom they work best, Borinsky admits, "I've always had success with the students in the gifted range." He does not attribute his success as a teacher to hard work or practice; he believes primarily that "teachers are born." However, he does think that it is helpful for teachers to never be satisfied with the jobs they are doing. A teacher who has the talent can become better. There is always room for improvement.

Challenges of Instructional Grouping

When Borinsky began teaching in 1972, his high school was quite different from what it is today. Located in a primarily middle class suburban neighborhood of reasonably well-educated citizens, many in high-tech fields, the school was primarily a prep school. It featured a college schedule in science, biology, and history that included one-hour lectures two days per week, as well as lab and recitation three days per week. Special education students were taught in their own program. Students in the college-prep track were nearly all taking biology; it was a fairly homogeneous group. "We didn't have students who couldn't read in biology or who couldn't speak English."

The School Reform Movement, with its emphasis on the heterogeneous grouping of students, began to mainstream special education students. These students, whose parents lobbied strongly for their placement into the least restrictive educational environments, were placed into regular biology classes. The Science Topics class, a more basic option, was phased out. Biology became a class for every student at the high school. Yet, Borinsky notes, the ability ranges grew so diverse that it became difficult to be effective at teaching.

After many years of teaching within this structure, the science department at Borinsky's high school started making changes, separating by ability. His high school offered two classes of Honors Biology, six to eight classes of regular Biology, and two classes of Basic Biology (for students with significant learning disabilities). Borinsky views the Honors Biology class as a pre-AP class that helps give students contact with some of the abstract concepts earlier. Although gifted students typically catch on quickly, others need more time with this material. However, Borinsky believes that it might actually be possible to take a group of bright students at the ninth-grade level and prepare them for an AP biology test! He thinks that more advanced classes for freshmen and sophomores should be available. Like many schools that offer AP courses, his high school has fewer advanced courses for underclassmen. He would prefer to offer them, as International Baccalaureate (IB) programs do, to prepare students for high-level coursework later. IB programs typically have a series of more challenging, honors level, Pre-IB courses.

Although three levels of introductory biology had been approved, Borinsky struggled to get the honors-level classes approved. "If we'd had to have two, the honors would have been scrapped and the basic and regular would have been offered," he states. "As a society, we do a great job with learning disabilities. We don't do a very good job with the other end of the spectrum. We don't have much pity for them." He hopes that three levels of classes will challenge all of the school's students.

Borinsky also has concern that the needs of some gifted students are obscured by their failure to be high achievers. The student who fails to achieve at a high level may not be granted access to opportunities that exist for those who do higher-level work and may not appear to need special services for the gifted. "Many kids are very, very bright but don't fit into the mold we have for students. Some won't do homework or are not organized enough to do well." They miss turning in some assignments, so they're not doing very well for a grade, but they're still learning the material. Adjusting the grading structure can help talented underachievers.

On Grading

Borinsky wants students' overall learning of the material to determine their final grades. Because Advanced Placement and International Baccalaureate classes both involve *exit testing*, in which a comprehensive test is given at the end of the class covering all of the material taught, the student's ultimate learning can be measured at the end of the class. Borinsky routinely allowed students who earned a 5—the top grade on the Advanced Placement Biology test—an A in his class, regardless of grades up to that point. "My goal is to put the emphasis on the learning and not the grade. You have to make them accountable for the work they turn in, but in the end, they either know it or they don't. The goal of the class is to learn enough to do well on that exam."

Borinsky likes the fact that the exit exam is externally evaluated; the students must prove their mastery of the course content. Doing well on the exam is a powerful indicator that students have successfully learned the necessary material in biology, even though they may have struggled to maintain high grades along the way or failed to turn in all assignments. Sometimes concepts that weren't fully understood when first tested become relevant and meaningful to the student later in the year. Scoring high on the AP exam documents that students, by the May test date, have reached a high-level understanding of the content. "If they do that, then they've accomplished the goal of the class."

Instruction—Empower Independent Learning

"I'm not a person who stands up in front of a room and lectures. I don't think I do that very well," Rich Borinsky insists. "I think I need to explain some things to [the students], but I need to find out what it is that they need explained." Each year, Borinsky assumed that he would have a variety of students "who know things in different ways, and some of them know it a lot better than others and are able to explain it maybe a lot better than I am." Because he also believes that "kids relate to kids probably better than teachers relate to kids," he tried to structure the class to allow considerable interaction between students. Most work was done in small groups of the students' choosing. "I give them things that they're able to talk about in class." He feels that a small group structure, with each group of students being more homogeneous, can best meet the learning needs of individuals. "I'm a student," he says. "I take a lot of classes. If I find myself in a classroom and I already know the material the professor is talking about, I want to go beyond that, ask questions, or it's very boring." Smaller groups allow for greater interaction about the course content at the level of the individuals in the group.

Borinsky tried to minimize lecturing in his class and maximize opportunities for students to talk to each other and solve a problem. "I try to go beyond the text—incorporate things that are relevant to the text and get them to think about things—use a lot of resources," he explains. He also used critical thinking approaches to ferret out misconceptions, knowing that students can easily parrot back information but need to understand it thoroughly.

As a result, his classes were quite variable. They weren't the same every day. Borinsky notes that some teachers have their entire year planned at the beginning; however, the structure of his class did not allow such long-term planning. "I know exactly what I'm going to be doing on a day-to-day basis, but not next week. Teaching is very difficult for me. I don't know how things will play out from week to week. I may have to work late at night to prepare." Allowing flexibility for students to pursue ideas requires more continuous planning and last-minute preparation, as adjustments must be ongoing. "My weaknesses may be good for gifted kids," he admits, as flexibility allows for meeting their unusual needs. "I've never taught AP the same way twice, although I've given out some of the same documents. It's difficult to be that way. It has its disadvantages."

In fact, every year brought concern for Borinsky that all topics wouldn't be covered in time for the AP test, and a great flurry of activity ensued as the test approached. "I've made videotapes for students to ensure they know something we don't have time to cover in class. It's another part of giving them responsibility." AP Biology involves a huge amount of content—more than is typically taught at the college freshman level, where instructors often leave out anatomy and physiology to meet time constraints. However, the necessary preparation must be done for the AP test. The level to which Richard Borinsky's students were always prepared is a testament to his high standards and annual accomplishment.

"One of the things I'm doing is I'm giving up a lot of control," Borinsky says of empowering his students to learn more independently. "I realize that some of the students are going to be smarter than I am. That doesn't threaten me; it intrigues me. I don't have a problem with that at all. I just happen to know more biology than they know, so I can still teach them something. I can help guide their enthusiastic questions."

"I'm willing to give up control in a lot of different ways," he explains. "I let the students determine a lot of the class." He routinely allowed students to decide when they would be tested. If tests on two subject areas were needed, did they want to take them on the same day or different days? He also gave take-home exams to save class time, trusting students to complete the tests without outside help. Sometimes he even provided students with the answers to check themselves. He found that open-book tests produce the best learning. "They're in the class for their own benefit, not for my benefit," he insists. "If they want to cheat, they're not going to get much out of it." Students frequently graded their own exams and other students' exams, and they seem to learn a lot from that. "I like to take work that's exceptional and share that work with other students. I photocopy papers or essays that are exceptional," Borinsky adds.

"I look at it as I'm a student, too. I'm a part of their group. I try to become a part of the group as much as possible," Borinsky explains. He treated his students as peers and fellow learners. "I'm trying to tell them whether they did well or didn't do well, and if they didn't do well enough, what they need to do to get where they need to be." Every day, Rich Borinsky approached his students as he would other responsible adults. "Here's what we're going to do today. Here's what we need to do. How are we going to do this? Here's my idea of what this concept means. What's your idea?" The result was considerable discussion in class that flowed back and forth. "I'm throwing things out, telling them a little bit, and getting feedback, then having them share their own ideas with students in their groups," he explains.

Borinsky also offered special support by trusting students with high-quality equipment. "When we do labs, I give them the lab and let them do what they need to do with it, trying to use computers and high-tech equipment as much as we can because they're usually fascinated with it. I reserve a lot of my best stuff for them, and they appreciate that and do a better job." His AP students appreciated being allowed to use special pipettes, Spec 20s, and interface software for the computer that allows them to see digitally what's going on in an experiment in terms of various measurements. He thinks that one of the best things that he did was "to challenge students to solve problems," while trying "not to take control of the class."

Another point of emphasis in Borinsky's classes was "Why are you here?" He explains, "It's really a difficult point to try to get across, because every class they've ever taken, they've taken for external reasons—not for their own benefit, unless it was a photography class or something really fun." He feels that most students have never taken an academic class for fun—and for self-benefit. Rich Borinsky believed in constant reinforcement of this principle in his classes: "Why are you here? If you're only reading this once, are you getting enough out of it?" Demonstrating his own curiosity and overt passion for his subject, and supporting his students as respected peers wanting to learn, Borinsky shifted the responsibility for learning to his students. As they experienced his style of teaching, they progressed from an external locus of control, in which they passively expected to be entertained and taught, to an internal locus of control, in which they actively pursued their own learning.

Resist Authoritarianism

How does treating high school students as responsible adult peers coexist with increasingly authoritarian high school rules? "This is the antithesis of that," Rich Borinsky admits. "Yes, I have to violate rules myself to do that. The first day I got bagels and cream cheese (students are not supposed to eat in class). I view them as peers. I have to kind of tiptoe around the administration."

Students are supposed to come to class after the AP test, but Borinsky didn't require it. He also violated rules to do his highly popular AP study weekend, allowing students to drive up to the mountains in their own cars. The chaperoned students studied and took practice tests, sometimes while in the hot tub of a mountain condo or enjoying dinner together. "In this class, they know they have accomplished something, and they can feel good about themselves," he believes. He also contends that these students need some humor. "They appreciate it and feel more relaxed." Borinsky occasionally gave such silly assignments as: "Write a love story about photosynthesis."

Maintain High Expectations

The expectation was always there that Borinsky's students were going to learn the material to a very high degree. "Mastery learning is something I'm very interested in," he notes, "not just to get a B on something and let it go. They need to know the material at the end." Although he knew that his students often wouldn't fully comprehend the material when first tested on it, he expected them to understand it by the end of the course. "You keep coming back to it in different contexts, and they see the relevancy of it. At the end, they know it. That's all I care about. I'm not too concerned as we go along if students don't get something."

One thing that Borinsky did that particularly aids gifted learners is he gave them considerable practice with multiple-choice tests, which constitute a substantial portion of the AP Biology exam. Because gifted students see many possible answers, they often make the questions more complex than the test author had in mind. Borinsky helped them to focus their answers more appropriately through sample tests. Once they become familiar with the tests and learn what knowledge is being assessed, they overcome this difficulty.

Establish a Strong Content Background

Like the other teachers profiled above, Rich Borinsky believes that another key to being a good teacher for gifted students is really knowing your subject well. A strong content background is essential. "You have to think well on your feet and direct their energy. If you have a surface level [of knowledge], they figure that out right away, and they will totally write you off. It's essential to have a tremendous background. You can't overemphasize that."

A seasoned veteran, Borinsky continuously takes classes and does "workshop after workshop after workshop." He states, "Everything you take from a workshop, you have to modify and make your own. Too much of the same thing and boredom occurs." Not only did his background prepare him for his most advanced students, but it also allowed him to model being a lifelong learner who is always curious to answer new questions. Gifted students usually have great respect for teachers who are both exceptionally competent and open to new ideas. "I've always been interested in improving myself. My background has broadened considerably." Borinsky worries because, "It's difficult to find people with a rich background in biology. Right out of college, they have a narrow background that needs to be broadened. I see teachers who need to learn so much, and it doesn't happen overnight."

Care about Students

Borinsky insists that he deserves no credit for his students' high level of learning. To him, the students' accomplishments are their own, and he always felt that he could have done a better job. His students knew that he cared about what they were doing. He recalls attending one workshop in which he was told that at least 80% of the reason a student will learn is because of the relationship with his or her teacher. He agrees. "It's more important than all other reasons together. If you have a positive relationship with students, they're much more likely to want to do things than if you don't. By giving up responsibility and creating an environment, I'm establishing positive relationships. I'm encouraging them to learn in their own way, at their own pace, and go as far as they can. So kids will go really far, way beyond." Borinsky was always willing to go with them.

He notes that there were always a lot of *why* questions. "I find myself saying 'I don't know' a lot. They ask great questions. If you don't say 'I don't know,' you are going to get killed. They know when you're bluffing; they can smell it." Sometimes, Borinsky admits, he said, "I don't know" 15 or 20 times and felt inadequate as a result. But he focused on how he and his students could try to find out. "There are resources which are great." He adds that another typical trait of gifted kids is the kind of questions they ask. They ask more abstract questions—for example, "Would the laws that apply to a certain biological process still apply in space?" He believes that kids who are simply high achievers don't ask those kinds of questions.

"When we get to some things that are really esoteric—abstract—the fun is in differentiating themselves because they do know that. I'm always making them feel special." Borinsky believes that there's nothing wrong with being elite because you know something that very few people know, and he was quick to praise his students for their accomplishments. "Go home and tell your parents about it. If they won't listen, tell your little sister or brother, or a pet," he told them, certain that their knowledge was worthwhile and should be shared. But, laughing, he also told them that their knowledge and high-level interest in biology were "going to ruin your life." He warned, "The people you hang around with now, who may be interested in how many home runs somebody hit, you're going to become less interested in." With a smile, he cautioned, "You're going to want to talk about the light/dark reactions of photosynthesis or how electrons are cycled between photosynthesis and respiration. Your girlfriend or boyfriend is not going to want to hear about this. So whatever your relationship is now, it's going to be trashed."

Be a Passionate Teacher

Borinsky is passionate about biology. He remembers memorizing one book in a series of children's books that his parents bought him—it was the book on science. "When I got to biology in high school, I thought, 'This is just so interesting.'" Borinsky says there are "hooks" all along the way in biology—fascinating things that make one want to learn more. "It may seem like it would not be interesting, but it is if you know how to frame it," he insists. "I was really interested in ecology when I first started. As I've continued to learn, I've realized every single part of biology is interesting." He says of his students, "Probably they think it's bizarre that you're so interested in something, but if *you* weren't, *they* wouldn't be."

Elizabeth Maxwell: Reflections on Gifted Education

The Senior Staff Director of the Gifted Development Center, Betty Maxwell is a woman of enormous experience and wisdom about gifted children. A teacher for 18 years, she taught the fourth, fifth, and sixth grades in a school for gifted students, as well as second grade, fifth- and sixth-grade language arts, and high school English in more typical schools. She also served as a resource room teacher for grades five through eight, working with special education students.

Maxwell earned a master's degree in gifted education, an experience that she feels significantly added to her expertise as a teacher of the gifted. Because she already had some background in learning disabilities, her master's work helped her realize how she could combine instruction for students with both giftedness and learning disabilities—students who are twice exceptional. It also helped her to see which qualities are essential to a good teacher of the gifted.

The Gifted Teacher's Best Characteristics: Appreciate Their Gifts

Maxwell believes that the ability to appreciate a gifted child is paramount. "Most children aren't able to open up to teachers who don't really see them—who don't recognize who they are and what they can do," she explains. The teacher must possess a general good will toward high intellect. "So much of the time, [gifted] children are getting false feedback that they are wrong in some way. They shouldn't raise their hands so much, should talk less, and need to be patient," she notes. "They are square pegs in round holes." Any teacher who recognizes a child's unusual grasp of things has to recognize giftedness, support it, and have good will toward that gifted child.

Maxwell also believes that effective teachers of gifted students need to have at least superior intelligence themselves, as well as imagination, creativity, and humor to fully appreciate the needs, along with the strengths, of their students. A large percentage of gifted children are intuitive as well. It's helpful for a teacher of the gifted to have a similar intuitive orientation to be sensitive to the emotional climate within the classroom.

Facilitate Learning

Maxwell notes, "It's already well known that gifted teachers need to be facilitators, not lecturers. They need to be promoting thinking and discovery on the part of their students; they must encourage questioning." In fact, the art of questioning and follow-up questioning is of crucial importance. The best teachers of the gifted view it as their obligation to ask questions that are provocative—that lead people to thinking.

Empower Students

Gifted teachers need to be empowering rather than placing limits. They should be delighted with the student's abilities and help the child expand them. "To do this, they must have a sincere enthusiasm for ideas, creativity, for what gifted children are revealing, for the opportunity to explore and expand beyond the usual parameters of the class."

Don't Tolerate "Meanness"

Just as Stuart Little proclaimed that he didn't like "meanness," gifted children need a classroom environment that is kind and supportive, not snide, derogatory, and hurtful, Maxwell cautions. Where the classroom or playground is out of control and children are allowed to routinely treat others roughly, unkindly, or in a bullying fashion, the gifted child is especially anxious and responds extremely poorly. Where the teacher is unkind to students, there is not only a lack of trust that the teacher will keep children safe, but also a sense of injustice that the teacher is violating the ethical demands of his or her position.

Gifted children can be highly tolerant of a range of situations when the atmosphere is kind. "I've seen gifted students be really patient with slower students if the teacher was positive and supportive; they liked that kind of handling of the situation," Maxwell recalls. Related to this, gifted children dislike strictness and harshness when gentle guidance is all they need. "You need to be very positive," Maxwell notes, "reinforcing their progress through praise."

Teach Research and Interview Skills

Gifted children "do want a teacher who is thoroughly knowledgeable," Maxwell insists, adding, "That's a huge stretch in an elementary school. They're likely to be asking quantum physics questions that go beyond the expertise of most teachers." However, she reminds teachers to always "be a facilitator and help them read or interview others who have those answers." Gifted students' need for information can be so insatiable that teachers must teach them to be resourceful. What resources should they turn to? "Give them practice in how to ask questions to get the most answers," she advises. Teach them how to interview, conduct polls, and speak to someone engagingly. They must learn to find things on the Internet, use computers, and locate resources in the library. Gifted students require a set of skills not usually taught in the regular classroom to become independent learners.

Be Sensitive to Affective Needs

The good teacher of the gifted also needs to have some innate counseling skills, be a good listener, and read signs of when someone needs to talk, Maxwell recommends. The affective side of giftedness requires support just as much as the cognitive side. "The teacher needs to create a class where there are a lot of independent projects going on so there's time to take someone aside to talk, or be willing to put in extra hours so they're available to talk," she advises.

Address "Being in the Gifted Class"

Maxwell believes that a major problem for many gifted young people is that they are placed into a gifted program with no thoughtful explanation about why they're there. The teacher needs to allow them to discuss what it feels like to be in this special class situation, being pulled out of their regular class, etc. Part of the teaching time ought to deal with emotional issues. Students should begin the year with a discussion of what it means to be gifted. "They need to talk about the ability to learn rapidly, move faster, ask more questions, how annoying that can be to others in the class, and why there's a real need to have separate classes," she suggests. "Discuss how to deal with taunting from classmates and self-consciousness."

Involve Students in Self-Evaluation

Maxwell also believes that it is important to involve students in self-evaluation of some sort; student input should be a part of looking at projects and grades. "Along with that comes a more level playing field—you're in more of a partnership with gifted children," she says. "The teacher needs to be getting their input, helping them understand themselves, and meeting their needs, but not in a position of command." The best gifted teachers, she believes, involve their classes in solving problems that arise. They use brainstorming techniques to work the problems out within the group (although emotional problems need to be dealt with individually).

Be Flexible: Allow Instructional Plans to Change

Betty Maxwell advises teachers to be extremely flexible. "Plans often get changed because kids will zoom through plans that you've made that you think will take more time, or there's a tremendous dislike of the approach, or something else comes up," she explains. "Go with the flow—the moment; do the same thing in a different way." This can be particularly disheartening to the inexperienced teacher who puts tremendous effort into a project or unit, only to see it succeed just minimally. It can be difficult to try again. However, knowing in advance that this is an expected pitfall can help teachers to prepare.

Help Students Stretch

"Aim high," Maxwell encourages, noting that gifted children perform so much better when asked to stretch. "Bring into the classroom some very real, high-level philosophical problems to solve," she explains. "Raise the bar high."

Be a Rebel

Maxwell notes, as other teachers have told us, that many excellent teachers of the gifted are rebels. They are more original thinkers and frequently question authority themselves. They like to promote thinking for oneself in their students. Simply by that orientation, they understand the gifted student's divergent thinking, resistance to authority, and need for choice. This also gives them an edge when other teachers disagree with their methods. Accommodating the gifted requires significant modifications in educational programming. These teachers are not afraid to take risks and to make changes.

Make Homework Meaningful

Maxwell sees several areas of concern for gifted students in the typical approaches that schools take. The first is with homework. Usually assigned to assist less capable children who need additional practice to master concepts, homework typically makes little sense for the gifted. "Gifted kids get concepts almost immediately, so their homework is almost always busywork. They are smart enough to realize it doesn't do them any good," she states.

Maxwell believes that most gifted children are patient and tolerant of homework in the primary and upper elementary grades, but beginning in the sixth through ninth grades, many become extremely reluctant to continue doing homework. "It doesn't make good pedagogical sense for them to do the same homework as other students. I think it builds resentment toward the schools," she insists. If homework consisted of novel ways of applying what they learn, their attitude toward it would change. "Continued pressure to do it even when the students are getting high test grades, and making their grade contingent upon doing homework, is creating dropouts from school and a lot of underachievers," Maxwell states.

Moreover, she notes, "There's some kind of unconscious perception that homework may *not* be actually teaching kids things, and yet there is a drive to preserve it." She believes that homework has become more of a moral issue—of building character—than of ensuring content mastery. "You learn how to do this thing that's difficult for you, but it's difficult in a bad sense—difficult because it's mindless. Teaching kids to do things that are mindless doesn't build character. The kids with the best character and integrity will rebel against this," Maxwell believes. This strong stance from some teachers about homework may be driving students of character and integrity away from school. They won't play the game. "I feel it's criminal the way we're really pushing some of our best students out of school," she concludes.

Betty Maxwell reminds us that "It isn't that these kids don't want to work. They don't want to be held back and treated unintelligently." We need to engage their minds at all levels. "They're willing to learn but not jump through hoops. They have a need for that inner direction of learning. That's the spark," she notes. Many who find little meaning in regular high school courses are willing to take college or advanced online coursework concurrently. The work ceases to be a burden when the level is correct.

Resist Authoritarianism at School

Maxwell also feels that schools miscalculate the effects on gifted students of authoritarian rules for behavior and attendance. Especially as children mature and move on to middle and high school, rules that don't make sense and a plethora of consequences begin to overwhelm some gifted students. Schools struggle to manage many high-spirited youth, but clamping down with strict rules, dress codes, and dictated "ways of being" may cause gifted students to rebel.

Those students most resistant to direction by others do better not going to high school, but rather to any college campus or online course because people are not telling them what to do. They want more choice. It's difficult in a regular classroom to give some students more choice than others, although that would suit varying individual needs.

In particular, Maxwell believes that "arbitrary attendance rules really don't work well" to keep disillusioned gifted students in school. These students need rich content and challenging teachers, along with a variety of music, art, and other options to explore. Gifted students will come to school for learning options that they value.

Understand the Characteristics of Giftedness

Maxwell is most grateful to her master's program for giving her a far greater understanding of the characteristics of the gifted. Before that, efforts with other educators to arrange mentors for gifted students were sometimes unsuccessful. She recalls, "We created wonderful projects and expected the kids to love them, but it didn't always work." Her graduate work made her aware that gifted students need more choices; they need more input to be passionate about their learning. Her studies also made her more comfortable with their emotionality, intensity, theatricality, and curiosity—those natural characteristics of giftedness. "I had a better sense of why some curricula worked better for them," she states.

Discover Dabrowski's Overexcitabilities

"Exposure to Dabrowski's Theory of Positive Disintegration helped me see [gifted children's] intensity and sensitivity as very positive things," Maxwell says. Kazimierz Dabrowski was a Polish psychiatrist, psychologist, poet, and musician. As a therapist to high-ability individuals, he noted that his patients had *overexcitabilities* (inborn intensities),[1] as well as a persistent internal need to evolve as persons. Dabrowski believed that such intensity and sensitivity enhance the self-actualization process and play a role in developing potential. These intensities add to the individual's potential for growth.

Maxwell believes that Dabrowski's work "honors emotionality and emotional development, honors the struggle that dealing with oneself can entail, honors positive maladjustment when your conscience exceeds the values of those around you. He honored that struggle in general." Maxwell adds, "You really see a lot of those characteristics, especially the overexcitabilities, in the makeup of gifted children. They do form deep attachments, are sensitive, intense, have very high highs and very low lows, an amazing imagination, etc." Supporting and nurturing such characteristics helps gifted children to fulfill their moral, as well as their cognitive, promise.

Following her teaching career, Maxwell went on to complete training in psychosynthesis counseling and psychoeducational evaluation. She has worked at the Gifted Development Center consulting, counseling, testing, and making educational recommendations for gifted children for many years. Gently articulate, she remains a formidable champion of the gifted, of their rebellion, of their right to resist what is hurting them, decry authority for authority's sake, refuse homework that is pointless, and jump through hoops to prove personal value that is inherent. She believes that education must never seek to break a student's will, but rather work in concert with it, empowering the individual and nurturing what is most important.

Teachers of the Gifted, by Quinn O'Leary

When I walked into the classroom for the first time, it seemed no different than any of the others in the eldest wing of the school. Its institutional cinderblock construction was sheathed by cheap plastic carpet and papered with the idiot avuncularism of inspirational posters. It was populated by a herd of cheaply built desks, showing the scars of years of use, and headed by a withered woman with the corners of her mouth drawn down slightly.

When asked to describe the room, I did so in the purple, florid prose of the cheapest pulp novels of a generation past, lashing everything present. The dingy, sad construction became menacing, the small windows unconsciously and invisibly barred. The buzz-saw vibrations that melt into buildings after years of the subconscious torture of youth reverberated strongly in my mind and on the page. The short page's worth of unrefined bile was returned a week later with a few impartial slashes of corrective red and a short, glowing praise of my ability and descriptiveness.

By the time I received that first telling assignment back, however, I had already realized how very different from my description this classroom was. Through the two years I had the pleasure of attending it, the room's shoddiness and disorganization became less distressing and more homey, closer to my ideal. The pent-up anguish of other rooms was here seen only as the mild, happy frustration of true intellectual challenge, of the actual education so rare in my scholastic experiences.

The teacher's name was Sharon Babb, and she remains in my memories like a mythical creature, timeless and dangerous, the distilled learning and wisdom of untold eons at her disposal. Hunkering atop her hoard of treasured knowledge, tolerant of and nurturing to the puppyish intellect of her students but managing somehow to convey the threatening consequence of her disappointment, she loomed like a dragon over her impersonal, surrogate hatchlings. Unlike a mystical lizard, however, Mrs. Babb gave her hoard to her students, more than willing to share. She required the best a student had to offer, unsubtly disdaining any idea she felt was beneath its originator. She forced knowledge upon her students like an overzealous grandmother cooking huge meals for visiting children, offering so much nourishment that I often stumbled away from class with a head groggily full of new language. While time whiled its lazy way through other classes, in Mrs. Babb's it hectically rebounded like a super-ball in a bathroom, always gone too quickly.

The atmosphere fostered by this woman's leadership was one of flitting intellectual stimulation. Arguments arose and laughter abounded, but the stories discussed and the pages penned were alive with the crackling energy of newly discovered academic excitement. The flow from one author to another, from one linguistic style, period, philosophy and medium to the next was unbroken, full of soft, frayed tributaries, shaking hands with other branches.

The lacy interconnectedness of all education became more and more clear under her expert illumination.

This glowing, encompassing flow, covering what it could reach and hinting at all that it couldn't, brought back what it was like to immerse myself in a library for days, leaving to eat and sleep but otherwise with a book always in hand, the musty smell of binding glue and the subtle scents of the last person to borrow it ghosting its pages.

Few other teachers have taught me as much in their chosen subject and none have come close to the tutelage I received in the myriad facets of language. Mrs. Babb prodded the books of the proverbial greats to the forefront of the herd clamoring for my perusal, showed me how I want to develop myself as a scholar, as a writer and, almost incidentally, as a teacher.

Chapter 10
Charter Schools—In Principle and Practice

When local educational options for gifted children are limited or virtually nonexistent, the creation of a charter school is a possibility that many states now offer. Charter schools are public schools, not private, that receive state funding similar to regular school district funding. They are created by citizens in the community who perceive a need for a certain type of school to meet the educational needs of a certain type of student. They may be oriented to disadvantaged students or any of a number of categories of students with a special need. Or they may simply reflect a concern within the community for a school with higher educational standards, a school that features the arts, a school that focuses on technology, or a school that strictly adheres to traditional curricula.

The individual or group wishing to begin the charter school writes a "charter" explaining the philosophy and organization of the school, mission statement, number of teachers and students, and budget details, and then submits it to the legislative body that approves such charters.

Not for the fainthearted, charter school organization is best attempted by parents who are relatively desperate ("We won't send another one of our children to that middle school!"), determined to see the process through ("We have no other options"), and have a good idea of what kind of school is needed (e.g., one that provides advanced coursework options). The planning process is lengthy and arduous; often fraught with conflict between organizers, with the local school district, and inevitably, some members of the community; and full of twists and turns from the time the application is submitted to the time the school opens. For the group that I worked with, it was a lesson in learning about and dealing with new obstacles as we crossed the minefield of application requirements, district regulations, and state laws. A positive aspect, however, is that charter school applications in our state always include a tenet that the children of the organizers will be accepted to the school (without this, no one would do the work necessary). Moreover, to see a school that embodies the hopes and dreams of people working together over a long period of time, and to watch students and parents love it, is tremendously satisfying.

The school that I helped organize was the first charter school approved within the Boulder Valley School District in Boulder, Colorado. The school began in 1996 and has been quite successful. It is a middle school for students in grades six through eight; however, it differs considerably from typical middle school philosophy. For those who might want to consider forming a charter school, here is how it came to be.

Creating a School from the Ground Up

The Call to Arms

As in other communities across the nation, the popularity of middle schools and new "middle school philosophy" spread to Boulder Valley, and the school district began the process of changing its junior high schools, which were designed for grades seven through nine, into middle schools for students in grades six through eighth. Junior highs, modeled after high school programs, were perceived as lacking in their ability to adequately support the younger students. The new middle school approach was supposed to provide a protective bridge between elementary school, in which students had one teacher for the entire day, and high school, in which students attend classes with several different teachers.

A friend wryly commented that the choice of middle school philosophies had a lot to do with which high-priced consultant a school district hired, because not all middle schools are alike. In the case of Boulder, Colorado, the school board approved a list of "Middle School Essentials" that would change middle-level education considerably. Not only would the new middle schools include sixth graders, but efforts would be made to group students within grade levels into "pods" or "families" and keep them together with the same group of teachers to provide a more supportive environment. For example, with 100 sixth graders, there might be four groups of 25 students each, and the students would stay together and have the same teachers for all of their subjects.

Our middle school had several pods per grade. The pods allowed teachers the opportunity to easily team-teach interdisciplinary courses in block-scheduled time periods. To maintain these close-knit, supportive groupings, middle school philosophy dictated that students would be taught in heterogeneous classrooms, "*regardless of ability, needs, and interests*."

More importance was placed on helping students adjust socially than on their intellectual needs. In order to keep students together, they could not take classes at different levels.

Because Boulder is a highly educated community with a large gifted population, the resulting virtual abandonment of honors classes (math was spared in most, but not in all, schools) was of concern to many, although another large cadre of community members felt that the highly egalitarian Middle School Essentials were appropriate. In short, this vocal community was divided. Do we educate all children to an "equal" level or try to educate each and every child optimally?

At the same time, a new International Baccalaureate (IB) program was beginning at a local high school. A group of parents at the middle school next door had realistic concerns that, just at the time when their students might need additional high-level preparation to enter the new IB program, district restrictions against honors classes would hinder efforts to provide that.

Support for gifted education was at an all-time low, as the superintendent who fully supported the Middle School Essentials had both cut the program and closed the gifted and talented office. Parents of gifted students were concerned because honors classes had not fully met their children's needs *before*, and the situation would become even more grave without them.

Because I was co-chair, at the time, of the district's gifted and talented advisory committee and was also volunteering in the IB program, I was invited to meetings that the parents had requested at the middle school to discuss how to best prepare students for the IB program. From the outset, teachers and administrators at the school were defensive, even though the conversations focused mainly on adding only additional high-level work in English. The school already had an excellent math teacher, renowned for his very challenging program. Not only did school personnel take issue with the parents' perception that there was a need to improve and augment the program, but they were also insulted that parents would question their judgment. After all, they were the "education professionals." Unfortunately, this disturbing theme was presented repeatedly in meetings that the parents tried to keep pleasant, and it was probably a strong call to arms for the parents.

This middle school's absolute refusal to consider changes in its program led directly to the creation of a charter school—an option that the school never would have chosen. Looking back at those meetings, it seems clear that the wonderful charter school that resulted from the parent's wishes for a more rigorous program might never have happened if the middle school's personnel had made even minimal changes in their English program. But for the sake of many students who attend the new school today, it is fortuitous that they did not.

The Organizing Committee

The first meeting of the "organizing committee" found a group of parents, none of whom had ever created a school, together in the same room shortly after the Christmas holidays. These individuals strongly believed that middle school programs needed to be more challenging to prepare students for advanced high school work (IB programs and Advanced Placement classes) and hoped to create a new middle school that would open the next fall. Faced with a restrictive district middle school policy, all of these parents had been frustrated in their efforts to achieve meaningful change. Of greatest concern was the danger of highly capable middle school students losing their motivation to learn due to an insufficiently challenging curriculum.

The concerns were numerous and varied: restriction of honors classes to math only, or being eliminated altogether in some schools; over-reliance on heterogeneous cooperative learning strategies using group grades; teachers teaching outside of their areas of specialization to facilitate block schedules and interdisciplinary work; an overemphasis on efforts to make students feel good about themselves, when at the same time good students were being socially ostracized; and too much time spent coloring and learning in a hands-on fashion without adequate higher-level discussion and critical thinking. Fourteen individuals signed the original application. They were a highly educated group; 10 had advanced degrees, and virtually all had gifted children (several had profoundly gifted children). The parents' expertise included backgrounds in the natural sciences (meteorology, chemistry, geology, physics), computer science, mathematics, psychology, child development, social work, education, and law (having two attorneys on the committee proved to be very helpful). Some were excellent writers. Their varied backgrounds and willingness to contribute time and multitudinous efforts were significant strengths of the school. Before long, the committee grew to more than 30 individuals.

Our school district provided the option of a school becoming a *focus school*, or a local school that follows district educational guidelines but has a particular focus to distinguish its program. Committee members were divided as to whether they wanted to create a focus or a charter school. A focus school, as a regular district school, would alienate district personnel less and would make a statement that the organizing committee was trying to "play well with others." However, a charter school would have the power to waive many district rules and enjoy more autonomy. Although the group was divided on this issue, application deadlines for each type of school figured in. The decision was made to apply for both, and if the focus school application was approved, the charter plan would be withdrawn. If the focus school application was turned down or could not be considered, the charter school application would then be considered. By state law, the local school board had to rule on charter school applications within 60 days of submission.

Writing the Application

Committees were formed to handle the application writing, advertise the school, lead public information meetings, and find a potential site. The group decided to base the curriculum on what we knew of the International Baccalaureate Middle Years Programme, which was just being released after trials in a number of schools around the world. Members led meetings to describe the goals of the program and to obtain letters of interest from students and their parents. By February 21st, a tired but very determined group of parents submitted a lengthy application, with sections keyed to the necessary state and district requirements for a focus school, as well as a charter school. The school district fairly quickly turned down the focus school proposal on the basis that there was not sufficient time to create the program by fall. This then activated the charter application, and enough antagonism had developed by this point between the local school district and the organizing committee to make virtually all of the committee's members happy to be taking the more autonomous charter route.

Unfortunately, the Boulder Valley School Board turned down the charter application as well, forcing an appeal to the State Board of Education and eliminating any possibility of the school opening its doors in the fall of that year. We would have to wait another year. Thanks to a determined lawyer on the committee who prepared and argued our case without charge, the state board sided with our organizing committee, complimenting us on an outstanding application and requiring the Boulder Valley Schools to try to accommodate its first charter school.

Site Challenges

Now the critical concern became finding a site for the new school. Because capital funding was not available for charter schools at that time in Colorado, the organizing committee struggled to find potential space; Boulder has very high lease rates. The school district was reluctant to put the new school in one of its buildings with available space, so a potentially outstanding program had no place to go. The State Board of Education then placed pressure on the Boulder Valley School Board to find space. The result was placement of the new charter school, as a school within a school, within the middle school that first refused to augment its curriculum. Because of its declining enrollment in recent years, this middle school had extra space; it could offer some classrooms, gym space, use of the auditorium, and the cafeteria. The additional needed classroom space would be provided by portable classroom buildings erected on site for that purpose. Another portable building would provide space for an office.

Choosing Curriculum

As these decisions dragged on, the school's curriculum became the next important issue. As we obtained materials from the IB Middle Years Programme, it became apparent that the program, at that time anyway, consisted mostly of goals but little developed content. We liked what we saw in the sciences, but materials were too sketchy in the other subject areas to fully adopt the program.

Our curriculum subcommittee generated ideas for the full committee to consider. Teachers from other schools who had developed advanced programs in various subject areas and were willing to talk to us were a great help. After some time, we gained confidence in our ability to discern what was needed. We knew that we did not want to create a detailed curriculum; none of us had the necessary expertise. Yet our children had been damaged too much by inadequate programs to leave that entirely to chance. The result was an agreement that we would establish basic parameters for the coursework we wanted to offer and expect quality teachers to do the rest.

The school opened one year later than originally planned. Below is an adaptation of an article that I wrote about the program for *Kaleidoscope*, a publication of the Colorado Association of the Gifted and Talented.[1] It describes the early formulation of the program, which has continued to undergo changes since its inception.

Summit Middle School in 1997

Boulder Valley's first charter school is giving us hope and options for all to copy in challenging the gifted middle-level student. Summit Middle School, which opened in the fall of 1996, began offering students an ability-grouped assortment of higher-level classes, and the results are stunning. Students at Summit are delighted with the work and relieved to be in an environment where being smart is not a curse and where friends with similar interests are easy to find.

The school came about due to a large parent committee whose members shared a common history of advocacy as they lobbied for more challenging educational programs. When the school was not responsive to their requests, the group decided to form a charter school. They began by waiving the district's Middle Level Education Essentials, which mandated heterogeneous grouping of a full range of students for instruction and restricted honors classes. They utilized the independence of a charter school to create a hiring plan for teachers, and they waived the requirement that teachers be hired from the district's union pool. Teacher certification was waived as a mandate, as long as teachers had adequate expertise to apply for "alternative" state certification. It was decided not to create a school for the gifted, but a self-selecting school "for students who feel they want or need more challenge."

Then began the enormous challenge of creating a diagnostic-prescriptive curriculum for the range of students that the school expected to attract. To the degree possible, the school also had to meet or exceed the district curriculum, conform adequately to district and state content standards, and provide a reasonable bridge from elementary schools in the area to a nearby International Baccalaureate program or other advanced high school programs.

There was early agreement that the curriculum would have a balanced emphasis on content and critical thinking skills. It would be based on the assumption that Summit students are good abstract thinkers and need this level of challenge to maintain their motivation to learn. Middle school education literature has stressed that a majority of students have not yet reached a level at which they can reason abstractly;[2] most middle schools believe that hands-on approaches (best for concrete learners) must be used for all students in a heterogeneously structured environment. Summit would emphasize meeting individual needs based on level of subject mastery, preferred pace, learning style, and areas of weakness.

The committee examined many types of curricula: the International Baccalaureate Middle Years Programme, curricula from schools for the gifted and magnet schools in the Denver metropolitan area, and other middle schools with higher challenge offerings in a particular subject area. Teachers who had developed innovative programs for high-ability students were invited to curriculum meetings.

The group set general parameters for the courses, but teachers were asked to create the details of course syllabi. It was agreed to offer more than three year-long courses (typically four to five) in each subject area to allow placement of students at different points in a flexible sequence. Courses reflected fairly traditional content areas to blend with high school work and facilitate transfers. Summit classes at the high end overlapped with high school offerings.

Courses were defined in five core subject areas: English, science, math, social studies, and foreign language. The first year, four literature-based English courses were offered, differing primarily by reading level. Courses were based on the excellent challenge language arts program developed by Gerri Masson and Kathy Barry at Prairie Middle School in Cherry Creek (a metro-Denver school district). Students studied quality pieces of literature, generally classics, at the pace of approximately one per month. They discussed the literature in depth within the classroom, moving from consideration of the concrete aspects of each piece to universal themes, thereby using a high level of abstract thinking.

Students wrote an essay with each piece, as well as completed creative writing assignments and "visual" and oral presentations. Each assignment offered a number of choices, and students were allowed to present an alternative idea for approval. Direct instruction in grammar and essay writing were an integral part of the program, with modification for students testing out of these units. The heavy writing emphasis, high level of abstraction, multiple types of assignments to address different learning styles, enjoyable creative aspects, and books of more appropriate reading level were all designed to meet the needs of this range of students.

In mathematics, four courses were offered, with tutorials for various levels an every-other-day option. Advanced Numerical Topics served as a first course of advanced arithmetic and pre-algebra topics for students not yet prepared to undertake algebra. Next were Algebra I, Geometry, and Algebra II/Trigonometry, with the order determined for individual students by readiness for symbolic logic and spatial relations. Tutorials were used for filling holes or enhancing and accelerating learning.

Science courses began with Biological Science and the Environment, and Physical Science and the Earth. These two year-long courses replaced three typical middle school years of study in earth science, biological science, and physical science. Students subsequently took a Chemistry/Physics class akin to a ninth-grade offering for Pre-IB students at the nearby high school, with Biology (high school honors level) and Chemistry likely later additions. The acceleration of students in math allowed the higher-level treatments of subject matter in science; students could handle the necessary formulas and calculations and utilize math as the language of science.

Social studies courses included the following four options: World Geography, History, and Culture; American History; World History; and U.S. Government and History. These courses emphasized both higher-order thinking skills and mastery of basic facts and information in these fields. By the time students left Summit, they would be expected to understand the complexity of these subjects—for example, the effect of different perspectives on history; the use of history as both an explanatory and predictive tool; the influences of geography, resources, and culture on history; the fragmentary nature of historical data; how ideas and individuals can shape history; the interweaving of moral and ethical issues in history; the nature of violence within and between societies; the organizing constructs for society; how to conduct research; and how to argue current issues analytically.

Foreign language courses were offered in Spanish, French, and German, with an emphasis on immersion. Each course consisted of Conversation, Level 1 (typical high school coverage), then Level 2 and Level 3. The committee agreed that using the typical middle school Level 1a/1b approach to extend the first year course to two years was too slow. With the Conversation course, a student had the option of beginning with either an immersion approach (without emphasis on correct spelling of vocabulary or a strict grammatical focus) or Level 1, if the student had some experience with a language or was particularly adept at learning languages.

The curriculum committee chose electives that would appeal to the students and support a lively exploration of a variety of fields. Astronomy and Climatology supplemented more typical offerings in art, drama, and physical education. Music performance classes grouped students by expertise, abandoning the typical orchestra, band, and chorus divisions for string quartets, jazz bands, and other combinations for the particular talent pool each semester.

Placements were based on ability, content mastery, motivation, and developmental level (for example, students took an algebra readiness test to ensure readiness for symbolic logic). Students' grade levels were not a factor in placement, and parents made ultimate placement decisions following an advisory conference.

In the spring of the year before Summit opened, the new principal met with each student and his or her parents to informally assess placement in each subject area for the following year. Information from the algebra readiness instrument helped with math placement, and a review of reading comprehension levels on standardized tests helped to corroborate placement advice in English.

Teachers were selected during the spring and summer for the fall opening. Those with the strongest resumes taught a sample lesson to volunteer students and members of the hiring committee (English teachers graded sample papers). After the sample lesson, the committee interviewed the students, then the teacher. The teachers who were chosen shared a number of characteristics: they had strong content-area expertise, they imposed no ceiling on the level of information that they would share with the students, they treated the students as equals and had good rapport, and they stressed critical thinking and a high level of abstraction. Most were high school and college teachers who were interested in teaching advanced students at this age and were relatively unaware of "what middle schoolers cannot do." They were highly intelligent themselves and passionate about their subjects.

Since the opening of the school to 250 students in the fall of 1996, the majority of families have been pleased. Textbooks chosen to be at approximately the ninth-grade reading level or above (many students have twelfth-grade reading comprehension levels) have been appropriate and successful, except for one geography book that some thought too difficult and an ancient history book some thought too simplistic. The curriculum has proven to be a reasonable match for the student body that is largely in the top quartile of ability. The flexibility to place students at different levels, regardless of age, has met most needs, although an Algebra Plus class has been added to increase the pace and depth that some students need.

Trusting parents to make placement decisions has proven to be reasonable. Some have worried that the approximate two hours per night of homework is stressful and inappropriate for these younger students; others, who have had an older student arrive at high school unprepared for an IB program, feel that this preparation is warranted. Students are clearly learning organizational skills necessary to handle their coursework.

Minor curriculum modifications are likely to continue as talks progress with local high schools to ensure a smooth transition for Summit students. One course change was brought about by the students themselves, who rallied with placards. Frustrated that their foreign language Conversation courses did not include textbooks and more specific help with spelling and grammar, they initiated the elimination of most of the Conversation sections. Their teachers agreed to modify the classes to include the Level 1 curriculum, and the students agreed to do the extra work in the second semester to obtain credit for completing Level 1.

Although evidence of the success of this school is still largely anecdotal, the satisfaction felt by even the most highly gifted students suggests that Summit has created a unique learning environment. A science teacher could not contain her joy as she talked to the parents of her Chemistry/Physics students at Back to School Night. "I want you to know what your students did," she said, holding up a small square of foil. After only a few days discussing the physical properties of matter, she had asked her students if they could find a way to determine the thickness of the foil. Each student in the class was able to figure out independently how to calculate the foil's thickness. "This is something many college freshmen cannot do, and your children did it!" The teacher, who had a Ph.D. in biochemistry, had come to us from a university and was accustomed to teaching college freshmen.

The English IV teacher has taken her class through *The Rhyme of the Ancient Mariner, Beowulf,* and *A Doll's House* at a depth that most of us experience in college, not middle or high school. While shaping their essay writing, grammar mastery, oral presentations, and knowledge of literary forms and devices, she invoked Joseph Campbell's notions of the universal hero and the hero's journey to broaden her students' experience, challenged them with the Anglo-Saxon warrior code and *comitatus* relationships, and explored issues of individuals who must reject their roles in society. One student commented to his mother that he had never discussed such high-level issues at school, only at home.

A particularly joyous aspect of the new school has been seeing the students blossom socially. Many who were previously isolated for their differences, known to be sensitive and introverted, and girls who had a tendency to "go underground" have flourished. One teacher commented, "There are no shrinking violets in my classroom." Summit students both work and play hard. The school has a volunteer Dean of Fun (a humorous father), and student council, dances, outings, carnivals, and sports flourish along with academic competitions. Hundreds of tickets were purchased for area plays that the students attend together.

The Summit model offers an alternative for the education of gifted middle-level students that ensures more appropriate programming and social development than can be provided by modifications in the heterogeneous classroom. The accelerated curriculum is more easily delivered with instructional approaches geared to these learners, combining high levels of abstraction and critical thinking with an energetic involvement of students and hands-on activities. Teachers from higher levels of education have the necessary expertise to offer instruction without a ceiling when students wish to move ahead. Students have opportunities to develop socially with friends who have similar interests.

Creating one or more such schools in a district is no more expensive than maintaining the same number of students in a typical middle school. Opening the school to students on a self-selecting basis allows those most at risk of underachievement or dropping out a clear alternative. The result is that gifted students can attend school in what most truly approximates a least restrictive environment.

Summit Middle School in 2003

By 2003, Summit Charter Middle School was flourishing from the point of view of its students, parents, and staff. It had struggled as well. Finding a comfort level between its parent governing board, principal, and staff was a challenge; the school hired three principals in its first five years. Yet as the school has matured and the interested parties have grown to view their efforts as joint, it has become easier. The success of the school has increased everyone's confidence and minimized overreactions when problems arise.

The school has made changes as needed. Curriculum development is ongoing, with great effort put into meeting specific needs of the student group in various subject areas. Unfortunately, teachers and administrators note a change from the first couple of years at Summit, when the parents and students really knew what the mission of the school was—to provide a highly academic environment for children and to make sure that the kids at the top end are not forgotten in the process. Summit became so popular and the school's test scores were so high that new parents ignored the mission of the school and chose to send less advanced students there so that they could earn high test scores, too. This trend triggered serious changes in the way in which the school functioned.

Summit's curriculum has clearly evolved since the school's first year of operation, when parent organizers created an outline, leaving teachers to fill in details. With the help of fine teachers and a standards-based approach, Summit built a carefully constructed, solid program. However, it is satisfying to note that the assumptions of the parent organizers are still very good. The instincts guiding the group to create an accelerated program to fit the level of an advanced student population seem right on target. Summit has done well offering courses that overlap with high school-level work, allowing students and their families the final say in placement decisions and, in general, diverging from middle school philosophy to offer many levels of instruction rather than grouping students heterogeneously.

Curriculum Changes

English

In English, the school has retained its four year-long, literature-based courses, with students placed at the level that is appropriate. The first two courses cover the content of typical (three-year) middle school coursework, and the third and fourth courses overlap with high school offerings. The English Level I course teaches students to develop skills in decoding literal meaning in a variety of literature texts while beginning to identify stylistic and structural literary elements, including plot, theme, and characterization. Students use the writing process to develop basic skills, such as creating and organizing solid expository paragraphs and five-paragraph essays based upon a thesis statement. Formal grammar instruction includes parts of speech and correct use of punctuation.

The language arts coursework culminates in English Level IV, in which students respond to literature on numerous levels, considering both universal themes and the particular cultural and artistic traditions that shape a literary work. In addition to the literary elements introduced in earlier levels, students learn to respond to and analyze stories, poems, plays, and novels with respect to genre, and they gain experiences with various rhetorical purposes, exposition of research, comparison/

contrast, analysis of literary style, and narration/storytelling. Grammar units focus on improvement of writing accuracy and style: spelling rules, internal punctuation, and embedding information using phrases and clauses.

To increase flexibility, the faculty has developed two separate reading lists for each course level. The lists are utilized in alternate years in which the course is offered, allowing a student to remain at the same level, if needed, for two years without repeating the same content. This is especially helpful for any student who struggled in English when entering the school or a student who began at a high level and needs to repeat English IV. The school is anticipating, for the first time, offering only one section of English IV in the fall, reflecting the lower proportion of highly advanced students now comprising the student body. In addition, for the first time, a remedial reading class is to be offered.

Science

In science, Summit continues to offer two year-long courses covering three typical years of middle school instruction: Biological Sciences and the Environment, and Physical Sciences and the Earth. This seems to work well, although it is challenging for some students. Those who flourish with their science instruction continue on to Chemistry/Physics, an advanced high school-level offering. Students who struggle take Advanced Topics in Science, a course designed to revisit selected content areas.

Social Studies

In social studies, students begin their coursework with World History, generally in sixth grade, which explores the development of the world's major civilizations on all continents from pre-history through the Renaissance. This is followed by American History, which covers the development of our nation from the initial contact between Europeans and American Indians to the present. This course sets the stage for the final course in the sequence: World Geography/International Relations. The goal of this course is to help students understand the complex political, economic, social, and environmental problems that face the world's nations today and to assess the role that the United States should play in shaping solutions.

Math

Courses in mathematics include Pre-Algebra, Algebra, Advanced Algebra and Introduction to Geometry, Pre-Algebra Honors, Accelerated Algebra, Proof Geometry, and Algebra II/Trigonometry to address the need for differing levels of content and instructional pace. Parents and students continue to make the final determination of course choice, with school recommendations to assist them. Students are advised to take the most difficult course in which they can succeed. All students should have a solid understanding of algebra by the end of eighth grade (whereas most middle schools allow only a small group of students to take algebra before high school).

Foreign Language

Foreign language instruction is still available in French, Spanish, and German. The equivalent of two full high school years of a language is now covered in three year-long courses at Summit: Beginning Language, Language I, and Language II. Students are prepared to begin high school Level III courses after completing Summit's coursework.

Electives

Electives at Summit continue to offer a combination of training in necessary modern-day skills such as computer literacy, talent development in the arts, and opportunities for exploration. Advanced students require higher-level support for talent development, and their exploratory behavior is more sophisticated. Summit utilizes its talented faculty to provide varying topics of interest (e.g., Introduction to Japan: A Portal to Nihon). Teachers at Summit know well that middle school students in a highly academic program still require their physical education classes (they need to run, jump, and bounce balls) and opportunities to express themselves in the arts. Especially in such a program, students need outlets and opportunities to keep stress in check.

There are three technology courses. Applied Technology offers units on structures, machines, energy, materials, flight, rocketry, communications, electronics, and computer technology. Introduction to Programming is the beginning computer programming class, followed by Advanced Programming, which emphasizes proper program design, including subroutines, data structures, and program control.

Liberal arts electives include Drama, Advanced Reading Techniques, Film as Literature, and Creative Writing. Art electives included

Art Forms, Pottery/Crafts, Sculpture, and Splash of Color. Music options continue to include an exceptional range of courses and talent groupings: Orchestra and Select Strings (the latter requiring three years of playing and an audition); Jazz Band I, Jazz Band II, and Jazz Band III (the latter requiring a minimum of three years of playing and an audition); Musical Theatre Workshop; and Choir, Starlight (advanced choir), and Silver Rain (choral ensemble by audition only).

Physical education classes continue to be taught, even though the school has only the use of a multi-purpose room for a gym.

Politics, Politics

With all of Summit's success, it continues to draw the ire of the school district that fought so hard against it. Continued intense pressure against the school's location from the middle school forced to share space with it and sympathetic school board members finally forced Summit to move to another site, residing in a former elementary school building that had been closed. Although the site contained only one large multi-purpose room that would have to serve as cafeteria, gym, and auditorium and still required some portable classrooms, staff members felt a sense of relief at having their own space and no unfriendly neighbors. The district stubbornly refused to let the program grow significantly, although Summit continues to have a lengthy waiting list every year. Interestingly, the school district did not try to copy or compete with it, even though this small charter school had the highest middle school test scores in the district.

Summit appealed several decisions made by the local school district to the State Board of Education. A three-to-three split decision by the board (one member sympathetic to Summit was absent) resulted in Summit's inability to prove its case. The local school board hurt Summit with these decisions: to restrict Summit's growth to only 50 students within the next five years, to restrict Summit from building a gym (one board member said that it was not needed in a highly academic program), to make Summit renegotiate its site each year, and to force Summit to relinquish all funds raised in internal fund drives to the district (Summit could no longer use these funds, in part, for teachers). In addition, the school district would decide how much financial support each school would be given from these drives. Of significant concern was the fact that Summit was ordered to develop a remediation plan for struggling students, even though the school's stated mission is to support students who require higher challenge and a more advanced program.

Can Charter Schools Meet the Needs of Gifted Students?

This chapter began as an effort to familiarize parents with the charter school concept as a viable option for meeting the needs of gifted students. Parents frustrated by their children's inability to learn appropriately in typical school programs need options desperately, and charters may offer a clear alternative. Charter schools exist to meet myriad different needs. One in Colorado even serves pregnant teens. Certainly, charter schools for gifted students make sense.

However, the problems that Summit has experienced emphasize the need for parents to proceed with caution. Certainly charters offer a publicly funded alternative that can, potentially, result in a school with a significantly different educational program. Yet charter schools are expected to be "open to all," and therein lies the problem. Whereas a school for pregnant teens, obviously not "open to all," is tolerated because it is perceived to meet a need in the community, a school for high-ability students may draw criticism because the need for it is largely unappreciated.

Summit organizers were initially divided as to whether to create a school for the gifted or a school appealing to a somewhat larger group. Some were clearly uncomfortable with the term *gifted* and felt that it would not be popular in Boulder, Colorado. The decision was made to create a self-selecting school "for students who feel they want or need more challenge," hoping that students and their families would choose wisely. Knowing that self-selecting schools for the gifted *can* work, provided that the school carefully advertises its program so that parents can choose wisely, this approach seemed possible for Summit.

However, the local school district changed the way it handles requests for schools of choice. In Summit's first years, parents wanting to request a school of choice were asked to turn in a request at their chosen school. When parents came to Summit, they were told of informational meetings and opportunities to visit the program. Now, parents are asked to turn in a request to the district office, listing their first, second, and third choices. If they were not granted their first choice, they automatically received their second. Some new families at Summit have never attended a meeting or learned much about the program, despite information on a website. Summit's principal has noted that many of the school's problems could be alleviated if only the parents would visit before enrolling their children.

What does a school do when the wrong students attend? Initially, Summit organizers felt that such students might need thoughtful "counseling out" because the program would be too stressful for them, and other more typical programs would be a better fit. They knew that the program was too small for teachers to stretch too much. Teachers also felt that to keep the level of the program high, they could not lower standards to the level of the least advanced learner. The school felt that it had the right to stay true to its mission.

Summit's teachers deserve credit for their efforts to meet the needs of a student body with ever-widening abilities. For example, science teacher Sharon Sikora, profiled in Chapter 9, modified her requirement that eighth graders do Science Fair projects to allow for a less rigorous, group-oriented activity that some students would benefit from more. The high-end students overwhelmingly chose Science Fair and individual projects. The lower-ability group, now a full 30% of the student body, chose a robotics project that was offered as more of a group activity. Critical thinking was emphasized in the group project as well. All projects culminated in a "Shine" night, in which all students who wished to could share their projects with parents. Sikora felt confident that she met the needs of more students in this way than requiring Science Fair for all eighth graders.

A $10,000 grant from Toshiba provided wonderful technology for the robotics project. Students had the opportunity to explain this advanced technology and the use of it to their parents, who were often in awe of their children because they were able to do such advanced work. Sikora believes that a critical piece in any student's development is the opportunity to shine. Adding this robotics option, she felt that "not every project was awesome, but every kid felt awesome because every one went up a couple of rungs on the ladder." Some students did not feel confident enough to present their work to parents but took a strong leadership role arranging the evening. "You can make it work on so many different levels. Now the clientele has shifted from these very gifted kids to a very different group—many emotionally disturbed, many with learning disabilities," Sikora notes. Summit had always embraced students with disabilities, but advanced students—the twice-exceptional and bright students with emotional or physical issues.

The question now is this: How far can the teachers and the program stretch? In Sharon Sikora's classes, she found it more difficult to shape critical thinking and to cover as much material as in her classes of previous years. She agreed that it would help if all families were made to come to Summit and hear about the mission and what the school is about. "You are going to have homework; you are going to have to work hard," she says.

The state board ruled that Summit would have to provide a plan to address the remedial needs of Summit's less successful students. However, Summit's mission statement calls for a primary focus on high achievement, and for some children, Summit is simply not the right environment. "Counseling kids out is difficult," Sikora states. "Few leave in the middle of the year, but some do leave at the end. And wherever they go, they're happier. It's an interesting challenge."

How can a charter school for the gifted remain effective? Charter schools specifically for the gifted do exist. One in Denver continues to use IQ testing as a part of its admissions program—clearly not complying with the *open to all* concept. IQ testing is an excellent way of determining need for a gifted program. Above all, it measures the degree of asynchrony of the child and is highly suggestive of problems of fit in a program designed for average children.

Although the *open to all* concept is more often a point of contention in schools for high-ability students, a local charter school attorney points out that a Colorado law allows charter schools to provide *any* program currently being provided by local school districts. Several school districts have self-contained schools for the gifted, or schools within schools. There are also a number of magnet schools for the arts, computing, International Baccalaureate, etc. Quite interestingly, all have extremely stringent entry criteria and are not *open to all*. The attorney's message is that there is room for some charter schools to meet the needs of specific groups for which enrollment criteria are appropriate.

However, whether or not a charter school organizing committee can anticipate wisely the challenges that it will face and put protective policies in place from the beginning is something else. Clearly, in the case of Summit, the organizing committee was not in agreement that this charter should be a school for the gifted. Although most of the organizers had gifted children, the need for a self-contained school was not understood, and some thought that an excellent school could work for everyone—a more egalitarian and comforting notion which led to real difficulties.

Amanda P. Avallone (2007) addresses the upside of charter schools for gifted students in "Unfettered Innovation: The Promise of Charter Schools." Avallone is a teacher of English and literacy who serves as assistant principal for curriculum and instruction and directs the in-house teacher training at Summit Middle School. She notes the relative freedom from district policies that charter schools enjoy: their ability to base an entire program on a specific educational mission, as well as their flexibility to determine the number and types of classes offered, whether classes combine mixed-age students, and whether students can accelerate mid-year. Charters can experiment with their school calendar and daily schedule for best results. They can choose their teachers differently and need not take teachers from the district pool. Charter schools can tailor their in-house teacher training to emphasize instructional strategies critical to their student population. "For example," Avallone writes, "the program requirements [at Summit] include training in promoting critical thinking; understanding learning styles; and meeting the needs of bright, gifted, and twice-exceptional students" (p. 193). The freedom to hire non-certified teachers allowed Summit to hire a variety of highly qualified teachers with unique skills—even university professors who did not have state certification to teach younger students.

Avallone emphasizes the ability of charter schools to react quickly to staff and student concerns. Needs can be brought to the governing board of a charter school and addressed quickly because "layers of bureaucracy, interminable studies, and focus groups do not hamper charter schools" (p. 194). For regular district schools, "Relatively minor changes—such as adopting a new textbook or retooling the curriculum of one course—can take months or years" (p. 194). At Summit, a variety of changes were made quickly enough for the parents to see positive results by the end of the school year in which the problems were discovered. And although Summit had to address remedial reading needs for some students, it could refuse to require remedial reading for *all* students in heterogeneous groups, as fellow district schools were instructed to do!

Parents in all states who may be considering charter school options for gifted students need to be aware of a possible uphill fight, as well as the possibilities and success that can result. Knowing that schools like Summit Middle School continue to support students with few other educational options may justify the effort required to create such schools. However, organizers need to do their homework, research state laws, choose fellow organizers wisely, be willing to continue their fight, and be sure to include attorneys in their groups!

Since the Colorado charter school law was passed in 1993, 133 new schools have been created in our state, with increasing opportunities for funding and support. Nationally, more than one million students are enrolled in more than 3,500 schools in 40 states plus the District of Columbia and Puerto Rico (see U.S. Charter Schools, www.uscharterschools.org/pub/uscs_docs/index.htm). As public schools increasingly strive to ignore student differences and teach to heterogeneous groups, communities are stepping up efforts to create schools to address divergent needs.

Summit, by Quinn O'Leary

> *So what can I say about Summit? It's a small school, one of those unimposing, ambiguously-designed products of an era bygone in all architectural study save that of schools. Orangeish brick, a single squat story, ringed with a band of windows that look like they pivot open from the bottom like a drawbridge. The surrounding schoolyard is caught between the philosophies of grammar and middle school playgrounds, the squatting hulk of the former's requisite equipment looking small and well-used in the trampled verdancy of the latter's requisite sports-sized field. It's a rather dull, cookie-cutter façade considering the ability it contains.*
>
> *I was frankly tired, a late night and an early morning ganging up on me, but my exhaustion was tensed and somewhat dispelled, made ignorable by the stomach-wrapping tentacles of excitement and the crackle and buzz of caffeine. My reason for attending, if only for a day and if only as a ghost, was to watch the expertise of Summit's teachers.*
>
> *After the usual rounds of smiles and handshakes, I was shuffled off to my first classroom, moving among the tide of kids five and six years younger than myself, feeling ancient and out of place. Walking through the halls of a middle school is usually like visiting a slaughterhouse long out of use. It's oppressive and unreal, the lingering flickers of simple anguish and elemental fear blending with the forgotten, ethereal and half-imagined smell of animalistic desperation.*

Summit, however, was different. The electrical charge in the air was still present, the slightly-needy touch of adolescence, but the fear and angst were absent, replaced by the open, breezy flow of comfortable youth. Abruptly, I found myself wishing I had attended this school.

I claimed a quiet, out of the way seat in my first classroom, English IV, a busily organized place run by a perfectionistic but rather kind and obviously competent teacher. The students were occupied with character dissections, peeling away layers of nuance and exposing desires and fears from the terse text of a short story. It was gratifying to a ridiculous degree to see the intelligence of these children tested and displayed.

In another class, I heard a discussion of Mark Twain that would have put many a high schooler to shame, followed by a discussion of the basis of heroism and a short mention of Metamorphosis, *a book I didn't get around to reading myself until far later in life than this lucky lot, and certainly not for credit.*

As I watched the kids interacting and enjoying their time in what was the least enjoyable of my scholastic eras, I was washed over again with the same soft jealousy and retroactive wishing. I grinned, knowing now that alternatives to the prison camp of most middle schools do exist. It's simply a matter of finding them.

For Further Reading:

Books and Articles

Avallone, A. P. (2007). Unfettered innovation: The promise of charter schools. In K. Kay, D. Robson, & J. F. Brenneman (Eds.), *High IQ kids* (pp. 186-196). Minneapolis, MN: Free Spirit.

Gilman, B. J. (1997, May-June-July). New challenge for middle schoolers. *Kaleidoscope*, 9-12.

Tomlinson, C. (1992). Gifted education and the middle school movement: Two voices on teaching the academically talented. *Journal for the Education of the Gifted, 15*(3), 206-238.

Website

U.S. Charter Schools (provides information about currently existing charter schools across the United States, state laws, startup and assistance, and federal resources)
www.uscharterschools.org/pub/uscs_docs/index.htm

For Further Reading

Books and Articles

Chapter 11
Planning Your Child's Program—Year by Year

Parents call us from around the world asking for recommendations for what should be done for their children. They call from large cities with plenty of resources, such as the parents who phoned from the Washington D.C. area whose child once attended a preschool program at the Smithsonian. They call from rural areas, like the mother from Nebraska whose son attended a one-room schoolhouse. Virtually none of these parents have access to a school for the gifted, which would be our first choice to meet their child's academic, social, and emotional needs. Most have only their neighborhood public school, perhaps a few additional public schools that they might consider, and possibly one or more private schools. Not seeing an easy way to meet their child's needs, they seek advice.

They call about the four-year-old who is already an avid reader and is begging to attend school early. They call about the second grader who reads at a fifth-grade level. They call about the fourth grader who seems to have an easy understanding of algebra concepts at home and is (of course) frustrated with arithmetic drill and practice at school. Often, they call because the gifted program at their child's school is minimal or nonexistent, or because being identified for gifted services requires high achievement, and their child is losing motivation to achieve. They call because low-level middle school coursework has resulted in their son refusing to attend school, or their daughter is going underground with her abilities in order to be popular. They call because their gifted high school student has attendance problems and is in danger of being expelled from school. The calls regarding older children and teenagers take on more urgency, because these kids are considerably more frustrated with their educational options than their younger counterparts.

Similar calls come in to state departments of education in all states and to other gifted education centers and gifted consultants in other cities. Parents aren't sure where to turn for help. What role should the parent play? How much advocacy is wise, and what form should it take?

Given the fact that gifted children are truly an at-risk population, advocacy is essential. Here are some ways to advocate for a gifted child sensibly and realistically.

The Diagnostic-Prescriptive Curriculum

Gifted children of all levels require a *diagnostic-prescriptive curriculum* geared to their advanced learning needs. They master concepts more easily, with little or no drill and practice, so they pace through material more quickly. Even adding depth and breadth (enrichment) to their programs, they still pace faster. Too much of a discrepancy between what they already know and what they are being taught threatens their motivation to learn. Parents cannot assume that the schools will know their child's level of achievement in all subject areas. So each year, the parent needs to advocate for accommodations that provide the best fit.

Such advocacy takes a different form with gifted children of different ages and different levels of giftedness. Children who are moderately gifted will need Individual Education Plans (IEPs) throughout elementary school to ensure that they are placed at approximately the correct levels in their various academic subjects. Although they stay in one classroom throughout the day, an IEP allows for accommodations within the room and possible opportunities to pursue some work at a higher grade level in another classroom or through a program outside of the school.

In middle school, the advocacy focus changes from ensuring modifications within a single classroom (although this could occur) to obtaining permission from a counselor, teacher, or administrator for the student to take higher-grade-level classes earlier. Appropriate class placement usually involves placing (or testing) out of some entry-level courses that the student has already mastered and taking classes that older students take. This typically results in students enrolling in some high school coursework during middle school. High school advocacy involves obtaining permission for the student to place out of entry-level courses, enter advanced high school classes earlier, and pursue college-level courses concurrently.

Children with even higher levels of giftedness need even faster progression. We have seen a wide range of accommodations work for these highly, exceptionally, and profoundly gifted children, from acceleration in the public schools of only a couple of years, provided that there are substantial opportunities for advanced work, to some profoundly gifted children graduating from high school before age 10 and beginning college courses, either online or by attending the actual classes. Much depends on what is available in the community and local school district, as well as whether nearby colleges or universities are willing to be flexible. Even more important, parents and children choose options that feel comfortable to them while ruling out alternatives that seem too risky or at odds with their carefully considered intentions.

With all gifted children, we must continually assess how their programs are working and make adjustments as needed. We should expect to hear satisfaction from the students about the majority of their courses, even if some will almost inevitably disappoint. Here are some guidelines for advocacy at the various levels of schooling, to add to the information presented in Chapter 7: Successful Programs, and Chapter 8: Models of Advocacy.

Elementary School

Early Entrance

For the child who is eager to begin school and has early reading skills, early entrance to kindergarten is an excellent accommodation in school districts that will allow it. It is a good idea for parents to inquire about the necessary requirements for early admission, as this is the easiest acceleration to accomplish. The child begins school with a group of children that he or she can remain with for some time. In addition, since reading is not taught seriously until first grade, a child who is advanced is likely to suffer significantly if forced to wait another year before even beginning kindergarten. In some cases, a placement in first grade makes even more sense, but it is rarely possible, as it depends on the willingness and flexibility of administrators. Some parents get around an inflexible system by enrolling the child in a private school kindergarten and are thus able to say the next year that their child is ready for first grade, having the record of kindergarten completion from the private school.

School districts that allow early admission usually require assessment of some sort. Unfortunately, some utilize a mock classroom situation to evaluate the social maturity of perspective new students. Yet when the criterion for maturity is willingness to readily join the group, introverted young gifted children may appear immature. This is not an appropriate requirement for a gifted child, since these children often need some time to observe and reflect before joining in. Children will appear to be no more mature in this regard if assessed the next year or the year after. They often are slow to join the group initially but will eagerly participate once they become familiar with classmates. As long as they are comfortable being placed with the older group and want to begin school early, then early entrance to kindergarten is an appropriate accommodation.

In school districts that refuse to allow early entrance, a child can sometimes grade-skip within a few weeks to first grade. The reasoning behind this is that the kindergarten teacher is in a better position to determine the need for acceleration after observing the child in the classroom. In such cases, it is wise to not only have the child tested on an individual intelligence test, but also on an individual achievement test to document the child's reading and math achievement levels. When the scores indicate advanced achievement as well as gifted abilities, there is a stronger case for acceleration to first grade.

Many parents worry that their children will not score high on individual achievement tests because they have not been taught higher-grade-level work. However, young gifted children tend to score higher than their classmates because they have learned age-appropriate concepts more thoroughly and can answer more questions correctly. Of course, at some point, exposure to new skills is necessary—for example, when learning to multiply or solve algebraic equations. However, these efficient learners usually outscore their grade peers with nothing more than the instruction that all have had.

Accommodations in Kindergarten and the Primary Grades

Once children are attending elementary school, regardless of their age, the most common modification needed is for advanced reading skills. More young gifted children are advanced in reading than in math, probably because most are read to as young children and have regular access to reading at home. Fewer are taught formal math skills beyond counting. Because primary grades emphasize the acquisition of reading skills, teachers spend considerable time on reading basics. Although we want to ensure reasonable coverage of phonics and sound blending, the child who is fully reading and sounding out words does not need the same instruction that beginning readers need. Moreover, the advanced child needs to read at a challenging level to progress further.

These children will benefit from a plan in which the teacher substitutes more advanced work for material that the student has already mastered. The teacher may divide the students into reading groups based on skill level. If the children are not grouped, or if none of the groups is reading challenging enough material, the teacher should look for opportunities to place the child with a higher-grade-level reading group, perhaps by asking another teacher if the child can join his or her classroom for a short time each day for reading. In addition, the child may be assigned advanced literature by the classroom teacher who is individualizing for this child. In some cases, a less advanced book that the class is reading has enough inherent value to be appropriate for the gifted child, provided that assignments related to the book are modified to require some higher-level thinking.

Children who learn to read early are also more likely to be aware of the correct spelling of words. Although perfectionistic gifted children also need to be encouraged to write before they know how to spell words, teachers may gently provide the correct spelling to help the child avoid learning a word incorrectly. A colleague recently noted that her school was seeing a problem for many children—not just those who are gifted—by encouraging inventive spelling for too long. As a result, the school started teaching formal spelling along with reading skills. Apparently, many children find this incorrect learning difficult to rectify.

Children who are advanced in math in the early grades need support to continue their progress in that subject, particularly if they have already learned advanced concepts. Some children are eager to learn arithmetic operations and question their parents at home to learn more. Answering questions to support a child's curiosity is always a good idea, so parents should not stop providing answers. However, the child who can add, subtract, and multiply in first grade is going to be underchallenged with a constant diet of beginning addition facts.

The IEP

Rather than hoping that schools will make accommodations voluntarily, perhaps following a conversation with the teacher, it is better if parents pursue a written plan. This can be called an Individual Education Plan (IEP), using special education terminology, a Personal Learning Plan (PLP), an Alternative Learning Plan (ALP), or something similar. Even though program modifications for gifted children are rarely mandated by law, a written plan improves the chances that realistic accommodations will be made. To create it, the parents, teacher, and student must agree upon needs, goals, and special programming for the year. Ultimately, the written plan clarifies expectations for all, but its real benefit is the careful consideration that goes into it.

Such a plan need not be complicated; in fact, teachers are more likely to follow a simple, straightforward plan. It should address the areas of the curriculum in which the child will need modifications. Leave other areas alone. Forms for the IEP vary. Two examples utilizing a simple form are completed below, but other forms will work, too, such as those in Karen Rogers' *Re-Forming Gifted Education* (2002), Susan Winebrenner and Pamela Espeland's *Teaching Gifted Kids in the Regular Classroom* (2001), or *The Curriculum Compacting Study* (1993) by Sally Reis, et al. In addition, the child's teacher or school may have a form that will serve the purpose.

The important thing is to complete a written plan that documents agreed-upon educational goals and lists principal activities to meet those goals for the school year. (A note of caution: In districts that create alternative learning plans for all gifted children that look essentially the same, try to incorporate any specific accommodations that an individual child needs.) It is not necessary for the plan to contain each and every lesson—the teacher needs freedom to plan as the year unfolds—but general goals should be defined.

Individual Education Plan: Lara

Consider the case of Lara, a first grader who started reading before kindergarten, currently reads chapter books at the third-grade level, and already knows how to spell many words. Her math is at grade level because she has not been exposed to formal, written math calculations at home. If her advanced reading needs are not accommodated, she may fail to progress in her reading this year. Moreover, she may even sense disapproval about her reading skill if it is not supported (some gifted children stop reading because they believe that the teacher or other students will not like it).

Lara is moderately gifted, with an IQ of 137. Her Wechsler IQ test profile indicates strengths in both verbal abstract reasoning and spatial reasoning (some schools address reasoning strengths and learning styles on student education plans). Like most gifted children, she is an introvert who is not likely to complain to her teacher about work that is too easy or risk calling attention to herself. Her parents and teacher would like to support her strengths in the classroom this year. Here is a sample IEP for Lara.

Individual Education Plan

Name: Lara **Age:** 6 years, 3 months

Grade: 1

Strong Subject Areas: Reading and spelling

Learning Characteristics/Style: Gifted verbal abstract reasoner and visual-spatial reasoner

Subject Areas Chosen to Provide Advanced Study: Reading and spelling

Weaknesses to be Accommodated: None

Goals: Lara will progress commensurate with her ability this year from her current level in reading and spelling. Her introversion will be supported in the classroom. She will be allowed to pace quickly, if needed, in math (her gifted visual-spatial strengths suggest that she will be good in math).

Activities:

1. Have Lara participate daily in an advanced second-grade reading group.
2. Exempt her from pre-reading activities and phonics instruction in the first grade, as her knowledge of phonics is already strong.
3. In writing assignments, encourage Lara to spell inventively, but also offer her the correct spellings for her own information (no penalties for misspelled words).
4. Admit Lara to the school's gifted program, especially to encourage contact with other gifted girls.
5. Have Lara participate in the Junior Great Books program, an extracurricular activity at the school. This program encourages thoughtful analysis of literature, emphasizing abstract reasoning—a strength for Lara.
6. Assess her frequently in math.
7. Keep drill, practice, and worksheets to a minimum.
8. Along with advanced verbal explanation, teach to her visual-spatial strengths—provide a conceptual framework before teaching, and use visual aids.

End-of-Year Evaluation: [Were Lara's accommodations successful? Does she enjoy school, and does she feel that she is learning mostly new material?]

Plan for Next Year: [Will the third-grade reading group suffice to meet her needs next year in second grade? Should full-grade acceleration be considered if math advances quickly as well? What are the next most logical steps for her?]

Such an IEP should provide reasonable accommodation for Lara's strengths this year. Her parents and teacher should review the plan several times during the year to make any needed changes. Before the end of the school year, they should meet again to evaluate the success of the plan and consider prospects to support Lara's progress next year. Her parents should avoid placing her in a second-grade classroom with the outcome unknown. A written plan will ensure that she will not be asked to repeat material—for example, participate in the advanced second-grade reading group again!

At this point, parents are wise to interview teachers at the next grade level to see which teacher is most eager to accommodate a gifted child like Lara so that planning can begin. The principal can help, too, by allowing some choice of the teacher or, better yet, suggesting one that would be appropriate. We were once told by an elementary principal, "If you don't like the teacher after a month, I'll put your son into another class." He explained why he thought that the teacher assignment was a good one, and he was right! It is a tremendous help to have such support from an administrator for a special needs child.

Individual Education Plan: Omar

Consider this next example. Omar is a highly gifted third-grade boy with advanced math abilities and interest in science. He has been diagnosed by a private psychologist as having ADHD and poor fine-motor coordination. He can compose stories fairly well if he can dictate them, but he hates the physical act of handwriting. He will, on purpose, write only brief compositions (by hand) at school. Omar reads at a high level but rarely reads books for enjoyment. He despises timed math tests because he cannot write quickly enough, and his math facts are not fully memorized. He is distractible in the classroom and needs to move around frequently. He sometimes forgets assignments and lacks organizational skills. His teacher wonders if he should even be in the gifted program—his IQ score is 146—because he is impatient with classwork and often does not do his best.

Omar needs a challenging, fast-paced program to minimize his ADHD-like symptoms and help him engage in his work. Conversely, if instruction is too easy and repetitive, his symptoms may worsen. It is important for his teachers to exempt Omar from instruction that he doesn't need and teach him at a level and pace that are somewhat difficult for him; he can engage and focus best with material that is largely new and novel, and this will encourage his best efforts. At the same time, he needs modifications for his fine-motor weaknesses and poor organizational skills.

Omar, because he has ADHD, is fortunate that he qualifies by federal law for a 504 Plan, which requires accommodations for individuals with disabilities. (IDEA 2004 also allows children with severe ADHD to qualify for regular special education assistance). Omar therefore has a legal right to accommodations in school or the workplace to allow him to succeed *if he needs them*. A 504 Plan might address Omar's organizational problems, fine-motor deficits, need for movement, and distractibility in the classroom with several mandated accommodations that would continue at school, year by year, with periodic review. For example, his 504 Plan might include having the teacher check his daily planner to ensure that assignments are written down, contact his parents if homework isn't turned in (and give him additional time to complete it before grades decline), allow him opportunities for movement in the classroom, let him dictate compositions or use a keyboard, and ensure preferential seating so that he is less distracted listening and when taking tests. Such accommodations can be changed as a child's organizational skills improve and other needs change. If Omar doesn't need this degree of help for his deficits, then the IEP developed with the teacher would be enough.

A frequent sticking point with 504 Plans for gifted children with ADHD is that accommodating the giftedness is also a critical part of addressing the ADHD-like behaviors, yet most states do not have strong legal mandates for the gifted portion. Some schools will refuse to include gifted accommodations, when they are so important in minimizing ADHD symptoms. As a result, Omar's 504 Plan and the suggested IEP below might differ between one another considerably.

Omar needs accommodations for his giftedness in any case. As a twice-exceptional student, he will likely thrive when his giftedness is supported first, then his ADHD is gently accommodated as well. In this particular case, Omar is highly gifted, and if his teacher opens doors for him and believes that he is capable, he may succeed brilliantly. Here, then, is a sample IEP for Omar.

Individual Education Plan

Name: Omar **Age:** 8, years, 5 months

Grade: 3

Strong Subject Areas: Math, science, and reading

Learning Characteristics/Style: Highly gifted, twice-exceptional visual-spatial learner with verbal abstract reasoning strengths; holistic learner

Subject Areas Chosen to Provide Advanced Study: Math, science, and reading

Weaknesses to Be Accommodated: Handwriting, attention

Goals: Teach Omar at the level of his advanced mastery in math and reading. Enrich science study. Accommodate fine-motor weaknesses through reduced handwriting demands. Address ADHD symptoms with a challenging, fast-paced program and support for organizational weaknesses.

Activities:

1. Place Omar in the fifth-grade challenge math group for math instruction.
2. Allow him to do in-depth projects in science, extending the topics studied by the class. Exempt him from simpler assignments that he has already mastered.
3. Place Omar in a fourth-grade reading group.
4. Add non-fiction books of his choosing in science.
5. Teach to his visual-spatial preference. Provide a conceptual framework before teaching, into which Omar can place new facts learned. Use visual aids and hands-on activities.
6. Teach Omar keyboarding skills.
7. Allow him to use a computer for his writing in class or at home.

8. Also allow Omar to demonstrate what he knows in other ways, such as through oral reports, class presentations with visual aids, creative projects, or dictation (trust his work).
9. Allow him to move around the classroom as needed.
10. Teach study and organizational skills, especially the use of a daily planner. Make sure that Omar has his assignments written down adequately, or provide assignments in writing.
11. Avoid timed tests.
12. Minimize drill and practice. When Omar masters a concept, he should move on.
13. Pre-test before teaching to avoid teaching what Omar already knows.
14. Arrange a mentor for Omar in science to support his interests and extend his knowledge of the field.

Evaluation: [Did the activities planned to challenge Omar engage him better? Did he progress in math and reading from his already-advanced levels? Did organizational skills improve? Is he keeping track of assignments and turning them in? Did composition skills progress once keyboarding was allowed?]

Plan for Next Year: [It is very important to ensure Omar's continuous progress. Avoid repeating coursework when he moves on to the next classroom. Support for ADHD may need to continue.]

The plan for Omar acknowledges his highly gifted learning capacity with accelerated work in math and reading, along with enriched science assignments in the classroom. He will engage more readily and do his best work when encouraged to stretch. At the same time, the plan supports his handwriting difficulties with an emphasis on keyboarding and demonstrating his learning in alternate ways. The plan also acknowledges his ADHD with opportunities for movement, help with study and organizational skills, and an effort to provide challenging, high-interest, novel material as consistently as possible.

Karen Rogers (2002) has done an excellent job describing how particular needs can be addressed in IEPs. For additional information and examples, consult her book *Re-Forming Gifted Education: How Parents and Teachers Can Match the Program to the Child.*

Integrating Outside Coursework into the IEP

What does one do when a child needs a level of instruction that is not available within his or her school? Although the limitations that schools impose may seem daunting (e.g., the school *refuses* to allow a child to accelerate in math or to substitute more advanced literature in language arts), there are usually options. Achievement testing can document the need for more advanced work at the child's actual level, and the needed coursework is usually within reach of most families.

Consider the student who needs algebra as early as elementary school. Courses may be available at a nearby middle or high school. If the upper-level school agrees to allow the student to attend classes and transportation and scheduling can be arranged (students may have to attend first or last periods), the younger student can successfully complete such coursework early. Distance-learning courses may also be used to substitute for grade-level math. For example, the Education Program for Gifted Youth's (EPGY) math coursework substitutes nicely for school instruction from the elementary school level to beyond high school (see http://epgy.stanford.edu). The lectures are available via CD-ROM and can be viewed on a family's home computer after school, or at school if the school agrees to offer the program. EPGY homework might be done during math instruction in the classroom, allowing the student to substitute advanced work for regular math instruction. Such substitutions must be included in the IEP. (It is never advisable to insist that the child complete regular coursework at school *in addition* to accelerated work.)

When the advanced needs of a child exceed what can be provided through a typical IEP, parents may choose partial home schooling. This solution satisfies the child who is accelerated in several subjects but resists full-grade acceleration and leaving friends. Parents can offer the advanced coursework needed in a portion of the school day and still allow the child to attend school for some subjects and social activities.

Full-Grade Acceleration

As some gifted children progress through elementary school, their advancement becomes more pronounced, requiring more substantial modifications. For a child who is advanced in virtually all subject areas, acceleration in one or two subjects of a grade level is no longer enough. When we see achievement test results that indicate that a child is at least two or more grade levels (as indicated by grade-equivalent scores on standardized tests) ahead of age peers in virtually all academic subject areas (we tend to ignore spelling), and the child voices concerns about being bored in school and frustrated by limited options, we suggest full-grade acceleration (whole-grade skip).

Because the research on grade acceleration is generally positive if the child concurs with the placement, we recommend that the child make the final decision, as long as the parents can accepted either the regular or accelerated placement options as reasonable. If the child wishes to accelerate and his or her current teacher concurs, the school should then agree. This usually requires the consensus of a team of teachers, staff, and administrators meeting with the parents. Consider asking an expert advocate to attend so that he or she can present the child's case and provide articles about acceleration to the committee members, because most will not have considered full-grade acceleration before. Generally, these committees deal with children who are struggling in some way. There is the risk that each committee member will be swayed by the limited experience that he or she has with acceleration—perhaps with a single acquaintance or family member. Most dangerously, schools assume that a decision not to accelerate the gifted child is *safer.* It is important to understand that the decision *not* to accelerate is just as serious as the decision *to* accelerate, and each option should be weighted equally in consideration.

The committee needs to both weigh the issues carefully and know that gifted children generally accelerate well and are happy with the results.

If parents and schools wish to have a research-based tool to guide the discussion about full-grade acceleration, the *Iowa Acceleration Scale,*[1] mentioned in Chapter 7, is something to consider. It systematically leads a child study team through a series of questions to determine whether a whole-grade skip or some other option should be recommended. The IAS Manual contains relevant educational and psychological research on whole-grade acceleration. It is important that the child want the acceleration, and also that the school will follow through to make the transition to the new grade as smooth and supportive as possible. The IAS Form acts like an IEP, in that it lists who is responsible for monitoring the child's progress and how to know if the skip is successful. The authors of the IAS also make it clear that no decision is irrevocable. If the child is unhappy after two months in the new classroom, he or she can always return to the previous class placement. However, research data show that gifted children typically thrive and are happy in their new setting.

When a child has a current IEP, it should include any needed preparation for grade skipping. If cursive or long division will be expected, some instruction can be added prior to the grade skip. Likewise, if the child will miss some material in the next grade level that would be enriching, plans can be made to include it, too, perhaps during the summer. For example, one local student planning to skip third grade would have missed the social studies unit on Colorado history and mining, so his teachers agreed to loan him the books over the summer.

Enrichment/Academic Experiences Outside of School

In addition to the individualized education programs that can be arranged with the child's elementary school, parents should also consider enrichment experiences outside of school. Many gifted children take summer classes in their areas of interest at local museums and universities. The programs may or may not be specifically designed for gifted children, but they tend to draw bright children with shared interests. They provide one means of finding like-minded peers.

Always popular are the science enrichment classes and creative writing groups. Foreign language camps, such as Concordia Language Villages in Minnesota (http://clvweb.cord.edu/prweb), offer summertime immersion learning experiences in many languages. A check of Hoagies' Gifted Education Page (www.hoagiesgifted.org) covers many other possibilities (see Academic Programs, and Summer and Saturday Programs).

Talent Searches and Related Programs

Talent Search programs offer advanced educational opportunities for students who can demonstrate high ability on tests. The practice of conducting searches for students who reason extremely well mathematically and/or verbally was begun by the late Professor Julian Stanley of The Johns Hopkins University in the early 1970s. Stanley believed that giving an SAT or ACT test to students who are much younger than the college-bound seniors for whom the tests are designed results in scores that measure differences among bright students who all score well on in-grade tests. He then designed an accelerated summer academic program for students who scored well on the tests. Now there are four regional talent searches conducted by The University of Denver, The Johns Hopkins University, Duke University, and Northwestern University.

Students may wish to consider the Talent Search program at the university in their designated area, though they may also attend the programs of other schools (entrance criteria vary). To participate in talent searches, students usually take the SAT or ACT exams in the sixth or seventh grade. If they score high enough, they are invited to attend classes at the university the following summer. These are fast-paced, intensive courses that these students usually love and that *may* confer credit at the student's home school if requested. Taken as commuter courses or with the students staying in dormitories, they usually offer a wonderful social experience, as well as challenging work. It is important to check with the Talent Searches early for details. The SAT or ACT must be taken early in the fall prior to the summer in which classes are sought. Talent Search offices can provide information about deadlines and registration for tests (websites are listed at the end of this chapter).

There are also opportunities for younger elementary students, utilizing tests such as the PLUS, EXPLORE, and SCAT. A range of classes exists, depending on the program, including distance learning and Saturday enrichment. Contacting the Talent Searches while the child is in the primary grades is a good idea so that parents know about possible options for the future.

In addition to the four major Talent Search programs, smaller regional programs also exist at colleges and universities. These may be accessed by an Internet search.

The Move to Middle School

Because most middle school philosophy stresses the instruction of students of all ability levels together (*heterogeneous grouping*), parents need to research options carefully. Does a middle school offer honors classes and, if so, in what subjects? Is it possible for a student to take a higher-grade-level class if it can be documented that the typical grade-level material has already been mastered? Some middle schools are particularly concerned about their students staying together for the entire school day with the same team of teachers; they believe that this provides additional support that middle schoolers need. Staff members may be concerned that if a student takes a course with an upper-level teacher and different students, it may undermine the student's confidence. However, one middle school in Colorado actually studied the effects of releasing some of its most advanced students from their within-grade groupings to facilitate taking higher-level classes. A poll taken of the students following their experience documented overwhelming support for the advanced classes. In no way did students feel that they lost confidence!

Providing Accelerated Middle School Coursework

When a student enters middle school, there should already be agreement about placement. If the student has been accelerated, he or she needs to be placed at the next level in each subject. Gifted students do not tolerate repeating classes well; inappropriate placement can cause anger, resentment, and the belief that the school is being unfair. There is virtually never a good argument for taking a grade-level class when the student has already mastered the content.

High School Courses for Middle Schoolers

Because middle schools usually serve three grades, there are few opportunities for accelerated courses within the building (unless the school offers multiple levels of coursework to improve differentiation). The advanced student who places out of one or more courses in a subject area sequence quickly needs high school work. Most frequently, accelerated middle school students go to the nearest high school to take the necessary course, generally working it into their schedules successfully. Unless the middle school and high school are near one another, transportation is an issue, and parents may need to be responsible. More than one class period is often needed to allow for transportation time, with the result that the middle school student often has little flexibility in his or her schedule.

Distance-Learning Courses

Other options may mesh with a student's schedule better. Online, computer-based, or correspondence coursework (such as the University of Nebraska's Independent Study High School or Stanford's EPGY) are options which eliminate the transportation problem. Utilizing such options, a middle school student can support his or her advanced abilities and still have a relatively normal placement for most of the school day.

College Courses for Middle Schoolers

Community college and university courses are not out of reach for many gifted middle school students (and sometimes even younger children). Colleges vary in their admissions policies; however, many have no administrative restrictions against young students attending classes. It is always wise to speak with the instructor of the course in question; some teachers are resistant to young students, whereas others are delighted with the unusual opportunity. It is important for the younger student to have a teacher who is enthusiastic and supportive.

With colleges that restrict younger students from attending courses, some parents have found approaching an individual faculty member to be effective. One father reported that his calls to a university physics department chairman, then later to the head of undergraduate physics, went unheeded for months when he wanted his 10-year-old profoundly gifted son to attend a Physics for Poets class (with little math). Yet when he met the well-known professor of the course at a party, he easily obtained an invitation for his son to visit the class. When the boy's visit went well, the professor invited him to take the course. The professor would simply *tell* his department head, he said. He added that if the boy wanted credit for the class and the university would not give it, he might be able to persuade them—or he would write a letter describing the young student's achievement that could be presented to an admissions office, if needed.

Credit for Accelerated Work

When a younger student takes coursework at the high school level or higher, it is important to ask about credit. Will the course confer credit toward high school graduation? Ideally, it should. However, some schools offer credit if the course is taken at the high school, but no credit if the same course is taken at the middle school. The school district may also have a policy that if the student is not yet full-time at the high school, the coursework counts only for high school placement—no credit is given toward a high school diploma—but the student will not have to take the course again and will be placed in a higher-level course once in high school. It may be impossible to fight such a regulation, but it is better to know ahead of time what will be done.

When a middle school (or sometimes elementary) student takes a high school course (algebra, geometry, biology, earth science, Spanish, or other foreign language), the course should appear on the student's high school transcript with the date completed. Parents should keep a record of the enrollment, such as a letter signed by the instructor indicating the grade earned, so that when the student enrolls full-time in high school, the student's transcript can show the course credit. If there is any problem, the principal or a department chair can explain to the registrar.

Issues of credit for successful completion of courses can also, ultimately, affect class rank if the student is not awarded "weighted" credit for difficult high school courses taken before formally entering high school. As a result, many gifted students relinquish their goal of becoming valedictorian in favor of moving on to college more quickly!

Grade Acceleration in Middle School

Middle school may be a good time to consider full-grade acceleration. There are generally no clear rules about the number of classes or credits needed to complete middle school. However, high school graduation requirements are quite rigid. For example, our school district requires 220 credits for graduation, with a typical semester course earning five credits (requirements vary by state). This assumes a four-year program in which the student takes 55 credits per year, or 25-30 per semester. To graduate in less than four years requires taking more than the usual five to six courses each semester—not a trivial undertaking. Most districts in our state are reluctant to modify this requirement for any student.

If the gifted student is learning quickly and seven years seems like too many to complete middle and high school, then *the time to skip a grade is in middle school.* This becomes an even better idea in middle schools in which few advanced classes are offered. Many gifted students have reached high school grade equivalents in reading or math while still in elementary school, leaving little or no gap between their level of achievement and that of typical students entering high school. With some of the most advanced students, we have suggested skipping middle school altogether, and it has been a good strategy. For others, reducing the time spent in middle school is reasonable.

High School

Different Offerings in Different High Schools

If a gifted student will need significant accommodations in high school, it is best to explore options with several high schools during the last year of middle school (perhaps in October or November to allow plenty of time). Parents should ask for the high school course catalog and look for advanced offerings in subjects of interest to the student. More advanced classes and the flexibility to take them earlier if needed suits gifted students well.

Does the school offer a large number of Advanced Placement (AP) courses? A large high school heavily committed to such offerings will have 20 to 30 AP courses—subjects like American history, American literature, British literature, English composition, various foreign languages, calculus, biology, chemistry, physics, and even music theory and art. Advanced Placement courses lead to an exit test taken nationwide on the same date in early May that, depending on the score earned (1-5) and the policy of the college or university that the student attends, can confer college credit to the student.

High school course booklets list the prerequisites for taking the AP classes. A student will normally need to have the prerequisite math courses (or test out of those courses) in order to take AP calculus, for example. Students who take several AP classes during high school and score well enough on the tests to earn college credit may enter college with sophomore status, thanks to the number of college credits they earned from AP classes while in high school. When younger students are accelerated and taking AP classes earlier—as freshmen or sophomores, it is good to know that the AP exams for credit are not age restricted. A freshman can take the exam.

Some high schools offer the International Baccalaureate (IB) program, an eleventh- and twelfth-grade comprehensive degree program with similar advanced courses that confer college credit. Most schools require students to complete the entire program for an IB diploma, but some schools allow students to pick and choose individual courses and earn certificates (similar to taking individual AP courses). IB exams must be taken in the junior and senior years, which can be a problem if the student is ready to take the test early. However, there are some excellent, rigorous IB programs that have met the needs of very highly gifted students beautifully. High schools offering IB programs usually have Pre-IB courses as well, which ensure high-level coursework during freshmen and sophomore years. This can be important. If the student will not be placing out of entry-level courses, are there honors or other advanced/accelerated offerings for underclassmen?

The Importance of Proper Class Placements

High schools usually offer some degree of placement flexibility to entering freshmen. For example, counselors often allow a sizeable group of students to skip the entry-level English class in favor of the sophomore course. Or counselors may recommend students for a higher-level freshman English course. This option normally depends on the student's past record—grades and teacher recommendation. Likewise, students routinely take the next level course in typical math and foreign language sequences. If the student has completed accelerated work, it is important to make sure that the high school course selection is appropriately accelerated when the student enters. Gifted students can usually qualify for such accommodations and should seek them.

For more extensive placement flexibility, the principal or a department chair may make a placement decision (for example, a department chair might administer a math placement test to determine the correct math class). If a principal is willing to get involved, he or she can be a wonderful ally for the out-of-sync student, determining placement levels (without the objection of the counselors), offering long-range planning tips, and suggesting appropriate classes or teachers to consider. In our state, the principal has the power to approve the granting of credit for independent studies, mentorships, and internships, so if a student wants such an option, it is worth inquiring about the possibility. The principal can also exempt students from some graduation requirements, which affect the gifted student's overall program. Sometimes a principal is pleased to be involved in such a proactive way for a special student; it helps to balance the more negative, problem-oriented aspects of the job.

Bob Martin, former principal of Broomfield High School in Broomfield, Colorado, offered the following help to one accelerated student. He suggested a four-year plan of courses, whereby the student could begin at the correct level in each subject area based on mastery. Because the young man had completed Geometry 1, Algebra 2, a high school-level Chemistry/Physics class, and was an advanced writer at the time he entered high school, he needed significant acceleration. The high school already had a suggested "Course of Study with Advanced, Honors, and AP Courses" to help college-bound students plan their schedules. The high school's suggested plan for such students looked like this:

Department	Grade 9	Grade 10	Grade 11	Grade 12
Language Arts	Freshman Core	Sophomore English	Advanced Composition, Shakespeare, etc.	AP English
Social Studies	Freshman Core (English, U.S. Govt., and Geography)	World History	American Studies Honors, [or similar course]	AP U.S. History or AP European History
Math	Geometry Honors	Algebra 2 Honors	Pre-Calculus 1 and 2	AP Calculus
Science	Biology	Chemistry	AP Biology, AP Chemistry, Adv. Physics,	Anatomy [or similar course]
Foreign Language	Level 1 or Level 2	Level 2 or Level 3	Level 3 or Level 4	Level 4 or Level 5 (AP)
Electives	PE/Elective	PE/Elective	PE/Elective/ Health	Elective/Elective or Health
Seventh Class	Optional	Optional	Optional	Optional

When the English department chair read the student's writing and suggested a junior-level English class, the principal modified the general schedule (above), resulting in the following plan for this student:

Department	Grade 9	Grade 10	Grade 11	Grade 12
Language Arts	Advanced Composition, Shakespeare	American Studies Honors	AP English	College
Social Studies	U.S. Government, Geography	World History	AP U.S. History	AP European History
Math	Honors Pre-Calculus 1 and 2	AB Calculus, BC Calculus	College	College
Science	Chemistry or Anatomy	AP Biology	AP Chemistry	Advanced Physics
Foreign Language	Spanish Level 4	College or a second foreign language	College	College
Electives	Stage Band, PE, Computer Program C++	Stage Band, PE	Stage Band, PE	Stage Band, Health
Seventh Class	Optional	Optional	Optional	Optional

A four-year plan acts as a roadmap to help the student get as much as possible out of his or her high school years. Naturally, the student described here ended up with a final schedule that varied from these suggestions, based on course availability and personal choice. Even so, the principal served as this student's primary advisor, suggesting courses that he thought the student would like. Teacher preference and availability played a role as well—for example, the student postponed AP Calculus while a favorite teacher took a sabbatical, and took Statistics in the interim. The experienced high school AP Chemistry teacher retired before the student could take that course in high school, so he took an Honors Chemistry course (instead of AP Chemistry) at the university in his first full year of college. (The student became a biochemistry major, so his university also preferred that he take their course.) Because he became aware that he had missed interesting cultural material in third-level Spanish by beginning with Spanish 4, he took Spanish 310 next (even though it was fairly easy for him). Here is what this accelerated student actually took. As you can see, he graduated in three years.

Department	**Grade 9**	**Grade ?**	**Grade 12**
Language Arts	Advanced Composition, Public Speaking	AP English [*Masterpieces of American Literature]	Discussion and Debate
Social Studies	World History	AP European History [*History of the U.S. to 1865, *History of the U.S. Since 1865, *American Political Systems]	[**World Regional Geography]
Math	Honors Pre-Calculus 1 and 2	Statistics	AB Calculus, BC Calculus (AP)
Science	Chemistry	AP Biology	Advanced Physics
Foreign Language	Spanish Level 4	Spanish 310	AP Spanish Level 5
Electives	Stage Band, PE	Team Sports	Racquet Sports, Health
Seventh Class	Stage Band		Photography 1 and 2, Honors Computer C++

*Courses taken at a nearby university in summer school.
** University continuing education course taken in the evening.

This student decided early in his second year to shorten his high school stay, primarily for social reasons. Initially placed with older students, he made friends, felt that he fit in quite nicely, and was comfortable. He watched some of them graduate at the end of his first year, however, and soon wanted to go with them. He took four courses at a university in the summer between his second and third years in high school, choosing classes carefully to meet high school graduation requirements, and another class in the fall of his third year when he had difficulty scheduling a similar required course at the high school. His principal approved the courses as meeting high school graduation requirements and signed a form for the university stating that the student was mature enough to handle college-level work. In addition, the school district waived 10 credits toward graduation to enable the student to move on to college (he was 10 credits short). (Some students that we have seen have been accepted to colleges without high school diplomas.)

The student began college full-time the following fall with almost enough credits to qualify as a junior (with his college coursework and credit for AP exams), and he was well placed and comfortable. Since he was planning on earning a Ph.D., he figured that he would still have plenty of time left in college!

When the school designates teachers or department chairs to make placement decisions, results can vary. If, for example, a student has a strong enough background to place out of a ninth-grade class but the department has designated the teacher of that course (who teaches nothing else) to make placement decisions, odds are that the student's request will be turned down. However, when the department head determines such placements and teaches classes at several grade levels, there is a better chance of a reasonable placement decision being made. Educators vary in their flexibility, and unfortunately, some will say, "I believe that all students will find my class valuable!"

The combination of classes and placements offered, administrative support, and teacher quality all help determine which high school is best. Students should visit classes, at least in subjects of greatest interest. In this way, they gain firsthand knowledge of the teachers, class sizes, and instructional approaches used. Even a school with an excellent reputation may not have the student's favorite teachers in preferred subjects. Meeting teachers and being a student in their classrooms, albeit briefly, can offer a wealth of information.

The size of classes not only figures into the comfort of the student, but may also determine admission policies to advanced classes. For example, in very large schools, entry into AP classes can be quite competitive. The young or underachieving gifted student is more likely to be welcomed into the AP class in a smaller high school which has barely enough students for the school to offer the class.

In our area, high schools vary tremendously. One school is trying to create an AP Scholar program, offering all of the 35 AP classes for which there are tests, as well as flexible placement options. The mother of one very advanced middle schooler was told that her son could take some AP classes there as a freshman. Such offerings and flexibility allow the unusually advanced student to take highly challenging courses throughout high school.

In contrast, at some other schools, few students take AP classes before their senior year and are forced to take typical grade-level offerings. A gifted student needs to find the right combination. He or she may choose a high school with only moderate AP offerings if there are good teachers for favorite subjects and the administration permits flexibility.

Maintaining Challenge

Once the student has chosen a high school and the initial placements have been made, the challenge is to ensure engaging coursework that continues to motivate. Gifted high school students thrive in classes that require them to think abstractly, deal with complexity, and occasionally struggle. They will usually gravitate to honors and other advanced courses unless the teacher requires too much drill and practice.

There is no way to avoid a few low-level classes that seem ridiculous to gifted students but are required for graduation. Often, these classes have regular homework that seems pointless. Ask for advice about the most engaging teachers and the least frustrating prospects. Gifted high school students perform better for teachers whom they respect, and they put forth less effort for those they do not. When choosing the health or "living on your own" class, the teacher who is at least reasonable and well-meaning will be best tolerated.

Concurrent College Enrollment

When the high school offerings need a boost or a student wants to complete high school quickly (as in the case above), consider concurrent enrollment in college courses. Such classes aim a little higher than most (but not all) of their high school counterparts, asking students to reason at a higher level. They often have more knowledgeable instructors, who conduct research or explore cutting-edge issues in their fields. The students love the discussions, realize how much more there is to be learned, and gain an enhanced view of higher education.

Gifted students are usually mature and responsible enough to handle college classes and appreciate the fact that few college instructors assign daily homework, but plan their courses instead around reading, written assignments, and a few quizzes and exams. Gifted students enjoy having more independence. At the college, they don't need to worry about unexcused absences for being five minutes late or about rigid dress codes. They appreciate being treated as adults who want to learn and are willing to work hard.

Concurrent enrollment in both high school and college offers dual credit. If the college course meets a high school graduation requirement or is perceived to be worthy of credit toward the student's high school diploma, it can count for credit toward both high school graduation and a college bachelor's degree. When students realize this, college classes become even more of a pleasure to take. A high school administrator will usually have to approve the college course for high school credit. Some school districts even pay for college courses that the accelerated student needs but the high school is unable to offer. Check requirements carefully for such programs to take advantage of this assistance. Colleges have requirements for the admission of high school students that vary from school to school, but they are less daunting than most parents would assume.

College courses can become a large part of a gifted student's program if the student wishes to graduate early. They are useful when the student is unable to schedule a high school course required for graduation, which is not uncommon with accelerated students who are taking courses out of sequence and where only one section of a high school course is offered at a particular time during the semester. High schools try to schedule classes so that the students who need them can schedule them along with other classes that they are likely to take. However, an accelerated student is often taking classes at atypical times, so the school's planning falls short. It can be a relief to find an appropriate college class offered—perhaps one night a week for half a semester—that fills such a requirement. Colleges usually offer coursework for high school students through their continuing education departments. Classes are scheduled at times when working people and full-time high school students can take them.

Finally, if an accelerated student is graduating early, the experience with college courses is invaluable. The student heading off to college may be young but is already practiced in navigating a college campus and handling college work. Such a student enters with far more experience with college than most average freshmen.

Taking college courses, along with AP and IB classes, can produce a large number of college credits by high school graduation. These credit hours shorten the time required for a bachelor's degree but may reduce scholarship opportunities open to freshmen. However, most students appreciate having to take fewer entry-level courses when they enter college full-time. Moreover, the student who begins college classified as a sophomore or junior enjoys some preference for classes, as seniors are generally scheduled first, then juniors, etc. The student may be eligible for a single dorm room sooner (important to gifted introverts) and may be eligible for research opportunities or teaching assistantships earlier than other students.

Other Course Options and Opportunities

The distance-learning options previously discussed (e.g., Stanford's EPGY) are also appropriate for gifted learners in high school; however, such students should avoid correspondence courses that may be designed for struggling students (although young gifted students may appreciate them). Even underachieving gifted high school students do better in challenging courses with significant complexity. Placing them in easier courses to improve grades usually backfires.

Independent study is another option. A supportive principal may be able to offer credit for a student to pursue an area of interest. Perhaps a faculty member knowledgeable in the area can supervise the independent study, monitor progress, offer suggestions when needed, and determine goals and objectives to result in the school credit. Gifted students often have the motivation for independent study but may need guidance with breaking the study down into smaller parts with benchmarks.

Internships are another option when an advanced student is eager to learn more about a particular field or when an underachieving gifted student's motivation is waning. Student placements for a few hours a week are often possible. The student is usually not paid but gains a valuable recommendation and, if possible, a few credits for the experience. Some schools have internship programs available to gifted students, usually organized by a teacher or counselor interested in gifted children. Internships allow students to be in the adult work world observing and working with a professional in a field that interests them (architecture, medicine, pharmacy, teaching, etc.). The student normally keeps a journal of his or her experiences, talks regularly with the high school liaison, and receives credit based on hours spent. The principal will need to be involved to approve credit if an internship program is not already in place or an unusual option is considered.

A Continued Need for Advocacy

High school-aged gifted students need parents as advocates as much as elementary students. Even though older students are more capable of advocating for themselves, it is still very difficult for them to obtain permission for atypical placements, shortened programs, and exemptions from the usual requirements. Requests like these strike terror in the hearts of some administrators who are concerned about making a wrong choice for the student or diverging from established school or district policy. Parents are able to argue more effectively in favor of the wisdom of a particular request.

Parents can also help their students keep track of graduation requirements, college admission tests, etc., as some gifted students have rather poor planning and organizational skills. Especially when the student will be graduating early, requirements seem to sneak up. Most students who graduate in three years, for example, do not plan to do so initially. It is only after some time in high school that they decide they would rather move on more quickly. If a student has the potential to graduate early, it is wise to at least discuss an alternate course schedule that meets graduation requirements more quickly to help avoid surprises.

Students should plan to take one or more of the college admission tests (the PSAT, SAT, or ACT) *early* to avoid a rush at the end to complete them all. The Preliminary Scholastic Aptitude Test (PSAT) is important because scores from this test determine National Merit Scholarship recipients. Students usually take the test at the beginning of their junior or third year in high school, unless they plan to graduate in three years. In that case, they may take it in their second year. However, if the student fails to take it in the second year because he or she has not yet decided to graduate in three years, it causes a one-year delay of scholarship opportunities. If the student is granted a scholarship, it is not available until the beginning of the student's second year in college.

Students usually take the Scholastic Aptitude Test (SAT) at the end of the junior or beginning of the senior year. The SAT and the PSAT may end up being taken virtually together at the beginning of the third and last year in high school if the student did not know to take the PSAT a year early. High school counseling offices have packets of registration materials for all of these tests, which include the dates on which the tests are given, deadlines for sending in registration fees, and information about the test itself. Such information is also available online. School counselors can advise students of which tests to take for which colleges; some colleges prefer the SAT and some the ACT. Often, the colleges will send representatives to large high schools to talk to students about their school. Parents and students should seek opportunities to learn about colleges and universities of interest.

Gifted students usually welcome ways to shorten their stay in high school, elevate their work (through college courses), or gain more responsibility (spending time on a college campus, away from the tight control of the high school). While the intricacies of such options are challenging, they are worthwhile for the advocate to pursue.

Twice-Exceptional Students

Support Both the Giftedness and the Deficit(s)

Children who exhibit both giftedness and learning deficits require special planning throughout their educational careers. Earlier, a sample IEP for Omar, an elementary twice-exceptional (2e) student, showed how accommodations could support reasoning abilities and also offer modifications for weak areas. Gifted children with deficits need a two-pronged approach, emphasizing and supporting the giftedness, but also accommodating the weaknesses. This can be tricky to ensure because school personnel often don't realize that a child with weaknesses can also be gifted. They may need help to learn that children who are twice exceptional depend on support for their strengths even more than for their weakness.

If a student's achievement is less impressive, especially when deficits are apparent, school staff may question the child's giftedness. It is essential to provide high-quality testing information that not only documents the dual exceptionality, but also offers recommendations for the classroom. A tester with considerable experience with twice-exceptional students, not just children with disabilities, should give a comprehensive individual intelligence test and achievement test, as well as any additional diagnostic tests that are warranted (discussed in Chapter 3). The resulting report can assist the classroom teacher in several ways: to clarify the child's weaknesses (perhaps the gifted "average reader" has subtle dyslexia which has evaded detection because the child compensates well), document strengths to justify including the child in gifted programming, and suggest specific recommendations. It may also be helpful to provide the school with articles or other materials about the twice-exceptional student to clarify the student's challenges.

When a gifted child with deficits has support for her strengths, her confidence remains strong. Having both gifted intellectual abilities *and* weaknesses can be destabilizing, and self-esteem suffers. The child is smart and has been told so by the adults in her life, but she also knows that certain classroom activities that other children do easily are difficult for her. She wonders if, indeed, she really *is* intelligent. It is crucial that the teacher recognize the giftedness and support the child's strengths. Once the child receives support (through modified coursework) for her advanced math or beautiful creative writing, she will more easily appreciate and tolerate modifications for her weak areas, while maintaining her self-esteem.

Twice-exceptional young people usually work very hard to compensate for deficits, which they hide fairly well. However, such effort is often exhausting, and achievement may be inconsistent. These students are typically late bloomers who master compensatory skills as they mature that allow their giftedness to become more apparent.

Consider IDEA (Special Education Services) and 504 Plans

Some twice-exceptional students have access to services for their deficits, but not necessarily their giftedness, at school. If their weaknesses are considered learning disabilities (e.g., reading or writing disabilities), they may qualify for special education services for the learning disabled (see Chapter 6). Special education can provide not only accommodations in the classroom (e.g., extra time for writing assignments), but also special teaching and therapeutic interventions in a resource room setting until students graduate from high school. If their deficits fall under the listed disabilities for a 504 Plan under the Rehabilitation Act of 1973 (related to the Americans with Disabilities legislation), then they have access to accommodations in the classroom or workplace as long as they need them.

Sometimes weaknesses are significant but do not qualify for either type of assistance—the overall functioning of the child is felt to be too high. In such cases, parents need to pursue outside interventions and work with teachers for voluntary accommodations. Children who receive these interventions usually find these efforts invaluable, and they perform progressively better in school as they mature.

Advocating for Children with Higher Levels of Giftedness

How does yearly advocacy differ for parents of children with higher levels of giftedness—the highly, exceptionally, or profoundly gifted? First, gifted children at these levels learn at an increasingly fast pace, easily outstripping their curriculum and surprising their teachers. The mismatch becomes so great at the higher IQ levels between their abilities and their educational programs that we can virtually expect increasing angst. Some students will even find that enrollment within typical school programs is impossible.

Personality characteristics that are typical for most gifted students increase in intensity with even higher intelligence and may appear so abnormal to some as to seem pathological. Socially, highly gifted students find it even more difficult to find true peers or to relate to age peers in meaningful ways. Parents often report that these children prefer adults and considerably older children. Most highly gifted students show strengths in both visual-spatial and verbal abstract reasoning abilities, so both learning styles are operating fairly well. However, most are holistic rather than sequential learners. Because most teachers have little or no experience with such children, parent advocates must play a more significant role.

Consider Even Higher Level and Faster Pace of Instruction

The level of instruction and pacing necessary for highly, exceptionally, and profoundly gifted children would surprise most people. At the highly gifted level (IQ 145 or higher on most tests), students will generally learn upon presentation, if they are paying attention. They do not need drill and practice, so if the teacher is cycling though the material eight or nine times (for the average student to reach mastery), highly gifted students are definitely struggling to maintain their attention. The problem grows worse for exceptionally and profoundly gifted students, who absolutely devour teaching materials.

One boy whom we tested, with a Stanford-Binet L-M IQ score of 192, took three achievement tests—in the summer prior to first grade, in the spring of second grade, and in the spring of third grade—covering a period of less than three years. While the tests have limited comparability, note his grade equivalency scores below to gain an idea of how rapidly he progressed.

The Academic Progress of a Profoundly Gifted Child as Measured by Grade Equivalents

	PIAT-R Age 6-1	K-TEA (Brief Form), Age 7-9	K-TEA (Long Form) (includes specialized subtests) Age 8-10
Math	2.6	10.9	Math Application 11.3 Math Computation 10.7
Reading	3.2	8.5	Reading Comprehension >12.9 Reading Decoding 10.8
Spelling	2.8	5.2	Spelling 10.9

Notice the dramatic and sudden increases as this student learned basic skills in reading and math in the primary grades. Few teachers would suspect that students could progress this rapidly. A teacher would only notice the rapid progress if she assessed frequently on above-level tests. On grade-level achievement tests, the child would simply earn a score at the 99th percentile for first, second, or third graders, and no one would know how high the child's achievement level actually was. If a child scores at the 99th percentile repeatedly, it is wise to administer achievement tests to see how high the child is actually performing. Scoring at the 99th percentile merely indicates that the child has "topped out" or "hit the ceiling" of the test, and we need another more difficult test to see how high the child is actually performing.

Provide Achievement Testing

In planning each year's program, parents can help by having individual achievement tests administered, perhaps every 1½ to 2½ years, throughout elementary school and somewhat beyond. Be careful to have a test administered with a ceiling score as high as the child's IQ score, or ceiling limitations may apply. The Woodcock-Johnson III (WJ-III ACH or WJ-III ACH NU) has a very high ceiling (beyond 200 at some ages on some subtests) and provides excellent information. The subtests needed include the following: Letter-Word Identification, Passage Comprehension, Calculation, Applied Problems, Spelling, and Writing Samples (or substitute a writing evaluation from another test). Remember, the subtests that measure the speed (not necessarily the comprehension) of reading, calculating, and writing—Reading Fluency, Math Fluency, and Writing Fluency—test very simple skills that do not represent the range of abilities of the gifted and may lower Broad Reading, Broad Math, and Broad Written Language scores, causing teachers to question the need for higher-level work in the classroom. However, if a child has a serious processing speed deficit and needs accommodations, have the tester give the fluency measures to document the problem.

Accelerate with Care

When is acceleration appropriate for highly, exceptionally, and profoundly gifted students, and how much should be skipped? The profoundly gifted child mentioned above skipped third grade after earning grade equivalents from the fifth- through tenth-grade levels in the spring of second grade. His acceleration was easy and comfortable, and it permanently moved him to somewhat higher-level material than he would have had if he had remained with age peers. We generally recommend accelerating one year at a time, but some children have fared well skipping two or three grades at once. Schools tend to be very reluctant to accelerate a child even one grade level, however, so multi-grade skips are unlikely options.

Sometimes a child placed far below his achievement levels balks at the idea of a grade skip, even though he is frustrated learning in his current classroom. When this occurs, provide him with all of the information needed to begin considering whole-grade acceleration, including an opportunity to visit the advanced class. Respect his resulting choice to make the full-grade skip, accelerate in one subject only, or just ponder the possibility for the future.

Consider Outside Coursework

Meeting the rapidly advancing needs of the very highly gifted will require other solutions as well, all of which have been described in detail previously in this chapter. Distance-learning courses to substitute for one or more courses at school, mentoring or tutoring, and partial or full-time home schooling are particular possibilities, as are Talent Search summer classes. College courses may be possible, even for elementary-aged highly gifted students (they may wish to audit first). We have seen profoundly gifted students take college courses successfully at age six or seven (with some help from parents), and we know high school graduates of nine, 10, and 11, as well as a 10-year-old college graduate. These were all children whose parents capitulated to serving their needs, giving in to their requests for more challenging coursework. Such parents rarely push, but instead struggle to meet the compelling needs of these children.

At the same time, there are highly, exceptionally, and profoundly gifted students who prefer to proceed more cautiously through school. Involving children in decisions about their education prevents an educational path that pressures the child too much to accelerate or that frustrates his or her desired progress. If, for example, a young teenager is not ready to leave home for college, he or she might live at home and attend a college nearby. Of course, parents are under no obligation to accept a plan that doesn't fit what the family holds dear.

Most children at the highest levels of giftedness have no access to any school program that comes close to meeting their needs. However, a thoughtfully conceived patchwork of successful options, created each year to address their needs, is quite an excellent substitute.

Help Teacher Advocates

The teacher who successfully supports a highly gifted student may encounter enormous resistance from other teachers who feel that acceleration is inappropriate or who otherwise disagree with the teacher handling the student with flexibility. Supportive teachers may even have difficulties with administrators and may need parental support for their efforts.

Parents must understand the limitations of teachers—that very few could teach *all* levels of every subject. Thus, a child who needs algebra in elementary school will probably have to find instruction outside of the school. Likewise, teachers will not be able to answer all questions posed by such children. The wise teacher will instruct the child in ways to research information independently via the Internet, books, or interviewing experts—or even guide the child to another educator's class. The teacher then becomes the advocate and facilitator of the child's learning, rather than the authority who knows all of the answers and can meet every need.

Support Personality Characteristics

The intensity of highly gifted children, along with their increased sensitivity and concern for injustice in the world, renders them especially vulnerable to ill-fitting programs. One third-grade girl with a 211 IQ score began to have "meltdowns" in the restroom, with uncontrollable crying. She had simply reached a point at which she felt that her teacher required her to be someone else. Unable to be a typical third grader who was satisfied with third-grade work, she was deemed "not gifted" by her teacher and labeled as having "emotional issues." This child was so sensitive and attuned to the need for kindness and fairness that she simply could not cope with this unfair treatment. She had to be removed from school and home schooled.

When teachers become defensive and punishing, our most highly gifted children suffer tremendous pain. They fare poorly in classrooms in which there is even subtle disapproval of their differences. More blatant criticism can require years of therapy to mitigate. Depression and even the possibility of suicide may occur when such intense personalities experience extreme rejection.

Parents need to ensure a healthy psychological environment for such a student. Does the teacher appreciate and nurture the child's special qualities? These children should never be criticized for their giftedness, nor should their strengths be ignored to avoid hurting the feelings of other children. All children's gifts should be acknowledged—though not overpraised—or the message of disapproval is conveyed.

It is helpful to educate teachers about the personality characteristics of very highly gifted children. In addition, teachers need to know that such a child is still able to be a child. The quality of childhood simply changes. The child will likely show a normal love of play, fantasy, and silliness, but interspersed with that may be an unusually sophisticated interest in a subject. This is normal childhood for very highly gifted children. Adult-level interests go with the territory and are not imposed by pushy parents.

Nurture Social Development

Assuming that gifted children usually gravitate toward mental age peers, it is clear that it is more difficult for children at the higher ranges of giftedness to find true peers and less likely that those peers will be of a similar chronological age. We have seen remarkable situations in which such children were integrated easily into classrooms of much older children. Indeed, they need mental age peers, who are more likely to have similar interests, in order to form friendships. Such friendships also provide the context in which children learn social skills and confidence to function at their appropriate level. However, when is the age mismatch too great? Certainly when the child feels that it is. In our experience, the ability of these most highly gifted children to assess what is best for them is impressive.

Becoming the Gifted Advocate and Educational Program Manager

Most parents of gifted children would rather find a perfect school placement for their child than to take on the role of essential advocate and educational program planner. It is a role that most accept only reluctantly once it appears that a child's needs won't be met within any available schools. Happily, letting go of the notion that the "school will do it" can be empowering and actually help us to see options that we might otherwise overlook. Viewing a child's education as a series of potentially interesting years, carefully crafted with options that come and go as needed, opens up a realm of new and exhilarating possibilities. Taking an active role—in partnership with educators—directly meets needs and limits damage.

This is the point at which the parent advocate must be at his or her best, gently educating and cajoling school personnel to try needed accommodations while releasing them from responsibility if plans do not produce perfect results. All have to make their best guess as to what will work and summon the courage to try.

For Further Reading

Books and Articles

Assouline, S. G., Colangelo, N., Lupowski-Shoplik, A., Lipscomb, J., & Forstadt, L. (2003). *Iowa acceleration scale* (2nd ed.). Scottsdale, AZ:Great Potential Press.

Colangelo, N., Assouline, S. G., & Gross, M. U. M., (Eds.). (2004). *A nation deceived: How schools hold back America's brightest students* (Vols. 1-2). Iowa City, IA: The University of Iowa.

Davidson, J., Davidson, B., & Vanderkam, L. (2005). *Genius denied: How to stop wasting our brightest young minds.* New York: Simon & Schuster.

Eide, B., & Eide, F. (2006). *The mislabeled child.* New York: Hyperion.

Gilman, B. J. (2008). *Challenging highly gifted learners.* Waco, TX; Prufrock Press.

Gross, M. U. M. (2004a). *Exceptionally gifted children* (2nd ed.). London: Routledge Falmer.

Gross, M. U. M. (2004b). Radical acceleration. In N. Colangelo, S. G. Assouline, & M. U. M. Gross (Eds.), *A nation deceived: How schools hold back America's brightest students* (Vol. II, pp. 87-96). Iowa City, IA: The University of Iowa.

Hollingworth, L. S. (1942). *Children above 180 IQ Stanford-Binet: Origin and developments.* Yonkers-on-Hudson, NY: World Book Company.

Karnes, F. A., & Marquardt, R. G. (2000). *Gifted children and legal issues: An update.* Scottsdale: Great Potential Press.

Kay, K., Robson, D., & Brenneman, J. F. (2007). *High IQ kids: Collected insights, information, and personal stories from the experts.* Minneapolis, MN: Free Spirit.

Matthews, D. J., & Foster, J. F. (2005). *Being smart about gifted children: A guidebook for parents and educators.* Scottsdale, AZ: Great Potential Press.

Reis, S., Burns, D., & Renzulli, J. (1992). *Curriculum compacting.* Mansfield Center, CT: Creative Learning Press.

Robinson, N. (1991). Early entrance to kindergarten and grade 1. In W. T. Southern & E. D. Jones (Eds.), *The academic acceleration of gifted children.* New York: Teacher's College Press.

Rogers, K. B. (2002). *Re-forming gifted education: How parents and teachers can match the program to the child.* Scottsdale, AZ: Great Potential Press.

Webb, J. T., Gore, J. L., Amend, E. R., & DeVries, A. R. (2007). *A parent's guide to gifted children.* Scottsdale, AZ: Great Potential Press.

Winebrenner, S., & Espeland, P. (2001). *Teaching gifted kids in the regular classroom: Strategies and techniques every teacher can use to meet the academic needs of the gifted and talented.* Minneapolis, MN: Free Spirit.

Wright, A. L., & Olszewski-Kubilius, P. (1993). *Helping gifted children and their families prepare for college: A handbook designed to assist economically disadvantaged and first-generation college attendees* (RM93201). Storrs, CT: University of Connecticut, The National Research Center on the Gifted and Talented. Also available at www.gifted.uconn.edu/nrcgt/nrconlin.html

Websites

ALEKS Math Instruction
www.aleks.com/?ref=web

Concordia Language Villages (a program of Concordia College, USA)
800-222-4750 or 218-299-4544
http://clvweb.cord.edu/prweb

Davidson Institute for Talent Development
www.ditd.org

EPGY (Education Program for Gifted Youth)
220 Panama Street, Stanford, CA 94305-4101
800-372-EPGY
http://epgy.stanford.edu/contact.html

Hoagies' Gifted Education Page (the advocate's most comprehensive website on a multitude of topics.)
www.hoagiesgifted.org

Hoagies' Gifted Education Page, Academic Programs
www.hoagiesgifted.org/academics.htm

Hoagies' Gifted Education Page, Summer and Saturday Programs
www.hoagiesgifted.org/summer.htm

Peterson's (colleges, graduate schools, online practice tests, financial aid, free online)
www.petersons.com

SAT Test Preparation (click on SAT Prep Center and Question of the Day)
www.collegeboard.com

Talent Searches (Websites)

Duke University Talent Identification Program (Duke TIP)
www.tip.duke.edu

Johns Hopkins Center for Talented Youth (CTY)
http://cty.jhu.edu

Northwestern Center for Talent Development (CTD)
www.ctd.northwestern.edu

Rocky Mountain Academic Talent Search at the University of Denver
www.du.edu/city

Afterword
The Call to Arms

Parents and teachers advocating for gifted children find themselves in the most curious situation. They must advocate strongly for significant educational accommodations to meet the needs of their gifted charges. However, they operate largely in an environment of limited knowledge about what those needs are. They must learn through their own efforts what a gifted child's education must accomplish. The fact that few states require significant study in gifted education for teacher certification ensures that there will be confusion in schools about what gifted students should be doing in the classroom and, therefore, insufficient concern about what will happen if the right things are not done.

At the same time, advocates for gifted students face charges of elitism within a society that is not sure whether it wants to nurture its most capable members or submit them to an egalitarian leveling process. Faced with society's often-harsh ambivalence, gifted advocates who are sensitive and compassionate about the needs of others hesitate to proceed. Dare they approach schools about gifted children, even those who are dangerously at risk?

The message that we must do *something* for gifted children has permeated the American educational system enough to bring about a plethora of gifted programs in schools that superimpose some type of enrichment upon the regular program. However, the addition of an hour or more per week of leadership training, thinking skills, art appreciation, or other unrelated enrichment does little to mitigate the effects of a vastly inappropriate education. Even when add-on gifted programs offer more substantial opportunities to do a project of interest, attend a weekly science enrichment class, participate in a writing workshop, or spend quality time with intellectual peers, they rarely lead to significant and needed changes in daily classwork. Too many gifted students still spend the bulk of their time in learning situations that restrict their forward progress and require little real effort—a situation that no parent wants for any child.

Admission to gifted programs presents its own special challenges. Most schools cannot offer comprehensive testing to gifted students due to limited funding, so identification must rely upon ability screeners that miss some students. The brief tests, often administered to groups, also offer little information about strengths and weaknesses that might be utilized to plan a child's individual program.

In addition, the discomfort that some school personnel feel with children who are more capable, more advanced, and more efficient learners can lead to restrictive admission policies and demanding, compassionless gatekeepers. It is difficult to forget the boy in Texas who was turned down for the gifted program when he scored low on his school district's creativity test, one of a battery of tests (mostly screeners) on which he needed to score high, yet he earned a Stanford-Binet L-M IQ score of 180 and high scores on the WISC-IV when tested privately. An IQ score from a major individual intelligence test is an excellent indicator of asynchrony and the need for educational accommodations.

Unease also appears to drive some school personnel to make gifted children "earn their giftedness" by a show of high achievement, task commitment, or general good citizenship. One mother reported that her son's teacher refused to nominate him for the gifted program, despite a phenomenal test score, because he had a messy desk. It is interesting to note that we impose no such behavioral requirements on children needing to be identified as learning or developmentally disabled. We simply accept their asynchrony—their capacities and limitations—and work to plan appropriate educational programs for them.

Some districts cope with the discomfort of identifying gifted students by trying to include as many children as possible. However, lowering score requirements to identify 10%, 20%, or even 30% of the school population can dilute programming options to a degree that they cannot possibly meet the unusual academic needs of some gifted children. Perhaps even worse, such a degree of inclusion calls into question whether all of these children actually need differentiation in their programs, or whether some are having their needs met already in the regular program. If some children do not need special accommodations, then there is good reason for deep resentment to develop among the parents of children not included. The seeds are sown for the eventual abandonment of all gifted services, poor as many are, due to parent pressure.

Sadly, some schools still disregard giftedness altogether. We still hear occasionally of the principal who insists that "every child is gifted," effectively ignoring any individual differences that might require an educational response. A child's needs cannot be met if they are not recognized, and it is no more true to say that "every child is gifted" than it is to say that "every child is retarded."

It is into this daunting world that advocates of gifted children—both supportive teachers and parents—must go, prepared to the extent that they can muster to fight for a child's right to an appropriate education. What kind of an education do we want for all children? Teachers must utilize a curriculum in which the child is taught at the appropriate level (based on current mastery) in each subject area and at approximately the right pace. The standard school curriculum is carefully designed for the majority of children in school, but is not a good fit for children at the extremes of ability. For these children, the level of difficulty is wrong, the pace doesn't work, and a variety of related skills fails to develop properly. Successful modifications for gifted children in school allow them to meet the same educational expectations that we have for all children.

The father of two very gifted elementary-aged sons, after hearing post-test recommendations for a variety of options, including acceleration, distance-learning courses, and alternate school choices, responded, "Tell me again, *why* should we do these things for our sons?" I suspect that although he was worried that his sons were underchallenged in school, he wasn't sure he wanted to push them to become academic whiz kids either.

"To normalize their experience in school," I said. These options are needed to teach them new material daily, make them stretch, present them with hard enough problems that they must develop strategies to solve them (not melt down), teach them organizational skills that they won't learn if the work is too easy, help them develop a reasonable work ethic, prevent them from being the 'smartest kid in the class' who earns A's but never has to work hard, allow them access to other students whose ideas they respect, and generally maintain their love of learning. The answer surprised him, but he readily agreed.

Advocates for gifted children must attempt to create their own programs by assembling a patchwork of options each year that come as close as possible to meeting more asynchronous needs. If they can accomplish this—usually without the benefit of desperately needed legal protection—then the child is likely to thrive intellectually and emotionally.

Teachers who value these unusual students must do extra work to individualize for them, increasing their own planning time, while they also deal with more typical learners and asynchronous learners at other levels of ability. They must assess frequently to avoid teaching what gifted students already know, and they need to find ways to ensure continuous progress so that the children's love of learning is supported. Teachers need to keep ceilings off the level of discussion, welcome any question, encourage abstract reasoning, maintain high expectations, and provide opportunities for gifted students to stretch. They must also deal sensitively with a range of personality traits, from heightened emotions to concern for injustice, and be intuitive about the issues that gifted introverts experience but may be reluctant to share.

For their efforts, supportive teachers face disagreements with colleagues and inevitable turf battles when a child needs accelerated work but the higher-grade-level teacher disagrees. They may incur the wrath of administrators. Yet these special teachers deserve our heart-felt appreciation for doing a critical—and at times life-saving—job for gifted students that some other educators would never attempt or even respect.

Parent advocates for the gifted face even greater challenges because their advocacy continues for the many years of their child's education, with no guarantee of success. The advocate must summon his or her warmest smile and most sincere willingness to work with each teacher, counselor, or administrator to find the best options for the child. Unswayed by superficial enrichment programs, the parent must go to the school knowing that significant classroom accommodations are essential. Much of the daily curriculum and instruction in typical schools is simply not designed for such learners. Gifted students are as different from average learners as are students who are developmentally delayed, so the regular program must be carefully modified for both. There is no need to apologize for such requests.

Parent advocates must be ready with their testing reports, their portfolios, their records of advanced classes taken in order to document special needs and qualify their children for modifications. They need to learn to say thoughtfully, "Here is what we are dealing with. What options do you have that might meet these needs?"

Because they may know more about the educational needs of the gifted than school personnel, parents must be ready to educate with a few well-placed comments about an important topic or by offering a helpful article or book. They may need to dispel common myths about gifted students. First, the notion that the gifted will be "just fine without special accommodations" is at odds with our experience that gifted students are at the highest risk when their learning is restricted and their needs are ignored. Second, "gifted children need to be with age peers for social development" is countered by seeing gifted children cherish their multi-age friends and learn social skills with all ages. Finally, "grade acceleration is to be avoided at all costs" is nonsense when we can witness an accelerated child re-engage in his or her studies because the level is finally right. Any child works best at the level of mastery, where mostly new material is being presented.

Both teacher and parent advocates need to remember that a child's program does not have to be perfect to be adequate. Maintaining motivation to learn is the bottom line. We must prevent the gifted student from becoming jaded about education—damaged enough that he or she flees the system and is too afraid to return. It is much easier to prevent such a negative outcome than to repair it once it is full-blown. Advocates need to know, however, that if they work to ensure a reasonably good program for a child each year, the results can be very good. Even profoundly gifted children—those most at risk of suffering from the poor fit of their educations—can complete public school with their love of learning intact. The result is worth every effort.

To accomplish this, parent advocates must chart a course for a gifted student through school, navigating the rules of the system, locating supportive teachers, and discovering appropriate options. Parents must ultimately manage their children's educations or the status quo will prevail—the gifted child will be expected to progress through school in the standard manner. It is highly unlikely that more than a few special teachers will pose the question: "Does this child need any modifications to his or her education?" The number of gifted high school dropouts and depressed or suicidal gifted students is testament to the danger inherent in ignoring their needs.

A friend whose profoundly gifted son, Jeremiah, dropped out of high school sent me this email:

> *...[F]or the longest time, [Jeremiah] remained adamant about not wanting anything to do with structured schooling. He was hoping to be a success with his band, but the other members weren't as committed to it as he was, and he could see that his friends who had opted not to go on to college were settling into lives that were less than what he would want. He finally called me in Tennessee (he was living with a group of friends in Boston) and asked me if he could come to Nashville with the goal of taking the GED, the*

> *ACT, and applying to Goddard [College in Vermont]. Goddard was the only school he would even consider applying to. It was the only one that he saw as allowing him the freedom to study what he wanted to study and devise his own program. When he arrived in Nashville, he spent three weeks studying for both tests, took the GED on a Friday and the ACT the next day, aced them both, applied to Goddard, and got in. The poor kid didn't have any ready recommendations because he had been out of school for so long. I got one letter from the Pastor of a local church, a second one in handwritten scrawl from Jeremiah's Boston guitar teacher, and a third from a doctoral student/teacher at Vanderbilt University who was a dear friend and offered to interview Jeremiah and write a letter on his behalf. I was SO grateful when he was accepted. And I'll never forget the way he hugged me when they called him. It was as if his life had been saved.*

Jeremiah became a model student at Goddard—constantly earning high praise from his teachers. In his third term at the college, they felt that he was working at the master's level.

As wonderful as this note was to receive, I was struck by the inherent danger in stories like Jeremiah's. Although he seemed well on his way to a life rich with promise, how many others like him never find their way? Our most able students deserve better.

Note: Just after this original manuscript went to press, students were notified that Goddard College had decided to discontinue the school's undergraduate residential program that had existed since 1938. Both Jeremiah and Quinn O'Leary were students.

For Further Reading

Page, C. (2002, June 30). The Goddard factor: Freethinking college exerts influence beyond small size. *The Burlington Free Press*, pp. 1A, 4A, 5A. Also available at www.burlingtonfreepress.com

Essential Resources

The following resources are popular with parents and teachers advocating for gifted children. The comprehensive Hoagies' Gifted Education Page website (www.hoagiesgifted.org) is always a great place to start.

Instructional Materials and Curricula

Creative Learning Press (resources for high-end learning)
    888-518-8004
    www.creativelearningprcss.com

Creative Publications/Wright Group (both McGraw-Hill)
    888-205-4444
    www.creativepublications.com
    800-648-2970
    www.wrightgroup.com

Critical Thinking Books and Software
    800-458-4849
    www.criticalthinking.com

Math-U-See
    888-854-6284
    www.mathusee.com

Science, Math & Gifted Products
    715-235-1840
    www.smgproducts.com

The Teaching Company
    800-832-2412
    www.teachco.com

Instructional Programs for Gifted Children (Or Programs that Work Well for Them)

Advanced Placement (AP) Program (AP course descriptions and syllabi. Students may take the AP exams without having been enrolled in an AP course.)
www.collegeboard.com/student/testing/ap/about.html

CalTech Summer Programs
www.yess.caltech.edu

Center for Talent Development
Northwestern University
(including Gifted Learning Links, K-12)
www.ctd.northwestern.edu

Center for Talented Youth (CTY)
Johns Hopkins University
http://cty.jhu.edu/cde/index.html

Distance Learning Programs
Hoagies Gifted Education Page
www.hoagiesgifted.org/distance_learning.htm

Duke University Talent Identification Program (TIP) e-Studies
www.tip.duke.edu/e-studies/index.html

Early Entrance College Programs
Hoagies' Gifted Education Page
www.hoagiesgifted.org/early_college.htm

EarlyEntrance.org (programs, comparisons, testimonials)
www.earlyentrance.org

EPGY (Education Program for Gifted Youth)
Stanford University
http://epgy.stanford.edu/courses/index.html

Independent Study High School
University of Nebraska
http://nebraskahs.unl.edu/index.shtml

International Baccalaureate (IBO)
www.ibo.org

Internet Academy (K-12)
www.iacademy.org

MIT K-12 Outreach
http://web.mit.edu/outreach

NAGC Resource Directory (listed by state)
www.nagc.org/resourcedirectory.aspx

Princeton Summer Programs
www.princeton.edu/main/news/archive/S18/15/77O28/index.xml

Program for the Exceptionally Gifted
Mary Baldwin College
www.mbc.edu/peg

Summer Enrichment Program for the Gifted and Talented (SEP)
University of Northern Colorado
www.unco.edu/sep

Westbridge Academy
www.westbridgeacademy.com

Journals (Giftedness in Children)

Gifted Child Quarterly (a publication of NAGC)
www.nagc.org/index.aspx?id=979

Gifted Child Today
Journal for the Education of the Gifted
Journal of Advanced Academics
Prufrock Press
www.prufrock.com

Gifted Education Communicator
California Association for the Gifted
www.cagifted.org

Parenting for High Potential (quarterly magazine for NAGC members)
www.nagc.org/index.aspx?id=1180

Roeper Review (order through Routledge, Taylor & Francis Group)
www.tandf.co.uk/journals/journals.asp?subcategory=ED200000

Understanding Our Gifted
Open Space Communications
www.openspacecomm.com

Journal (Giftedness in Adults)

When you need support for your own giftedness!

Advanced Development Journal
Gifted Development Center
www.gifteddevelopment.com

Organizations

American Association for Gifted Children
Duke University
919-783-6152.
www.aagc.org/main.html

Belin-Blank Center for Gifted Education
The University of Iowa
800-336-6463 or 319-335-6148
www.education.uiowa.edu/belinblank

Davidson Institute for Talent Development
Reno, NV
775-852-3483
www.ditd.org

European Council for High Ability (ECHA)
www.echa.ws/modules/news

Gifted Canada – Douance Canada
www3.bc.sympatico.ca/giftedcanada

Gifted Development Center
Denver, CO
303-837-8378
www.gifteddevelopment.com

Gifted Education Resource Institute (GERI)
Purdue University
765-494-7243
www.geri.soe.purdue.edu

Gifted Resource Center of New England
Providence, RI
401-421-3426
www.grcne.com

The Hollingworth Center for Highly Gifted Children
www.hollingworth.org

Institute for Educational Advancement
South Pasadena, CA
626-403-8900
www.educationaladvancement.org

National Association for Gifted Children (NAGC)
202-785-4268
www.nagc.org

National Association for Gifted Children (NAGC) UK
www.nagcbritain.org.uk

National Center for Learning Disabilities
www.ld.org

National Gifted Children's Fund
www.ngcfcharity.org

National Network of Families with Gifted Children
www.coe.unt.edu/GIFTED/parents/resources.htm

National Research Center on the Gifted and Talented (NRC/GT)
University of Connecticut
860-486-4676
www.gifted.uconn.edu/NRCGT.html

Supporting Emotional Needs of the Gifted (SENG)
845-226-4660
www.sengifted.org

World Council for Gifted and Talented Children
818-368-7501
www.worldgifted.org

Publishers of Books and Periodicals

Free Spirit Press
800-735-7323
www.freespirit.com

Gifted Education Press
10201 Yuma Court
P.O. Box 1586
Manassas, VA 20108
703-369-5017
www.giftededpress.com

Great Potential Press (formerly Gifted Psychology Press)
P.O. Box 5057
Scottsdale, AZ 85261
602-954-4200 or 877-954-4200
www.giftedbooks.com/contact.asp

New Moon Girl Media
800-381-4743
www.newmoon.org

Open Space Communications
P.O. Box 18268
Boulder, CO 80308
800-494-6178
www.openspacecomm.com

Prufrock Press
P.O. Box 8813
Waco, TX 76714-8813
800-998-2208
www.prufrock.com

State Associations

Search Hoagies' Gifted Education Page (www.hoagiesgifted.com) or do an Internet search for information about your state association and (possible) city affiliate. Most have annual conferences and may provide access to other resources throughout the year (publications, speakers, support groups, etc.).

Talent Searches

Duke University TIP (Talent Identification Program)
919-668-9100
www.tip.duke.edu

Johns Hopkins University
Center for Talented Youth (CTY)
410-735-4100
www.jhu.edu/gifted

Northwestern University
Center for Talent Development
847-491-3782
www.ctd.northwestern.edu

University of Denver
Center for Innovative and Talented Youth (CITY)
Rocky Mountain Academic Talent Search
303-871-2983
www.du.edu/city

Websites

Eric Clearinghouse on Disabilities and Gifted Education (articles on the education of gifted and gifted/learning disabled children)
www.ericec.org

Gifted Development Center
www.gifteddevelopment.com

GT-CyberSource (online library of articles on the highly gifted)
Davidson Institute for Talent Development
www.ditd.org (click on PG-Cybersource)

GT-Special List (for families of twice-exceptional children)
www.gtworld.org/gtspeclist.html

Hoagies' Gifted Education Page (resource site for parents, educators, and children)
www.hoagiesgifted.org

TAGFAM (Families of the Talented and Gifted) Home Page
www.tagfam.org

Uniquely Gifted (twice-exceptional resource site)
www.uniquelygifted.org

Websites about Home Schooling

Hoagies' Gifted Education Page
www.hoagiesgifted.org/home_school.htm

Home Education Magazine
www.homeedmag.com

Home School Legal Defense Association
www.hslda.org

Kearney, K.
Gifted Children and Homeschooling: An Annotated Bibliography
www.hollingworth.org/homebib.html

References

American Psychiatric Association. (1994). *Diagnostic and statistical manual of mental disorders* (4th ed.). Washington, DC: Author.

Assouline, S. G., Colangelo, N., Lupkowski-Shoplik, A., Lipscomb, J., & Forstadt, L. (2003). *Iowa acceleration scale, 2nd ed.* Scottsdale, AZ: Great Potential Press.

Avallone, A. P. (2007). Unfettered innovation: The promise of charter schools. In K. Kay, D. Robson, & J. F. Brenneman (Eds.), *High IQ kids* (pp. 186-196). Minneapolis, MN: Free Spirit.

Ayres, J. (1979). *Sensory integration and the child.* Los Angeles: Western Psychological Services.

Bloom, B. (Ed.). (1956). *Taxonomy of educational objectives: The classification of educational goals: Handbook I, Cognitive domain.* New York: Longmans, Green.

Callihan, D., & Callihan, L. (2000). *The guidance manual for the Christian home school: A parent's guide for preparing home school students for college or career.* Franklin Lakes, NJ: Career Press.

Carlin, G. (Writer/Performer), Urbisci, R. (Director), Hamza, J., & Carlin, B. (Executive Producers). (1990). *Doin' it again* [Videotape]. (Available from Columbia Tristar Home Video, 3400 Riverside Drive, Burbank, CA 91505)

Carson, D., & Roid, G. H. (2004). *Acceptable use of the Stanford-Binet Form L-M: Guidelines for the professional use of the Stanford-Binet Intelligence Scale, Third Edition (Form L-M).* Itasca, IL: Riverside.

Cattell, R. B. (1963). Theory of fluid and crystallized intelligence: A critical experiment. *Journal of Educational Psychology, 54*, 1-22.

Colangelo, N., Assouline, S.G., & Gross, M. U. M., (Eds.). (2004). *A nation deceived: How schools hold back America's brightest students* (Vols. 1-2). Iowa City, IA: The University of Iowa.

Colorado Department of Education. (n.d.) Retrieved April 20, 2008, from www.cde.state.co.us/gt

Columbus Group. (1991, July). Unpublished transcript of the meeting of the Columbus Group, Columbus, OH.

Eide, B., & Eide, F. (2006). *The mislabeled child.* New York: Hyperion.

Feagans, L. V. (1986). Otitis media: A model for long-term effects with implications for intervention. In J. Kavanaugh (Ed.), *Otitis media and child development.* Parkton, MD: York Press.

Flanagan, D. P., & Kaufman, A. S. (2004). *Essentials of WISC-IV assessment.* Hoboken, NJ: John Wiley & Sons.

Flynn, J. R. (1984). The mean IQ of Americans: Massive gains 1932 to 1978. *Psychological Bulletin, 95*, 29-51.

Flynn, J. R. (1999). Searching for justice: The discovery of IQ gains over time. *American Psychologist, 54,* 5-20.

Gardner, H. (1983). *Frames of mind: The theory of multiple intelligences.* New York: Basic Books.

Gardner, H. (1999). *Intelligence reframed: Multiple intelligences for the 21st century.* New York: Basic Books.

George, P. (1992). *How to untrack your school.* Alexandria, VA: Association for Supervision and Curriculum Development.

Gilman, B. J. (1997, May-June-July). New challenge for middle schoolers. *Kaleidoscope*, 9-12.

Gilman, B. J., & Falk, R. F. (2005, August). *Research-based guidelines for use of the WISC-IV in gifted assessment.* Paper presented at the 16th Biennial Conference of the World Council for Gifted and Talented Children, New Orleans, LA.

Gilman, B. J., & Greene, L. (1994). Challenging Ben. *Understanding Our Gifted, 6*(6), 1-17.

Hallowell, E. M., & Ratey, J. J. (1994). *Driven to distraction.* New York: Simon & Schuster.

Hammond, L. J. (2007). How well do homeschoolers perform? *Mensa Research Journal, Homeschooling for the Gifted, 38*(3), 80-81.

Jones, P., & Gloeckner, G. (2007). First-year college performance: A study of home school graduates and traditional school graduates. *Mensa Research Journal, Homeschooling for the Gifted, 38*(3), 62-65.

Kerr, B. A. (1997). *Smart girls: A new psychology of girls, women, and giftedness.* Scottsdale, AZ: Great Potential Press.

Kranowitz, C. S. (1998). *The out-of-sync child.* New York: The Berkley Publishing Group.

Kurcinka, M. S. (1992). *Raising your spirited child: A guide for parents whose child is more intense, sensitive, perceptive, persistent, energetic.* New York: HarperCollins.

Kurcinka, M. S. (1999, June). *Raising your spirited child.* Keynote presentation at the 20th anniversary conference of the Gifted Development Center, Denver, CO.

Lind, S. (2001). *Overexcitabilities and the gifted.* Retrieved April 24, 2008, from www.sengifted.org/articles_social/lind_overexcitabilityandthegifted.shtml

Lovecky, D. V., Kearney, K., Falk, R. F., & Gilman, B. J. (2005, August). *A comparison of the Stanford-Binet 5 and the Stanford-Binet Form L-M in the assessment of gifted children.* Paper presented at the 16th Biennial Conference of the World Council for Gifted and Talented Children, New Orleans, LA.

Margolin, L. (1994). *Goodness personified: The emergence of gifted children.* Hawthorne, NY: Aldine de Gruyter.

Maxwell, E. (1998). "I can do it myself!" Reflections on early self-efficacy. *Roeper Review, 20,* 183-187.

Mendaglio, S. (2008). *Dabrowski's theory of positive disintegration.* Scottsdale, AZ: Great Potential Press.

Miller, L. J. (2006). *Sensational kids: Hope and help for children with sensory processing disorder.* New York: Putnam Adult.

National Association for Gifted Children. (2008). *Use of the WISC-IV for gifted identification.* Retrieved January 27, 2008, from www.nagc.org/CMS400Min/index.aspx?id=375

Oakes, J. (1986). *Keeping track: How schools structure inequality.* New Haven, CT: Yale University Press.

Pegnato, C. W., & Birch, J. W. (1959). Locating gifted children in junior high schools: A comparison of methods. *Exceptional Children, 25,* 300-304.

Pipher, M. (1994). *Reviving Ophelia: Saving the selves of adolescent girls.* New York: Putnam.

Ray, B. D. (2007). Homeschooling systemically amenable to gifted and talented students? *Mensa Research Journal, Homeschooling for the Gifted, 38*(3), 18-25.

Reis, S. M., Westberg, K. L., Kulikowich, J., Caillard, F., Hébert, T. P., & Plucker, J. A. (1993). *Why not let high ability students start school in January? The curriculum compacting study* (RM93106). Storrs, CT: National Research Center on the Gifted and Talented, University of Connecticut.

Rivero, L. (2007). Progressive digressions: Home schooling for self-actualization. *Mensa Research Journal, Homeschooling for the Gifted, 38*(3), 47-54.

Roid, G. H. (2003). *Stanford-Binet Intelligence Scales interpretive manual: Expanded guide to the interpretation of SB5 test results.* Itasca, IL: Riverside.

Roid, G. H., & Carson, A. (2004). *Special composites scores for the SB5* (Assessment Service Bulletin No. 4). Itasca, IL: Riverside.

Rogers, K. B. (1991). *The relationship of grouping practices to the education of the gifted and talented learner* (Research-Based Decision Making Series). Storrs, CT: National Research Center on the Gifted and Talented, University of Connecticut.

Rogers, K. B. (2002). *Re-forming gifted education: How parents and teachers can match the program to the child.* Scottsdale, AZ: Great Potential Press.

Rudner, L. M. (1999). Scholastic achievement and demographic characteristics of home school students in 1998. *Education Policy Analysis Archives, 7*(8).

Ruf, D. L. (2003). *Use of the SB5 in the assessment of high abilities* (Assessment Service Bulletin No. 3). Itasca, IL: Riverside.

Ruf, D. L. (2005). *Losing our minds: Gifted children left behind.* Scottsdale, AZ: Great Potential Press.

Sapon-Shevin, M. (1994). *Playing favorites: Gifted education and the disruption of community.* Albany, NY: State University of New York Press.

Seeley, K. (1993). Gifted students at risk. In L. K. Silverman (Ed.), *Counseling the gifted and talented* (pp. 263-275). Denver, CO: Love.

The Sensory Processing Disorder Network (SPD Network). (n.d.). Retrieved February 16, 2008, from http://spdnetwork.org

Silverman, L. K. (1988, October). The second child syndrome. *Mensa Bulletin, 320,* 18-20.

Silverman, L. K. (1989). Invisible gifts, invisible handicaps. *Roeper Review, 12,* 37-42.

Silverman, L. K. (1990). *Characteristics of giftedness scale.* Retrieved February 27, 2008, from www.gifteddevelopment.com/What_is_Gifted/characgt.htm

Silverman, L. K. (1995). The universal experience of being out-of-sync. In L. K. Silverman (Ed.), *Advanced development: A collection of works on giftedness in adults* (pp. 1-12). Denver, CO: Institute for the Study of Advanced Development.

Silverman, L. K. (1998, January). *Giftedness in adults.* Retrieved February 27, 2008, from www.gifteddevelopment.com/ADJ/scale.htm

Silverman, L. K. (2002). *Upside-down brilliance: The visual-spatial learner.* Denver, CO: DeLeon.

Snyderman, M., & Rothman, S. (1988). *The IQ controversy, the media and public policy.* New Brunswick, NJ: Transaction Books.

Southern, W. T., & Jones, E. D. (1991). Academic acceleration: Background and issues. In W. T. Southern & E. D. Jones (Eds.), *The academic acceleration of gifted children* (pp. 1-28). New York: Teacher's College Press.

Stanley, J. C. (1976). The case for extreme educational acceleration of intellectually brilliant youths. *Gifted Child Quarterly, 20*(1), 66-75.

Start, K. B. (1995). *The relationship of learning pace and ability in concept acquisition.* Paper presented at the Annual Supporting the Emotional Needs of the Gifted (SENG) Conference, San Diego, CA.

Teasdale, T. W., & Owen. D. R. (2005). A long-term rise and recent decline in intelligence test performance: The Flynn effect in reverse. *Personality and Individual Differences, 39,* 837-843.

Terrell, S. K., & Terrell, K. (2007). What are four myths about homeschooling? *Mensa Research Journal, Homeschooling for the Gifted, 38*(3), 82-84.

Tomlinson, C. (1992). Gifted education and the middle school movement: Two voices on teaching the academically talented. *Journal for the Education of the Gifted, 15*(3), 206-238.

U.S. Department of Education, Office of Special Education and Rehabilitative Services. (2006). *Assistance to states for the education of children with disabilities and preschool grants for children with disabilities.* Retrieved April 25, 2008, from http://idea.ed.gov/download/finalregulations.pdf

U.S. Department of Education, Office for Civil Rights. (2007, Dec 26). *Dear colleague letter: Access by students with disabilities to accelerated programs from Assistant Secretary for Civil Rights Stephanie Monroe.* Retrieved February 17, 2008, from www.ed.gov/about/offices/list/ocr/letters/colleague-20071226.html

Wasserman, J. D. (2007). *The Flynn effect in gifted samples: Status as of 2007.* Unpublished manuscript retrieved February 16, 2008, from www.gifteddevelopment.com/ Whats_New/flynn.htm

Webb, J. T. (1993). Nurturing social-emotional development of gifted children. In K. A. Heller, F. J. Monks, & A. H. Passow (Eds.), *International handbook of research and development of giftedness and talent* (pp. 525-539). New York: Pergamon.

Webb, J. T., Amend, E. R., Webb, N. E., Goerss, J., Beljan, P., & Olenchak, F. R. (2005). *Misdiagnosis and dual diagnoses of gifted children and adults: ADHD, bipolar, OCD, Asperger's, depression, and other disorders.* Scottsdale, AZ: Great Potential Press.

Wechsler, D. (1991). *Wechsler Intelligence Scale for Children: Third edition manual.* San Antonio, TX: The Psychological Corp., Harcourt Brace.

Wechsler, D. (2003). *The WISC-IV technical and interpretive manual.* San Antonio, TX: The Psychological Corp.

Whitmore, J. (1980). *Giftedness, conflict and underachievement.* Needham Heights, MA: Allyn & Bacon.

Winebrenner, S. (1994, July-August). How gifted kids can survive in inclusion classrooms. *Understanding Our Gifted, 6*(6), 1, 8.

Winebrenner, S., & Espeland, P. (2001). *Teaching gifted kids in the regular classroom: Strategies and techniques every teacher can use to meet the academic needs of the gifted and talented.* Minneapolis, MN: Free Spirit.

Zhu, J., Cayton, T., Weiss, L., & Gabel, A. (2008). *WISC-IV technical report #7: Extended norms.* The Psychological Corp. Retrieved February, 7, 2008, from http://harcourtassessment.com/NR/rdonlyres/C1C19227-BC79-46D9-B 43C-8E4A114F7E1F/0/WISCIV_TechReport_7.pdf

Endnotes

Chapter 1

none

Chapter 2

1 (1994)

2 (1990)

3 The normal bell-shaped curve is customarily expressed in standard deviation units, which describe how scores fall above or below the average. The Wechsler scales used a standard deviation of 15. Thus, two standard deviations of 15 above the average of 100 equal a score of 130 for the beginning of the *gifted* or *very superior* range. The earlier Stanford-Binet tests utilized a standard deviation of 16 (later changed to 15), so 132 was considered the *gifted* level.

4 Snyderman & Rothman (1988)

5 (1991, p. 1)

6 Cattell (1963)

7 See, for example, George (1992), Margolin (1994), and Sapon-Shevin (1994).

8 Silverman (1990)

9 In fact, when Linda Silverman taught at the University of Denver, she and colleague Ken Seeley proposed (with tongue in cheek) the Silverman-Seeley Pun Test of Giftedness, in which a teacher makes a rather sophisticated, humorous comment to the class and watches to see who falls out of their chair.

10 Silverman (1998)

11 POGO was created in January of 1985 by Dr. Linda Silverman. For more information, contact the Gifted Development Center at gifted@gifteddevelopment.com.

Chapter 3

1 Snyderman & Rothman (1988)

2 Wechsler (2003, p. 77)

3 Flanagan & Kaufman (2004); Gilman & Falk (2005)

4 Zhu, Cayton, Weiss, & Gabel (2008)

5 Later versions used a Deviation IQ, in which the ratio-based scores were forced into a normal distribution with approximately equal intervals. This was done largely because the ratio-based IQ scores became progressively less appropriate and accurate as a child became older and entered adolescence.

6 SB5 author Gale Roid also notes that questions from one section out of the five (e.g., Working Memory) might be omitted and an overall score prorated from the other four sections, if those questions prove to be less relevant in identification of gifted children (G. Roid, personal communication, February 12, 2003).
7 See Roid & Carson (2004), or visit www.assess.nelson.com/pdf/sb5-asb4.pdf.
8 See Ruf (2003), or visit www.riverpub.com/products/sb5/pdf/SB5_ASB_3.pdf.
9 Carson & Roid (2004)
10 Flynn (1984, 1999)
11 See, for example, Teasdale & Owen (2005) and Wasserman (2007)
12 Zhu, Cayton, Weiss, & Gabel (2008)
13 Roid (2003)
14 G. H. Roid, personal communication, February 13, 2008
15 For information on the Rasch model, visit www.rasch-analysis.com.
16 Roid & Carson (2004); Ruf (2003)
17 Webb (1993)

Chapter 4

1 See "Public School Expectations by Grade Levels" in *Losing Our Minds: Gifted Children Left Behind* (Ruf, 2005) for a list of elementary skills.
2 Dr. Charlotte Mendosa, personal communication, 1993
3 Start (1995)
4 Reis, Westberg, Kulikowich, Caillard, Hébert, & Plucker (1993)
5 Colangelo, Assouline, & Gross (2004)
6 (1986)

Chapter 5

1 Pipher (1994). Barbara Kerr's 1997 book *Smart Girls: A New Psychology of Girls, Women, and Giftedness* also provides an interesting perspective.

Chapter 6

1 Silverman (1989, p. 37) constructed this list based on information from Whitmore's book.
2 Silverman (1989, p. 37)
3 U.S. Department of Education (2006, p. 46786)
4 Adapted from U.S. Department of Education (2006, pp. 46786-7)
5 Section 504 is a plan designed to accommodate the unique needs of an individual with a disability, as part of the Rehabilitation Act of 1973 and related to the Americans with Disabilities Act.
6 U.S. Department of Education (2007)
7 Eide & Eide (2006, p. 114)
8 Eide & Eide (2006, pp.118-119)
9 Eide & Eide (2006, pp. 132-146)

10 Additional relevant information can be found in the book *Misdiagnosis and Dual Diagnoses of Gifted Children and Adults* by Webb, Amend, Webb, Goerss, Beljan, & Olenchak (2005), listed in the References section of this book.

11 One excellent resource on this diagnostic dilemma is the book *Misdiagnosis and Dual Diagnoses of Gifted Children and Adults* (Webb, et al., 2005).

12 American Psychiatric Association (2000, p. 83)

13 Some research suggests that virtually all children and adults are able to concentrate better after receiving low to moderate amounts of a stimulant. See Webb, et al (2005) for more information.

14 Hallowell & Ratey (1994)

Chapter 7

1 Assouline, Colangelo, Lipscomb, & Forstadt (2003)

2 Stanley (1976)

Chapter 8

1 Hammond (2007, p. 81)

2 Terrell & Terrell (2007, p. 84)

3 Jones & Gloeckner (2007, p. 64)

4 Ray (2007)

5 Callihan & Callihan (2000)

6 Rivero (2007, pp. 47-48)

Chapter 9

1 For more information on Dabrowski's overexcitabilities, see Mendaglio (2008) and Lind (2001).

Chapter 10

1 Gilman (1997, pp. 9-12)

2 Tomlinson (1992)

Chapter 11

1 Assouline, et al. (2003)

Index

About the Author

Barbara ("Bobbie") Gilman, M.S., is Associate Director of Denver's Gifted Development Center (GDC), a service of the non-profit Institute for the Study of Advanced Development, dedicated to "supporting giftedness through the life span." Since 1979, the GDC, directed by Linda Silverman, Ph.D., has provided in-depth, individual assessment and educational guidance for more than 5,500 children. Bobbie joined the GDC in 1991 with degrees in Child Development from Purdue and Psychology from Duke and has assessed hundreds of children. She determines testing needs for children who come to the center, serves as a senior partner in post-test consultations with parents, supervises testers and doctoral interns in the intricacies of gifted assessment, and ensures that reports will provide a solid basis for school advocacy. She specializes in work with highly gifted children; gifted children with learning disabilities, sensory deficits, and ADHD; and gifted underachievers.

A parent of gifted sons, Bobbie is a veteran of gifted committees and school improvement teams, and she has experienced the heartbreak of having a gifted child drop out of school, as well as the challenges of the radically accelerated student. She is one of the founders of Summit Middle School in Boulder, Colorado, an award-winning, accelerated charter school.

Since the original release of this book in 2003 (formerly titled *Empowering Gifted Minds: Educational Advocacy that Works*), she has devoted more of her time to school advocacy consultation, helping parents worldwide to document the unique instructional needs of their gifted students, find curricular options that meet the children's needs, and negotiate with school personnel for programming accommodations. Her book for teachers and parents, *Challenging Highly Gifted Learners* (2008) in the series by F. A. Karnes and K. R. Stephens (Eds.) *Practical Strategies Series in Gifted Education,* explores the educational issues of our most highly gifted students.

Bobbie currently serves on the National Association for Gifted Children Task Force for IQ Test Interpretation and created the draft of NAGC's Position Statement on "Use of the WISC-IV for Gifted Identification." She participated in special population studies of the Stanford-Binet 5, the NAGC study of 334 gifted children on the WISC-IV, and she has worked with test authors to create alternative scoring techniques and extended norms to document abilities previously hidden by scoring limits. Bobbie writes and speaks extensively on the appropriate use and scoring of the newly revised and renormed major IQ tests with gifted children. Without strong, individualized programs to reduce the risk for gifted learners in school, she believes that the success of gifted students can only come from educated parent advocates and supportive teachers willing to think outside of the box. This fully updated and enhanced version of her award-winning advocacy book, originally published under the title *Empowering Gifted Minds: Educational Advocacy that Works,* is meant to provide the necessary tools for action.